WITHDRAWN
WRIGHT STATE UNIVERSITY LIBRARIES

School-Based Prevention for Children at Risk

School-Based Prevention for Children at Risk

THE PRIMARY MENTAL HEALTH PROJECT

Emory L. Cowen
A. Dirk Hightower
JoAnne L. Pedro-Carroll
William C. Work
Peter A. Wyman
with
William G. Haffey

AMERICAN PSYCHOLOGICAL ASSOCIATION • WASHINGTON, DC

LB
3430
.S45
1996

Copyright © 1996 by the American Psychological Association. All rights reserved. Except as permitted under the United States Copyright Act of 1976, no part of this publication may be reproduced or distributed in any form or by any means, or stored in a database or retrieval system, without the prior written permission of the publisher.

Published by
American Psychological Association
750 First Street, NE
Washington, DC 20002

Copies may be ordered from
APA Order Department
P.O. Box 2710
Hyattsville, MD 20784

In the UK and Europe, copies may be ordered from
American Psychological Association
3 Henrietta Street
Covent Garden, London
WC2E 8LU England

Typeset in Goudy by PRO-IMAGE Corporation, Techna-Type Division, York, PA

Cover designer: Berg Design, Albany, NY
Printer: Port City Press, Inc., Baltimore, MD
Technical/Production Editor: Miria Liliana Riahi

Library of Congress Cataloging-in-Publication Data
School-based prevention for children at risk : the Primary Mental
    Health Project / by Emory L. Cowen . . . [et al.].
        p.   cm.
    Continues: New ways in school mental health. c1975.
    Includes bibliographical references and index.
    ISBN 1-55798-353-4 (hardcover : alk. paper).—ISBN 1-55798-374-7
(softcover : alk. paper)
    1. Primary Mental Health Project.   2. School children—Mental
health services—United States.   3. Student adjustment—United
States.   4. Problem children—Education—United States.   I. Cowen,
Emory L.   II. New ways in school mental health.
LB3430.S45   1996
372.14'6—dc20   96-23913
                                                                              CIP

British Library Cataloguing-in-Publication Data
A CIP record is available from the British Library.

Printed in the United States of America
First edition

CONTENTS

v

FOREWORD

The Primary Mental Health Project (PMHP) has been operating in a steadily expanding number of school systems for almost two score years. Clearly, it is the gold medal champion for those of us who watch and cheer programs that are designed to promote wellness (mental health) and reduce emotional damage in groups of children at risk. The PMHP serves as a powerful model for the field. Originally, it was conceived as a rational alternative to the traditional one-to-one therapeutic intervention between a single professional therapist or counselor and a single disturbed school child. Clearly, the unavailability of enough school-based professional therapists and the ineffectiveness of this one-to-one model cried out for a system change. PMHP was developed to be this mode for change. It focused on very young school children who were screened to be at risk. The new interviewers were carefully selected child associates who were nonprofessionals. School-based mental health professionals could now serve as trainers, consultants, and supervisors.

It was a brilliant idea—breaking away from the tradition of one-to-one therapy by (scarce) professionals and, perhaps more challenging and original, setting the goal of building wellness rather than treating pathology.

This volume reviews the progress of PMHP since the earlier book in 1975 (Cowen, Trost, et al., 1975). It is a detailed and objective examination of a program that towers above all others in terms of clear goals, clear methods of implementation, widespread acceptance, and unflinching and honest evaluation.

PMHP continues to be and will always be the core program but, like a few other successful programs in wellness promotion and prevention of distress, it continues to generate spin-offs. One example is the Study Buddy program that pairs children for the entire school year to work together at least three times a week, learning to help each other and developing social skills. Design and evaluation problems are being addressed as this program evolves.

Long continuing experience with PMHP has also engendered increased awareness of the strong influence of outside-school factors that strongly affect children's emotional wellness. It is clear that the overarching goal must be to promote wellness generally. A caring school community is important, but cannot compensate for poverty, bad neighborhoods, incompetent or neglectful parents, and early continuing trauma like sexual abuse. Accordingly, PMHP has recently assumed leadership in a community project aimed at broad-based wellness programs from before birth.

The book is full of keen insights and suggestions for further research. There are seminal discussions of the importance of a focus on wellness promotion. This view is crucial to understanding a critical current issue in the field of primary prevention. The powerful Establishment view holds that prevention programs must focus separately on a specific *DSM-IV* (American Psychiatric Association, 1994) diagnostic category. This view neglects, or even argues against, competence enhancement or wellness programs. At the core of the argument is the question of continuity–discontinuity of mental conditions. If discontinuous separate mental illnesses exist, then they must have separate organic causes (like real illnesses). On the other hand, if emotional disturbances are learned and are continuous with normalcy, then competency-enhancing programs can work. PMHP gives comfort to those of us on the side of continuity.

The Acknowledgments section gives well-deserved praise and recognition to the many talented people who have participated in the PMHP program over the years. The name that must be added for special recognition and praise is that of Emory Cowen. Cowen stands like the tallest oak in the forest of prevention—sturdy, productive, deeply-rooted—and a guide to those unsure of their way. It is difficult not to become too poetic and flowery in his praise. When the history of prevention is written a hundred years hence, Cowen's ideas, achievements, and influence will lead all the rest.

GEORGE W. ALBEE

PREFACE

Virtually every school in America has in it children with adaptive or behavioral problems that seriously impede their learning and optimal development. Indeed, in many schools such problems are so rampant and demand so much of the time and energies of school personnel that they dilute the educational experience of other children.

Children's early school adaptation problems may reflect many different sources (e.g., difficult prior life experiences, preformed negative views of school and the educational process, inability to cope with school realities and demands, and ongoing life stressors). These problems come packaged in diverse forms, including hostile, aggressive, sullen, uncooperative behaviors; fearful, anxious, withdrawn behaviors; disinterest in learning (tuning out); and combinations of the preceding. Whatever the source or mode of manifestation of these early problems, they share two common negative features: They restrict the learning and personal development of children who experience them and, by diluting the educational opportunities of classmates, they hamper the school's pursuit of its prime educational mandate.

The foregoing is reality. What to do about it is another matter! The most common practice in the past has been to ignore early problems in hopes that they would go away. Sometimes, that does in fact happen! Unfortunately, however, many early adaptive problems persist and increase the likelihood of educational failure. The latter, in turn, predisposes later, serious, and far-reaching life problems. Hence, an appealing alternative, in principle, is to identify children's adaptive problems as soon as possible, before they exact heavy negative tolls and, on that basis, to provide a corrective experience that helps children overcome early false starts and come ultimately to profit from the school experience. This process embodies a basic shift in orientation from after-the-fact patchwork or repair to before-the-fact prevention. Because young children are flexible and malleable and because early problems have not yet had a chance to root or fan out, targeting preventive interventions to young children offers many potential advantages. The primary grades of schools are ideal settings in which to conduct such programs.

The preceding views led to the launching, in 1957, of an innovative school mental health program called the Primary Mental Health Project (PMHP), built on the yoked objectives of systematic early detection and prevention of young children's school adjustment problems. One unique aspect of PMHP is that it has remained in continuous operation for nearly 40 years—indeed, it has grown and expanded greatly during that period. That that has happened, despite ongoing changes in PMHP staff and, even more so, in staff in PMHP schools testifies to the program model's viability, usefulness to schools, and adaptability to diverse school situations. Schools have thus viewed PMHP as a sensible and utilitarian approach that addresses the real, everyday problems they face.

Other significant elements in PMHP's evolution include its (a) ongoing, critical self-scrutiny, and the program refinements and new program developments stimulated by that process; and (b) program evaluation and other types of research designed to strengthen the project's offerings. This special blend of features paved the way to widespread adoption of the PMHP model and, with that, visible change in how school mental health services are conceptualized and delivered.

This volume narrates the PMHP story with special emphasis on the period between 1975 and the present. As such, it builds on the base set down in a prior volume, *New Ways in School Mental Health: Early Detection and Prevention of School Maladaptation* (Cowen, Trost, et al., 1975), describing PMHP's early unfolding. Since 1975, PMHP has grown, flourished, and taken on important new challenges, such as refining and expanding the basic program model in several new directions, promoting widespread program implementation, and developing new cutting-edge primary prevention program modules that can extend the scope and practices of PMHP's basic program model. These latter approaches can be either implemented in their own right or built on to the base of existing PMHP programs.

Because the sum of these post-1975 developments is considerable, we believe that the time is again ripe to take stock of what PMHP has accomplished and the implications of these accomplishments for future school mental health programming. Although the book does not ignore PMHP's roots, rationale, or early history, its prime focus is on program evolution since 1975 and how this development may inform school mental health practice in the twenty-first century.

Chapter 1 describes the climate in which PMHP originated and issues that the program sought to address. As such, it provides a conceptual matrix that sets the stage for all that follows. The next five chapters (Part I) deal with the core PMHP program: how it developed, its basic components, how to set up a new PMHP and how such programs function in a school, new program options that expand PMHP's reach and effectiveness, and the program's justifying research base.

Part II of the volume focuses on two major, post-1975 thrusts that grew logically out of PMHP's initial accomplishments (and limitations): (a) disseminating the program model; and (b) developing and evaluating several new, primary prevention program initiatives in social problem-solving training, preventive programming for children of divorce, cooperative learning, and enhancing the resilience of profoundly stressed children. Although these new programs are not literally part of the basic PMHP, they expand the preventive programming options that a school can offer. The book's final chapter looks back panoramically at the total PMHP experience, taking stock of the project's accomplishments and nonaccomplishments as realistically as possible and, on that basis, identifying needed directions for future mental health programming.

PMHP's special combination of elements—particularly its prime foci on prevention and wellness enhancement as objectives, young children as prime targets, and elementary schools as the main loci of operation—offers a cohesive framework for advancing some of mental health's most basic goals.

ACKNOWLEDGMENTS

By the time this volume appears, the project it describes, the Primary Mental Health Project (PMHP), will have been in active, continuous operation for nearly four decades. PMHP has grown from a tiny, ever-so-frail seedling to a highly viable program now functioning in several thousand schools in many hundreds of school districts around the country—indeed, around the world. This enormously complex endeavor evolved as it did as a result of the contributions, some quite visible, others not, of many hundreds of people. This volume was written by six among those many hundreds, who have functioned as key members of PMHP's central staff for at least a decade and have made major contributions to one or more elements in PMHP's complex story.

For central PMHP staff and its school-based programs, turnaround among key players in the scenario has been part of the nature of things from the very start and has continued unabatedly ever since. As one small case in point, we note that of the 12 listed coauthors of the two PMHP volumes (the first published in 1975 and this one, two decades later), only one name is common to both.

The preceding observations pave the way to an apology. We cannot do what we would like to have done here, that is, to acknowledge the contributions of all the many people who, in the course of PMHP's long history, have contributed meaningfully to the project's emergence as a visible force on the school mental health scene. Truth be told, many different categories of people—each with a current, cross-sectional constituency and many different past constituencies—have been important elements in that process. These clusters of players include (a) members of PMHP's central professional and support staffs; (b) colleagues who have served as PMHP consultants, extending the staff arm; (c) members of PMHP Inc. Board of Directors; (d) school district administrators and planners; (e) school building administrators; (f) PMHP school-based professional staff members; (g) PMHP school-based child associates and senior associates; (h) PMHP classroom teachers; (i) Regional Dissemination Center coordinators and staff; (j) administrators and staff of state dissemination programs; and (k) agencies and organizations whose confidence in and literal support of PMHP have been major factors in the project's healthy evolution.

From this dazzling array of thousands of unnamed people, the most we can hope to do is to select a relatively few to cite and thank for their seminal contributions to PMHP. In so doing, we run the risk of incurring the (justifiable) wrath of many others who have also contributed importantly but who are not cited individually here because of the need to be finite.

Acknowledgments, understandably, often reflect the bias of contemporaneity. Ours will be no different. Even so, this is a moment to reflect on the full panorama of PMHP's history and to cite those relatively few people, in several categories, without whose focal contributions the project could not have evolved as it did. In that spirit, we begin with two of PMHP's three founders, going back nearly 40 years to when they comprised PMHP's original school-based team: the late Louis D. Izzo, PMHP's first chief psychologist; and Mary Ann Trost, PMHP's first chief social worker. Those two people functioned for over 20 years in these emergent, trailblazing roles, carving out the prototypic roles of PMHP psychologist and social worker that have since served as a model for many hundreds of PMHP schools. The third member of the project's founding troika, ELC, remains actively involved with PMHP.

In like manner, each of PMHP's first four research coordinators, Darwin A. Dorr, Raymond P. Lorion (both coauthors on the initial PMHP volume), Ellis L. Gesten, and Roger P. Weissberg contributed greatly to the crucial empirical strand of the project's evolution and success. PMHP's more recent Research Coordinators, ADH (now Director), WCW, and PAW, are coauthors on this volume.

One of PMHP's novel and important contributions was to articulate and develop the child-associate role, built around careful selection, training, and supervision of nonprofessional help agents (most were alumni–homemakers). In PMHP's extended history, locally and elsewhere, literally thousands of women have functioned nobly as associates, in child-serving ways. We cite only five of these women. Four were long-term members of PMHP's first ground-breaking wave of child associates who served from 10 to 25 years in that role: Frieda Behrman, Norma Finzer, Ruth Zax, and the late Dina Zwick. The fifth, Betty Salzman, has served effectively for 24 years as a child associate, senior associate, workshop spokesperson, and group leader in several primary prevention projects.

A number of sensitive, caring clinicians have contributed importantly to PMHP as consultants. We express our gratitude to PMHP's two current, longevitous consultants, Angelo Madonia and James Michael, both for their many direct contributions to the project over the years and as representatives of the broader genus of PMHP consultant. Our warm thanks also go to Arthur Orgel for his training and clinical-supervisory contributions, for more than 20 years, in preparing child associates to work with acting-out children.

Several people who have functioned in key PMHP administrative–coordinating roles (Ruth Zax, Kay Leary, and Jessie York) merit special recognition and expression of gratitude, as do two members of PMHP's current core social work staff, Ann Farie, PMHP's Chief Social Worker, and Lynne Mijangos. A special thanks also to Ellie Eksten, who both served as a social worker in a PMHP core school for several decades and produced a number of videos that faithfully and sensitively depict core aspects of PMHP.

Within PMHP's central structure, two people have long been unsung heroes in very different domains. One, Sharon DeVita, who has been on PMHP's staff for nearly two decades, functions exquisitely as administrator and budget coordinator—two very demanding roles. The other, Bohdan Stanislaw (Stas) Lotyczewski, PMHP's Senior Information Analyst has, for 16 years, been keeper of the faith for all building computer systems, equipment, and programs, and a repository of wisdom and troubleshooting skills in that hallowed domain. Stas has had a benevolent, albeit often unseen, hand in many PMHP research studies. Sharon and Stas are among PMHP's silent, behind-the-scenes expediters (shakers and bakers). We take them for granted, but without their steadfast if often silent and invisible contributions, the efficiency and effectiveness of PMHP's operations would suffer greatly.

Thanks also to Deborah Johnson, both for her informed leadership of the California's PMHP dissemination program for 7 years and for her editorial contributions to this volume.

As noted above, PMHP has been supported by many funding sources over the years. This ever-changing, patchwork funding-quilt, essential to PMHP's survival and development, has included large, medium-sized, and small awards from government agencies, school districts, foundations, community agencies, and individuals. Although it is infeasible to cite each of these many contributions, we acknowledge, with gratitude, the long-term support of the Rochester City School District, Monroe County Board of Cooperative Educational Services (BOCES) No. 1, and the University of Rochester.

The National Institute of Mental Health was PMHP's main outside funding source both in its early developmental period and in starting a national dissemination program. Since then, the New York State legislature, in concert with the State Education Department, has been a primary support source for PMHP's development and dissemination. Other New York State agencies and initiatives, including the Office of Mental Health, through its Coordinated Care Services, the Youth Bureau and Youth At Risk programs, Transferring Success, and the Office of Alcohol and Substance Abuse Services have provided support for PMHP. At the local level, significant governmental support for the project has come both from the City of Rochester and the County of Monroe.

Awards from private foundations have also contributed vitally to the project's wholesome evolution. Two major primary prevention initiatives, the Children of Divorce Intervention Project and the Rochester Child Resilience Project, have had major support from the W. T. Grant Foundation. Both in the past and currently, the United Way of Rochester has supported PMHP generously. Facets of PMHP programming have also been supported by the Daisy Marquis Jones Foundation, the Gottschalk Foundation, the Rochester Female Charitable Society, and the Rochester Area Foundation. Our sincere thanks to each of these funding sources and to others not mentioned here.

Finally, we acknowledge the yeoman contributions that five people made to the mechanics of this volume's evolution. Janet James worked diligently to produce the volume's appendixes and references. The other four are the women whose magic fingers on the keyboard, through many long, arduous (yea, even obsessive) revisions, including an endless stream of last-minute changes, produced this manuscript: Paula Assenato, Eva Galambos, Kristine Ryck and, without a doubt, Jo Ann Taliento, who not only did a great deal of this "dirty work," but even seemed, at times, to ask for and enjoy it.

1

THE PRIMARY MENTAL HEALTH PROJECT: ROOTS AND WELLSPRINGS

Twenty years ago we wrote a book to describe the activities and accomplishments of a then relatively young, innovative school-based program in early detection and prevention of young children's adjustment problems (Cowen, Trost, et al., 1975). The program was called the Primary Mental Health Project (PMHP). The word *primary* in its title was intended only to reflect the fact that the program was developed for children at the primary grade levels. Because the name Primary Mental Health Project was long and cumbersome, the project acquired the acronym PMHP early on. That acronym has stuck through the life of the project.

Innovation in PMHP was intended at two levels. The first, and probably more important, was the conceptual level. PMHP's focus on prevention was intended to provide a meaningful contrast to mental health's longstanding, dominant emphasis on the diagnosis and treatment of established dysfunction. The decisions to target young children and school sites were based on the conviction that these foci would provide maximally utilitarian and pragmatic conditions for implementing effective prevention programs.

At a second level of innovation was the specific body of technology that defined PMHP's operations. This technology, as it evolved, was built on the base of four structural components: (a) a focus on very young school children; (b) the use of systematic, outreaching early detection and screening procedures with primary graders; (c) the use of a new breed of intervener, that is, nonprofessional "child-associates," selected for their human and experiential qualities (Cowen, Dorr, & Pokracki, 1972) as the prime providers of direct helping services to children; and (d) modification of the role of school-based mental health professionals toward training, supervision, and consultation. Our hope, when we first fused these elements into a programmatic form, was that they would pave the way toward a major expansion in the delivery of early, effective, preventively oriented services to young children in need. We believe that hope has, in good measure, been realized and for that reason these same structural components have remained central to PMHP's functioning for 38 years.

At another level, it can also be said that these four elements, collectively, offered an inviting contrast both to the predominant ways in which mental health services had always been conceived and delivered and to typical everyday practice in the then-existing mental health system, including particularly the school mental health delivery subsystem. Within all prior mental health delivery frameworks, most of the system's limited energies and resources had been invested in efforts at psychological restoration. Moreover, the limited restoration services that the system had to offer were directed primarily to adults already experiencing psychological problems. Many of the latter were deeply rooted and serious at the time help was sought and, precisely for that reason, even the most sophisticated intervention methods were at best limited in their effectiveness.

At the time PMHP started, children were not an important focus within the larger mental health services picture (President's Commission on Mental Health, 1978). Moreover, the relatively few services that were available to children, including school mental health services, were heavily shaped by the same "casualty-repair" orientation that dominated the existing, adult-centered mental health system.

Since the 1975 volume appeared, PMHP has survived, grown, and logged an additional 20 years of experience in the schools. During this more recent period, PMHP's early formats and procedures have steadily evolved; the scope of project implementation has expanded dramatically; and several new, cutting-edge, primary prevention program modules have been developed, field-tested, and evaluated within PMHP's broader framework. Several of the latter now stand as viable, utilitarian program models that can either be implemented in their own right or be attached to an existing PMHP structure.

Several structural common denominators bind the preceding developments. More concretely, it can be said that each offers a contrast to mental health's prior established ways in its (a) focus on young children; (b) equipotential applicability in multiple settings, and for many different groups, including the heretofore underserved; and, most importantly, (c) embodiment of before-the-fact, preventively intended steps as opposed to after-the-fact efforts in damage control.

THE DURABILITY OF PMHP

Schools are complex entities. They are charged with responsibility for the formal education of our children, that is, those who will shape society's future. Schools are also fishbowls. Their noteworthy accomplishments and, perhaps even more so, their untoward happenings and nonaccomplishments, provide grist for the media mills and for vocal consumer reactions. Moreover, many people fancy themselves to be self-styled experts when it comes to education and to how a school should be run and are not hesitant to express those views forcefully (Sarason, 1995). This may be one reason why many teachers report that the "care and feeding" of parents is often a difficult and anxiety-producing part of their job (Cowen et al., 1975; Sarason, 1971). Not only do they often face the touchy task of breaking bad news to parents, with the threat of ensuing parental wrath hanging over their heads, but there is always the specter and the reality that an upset parent may materialize at any time with grave concerns about how the school or class is managing its business or, more specifically, how his or her child is being handled.

In such a context, teachers and other school personnel, who witness daily the inevitable difficulties or failings of children either to master educational materials or to adapt to a school's behavioral guidelines, are continually pressed to find new and better ways to conduct their classes and to join a bandwagon of educational reform (Sarason, 1983, 1990). Interested external parties, such as colleges of education, often beam on a similar wavelength. Small wonder then that schools are the targets of a steady stream of new trial balloons designed to improve educational strategies and outcomes, and to foster changes in children's behavior and adaptation that will make for a more wholesome educational experience.

So, change and exploration of change, at least at a surface level, is the rule rather than the exception in schools. The number of approaches toward a brave new school world that have been tried cannot be counted. Only a small fraction of the latter represent real, as opposed to cosmetic, changes. Only a few of those real changes have survived to become an integral part of an improved system. These are the realities behind Sarason's (1971) reminder that, in schools, "the more things change, the more they stay the same."

For all the preceding reasons, the mere fact of PMHP's survival for 38 years is a noteworthy accomplishment—certainly for a school mental health program. The latter typically have relatively brief half-lives. PMHP's longevity, indeed the extent to which the project has grown and flourished over the years quietly but convincingly suggests that what the program offers makes eminently good sense to consumers because it addresses real problems and meets important everyday needs in the schools.

Although program survival is not per se a sufficient reason for writing a book, the latter decision is better justified by the fact that the PMHP model has, by now, genuinely taken hold and expanded, that is, it has been widely adopted by many school districts around the world. Currently, more than 700 school districts from the bush in Australia to the Wailing Wall in Jerusalem are implementing PMHP. There are over 130 implementing districts in the state of New York, ranging from turbulent, high-risk inner city settings to innovative rural consortia serving underresourced districts. Three other states (California, Washington, and Connecticut) have passed specific PMHP-enabling legislation with supporting budgets. Each year, these programs bring effective, preventively oriented services to tens of thousands of young children in need. Because the sum of important new project developments over the past 20 years has been considerable, we believe that it is again time to take stock of what PMHP has accomplished, what these accomplishments mean, and what kinds of agenda they set up for future school-based prevention programming and research.

The preceding issues provide the integrative framework within which the project's emphases and specific ways of operation can best be understood. Although it will be important and instructive to consider PMHP's roots, including the issues that gave rise to the project in the first place and a brief account of the early unfolding of the project, the volume's main emphasis is on PMHP's development and evolutionary course from 1975 to 1995, the issues that fueled these ongoing developments, and the implications of what we have learned in this more recent period for (school) mental health practice in the 21st century.

SOIL AND ROOTS

PMHP, in a brief overly simplistic phrase, is a school-based preventive program for young children. Although conceptualizing the approach as a "mini" paradigm shift in school mental health may well be a form of "languaging-up" that borders on the grandiose, it at least helps to establish a framework for viewing how, and why, the project came about and the issues it seeks to address.

Otherwise put, PMHP did not suddenly spring from nothing. Rather, it was a logical outgrowth of the realities of its time—one that developed in a special type of soil that took centuries to evolve into the form it had taken by the early 1950s. A poor-man's soil analysis, at that time, identified some long-standing, serious problems facing the mental health fields—problems that called for conceptually different approaches (ergo the rationale for speaking of a small paradigm shift in mental health). Although those issues have been considered in some depth in other sources (Cowen et al., 1975; Zax & Cowen, 1976), they bear at least superficial review in this context, if only because an awareness of the evolutionary course of the mental health field, and the unresolved problems that were residues of that course in the 1950s, establishes a historical matrix that helps to clarify the thinking that catalyzed PMHP's birth and early development.

In the beginning, mental health matters were hardly among the most prominent preoccupations of humankind; survival, understandably, was a far more basic concern (Zax & Cowen, 1976). As a rough rule of thumb it can be said that the more evolved a society becomes, and the more people's lower-order needs are met, the more likely is it that mental health issues or concerns about the vagaries and complexities of human behavior will attract serious attention. Accordingly, notions of what a mental health issue is, and appropriate ways for dealing with such issues in our society, have broadened considerably, albeit slowly and gradually over time, paralleling evolutions in technology, meeting material needs, and, in some quarters, greater affluence and the availability of more leisure time (Zax & Cowen, 1976).

Early humans, in struggling for a meager survival, had few concerns about behavior. The first and strongest such concerns to develop were with grossly atypical, aberrant behaviors that were threatening because they deviated floridly and indisputably from established behavioral norms. Even today, extreme departures from such norms gain widespread attention in modern societies as well as primitive ones. Because such behaviors are not well understood, they are often frightening (Zax & Cowen, 1976).

The lack of understanding of profound aberration in human behavior gave rise to a need for notions that might explain, or at least somewhat demystify, such conditions. Evolving explanations reflected regnant world views and belief systems of the times. The earliest of these explanations centered around notions of possession by dark forces (e.g., the devil or demonic spirits). That way of understanding or explaining certain behaviors is still evident in some primitive societies.

In modern society, such primitive views yielded first to religious explanations of aberrant behaviors and later to the biological and medical discoveries of the 18th and 19th centuries, either by themselves or in combination with more recent emphases on environmental determinants of human psychological dysfunction. However, even in the face of these massive changes in explanatory systems (ways of understanding) for psychological problems, unsolved, indeed baffling, mysteries about the cause and cure of many profound psychological disorders remain fully evident as perplexing problems on the current mental health scene and stand as prime targets for the field's change-efforts. The point to underscore is that mental health's earliest, strongest, and remaining prime cathexes, interests, and commitments of resources have always been directed to major psychological dysfunction and the ways in which such dysfunction might be contained or repaired.

Along with these slowly changing notions of causality of dysfunction came a gradual broadening of the boundary definitions for psychological dysfunction and its forms of manifestation. The overall direction of this steady and important shift was toward an ever-growing inclusion of conditions that are less obvious than the florid, extreme deviations that had long been the exclusive focus of the mental health fields and its precursors. Examples of such subtler problems include loneliness, anxiety, depression, damaged interpersonal relationships, chronic unhappiness, and failure to realize one's potential. Such behavioral or phenomenological problems, each reflecting a more subtle failing in the human condition, came more and more to be matters of concern both to students of pathology and mental health practitioners.

New, more finely articulated types of disordered states were recognized, that is, conditions that now go under such rubrics as the neuroses, antisocial personalities, psychosomatic disorders, and, more recently, even more subtle entities such as existential or philosophical neuroses that pivot around preoccupation with the meaning of life and one's place in the cosmos. With those changes in view came the development of a growing tide of ever more specialized, differentiated treatment strategies designed to provide different curative strokes for different problem-smitten folks. One highly palpable reflection of this inexorable process of broadening the definition and of highlighting the nuances of psychological perturbation is the significant expansion in the numbers of maladaptive conditions formally recognized in the diagnostic manuals developed by the American Psychiatric Association over the past half-century.

A point to highlight from the preceding discussion is that these slow broadening steps toward recognizing less florid conditions as relevant to mental health field's scope and mandate have had important practical consequences for the field. One such consequence, in parallel with the emergence of a more affluent society with more leisure time, was a significant increase in the numbers of people who sought help from mental health professionals and/or other types of help agents for personal problems. This same evolutionary process also stimulated an ever-widening search for new ways to understand and deal with such conditions both within the traditionally defined mental health fields and ever-increasing numbers of related fields that believed they had something to offer in this regard.

Within mental health, psychotherapy is a prime example of one highly influential way that flowered in the past century. This process is built around verbal interactions between a trained mental health professional and a person experiencing psychological problems. The long-term objective of these interactions is to at least contain, and at best remediate, those problems. Many of mental health's more recently developed ways, psychotherapy included, have been very helpful, certainly for individuals beset with substantial and sometimes disabling personal problems.

At the same time, what is helpful for one individual, indeed for many individuals, is not necessarily the most helpful or utilitarian thing that can happen at a societal level. Thus, even with regard to today's vastly expanded family of psychotherapies—some of which have been extensively field-tested—important questions can be raised such as: Just how effective are they for the people who do have access to them? Which people do not have access to them? Why not? And to what extent might earlier preventive or competence enhancement approaches (Strayhorn, 1988) increase human effectiveness, reduce the need for restorative approaches such as psychotherapy, and, in the long run, be more humane and cost effective than even the most efficient and effective restorative approach? The difficult questions posed above had not been well answered in the early 1950s nor perhaps are they well answered even in the mid 1990s. Nagging doubts about whether there were good answers to them stimulated the need to consider conceptual alternatives to mental health's classic dominant ways of restoration and repair.

Other recent developments and social forces have also affected how we think about human psychological dysfunction. Modern society's technological evolution, improved standards of living, and consequent availability of more leisure time, have given many people more opportunities than ever before in the history of humankind to reflect upon themselves as psychological beings. Rieff (1959), commenting on this evolution, spoke of a then-emerging era of invasion and conquest of man's inner life and psyche or, as he put it, the emergence of a psychological man who seeks to "master his own personality." His observation reminds us once again that as humankind's survival needs are better met and as living conditions improve, people have more free energy to ponder psychological matters such as their happiness, effective functioning, and sense of security and belongingness.

We are thus living in an era in which we can perceive, in a "main-effects" sense, even though it may be subject to ups and downs as political forces wax and wane, the slow emergence of a social philosophy that recognizes the right of all people, including heretofore underserved, underrepresented groups such as children, retirees, women, ethnic and racial minorities, and disabled people, to have their basic and higher order needs met or, more earthily, to have a "fair shake" from life (Albee, 1982). However, the emergence of this way of thinking and behaving is indeed slow and still very much in the process of unfolding. Although the changes predisposed by this gradually shifting view are likely to be seen initially in concrete areas such as schooling, housing, job opportunities, and civil rights, the change in social philosophy they imply also importantly affects how we look at mental health issues and how we pursue the challenging task of enhancing people's psychological wellness (Cowen, 1991, 1994).

In parallel with, and in part because of, society's technological evolution, the mental health fields have broadened the range and types of problems that they accept as falling within their purview. Moreover, the earlier view that people's problems have primarily internal points of origin has been sharply modified to reflect the place of significant environmental roots and determinants. The latter range broadly from microsystem inputs (Bronfenbrenner, 1979) such as those that come from family milieu and family interaction variables, to the ways in which high-impact social institutions (e.g., schools, churches) go about conducting their mandated business, to the very heart of a society's macrostructure including the extent to which a society offers people access to such crucial, if abstract, entities as hope, justice, opportunity, and empowerment (Rappaport, 1981, 1987).

Concrete manifestations of these changing realities (expanding horizons) are evident in many forms and in many settings. For example, agencies or social institutions whose main purposes and functions are well outside of the mental health sphere (e.g., schools, industrial organizations, the legal system, the welfare system, police, the military, antipoverty organizations) have become more sensitized to the integral wholeness of people. To the extent that that is the case, an agency's success in meeting its mandated responsibilities may be closely intertwined with, or indeed depend heavily on, the mental health and well-being of the people it serves.

As these awarenesses have formed, agencies have increasingly come to recognize that the mental health fields can contribute significantly to the effective discharge of their (i.e., the agency's) roles and functions. One by-product of this growing awareness is that agencies of the type noted have increasingly hired mental health professionals directly to their staffs or, short of that, used such professionals as consultants. This changing scenario is one factor in a set of process changes that has drawn professionals out of their offices into community settings, where new needs, new issues, and new ways of looking at old problems have been identified. These latter observations and processes form a base on which innovative solutions to long-standing, refractory problems begin, if only dimly, to be perceived. When such solutions are found to work effectively across many contexts, they take on the air of a more substantial paradigm shift, or even a mental health revolution.

It is still too soon to know whether the changing orientation that PMHP reflects will prove ultimately to be part of a major paradigm shift or mental health revolution. What has become clearer is an awareness of the cumulation of unresolved problems facing the mental health field—a reality that calls for the conceptualization and exploration of innovative alternatives. Put in gross, global terms, the view that led to the birth of PMHP is that the sum of society's mental health efforts (i.e., its clinics, hospitals, and private practitioners), focused as it was on restoration or damage control, was then, and always would be, insufficient. Those efforts, directed primarily to evident, entrenched problems, led to a situation in which demand for help in dealing with problems far exceeded resources for providing such help (Albee, 1959). As a result, limited existing resources were distributed inequitably. Given such a state of affairs the theoretical alternatives of fostering sound development and building toward wellness from the start (Cowen, 1991, 1994) took on much abstract appeal.

The discussion to this point has several times spoken globally of perceived shortcomings (i.e., unresolved problems) of the then-existing mental health system as factors that stimulated thinking, in the early 1950s, in directions that ultimately spawned the PMHP development. We shall briefly overview those problems to make the mental health context in which PMHP surfaced more palpable. Thus, in the 1950s and, to a considerable extent still today, the following were major unresolved problems facing the mental health fields:

1. Mental health (repair) resources were insufficient to meet spontaneous demand for services, much less underlying need (Albee, 1959; Arnhoff, Rubenstein, & Speisman, 1969; Levine & Perkins, 1987; Zax & Cowen, 1976).

2. De facto allocations of mental health services, for overdetermined reasons, followed the rule that help was least available where it was most needed (Cowen, Gardner, & Zax, 1967; Lorion, 1973, 1974; Manson, 1982; Rappaport, 1977; Ryan, 1971; Sanua, 1966; Schofield, 1964). These glaring distributional inequities led the President's Commission on Mental Health (1978) to focus centrally on the unmet needs of the unserved and underserved, throughout its final report.

3. Major mismatches between mental health's traditional service delivery modes and the ways in which large segments of the population defined, perceived, and dealt with their problems, created conditions under which the affected groups saw traditional mental health services as inappropriate or irrelevant to *their* needs and life circumstances (Rappaport, 1977; Reiff, 1967; Reiff & Riessman, 1965; Ryan, 1971; Zax & Cowen, 1976).

4. Notwithstanding dedicated efforts by competent, committed mental health professionals, most of the serious problems that major mental disorders (e.g., schizophrenia) posed could not be solved (Cowen, 1986; Goldstein, 1982; Zax & Cowen, 1976).

5. Mental health's most finely honed repair strategies (e.g., psychotherapy) had limited efficacy, not because of default in skills or effort but because the conditions they were called on to remediate were rooted and change resistant (Albee, 1982; Cowen, 1973; Levine & Perkins, 1987; Rappaport, 1977). Under such circumstances even the most sophisticated, costly, and time-consuming repair efforts have guarded prognoses.

It was, of course, not just the condition of the overall mental health system that concerned us. Rather, our more specific concerns pertained to the smaller, but more directly relevant, world of school mental health. That domain was experiencing many of the same issues—and headaches—as the broader field of mental health, with perhaps more serious consequences since children's mental health services were sorely underrepresented at that time. The fact of the matter, however, was that the existing school mental health service system had been conceived in the image of and had, to a major extent, been imprisoned by the parent mental health field's views of dysfunction and the resultant ways of delivering services.

Looking at the opposite side of that coin, however, one might say that school mental health services had not sufficiently capitalized on the special attributes and potentials of the young child or the special opportunities for constructive intervention that schools offer. Children spend major portions of their early lives in school. There they are called upon continually to meet two stage-salient sets of demands: (a) mastering increasingly complex bodies of knowledge, that is, they must *learn*; and (b) doing so effectively within an existing set of rules about appropriate behavior, that is, they must *adapt*. Thus, for better or worse, schools exercise a powerful influence on children's personal and educational development (Task Panel Report: Learning Failure and Unused Learning Potential, 1978).

School mental health services arose originally, and developed later, in specific problem-oriented contexts. Social workers, or visiting teachers as they were known, entered the schools at the turn of the century, when compulsory attendance laws were first passed. Their job was to establish contacts with difficult-to-reach families so as to get "truant" children back to school. Doing so, it was hoped, was the key to reducing the then-rampant, adverse social consequences of noneducation. In like manner, the initial focus of school psychology, born in the psychometric tradition of the early 20th century, was also overwhelmingly problem oriented. Its earliest goals were to diagnose and remediate the school adaptation problems experienced by slow-learning and skill-deficient children, in the best possible manner.

Although these initially narrow and specific notions of professional roles have since been liberalized significantly, everyday school mental health practice in the days before PMHP reflected the predominant focus of doing whatever could be done to identify and remediate evident, established problems. By definition, such an approach allocates most of a school's limited "mental health" resources to the visibly troubled few. Learning and adaptive problems among school children are so widespread and professional resources for dealing with them so thin (Glidewell & Swallow, 1969; Task Panel Report: Learning Failure and Unused Learning Potential, 1978) that mental health services in most school settings are limited to a small fraction of children in dire need, that is, those with the most serious, vivid, nonpostponable problems. Many others, whose difficulties are less apparent or socially disruptive are left to struggle as best they can, or simply to sink into a maelstrom of failure. Alas, it is an unfortunate reality that many early school difficulties, left unattended, mount and fan out rather than disappear as time passes (Cowen, Pedersen, Babigian, Izzo, & Trost, 1973; Ensminger, Kellam, & Rubin, 1983; Kellam, Simon, & Ensminger, 1983). Thus, microcosmically, school mental health services in the 1950s well reflected the same troublesome problems that adult mental health services faced, that is, insufficient resources were being allocated disproportionately to the most serious, pressing problems (with the poorest prognoses) requiring major time investments.

School failure, whether defined educationally or behaviorally, has long been a rampant destructive problem in America (Task Panel Report: Learning Failure and Unused Learning Potential, 1978). Fleshing out that observation with relevant empirical findings from 27 separate incidence studies, Glidewell and Swallow's (1969) survey for the Joint Commission on the Mental Health of Children concluded that 1 in 3 American school children had school adjustment problems and 1 in 10 had sufficiently serious problems to need professional help. These already frightening overall base rates were considerably higher in the urban megalopolis. The Chicago–Woodlawn studies (Kellam, Branch, Agrawal, & Ensminger, 1975; Kellam, Branch, Agrawal, & Grabill, 1972), for example, reported a 7 in 10 school maladjustment figure in the inner-city areas of one megalopolis. That staggering incidence figure painted a somber profile for the urban inner city 20 years ago; that picture is even more somber today. If education, as Glidewell and Swallow (1969) suggested, should be viewed a major national resource, the conditions and survey data cited in their review reflected a tragic national waste.

These stark findings posed several important challenges. One concerned the extent to which informed early preventive efforts might cut back the flow and development of these early problems before they rooted and flowered. Closely related was the challenge of how to develop prevention programs that could bring much needed help to a rapidly swelling tide of urban children who, historically, had gotten short shrift both generally (i.e., in terms of the opportunities that society afforded them) and specifically (i.e., in terms of access to all facets of the mental health and other human service systems).

The preceding considerations raised important issues of tactics and policy in our minds, however vaguely and amorphously. The philosophical questions that absorbed us, with many subthemes, were (a) How *should* finite school mental health energies and resources be allocated as between: the visibly hurting few versus the less obvious many who suffer quietly; older and younger children; individual children versus the systems that shape their well-being; restoration versus prevention? and (b) How might meaningful early helping services be upgraded for those who are destined to be last in line when it comes to allocation of society's limited helping resources?

Although we had no pat solutions to these problems, the need to explore and develop such solutions was well established in our minds by the mid 1950s. We had, by then, begun to form a "gross cognitive map" (to use E. C. Tolman's then-popular learning-theory concept) of what might be done constructively to address the issues and problems we had come to perceive. Even so, at that early and still unstructured point in time, there were, no doubt, many different ways in which we might have proceeded—consonant with Sarason's (1971) heuristic concept of "universe of alternatives." In that kind of crucible, the initial contours of a PMHP plan that had begun to form in our minds was hardly a finely articulated master plan or blueprint; rather it was an initial gross approximation based on three guiding directional emphases: (a) prevention, (b) young children, and (c) schools. In the quest to develop a more meaningful, utilitarian, program paradigm in school mental health, prevention was to be the goal, young children the prime program targets, and elementary schools the prime activity sites. Although we have hinted at several of the rationales that fueled this particular combination of emphases, there is need to say more about why these same three directional beacons have remained central in our work since Day 1.

The concept of prevention captivated us because it seemed to harbor potentially meaningful solutions to vexing problems (insufficient resources, and inequitable distribution of those limited resources) that plagued the classically defined mental health field. Even more insipid was the fact that actions by mental health (including school mental health) professionals came into play only when evident dysfunction was brought forcibly to their attention. That is not an optimal time, prognostically, to intervene, because rooted dysfunction resists change tenaciously.

Prevention vivifies the conviction of many military strategists and athletic coaches that a good offense is the best defense. Among its most basic strategies are efforts to (a) minimize the development of dysfunction by building strengths and competencies in children from the start and/or (b) avert the predictably adverse outcomes that many situations of heightened risk are known to predispose. Effective early prevention programs thus hold promise for cutting down the flow of dysfunction and thus reducing the heavy human and societal costs associated with maladaptation (Kiesler, 1992; Kiesler, Simpkins, & Morton, 1989). Another virtue of prevention approaches is that because they can be equally targeted, via policy-making decisions, to all sectors of society, they can help to redress chronic problems created by de jure or de facto inequities in the distribution of society's limited mental health resources. Thus, we could perceive both the need for, and commonsensical appeal of, preventive approaches, in the period before PMHP started. The project grew out of that vision; indeed prevention by then was clearly established as an abstract deity at whose altar we would long worship.

Even granting the logic and compellingness of generalized arguments in favor of prevention, issues remained as to how and where such efforts could be directed most meaningfully. Our strongly held view at the time was that young children be the prime targets of prevention efforts. The reasoning behind that view went roughly as follows. Young children are, relatively speaking, flexible, malleable organisms. Whatever the nature of the difficulties they experience in their early development, those difficulties are less likely, than for older children, to have rooted or fanned out. Thus, the facilitating qualities of having (a) less crystallized problems; (b) fewer set, maladaptive ways of coping with such problems; and (c) the ability to pick up flexibly on new learnings and alternatives, each characteristic of the young child, made that age group, for us, the logical, indeed ideal, target for informed prevention programming. In the lingo of energy conservation strategies, a matter of major public concern when PMHP began, our thinking was powered by the belief that young children had the potential to yield maximal miles per gallon for a given investment of preventively targeted mental health time and effort.

Finally, there was the question, Why schools as the prime sites for prevention programs? Several considerations spoke in favor of such a location. Schools, in our view, are entirely natural settings for conducting prevention programs for children because many such programs are educational in nature. In Western society, schools also are a key force, second only to the family, in the child's early molding and development. For a dozen or more years, during a highly formative period of their lives, children spend up to one third of their waking hours in school. There, they have vital shaping experiences and continuing exposure to key mentors and identification models. Moreover, schools bring large numbers of children together under a single roof and administrative aegis. Thus, both by legal mandate and by the prerogatives and leeways that schools hold in exercising that mandate, schools have ongoing opportunities to make key shaping determinations about the type of educational experiences and environments to which children will be exposed.

Although none of the preceding is intended to suggest that schools are more important than the home and family in the child's early development, it at least highlights the facts that schools are extremely important in their own right and offer much better, and more systematic, access to large numbers of young children, than do individual families. As such, schools provide special opportunities for taking actions and developing (prevention) programs, that strive, from the start, to optimize young children's cognitive and behavioral development.

Because the adopted "Holy Trinity" of prevention, young children, and the schools "clicked in" and made eminently good sense to us very early, the main practical issues we faced in starting PMHP were less to identify a guiding leitmotif than to develop effective technologies embodying the three emphases (cf., above) that comprised an already adopted leitmotif. The work that has been done over the course of PMHP's multidecade existence represents one systematic, indeed stubbornly persistent, effort to achieve that goal.

Although we have many times in the course of that voyage (a) proceeded naively or uninformedly, (b) been guilty of egregious tactical errors, (c) flown by the "seat of our pants," (d) been obliged to modify practices or to pull in our horns, and (e) caulked weak spots, during this entire complex process of exploration and expansion of project efforts over the years, including some recent, significant, qualitative changes in the nature of PMHP's programming efforts, we have never really lost sight of an overarching and thoroughly persistent commitment to the keywords prevention, young children, and the schools. Thus, it has been technology and strategy, rather than the project's basic conceptual thrust or ultimate objectives, that have changed, evolved, and hopefully been strengthened in the overall process of PMHP's evolution. If this evolutionary experience has, as we believe to be the case, led us more clearly to visualize innovative, promising new options for school mental health, these options are, in the main, a by-product of PMHP's unswerving, nearly 40-year-long commitment to the development and evaluation of effective school-based prevention programming for young children.

I

PMHP: THE CORE PROGRAM

INTRODUCTION

It would be misleading to depict the Primary Mental Health Project (PMHP) as a static program. Although there is, to be sure, a basic PMHP entity, the program model has continued to evolve as a result of observation, research findings, and an attitude of critical self-scrutiny. Always paramount in our minds have been the questions of what's working well, what not so well, and what can be done to improve on the latter. Extending viable program options, reaching more children, and serving them more effectively in a preventive mode, rather than enshrining early PMHP practice, are the wellsprings that have stimulated our activities over the years.

This orienting-set has stimulated the development of (a) new program options within PMHP's basic framework, designed to enhance its reach, flexibility, and, in the last analysis, effectiveness; and (b) qualitatively different primary prevention program options. Although the latter share the goals of enhancing children's wellness and school adaptation, they embody different practices and targeting than the ontogenetically early secondary prevention approach that defines the core PMHP. This distinction establishes a rough line of demarcation between Parts 1 and 2 of the volume. Whereas Part 1 (chapters 2–6) focuses exclusively on the classic PMHP, Part 2 (chapters 7–11) describes developments that go beyond that entity.

Chapter 2 first describes the administrative framework within which PMHP developed and now operates, and then provides a preliminary overview (X ray) of how the program actually works. Chapter 3, in describing PMHP's early evolutionary course, recapitulates material from the earlier PMHP volume. Chapter 4, perhaps the most important in the book for practitioners and aspiring implementers, offers a concrete overview of the PMHP approach and provides a user-friendly description of essential steps in setting up and conducting such a program. Chapter 5 describes five offshoot programs, each of which extends PMHP's classic framework and enables the approach to work more effectively for some children. These newer mini-programs include work with small groups of children; crisis intervention; work with acting-out children; planned short-term intervention; and training nonprofessional child "associates" to work with parents. Chapter 6 overviews PMHP's extensive research efforts with special emphasis on program evaluation (outcome) studies that we ourselves and others have done. Evaluations of later primary prevention programs (Part 2) have been incorporated into the respective chapters describing them.

2

HOW PMHP OPERATES: AN X RAY

Chapter 1 provided background information about the climate in which the vestigial PMHP rooted, the problems it sought to address, and its intended place on the evolving school mental health scene. This chapter offers a brief overview (X ray) of PMHP's basic defining features. It is, in effect, a preview of coming attractions. It begins with a description of the project's current administrative structure and housing arrangement. This is followed by a global overview of the elements that define PMHP's basic modus operandi. The chapter is intended to be only a bare-bones summary of what PMHP is all about; later sections of the volume, particularly chapter 4, add more meat to those bare bones.

ADMINISTRATIVE STRUCTURE AND PHYSICAL LAYOUT

One element to consider at the very outset, is the administrative–organizational framework within which PMHP operates. The latter is unique, and probably implausible. How this particular arrangement evolved and the purposes it serves are relevant matters that will be addressed presently. For now, we wish only to note that PMHP, as a project, must deal with, and account to, an unlikely troika of masters: (a) the school districts in which the project is set, (b) the University of Rochester, and (c) a not-for-profit agency, called PMHP Inc., which is actively involved in important fund-raising and advocacy roles designed to ensure the project's survival, integrity, and healthy development. The first two of these masters have been part of PMHP's fabric since Day 1 (indeed even earlier, during the planning period before the project actually started). The third administrative entity of relevance, PMHP Inc., is a relative "newcomer" that has existed for "only" 27 years.

The overall PMHP operation has two main components. All central planning, coordinating, program development, training, and evaluation activities take place within a project headquarters building (cf. below). All program implementations, however, are set in school buildings. The section to follow describes the housing arrangement for PMHP's program development and research (i.e., non-school-based) activities. For those, PMHP's headquarters and nerve center, for the past 27 years, has been located in an ancient three-story building which, in a prior incarnation, a century back, was a fashionable private dwelling. The building, provided by the University of Rochester (UR), is called the UR Center for Community Study. It is located on a main thoroughfare in a residential city neighborhood, about one mile from campus in one direction and one mile from downtown Rochester in the other. Thus, geographically, the Center melds "town and gown" and its ready accessibility to campus facilitates student involvement in project activities.

Although one can see traces of the "elegance of yesteryear" in the Center's exterior structure and trappings, it is also clear that the building left its glory days behind long ago. The building's ornate exterior is painted a somber, unappealing dark purple. This combination prompted a wag once to describe the Center as a clone of Charles Addams's classic bat-infested mansion. It would be generous to describe the building's exterior as "a bit shopworn." A more accurate, albeit a tad more painful, descriptor is "seedy."

The building's interior also bears comment, both for its good, and not-so-good, features. Work space in the building consists of 14 offices and one (heavily used) multipurpose seminar room. The latter, with a gracious, broad, wood-beamed ceiling, functions as a classroom, training center, cinema, library, and overflow storage area for countless test forms, program manuals, and literally hundreds of thick computer data binders. Clutter in the seminar room has gotten sufficiently dense to make successful locomotion through it an heroic athletic achievement.

Most Center offices are good-sized—roomy enough to invite pack-rat saving behaviors, a commodity of which the building is in good supply. Besides its office space, the building provides several welcome common areas, for example, an oft-frequented coffee alcove and a large kitchen that serves as a congregating and conversing area at lunch and other times, for members of project staff and visitors.

As might be surmised from this account, most of the building's 14 offices are seriously overcrowded—necessarily so because they are occupied at various times by approximately 30 people. Indeed, the ravages of overcrowding, several years back, made it necessary for survival for PMHP to rent additional space in a nearby building and detach one contingent of staff members to this new annex. Because program growth continues to be a tail which, in some ways, wags the dog, we were obliged in Fall 1994 to move major segments of the PMHP operation into a much larger (4,000 sq. ft.) new space annex, half a mile away from the main building.

Much about the main building's interior, like its exterior, conveys the aura of having been around, and heavily used, for a long time. Interior walls have not been offended by fresh paint in eons. Last (foolishly) painted in pastel colors, those walls now bear the unmistakable imprimatur of fading, aggravated by the inexorable process of cumulation of dirt. Windows have also acquired their fair share of dust and grime, to the point where it is a challenge to see through some of them. Few if any offices are without evidence of fallen plaster; indeed several people have been reported to have been hit on the head with minor fragments of falling ceiling plaster in the course of within-building locomotion.

The building's floor coverings are a motley mix of very old and relatively less old carpets. The olds include some of the ugliest, most frayed, tattered rugs known to humankind. The more recently carpeted areas, in a relatively lesser state of disrepair, consist of lightly colored broadloom (bad mistake) that now shows countless coffee-spill scars—by-products of the never-ending treks, overflowing coffee mug in hand, from the coffee alcove back to building dwellers' offices. Coffee-spill offenders can be readily identified by observers much less skilled or experienced than Sherlock Holmes, via the specific directional trails of broadloom stains they leave in the wake of their frequent pilgrimages to the coffee machine.

Certainly, the overall building *gestalt* is one of striking contrasts. Thus, whereas its interior and exterior structures, and ornateness take one back directly to the Victorian era, other signposts (e.g., multiple computer workstations and laser printers humming away cheerfully at all times, electronic test-scoring machines) stand as markers of the late 20th century and harbingers of the 21st.

The massive, rather forbidding, thick-walled nature of the building, along with the anachronisms and relics of yesteryear that define its interior structure, prompted one fellow traveler, many years ago, to dub it "The Bunker." And that's exactly how central staff and local area project veterans have referred to it ever since. To the extent that the term *bunker* also conveys the notion of the project nerve center, that image too is appropriate in the sense that the building is "home base" for project planning, evaluation, and other research, and a broad range of project communication, training, and dissemination activities. It is also home for local school-based personnel who receive training there, and it is very much a "home-away-from-home" for scores of people from regional training centers and closely affiliated state programs, who visit PMHP, attend its workshops, and plan and do research with its staff. Thus, notwithstanding the building's many foibles, inadequacies, peculiarities, and weak points (as noted above)—indeed perhaps even because of them—the bunker is a safe, secure, loved project home to PMHP staff and project-related folk from near and far.

BASIC PROJECT OPERATIONS

Although it would seem, on the surface, that a description of PMHP's basic (i.e., school-based) project operations should be a reasonably straightforward task, it is in truth much more complex to do that today than it was when the project first started, or even 20 years ago when the initial PMHP book appeared (Cowen, Trost, et al., 1975). In those earlier days, PMHP's operations could be described primarily in terms of the program's *service* components, with a dash of training and research thrown in. That is no longer the case. Although service and research elements remain central to PMHP's functioning, the project's demonstrated early success (i.e., its ability to address real, vexing, everyday problems experienced by schools, and children in their adaptation to schools) has fueled a continuing process, still very active, of project growth and expansion. The latter, in turn, led to an ever-broadening conception of PMHP's operations that feature such new functions as training and metatraining; program dissemination; and pursuing a number of new program initiatives—both those designed to strengthen the options and expand the scope of the basic PMHP program and those designed to develop new primary prevention modules that seek to go an important step beyond what vintage PMHP can offer.

These change and expansion steps have contributed importantly to PMHP's current functioning and, if our crystal ball-gazing is at all accurate, such directional adaptations may be even more important in the future. Accordingly, each of those new directions will be considered in depth later, both in terms of the needs, rationales, and historical events that stimulated movement in their directions and the actual operations that define them. Hence, the X-ray glimpse of PMHP's main elements that this chapter provides is targeted primarily to the program's classic service components.

But even at that level, a name-rank-serial-number description will be somewhat more complex than it would seem it should be (or than it once was)! From 1957 to 1969, PMHP was essentially unidimensional and therefore relatively easy to describe. During that period, which we speak of in retrospect as PMHP's pilot–experimental stage, the project existed in only one school building under the loving, everyday surveillance of its three founders. The operation was very much a "Ma and Pa" shop. Everybody knew everybody else on a first-name basis and communication about project matters was extensive and wholesome.

"Them" days, however, are long gone! One project school building in one medium-sized city has become thousands of project school buildings—large and small; urban, suburban, and rural—in many different (geographically and sociodemographically) school districts around the country, indeed around the world. Part of the fabric of this major growth and expansion process has been steady change and evolution in PMHP's operating ways—most quite natural and foreseeable. One evolutionary difference, for sure, is that firsthand contacts and communication between project headquarters and implementing schools has diminished overall and, in some cases, virtually disappeared. With that change has come marked reduction in the direct inputs that the bunker makes to emerging programs and in the direct program quality-control steps that the parent program can take. One undesirable, yet inevitable, consequence of this shifting reality is dilution in fidelity of program implementation in some settings.

That same "coin of program expansion" has an opposite side as well. Understandably and importantly, as more and more districts implemented PMHP an ever-widening range of differences in needs, resources, personnel and staffing situations, and patterns of skills and predilections among key project personnel became apparent. New school programs—leastwise those with hopes of surviving—cannot develop wholesomely without full awareness and respect for their own defining "ecological realities." Hence, in the Darwinian sense, program survival requires that program implementations fit in well with, that is, be adapted to, their environs (pond ecologies).

This need has certainly been evident in the history of PMHP's unfolding. Programs out of tune with their environmental contexts have not survived, and with enormous expansion over the years, there now exist countless "variations on a basic theme" in the defining operations of specific program implementations around the world. These many variations are, in some ways, mindful of the variations within species that Darwin first observed in the Galapagos Islands. They are not, however, simply random environmentally adapted program variants; rather they are variants in which the observer can continue to see linking common denominators, through their adherence to PMHP's four guiding structural themes: (a) a focus on very young children; (b) using systematic early detection and screening methods; (c) using carefully selected nonprofessionals as the program's prime direct help agents with children; and (d) changing professional roles to the kinds of educative and consultative activities that support a more widespread delivery of early, effective preventively oriented services to young children in need.

The point to stress in this discussion, however, is that program variation and program relevant adaptations to the realities of particular school and community environmental surrounds—characteristics that epitomize many individual PMHP implementations—are the rule rather than the exception. Thus, no single program description can faithfully represent *all* the many operational programs in the extended PMHP family. Indeed even the parent PMHP, around which our account is built, has substantial heterogeneity in its more than 30 urban and suburban participating schools.

In any case, one reason for building this introductory overview around the parent PMHP, beyond the obvious fact that it's the version we know best, is that it stands as an ideal, or model, for other implementations, and as a source of credibility because of its decades of cumulated field experience and extensive research documentation. However, this decision is not made without several "pangs of misgiving," both because the parent PMHP is just one of many existing program "realities" and because doing so may paint an intimidating picture, in that the parent program is larger, more adequately resourced, and has had more battle-line experience than most other operating programs.

To counter the one-sidedness that this level of project depiction entails, we shall consider more fully, later in the volume, practical questions about how less well-resourced, aspiring new school districts can draw from the PMHP experience, and a range of concrete project modifications that can be considered that are calibrated to different levels of resource realities within a school district or specific school building.

PMHP SERVICES: A SYNOPSIS

The ultimate goal of PMHP services is to optimize school adaptation and learning in young children who have shown signs of risk for school maladjustment and/or failure. Thus, PMHP embodies the goals and methods of ontogenetically early secondary prevention. The phrase "ontogenetically early" in the preceding sentence is a crucial differentiator.

The term *secondary prevention* has been used in several different ways, that is, to describe interventions that take place (a) early in the unfolding of a given episode of disorder or (b) early in an individual's life history. As an approach, PMHP exemplifies the second of these two usages. Correcting early school adaptation problems and helping to build adaptive competencies in young, at-risk children from the start, can serve an immediate and important secondary preventive function and, in so doing, can help to lay down a firmer base for the child's later years in ways that take on a more primary preventive meaning.

The advantage of ontogenetically early secondary prevention (e.g., strengthening the adaptation of a 6-year-old school child showing early signs of being at risk) over entirely worthwhile, but ontogenetically later, secondary prevention (i.e., identifying a preinvolutional reaction pattern in a 47-year-old adult 3 days, rather than 3 weeks, after its first prodromal signs appear, thus making it possible to initiate correctives sooner), is that it holds within it greater potential for lifetime good. Otherwise put, there may be greater potential for radiation of the positive effects of effective early secondary prevention programs in younger, less chronically troubled, organisms.

Thus, PMHP's prime focus is on young children who show early signs of risk for adaptive or academic problems in school. Setting the project in schools offers ideal access lines for identifying such youngsters promptly and, given the necessary resources, a natural, relatively nonobtrusive framework in which to embed a preventively intended program.

Direct PMHP program services to young school children can most readily be considered within the preceding framework. Two reminders, however, are pertinent before those services are actually described. The first is that we shall (intentionally) be describing the program's major defining marker elements briefly and superficially, simply to provide the reader a gross cognitive map of the entity about which this book is written. Behind that incomplete description lies the promise that more fully fleshed out, concrete, "how-to-do it" information will be offered at several later points in the volume. Second, the particular, oversimplified overview offered here is based on how the parent PMHP project has operated. Project implementations elsewhere, even those that faithfully reflect PMHP's most fundamental assumptions and objectives, are characterized by different variations on a theme, in terms of the concrete program technologies and the specific ways used to deliver program services. Those variations are necessarily shaped by the implementor's needs, resources, predilections, and more broadly, by the specific "pond ecology" of the school building in which a given implementation is set.

Although the description of PMHP services to follow includes a number of discrete points, an "eyeball factor analysis" of those points suggests that they comprise three main clusters. The first two, which are at the heart of PMHP's active efforts, are (a) systematic, outreaching, early detection and screening and (b) the use of a relatively new breed of help agent, that is, the nonprofessional child associate, as the prime direct provider of early, effective helping services to young children in need. The third cluster is made up of several less readily classifiable, "instrumental" procedures, practices, and styles that share as common denominators the goals of maximizing the value of the project's active components and optimizing receptivity of the school context within which the project is set.

Early Detection and Screening

The PMHP process begins with systematic early detection and screening of primary graders for actual or incipient school adjustment problems. This step provides a necessary base on which to build early, effective preventively oriented interventions.

Several data sources (e.g., parent inputs, meetings with teachers, direct observation of the child in the classroom) feed into the overall early detection process. Its backbone however, in the sense of being an active, systematic, and outreaching effort to provide relevant information about school adaptation for *all* primary graders in a school, comes from a set of brief, PMHP-developed objective screening measures that profile young children's school problem behaviors and competencies.[1] We have learned that the keys to the usefulness of these measures in a complex, often overburdened school world are that they must be brief, objective, and easily completed and consist of items that are meaningful and relevant to classroom teachers. Over the years, PMHP has invested much time and effort in developing and refining such measures, always with an eye toward keeping them maximally streamlined and realistic for teachers, while at the same time strengthening their clinical sensitivity and psychometric properties.

We at PMHP have been pleased with the development of these early screening and assessment tools, which contribute importantly to the program's efficient and effective conduct. Because many implementing school districts have come to feel similarly about these measures, they are now widely used within PMHP's overall framework. On the other hand, even though we consider them to be sound measures, well adapted to the screening tasks at hand, it is not essential that implementing schools use these literal measures. What is essential to PMHP's underlying concepts and ways of functioning is that implementing programs use some systematic mechanism or process that provides an accurate picture of relevant aspects of all children's school functioning, early on.

The Referral and Assignment Processes

Early in the school year (October), a referral process to PMHP begins. This process grows out of the program's screening and early detection components. Most referrals are initiated by the classroom teacher on the basis of perceived indicators of ineffective functioning in the child. The latter may include any of a number of different problems, such as (a) aggressive,

---

[1]These measures are described in greater detail in chapter 4.

disruptive, acting-out behaviors, often readily observable and quite vexing for teachers because such problems impinge on other children and undermine class manageability (Sarason, 1995); (b) timid, anxious, withdrawn behaviors, including limited interaction with classmates—sometimes overlooked because such problems tend to be internal to given children and are not typically "boat-rocking" for the class at large; and (c) difficulties in learning, which are both obvious and worrisome to teachers because they reflect, very directly, a failure to meet the school's prime mandate. In more than a few cases, however, the reasons for referring a child straddle several of the areas noted above.

Although spontaneous teacher referrals for these types of school adjustment problems comprise the lion's share of referrals in PMHP schools, several other referring sources also bear mention. Some teacher referrals, for example, evolve from a process whereby teachers receive concrete feedback on children based on the screening information that PMHP collects. Thus a teacher, who may have previously had only a marginal or borderline concern about a child's status, might refer that child on the basis of additional confirmatory screening information. If, as sometimes happens, there is disagreement between the teacher's impressions of the child and the child's apparent status based on information gathered during the screening process (e.g., if the teacher believes that the child has significant adjustment problems but indicators of such problems are *not* evident in the screening data), the teacher's judgment typically supersedes the test data. Otherwise put, the project is responsive to perceived teacher need as well as teacher readiness.

Other school personnel also refer children to PMHP, often in relation to situational problems they observe in specific domains of school-related functioning (e.g., in the gym, on the playground, in the lunchroom, on the school bus). These referral sources include the principal, school nurse, specialty (e.g., art, physical education) teachers, street-crossing monitors, or lunchroom monitors. As PMHP gets to be known, and indicators of its effective functioning become evident in a school, parents sometimes refer their own children to the program. Indeed, there are known instances in which a parent's decision to move to a particular catchment area has reflected, in substantial measure, the knowledge that a PMHP, which they very much wanted their child to have, was in operation in the elementary school located in that area.

Once a referral to PMHP is to be made, a member of the school mental health team contacts the home to review the child's current school situation with the parent(s), describe how PMHP works, and explain to the parent why it may be helpful for their child to take advantage of PMHP's services. Parent permission is mandatory before a child can be seen through PMHP. In almost all cases, such permission is given readily. Every so often, however, a parent asks for more information about the project and the reasons for the child's referral. In such cases, school mental health personnel will attempt to provide whatever additional information is requested. And indeed, in any given year, one or two parents may decide that they do *not* want their (referred) child to participate in the project. That choice is, of course, honored. It should be noted, however, that some parents who initially decline later consent to their child's participation if evidence of the child's school adjustment problems continues to mount.

Relatively early in the school year, after parent permissions for the child to participate in PMHP have been received, screening and referral data are reviewed at an initial assignment conference in which members of the school's basic PMHP team participate. Although the exact nature of this team varies somewhat from setting to setting, it usually includes PMHP school mental health professionals, child associates, referring teachers, and, depending on interest and time availability, the building principal. Assignment conferences typically consider a number of children in any given session. Even though children can be, and in fact are, referred to PMHP throughout the school year, most assignment conferences and most of the allocation of child associates' available time for the year occur in the first several months of the school year.

Viewed broadly, the assignment conference has two main goals: (a) to review all information and data available for a referred child in seeking to reach a clear understanding of the child's situation and problems and, on that basis, (b) to establish overall intervention goals and consider intervention strategies and tactics that can best achieve those goals.

The Child Associate

The involvement of the nonprofessional child associate as the program's prime, direct help agent with young children is one of PMHP's most important distinguishing features. The modal PMHP associate is between ages 40 and 50 and is the mother of several children. There are, however, many exceptions to that modal profile, including both older and younger associates, some who are not mothers, and indeed a few who are not women. The range of educational backgrounds among associates is substantial.

The human qualities of caring and compassion, enjoying children, and having experience and relevant skills for working with them have for us been far more important criteria in selecting child associates than past traditional criteria (e.g., formal education, advanced degrees, years of supervised clinical experience) used to hire those who function as help agents with children. Criteria for selecting child associates are elastic in the parent PMHP and are even more elastic and diverse as one goes across school districts and considers implementations in different parts of the country, indeed around the world. For example, in some school districts with predominantly ethnic minorities, strong efforts have (appropriately) been made to hire child associates who are representative, ethnically, of the children served and thus have a clearer picture, often based on direct first-hand experience, of the styles and values of the group with whom they will be working.

Although child associates do, in fact, receive (time-limited) training in preparing for work with children in schools (the specific nature of this training is described in detail in chapter 4), the point to stress here is that the first consideration in selecting associates pivots around clinical judgments made about their human and experiential qualities (e.g., warmth, caring for children) as opposed to formal education, advanced degrees, or prior involvements in more traditional clinical roles.

The child associate seeks to establish a caring, trusting relationship with the children whom she sees. Such a relationship lays down the base on which children's progress in PMHP rests. Some children referred to PMHP lack such a stabilizing anchor point elsewhere in their lives. The specific technology that associates use in seeking to establish a trusting relationship varies and is, in any case, less crucial than the need for such efforts to be sincere and to unfold in natural, meaningful, ego-syntonic ways for the involved parties.

Among the vehicles used to establish a sound relationship with the child, and thus form a base for continuing productive associate–child interactions, are words and conversation, reading books, using puppets and other expressive media, and doll play. In our experience, associates vary greatly in the degree to which they are comfortable and invested in these diverse modes of interaction with children. Some depict themselves as "arts and crafts" types, others are more skilled and comfortable interacting as puppeteers, and still others feel especially at home in the book and story world. Such skills, however, are fundamentally tools, within the context of a meaningful relationship—tools designed to help children to get in touch, and deal effectively, with pertinent problem areas and important feelings. In the last analysis, it is the nature (i.e., the wholesomeness) of the associate–child relationship, far more than the medium through which it happens to gain expression, that is important in PMHP.

Moreover, going across hundreds of PMHP schools in many places around the world, it is surely the case that school-based mental health professionals differ greatly in their clinical styles and emphases, and certainly in their theoretical predilections (e.g., psychodynamic vs. behavioral vs. nondirective). That is, and will undoubtedly remain, a reality. But, notwithstanding these differences, the associate–child relationship remains pivotal in all program implementations. And clearly, experience with PMHP over many years, in many settings has shown that warm, effective associate–child relationships can, and do, form within a number of different theoretical frameworks. For that reason, the preferred (if not mandatory) conceptual–theoretical intervention framework within which to work in a PMHP school is the one in which program supervisors feel most comfortable and are best informed.

In PMHP schools, most of the associates' training after the initial round, and all of their supervision, comes from the school's mental health professionals. Some additional training comes about almost automatically by virtue of the associate's participation in a continuing stream of project clinical conferences as well as, in some cases, meetings conducted by program consultants. Supervision of associates is a vital aspect both of program quality control, and growth of associates in confidence and competence. As associates come to develop a better feel for the range and types of PMHP role demands, and become more comfortable and adept in those roles, they are provided with other more specific advanced training options (e.g., techniques for working with acting-out children, seeing children in groups, crisis intervention).

School-based PMHP programs vary in terms of how many associates they have, and how specifically associates are used and deployed. Many programs (modally perhaps) use part-time (16–24 hr/week) child associates, paid at a district's prevailing rates for such nonprofessional personnel. A smaller number of programs use paid, full-time associates. A significant number of districts have built programs around the use of volunteers as child associates. Programs in schools with large numbers of primary graders may have six or seven part-time child associates; whereas, at the other extreme, some very small programs have only one associate. Our experience, however, suggests that the presence of at least two associates in a program is useful in terms of providing discussion and feedback opportunities as well as a mutual support mechanism.

Most associates in the Rochester PMHP are hired on an approximate half-time, paid basis. Once they have become comfortable in their new role, associates attend relevant project conferences and carry caseloads of a dozen or more children. One can see, in that way, how a cadre of four or five associates in a given school can significantly expand the reach of early, effective preventive services. Specifically, four part-time associates, each seeing 12 or 13 children, can serve 50 or more children at any one time. The Rochester program has operated on the premise that the child associate's prime task, in the first year, is to become knowledgeable about and comfortable with her role in relation to a broad range of young children with diverse needs. In later years, the program offers other training options for associates to expand the scope of their activities and refine their skills. These options are described in chapter 5.

The role of being a child associate in the schools is an intrinsically satisfying one for many women who have raised their own children and are now seeking rewarding, new work involvement. One earthy, operational affirmation of that view is the fact that the parent PMHP now has a substantial number of associates who have logged 20 or more years of service in that role.

PMHP Conferences and Communication Mechanisms

There is an ongoing process, in PMHP schools, of exchange of information and coordination of goals on the child's behalf that involves teachers, school mental health professionals, child associates, and other pertinent school personnel. There are both formal and informal aspects of this interchange process. The formal components center around the program's major clinical conferences (cf. below), at which team decisions are made about the nature and course of child interventions. Informal contacts about children among key project players (e.g., teachers and child associates) take place continually in classrooms, hallways, and teacher lounges.

This interchange and communication process among team members offers important potential benefits to PMHP-seen children. As a result, referred children can be approached more knowledgeably and sensitively, in a way that reflects a coordinated school effort. These same interaction processes also offer indirect benefits to the school. One such benefit is that they help to weld a sense of community, or "teamness," built around working together on behalf of the children. A second is that this form of communication broadens the knowledge base of key program participants. Child associates continue to grow on the job and to enlarge their repertoire of child-serving skills. Teacher involvement in PMHP's clinical conferences and consultation meetings increases their understanding of, and sensitivity to, the sometimes complex connections between psychological factors and situational occurrences in the child's life on the one side, and the child's classroom behavior and readiness for learning on the other. Ultimately, some teachers are able to translate such new learnings into more sensitive, effective forms of class handling and management. To the extent that that happens, a program in ontogenetically early secondary prevention (i.e., PMHP) spawns initiatives and actions that move appreciably in the direction of primary prevention.

At the more formal level, three types of clinical conferences take place within PMHP's larger programmatic framework. These conferences are linked temporally with the child's progression through the program, and for that reason, tend to occur within relatively narrow time bands during the school year. Conference participants include the project's school mental health professionals, child associates, relevant teachers, and whenever possible, the principal. Other school personnel (e.g., specialty teachers, lunchroom or street-crossing monitors) also attend when pertinent and feasible.

The first such conference is the assignment conference (cf. above). Most of these occur early in the school year (October–November). At the assignment conference, screening data, teacher observations and impressions, and parent inputs are discussed, intervention goals are established, and strategies for working with the child are developed. Finally, the child is assigned to be seen by a child associate and shortly thereafter regular associate–child meetings begin.

Midyear conferences (January–February), involving the same personnel as the assignment conference, are designed to assess from all relevant perspectives, how the child has been progressing in the program. Questions pertinent to these conferences include: How is the child doing with regard to the problems for which she or he was referred? What is his or her current situation with respect both to classroom behavior and academic progress? Have there been important changes in his or her life situation?

If the child appears to be moving in the direction of achieving the initially established goals, the decision may be to continue on that course or perhaps to begin considering termination. Sometimes, however, the child is found not to be showing signs of progress, or perhaps new problems or sources of concern have been identified. In the latter cases, the midyear conference seeks to understand why progress has been limited. In some instances, it is necessary either to realign goals or to consider changes in tactics and strategy that can better help to realize earlier established intervention objectives.

The final conference, attended by the same "players," occurs late in the school year. It is called the end-of-year termination conference. The purposes of this conference are to take stock of the child's current status, behaviorally and academically, and to make determinations about the extent to which the initially established referral goals were met. Answers to these questions frame decisions about whether the child is ready to terminate from the program or should continue in it during the upcoming school year.

Two types of consultation in PMHP, program consultation and clinical consultation, are designed to augment the preceding set of conferences. Program consultation is characteristically done on a longitudinal basis over at least one, and more often several, school years, by the same person, usually a member of PMHP's central staff. The program consultant's roles are to (a) support the school's efforts to conduct the project; (b) provide information, as needed, about program practices and options to facilitate the job performance of team members; and (c) work toward maintaining high quality-control standards for the program. The frequency and nature of the program consultant's visits vary as a function of how long the program has been in operation and the extent to which it is "on top of things." For a young (i.e., just starting) program, monthly program consultation is not atypical. An initially important, early-in-the-year (e.g., September) visit is made to consider the program's resources, needs, child-serving potential, deployment of personnel, and use of space. Later visits are used to deal with specific problems the new program may be experiencing and for quality-control purposes.

The two main objectives of clinical consultation, by contrast, are program enrichment and troubleshooting around clinical issues encountered in working with young children. Although the initial training of child associates covers many relevant topics, such training cannot possibly anticipate or provide preparation for the many idiosyncratic situations that associates will ultimately encounter in working with referred children. Hence, as new situations foreign to their prior background and training come up, a need (indeed, sometimes a thirst) for new information on special topics surfaces. Such needs fuel many specific agenda requests for clinical consultation sessions. The latter, often topically focused, are designed to enrich the background and repertoires of project personnel in specific domains (e.g., how to deal with certain sensitive child behaviors, as for example lying, cheating, and stealing; the child who wets or soils himself or herself in the playroom; child initiation of sexually tinged physical contacts with others).

A second important focus of clinical consultation is in-depth consideration of particularly vexing or challenging cases. Sometimes, an associate finds it hard to establish a good relationship with a child, that is, she seems to be "spinning wheels" in that regard. Sometimes, a child's scenario unfolds in a way that identifies serious everyday family problems or home situations that seem to be limiting what PMHP can hope to accomplish with that child. Whatever the specific reason, the common denominator in these situations is that the associate and other project personnel feel that progress is not being made, indeed that they are up against a formidable, often frustrating, stone wall. These are the types of situations about which school-based program personnel have major concerns and for which they feel the greatest need for a fresh view (set of inputs) and help. Hence, a clinical consultation session of 2½ to 3 hours often pivots around in-depth consideration and review of several of the program's most baffling and difficult children.

The ultimate goal of both types of consultation meetings, beyond the immediate support and enrichment they offer, is to expand the horizons and knowledge base of key program personnel and to upgrade their basic skills in ways that translate ultimately into more effective program services for PMHP-seen children.

PMHP Professional Roles

A final important element in the configuration of a PMHP school is the significantly changed role of the school mental health professional. We once used the term *mental health quarterbacking* to describe this role. Rather than functioning as diagnostician and therapist with a limited number of the school's most evident and florid casualties, as in the traditional school mental health role, the PMHP professional devotes relatively little time to direct one-to-one services with identified problem children, and rather invests effort in (a) selection, training, and supervision of child associates and (b) consultative and resource roles with teachers and other school personnel. This modus operandi enables the professional, and the school, to identify young children's problems sooner and more systematically, and to be in a position to provide correctives early on when such problems are prodromal rather than entrenched and can thus be approached with a greater sense of hope. This major shift in professional role makes it possible not only to get at problems earlier, when less damage has been done and prognoses are less guarded, but also to expand geometrically the reach of effective early preventively oriented services. In this manner, the project once again vivifies the popular aphorism that "an ounce of prevention is worth a pound of cure!"

Nothing about this changed professional role (i.e., its move away from provision of direct one-to-one professional services to children) is to imply professional obsolescence. Rather, what it suggests is a composite picture of more socially utilitarian roles for school mental health professionals. These emerging roles hold potential both for expanding the reach of early needed services and, importantly, for bringing such services coequally to all segments and strata of the targeted school children in need. This breadth of potential applicability holds a key to bringing early effective services to broad segments of the population that have always fallen into that vast, often repressed, category of the underserved.

SUMMARY

The superficial, fast-paced, preliminary tour of PMHP that this chapter has provided describes the core of the parent PMHP's practices as the project has evolved after nearly four decades. Although this core, at least structurally, is still in clear evidence, there has been significant change and refinement in the technology and operation of several component PMHP processes. For example, the early detection and screening measures that PMHP uses today are broader in scope, more streamlined and efficient in style, and sounder psychometrically than those used in the 1960s. Also, child associates now receive more extensive and sophisticated initial training and are kept more au courant of new project technology as it develops, than was the case 30 years ago.

Despite some enduring constancies in PMHP's approach, the preceding account should not be taken to mean that PMHP is the same today as it was 30 years ago. Far from it! The project, from the start, has looked carefully and continuously at its practices and their consequences, by re-viewing program outcomes both clinically and empirically. This ongoing process has given PMHP staff a clearer sense of what the project could, and could not, do effectively at any given cross-sectional point in time. Throughout, close communication between PMHP's school-based field set-tings and its central program development and evaluation units has been encouraged. We have also been responsive (indeed aggressively self-corrective) to identified program shortcomings and areas of needed further development that earlier forms of the project had either not perceived or not been able to resolve.

Hence, although core segments of the original PMHP remain in clear evidence, the project has expanded its programming and training bases and is a much more embracing, comprehensive entity than it was 30 years ago. This ongoing evolutionary process has moved in two directions, that is, developing new program units that (a) expand the scope, reach, and effi-cacy of the basic PMHP process and (b) go well beyond project orthodoxy in new primary prevention directions. Both these important developmental processes, which together have significantly modified PMHP's smorgasbord in the past 20 years, are described in more detail in later chapters.

A way-station summary of the practices that have guided the ortho-dox PMHP approach should underscore several points. PMHP's most basic commitments are to the processes of systematic screening and early detec-tion of young children's school adjustment problems (and/or seeming risk for such problems) and following up that process with an effective, broad-reaching set of early secondary prevention steps. In our view those yoked strategies can greatly increase the likelihood of sound educational and per-sonal development for young children at early risk of school maladaptation and failure. In the PMHP model, the use of carefully developed and refined screening procedures is the key to early identification, and the use of non-professional child associates as the prime direct help agents with young children is the key to dramatic, much needed, expansion of early preven-tively oriented helping services.

Behind this combination of early services lies the further assumption that the early effective resolution of children's already visible or incipient school adjustment problems makes it much more likely that the child will adapt to, and profit from, the school experience. Effective school adapta-tion, in turn, is a major stepping-stone toward rewarding personal and social outcomes and productive accomplishments in later life. This way of thinking is mindful of explanations advanced to account for the impres-sively positive, long-term outcomes that have grown out of the Perry Pre-school Program (Berrueta-Clement, Schweinhart, Barnett, Epstein, & Wei-kart 1984; Schweinhart, Barnes, & Weikart, 1993). If there is merit and justification to the preceding assumptions, it follows logically that the PMHP model offers a bona fide and important alternative to past dominant modes of delivery of school mental health services. Beyond this common-sensical appeal, it should be noted that PMHP is also a cost-effective approach—a point further developed and documented in chapter 4.

3

PMHP'S EARLY EVOLUTION

Although this volume is not primarily about history, we shall consider enough of PMHP's early evolutionary course to highlight factors that shaped how and why the project evolved as it did. We touch on that history not so much to describe the stages through which PMHP proceeded, but rather to clarify the logic of its evolution; that is, how these stages are layered and the issues and needs that fueled each major scope-broadening change in PMHP's development.

Although it is handy to describe this evolutionary process within a step–stage framework, it is misleading, on several counts, to do so. For one thing, PMHP's overall course, certainly as any day-to-day observer would see it, is characterized much more by a perception of constancy than of change. An analogy comes to mind: Although a person looks very different at birth and age 40, a parent sees little if any of that change on a day-to-day basis. Second, to extend the child development analogy, what can arbitrarily and after-the-fact be depicted as discrete PMHP evolutionary stages, in reality reflects blends and overlaps among periods, just as the stages of child development do.

Within the framework of these limitations, the next section overviews the early stages of PMHP's evolution. Looking back panoramically at a smoothed over version of that evolutionary course, one can arbitrarily divide a complex trajectory into six major, somewhat overlapping periods with labels and approximate dates as follows: (a) the pilot–developmental period (1957–1963), (b) child associates and their emergent role (1963–1968), (c) the formation of PMHP Inc. and expanding the local project (1969–1976), (d) national dissemination (1972–1977), (e) state level and regional dissemination (1977–current), and (f) primary prevention steps (1976–current). Because the earlier PMHP volume (Cowen, Trost, et al., 1975) included four chapters describing the first three of these six stages, we shall summarize those stages only briefly here.

STAGE 1: PILOT–DEVELOPMENTAL PERIOD (1957–1963)

For its first 11 years, PMHP was a pilot–experimental project in a single elementary school in the Rochester City School District (RCSD). This period includes two essentially nonoverlapping subperiods. The first, described in this section, was dedicated to the development of prototypic versions of PMHP's early detection, screening, and intervention procedures. The second, considered in the next section, involved the piloting and early development of what has proven to be PMHP's most distinctive ingredient, that is, the use of the nonprofessional child associate as the project's prime direct help agent with identified young school children in need.

Chapter 1 considered sociocontextual factors that moved us to start PMHP. To recapitulate briefly, those included perceived insufficiencies in the existing mental health and school mental health systems (i.e., too little and too late) and the belief that systematic early detection followed by prompt, preventively oriented ameliorative measures represented an appealing conceptual alternative to the then-dominant, damage-control mode of the mental health fields.

The real task at hand, given those views, was to translate from reasoned theory to effective practice. Our loosely formulated belief then was that such practice would need to pivot around successful development of (a) technology to identify children at risk, early on, before such risk exacts a heavy toll and (b) a realistic service delivery framework that could short-circuit the often deleterious effects of early identified risk factors and thus point young children toward more effective, adaptive school experiences. PMHP's first efforts, however primitive, sought to advance those two key objectives.

At the time PMHP started, two concrete, largely clinical, observations rather than the reasoned, smoothed-over, after-the-fact reconstructions that this volume has so far offered, were the project's most important de facto wellsprings. One was a variant of the following observation, made by many teachers: "In my class of 25–30 children, management problems with 3–4 children consume at least 50% of my time, attention, energies, and certainly my worries." Behind this observation lay three serious negative consequences. The first and most visible was that these identified children were not profiting, as they should have, from the school experience. Somewhat less visible, but nevertheless quite upsetting, was the fact that the pressures these youngsters placed on the teacher (e.g., management problems that ate heavily into the productive time available to pursue the class's mandated educational objectives) significantly restricted progress of the rest of the children in the class. And finally, there were hidden, but important, negative consequences of this situation for teachers, including (a) feeling frustrated or "hog-tied" in pursuing educational goals for the whole class and (b) having a personal sense of guilt or failure because classroom progress, in the light of these management burdens, fell short of the teacher's image of ideal (anticipated) progress.

A second vexing concrete problem, also apparent, was the peaking of referrals, some quite serious, to school mental health services during the transition period between elementary and high school. The sum of such referrals was substantial; indeed it exceeded considerably the maximum level of helping services that could be provided. This paradox prompted a small, informal study of the school records of a sample of youngsters who were first-time referrals to school mental health services at the high school entry point. The most striking finding of this survey was visual: Most of the cumulated dossiers of these late-referred youngsters were thick and "dog-eared," often reflecting a long history of teacher-perceived difficulties that went back as far as kindergarten or first grade. The point to stress is that although significant early problems had been clearly noted in many cases, little had been done to provide helping services that might reduce them. Insofar as we could judge, this inaction was due either to the fact that people hoped that the problems would go away spontaneously over time, or because resources for dealing with them were simply unavailable. Far from extinguishing naturally, many of these early brushfires mounted and fanned out over time, becoming forest fires that affected many areas of the child's later functioning—indeed forest fires that could not be put out 6–8 years later, given the limited repair resources available to schools.

These two sets of concrete observations converged in leading to PMHP's start. Our abstract hope was that the project would operate first to identify, and then alleviate, young children's early school adjustment problems, and in so doing would cut down the flow of later damaging and costly (both to individuals and to the system) difficulties. This way of thinking, in turn, led to a decision to focus PMHP's finite resources and efforts on primary grade children, even at the risk of having to cut back on repair services for older children.

Given this set of views, PMHP's first 5 years were directed to the onerous challenges of developing systematic, sensitive, early detection and screening procedures and, on that basis, providing meaningful early preventively oriented help to children identified through screening as being at risk. This pilot–formative work took place in a single elementary school that well represented Rochester's sociodemographic makeup at the time. A small grant from the New York State Department of Mental Hygiene made it possible to hire a full-time psychologist and social worker exclusively for the primary grades of that school. Although that staffing format was luxurious for the time, just as it would be today, it was intended to facilitate in-depth exploration of the new approach.

The pilot project proceeded simultaneously on several fronts. Although each of those steps seems crude in retrospect, each was important as a precursor (and shaper) of later, more finely honed project formats. At that early point in time, school children were not formally evaluated until third grade. Indeed, the main potential source of information about a child's ability or psychological status then came from happenstance, nonsystematic teacher comments. Although that was a reality of the time, there was also a growing recognition that many children with serious academic or adaptive problems at third grade were destined for unrewarding subsequent school careers. Accordingly, one major thrust of this unfolding period was to develop early detection and screening procedures that (a) provided systematic, relevant assessment information for all children, from the start and, in so doing (b) identified promptly youngsters already experiencing school adaptation and learning problems, or who seemed to be at serious risk for such problems.

We did not, at that early point in time, carefully consider the many possible alternatives for achieving the preceding important goals. Rather our immediate goal was to "glom" onto an action plan that seemed to have promise for accomplishing what we were after (i.e., systematic early detection), and with which members of the initial PMHP team could live comfortably. The first, approximate "game plan" that emerged for achieving those ends had three active components, two of which, child assessment and social work interviews with parents, were information gathering, and the third, "red tagging," was information synthesizing.

Two measures constituted the initial screening battery: the short form of the California Test of Mental Maturity (CTMM; Sullivan, Clark, & Tiegs, 1957) to assess young children's intellectual functioning and the Goodenough Draw a Person (DAP; Goodenough, 1926) test, to provide preliminary estimates of adjustment status. These tests were administered by the project psychologist early in the school year in small groups in the classroom. During the testing sessions the psychologist also recorded observations of individual children's reactions and behaviors. The information that this assessment package yielded was shared with classroom teachers and with the PMHP social worker before his or her interview with the parent.

After testing was completed, parents of all first grade children were interviewed individually by the school social worker. Beyond the expression of interest in the child that this contact conveyed, the meeting sought to gather information about aspects of the child and family situations that might shed light on the child's school performance and, conversely, to provide information to the parent about PMHP's purpose and procedures.

A serious effort was made to see all parents early in the school year. Most were seen at school, though home visits were made when necessary or more appropriate. Before the actual parent contact, the social worker became familiar with the child's project folder, which included (a) health and attendance data, (b) observations by kindergarten teachers, (c) reading readiness test data, and (d) a summary of the psychologist's test findings and observations. The ensuing parent interview sought to gather additional information about (a) the child's developmental history; (b) parenting styles and practices; (c) interactions among family members, particularly as they involved the target child; (d) the child's relationships with peers, siblings, and adults outside the family; and (e) information about the parents' own background and history, and the goals they had for themselves and their children. In summary, the interviews sought to gather systematic information in diverse areas that might be pertinent to understanding the child's early school adaptation and any early problem identified in that context.

The interview also had several important "structural" objectives, including (a) establishing contact with parents of all first grade children; (b) presenting an image of the school as a caring entity; (c) providing each parent an opportunity to express attitudes about the school and his or her child's education; (d) explaining the school's educational goals and objectives, and the project's place in that matrix; and importantly, (e) encouraging parents to feel free at any time to contact relevant school personnel about issues relating to the child's educational or personal development. In instances when parents spontaneously raised serious concerns about the child in the interview, the social worker acted in a bridge role to encourage an appropriate referral to PMHP and/or other appropriate community agencies (e.g., testing for hearing loss). After the interview ended, the social worker entered a summary of his or her impressions in the child's confidential project folder, noting both manifest and incipient problems identified.

After all early identification procedures were completed, a final data-synthesizing step was taken. Information available for each child (cf. above) was brought together and reviewed by the project psychologist and social worker and a binary clinical judgment was made about the child's current school adjustment. The quaint terms used to describe these two adjustment groups were *red-tag* and *non-red-tag*. The former designated children who had either already shown moderate to serious school adjustment problems or seemed to be at serious risk for such problems. All others were called non-red-tag, meaning either that all available information pointed to normal early progress or, perhaps, that not enough data were yet available to document an early maladaptive process.

There was no hidden profundity behind the use of the term *red-tag*. In truth, it reflected only the accidental (concrete) fact that some army surplus red tags on hand were used for quick-and-easy visual identification of the confidential project folders of the designated at-risk group. The latter, by the way, comprised about one third of each annual cohort of school children through each of the project's first several years. That 33% figure closely approximated a national school maladjustment figure provided a decade later by a Task Force of the Joint Commission on the Mental Health of Children (Glidewell & Swallow, 1969), based on a review of 27 school maladjustment incidence studies.

Soon, however, it became clear to us that the term *red-tag* offered, at best, a relatively arbitrary (in some cases, fallible) judgment of the child's early school adjustment status. That awareness prompted us to retire the term from active usage about 30 years ago. The real issue was that although we were concerned about a current child-status variable, school adjustment, that is much more nearly continuous than binary and complex (multidimensional) rather than simple (unidimensional), we had reduced all that complexity into an overly simplified "fish or fowl" classification system.

In historical perspective then red tagging can be seen as an early "handiwork of convenience"—a harbinger of an early detection process that, through continuing effort and persistence, has evolved into a considerably more sophisticated, sensitive assessment framework. Thus, although the literal concept of red tagging has long since been relegated to the "elephant's graveyard," it stands as a significant historical marker point, that (a) spotlighted the importance of systematic, outreaching, early detection efforts in PMHP and (b) offered a framework, however oversimplified, both for tracking children's progress in the early school years and for targeting PMHP's early, active, preventive intervention steps. We turn next to a brief overview of the latter.

Although the elements that constituted PMHP's first prevention efforts seem primitive in retrospect, they can, with the special clarity of vision that hindsight offers, be viewed as initial gropings that have since moved in more sophisticated, clearly articulated directions. Four elements made up the initial prevention package. Two were built around sets of educationally oriented meetings (i.e., for teachers and parents, respectively) that sought to (a) clarify PMHP's goals, scope, and ways of operating; and (b) consider salient issues of child development and mental health. Specific topics for the dozen or so teacher meetings held each year were selected by a small committee consisting of several project staff members and teachers. These topics were diverse; they included classroom management, teacher mental health, neighborhood sociodemographics, emotional deprivation in children, and child development issues. The meetings provided opportunities for teachers to strengthen their backgrounds in those substantive areas and to discuss child and class management issues of concern to them.

Also, parent coffee hours, each lasting about 2½ hours, were held during the school year. These meetings, for parents of all primary students, attracted 25–70 parents. Led by project staff members or an outside consultant with expertise in a specific area, the meetings covered a range of topics, including family relationships, child development norms and expectancies, discipline approaches, and children's social relationships. Each meeting provided opportunities for discussion using a buzz-session format, in which parents first met in small subgroups with "recorders" and then came together as a large group to listen to, and discuss, inputs from the other subgroups. These two sets of meetings were designed to (a) provide relevant background and information about children, families, and the project and (b) forge teams of interested parties with the shared goal of maximizing young children's educational progress.

A third feature of this early intervention package was to develop the then-novel role of the school mental health professional as a consultant, rather than as someone whose prime responsibility was to provide direct diagnostic and therapeutic services to children. Specifically, after the child testing and parent interviews steps had been completed, PMHP's professional team (one psychologist and one social worker) set up meetings with teachers to talk in greater depth about youngsters for whom early concerns had been raised either by them or through the screening process. These meetings considered what could be done to facilitate the progress of children with early detected difficulties. Starting with youngsters who presented the most immediate and serious problems for the teacher, up to 30–40% of the children in each class were reviewed in depth by the end of the school year.

These consultation meetings with teachers had several purposes. One was to give teachers a chance to raise issues of concern to them around such matters as class management techniques, children who were not progressing in class, or the role demands of being an effective teacher. The team's willingness to focus on such issues, and its efforts to establish open lines of communication, were intended to convey interest and support to the teacher. The most basic objective of the meetings, however, was to share pertinent information gleaned about children through the early detection process and, on that basis, formulate ways to enhance their learning and school adaptation. The latter efforts included suggestions to teachers about specific ways of working with children who were presenting problems, and considering children who might be helped by participating in a special after-school activity group, described below.

Some of the PMHP professional's consultation activities involved school personnel other than teachers; for example, principals and school nurses. Those contacts were less frequent than the ones with teachers and they tended to occur in ad hoc, rather than systematic, ways. Sometimes, at a teacher's request, a team member or outside consultant observed children directly in the classroom. This enabled the viewer both to form his or her own impressions about a child of concern and to develop a first hand "feel" for the classroom atmosphere and the teacher's style in relation to the class at large and the target child. Such observation provided a base on which teacher and consultant could (a) discuss the child from multiple perspectives, (b) consider appropriate class management and handling strategies, and (c) exchange thoughts about enhancing children's educational and adaptive experiences in class.

After-school activity groups were the final element in the early prototypic PMHP program. The wellspring for starting these groups came from the awareness that some young children who were floundering seemed to need special interest and prompt, effective help to profit from the school experience. Because the sum of this need, schoolwide, far exceeded the availability of school mental health services, PMHP's first attempt to address this problem was to establish relationally oriented, after-school activity groups for such early identified youngsters. Decisions about children's referral to such groups were made jointly by the PMHP team and classroom teachers, on the basis of evidence and impressions gained about children both in the classroom and through the project's early detection and screening activities.

Several specially selected teachers served as group leaders, working closely with the professional team. Teachers were chosen for their warm caring qualities, interest in children, and a history of having worked effectively with problem children. Before the groups began, leaders were given resumés of what had been learned about the children's school histories and current problems through the early detection and screening processes. Specific goals were developed for each child on the basis of that information.

The after-school program was targeted primarily to second and third graders at risk. Groups met for 20 weekly, 1-hour after-school sessions; they used engaging activities such as arts and crafts, soap carving, cookie baking, woodworking, group games, and an occasional outside trip. While the program was in progress, leaders met regularly with PMHP professional team members to discuss their impressions of the children; assess their progress; consider new ways of approaching children who were progressing slowly; and, toward the end, make suggestions for the future including ones pertaining to optimal class placements for the next school year. Although the after-school activity program model was helpful for some youngsters, others profited less from it. Even so, this early exploratory program step had an important place in PMHP's history: it laid the groundwork for what later became the backbone of PMHP's intervention system, that is, the child associate program (cf. below), launched during the 1963–1964 school year.

We have said before, and will undoubtedly say several times again, that program evaluation research has been part of PMHP's fabric from Day 1 (see chapter 6). Hence, even though these early PMHP exploratory steps involved much groping, serious efforts were made to evaluate the outcomes of these germinal programs. Specifically, two major program evaluation studies were conducted to evaluate these initial PMHP steps (Cowen et al., 1963; Cowen, Zax, Izzo, & Trost, 1966). These studies, described more fully in chapter 6, focused on three questions: (a) What is the frequency of occurrence of moderate to serious school adjustment problems among primary graders? (b) In the absence of intervention, how do children with early detected risk compare in outcome with their "not-at-risk" peers? (c) And, importantly, how effective was the new PMHP early detection and prevention package?

The program evaluation done was hardly elegant by modern standards, nor were all of its findings overwhelmingly positive. At the same time, what was learned about the project's de facto functioning from those studies and concurrent clinical feedback served importantly both to confirm that PMHP had been steering a reasonable early course and to provide a more specific sense of direction for the future.

The following main conclusions came out of these early studies:

1. systematic early detection and screening showed that one third of all primary graders were experiencing at least moderate school adjustment problems;
2. left unattended (i.e., without preventive intervention), the problems of these early detected children got worse by third grade; by then, many were at risk for long-term school failure; and
3. by the end of third grade, program children exceeded demographically and adjustively matched comparison children on several important indicators of educational and behavioral functioning (Cowen, 1971; Cowen et al., 1966).

Although we realized that some of these findings were "soft" and viewed them conservatively, they nevertheless suggested that PMHP had gotten off to a sound start and was on the "right track." The main conclusions they highlighted were that (a) children's adjustment problems were widespread, even in the early school years; (b) ignoring these problems had potentially serious negative consequences; and (c) a reasoned, if still insufficiently developed, school-based prevention program showed promise for short-circuiting some of those unfortunate early outcomes.

The challenge this early research put into focus—indeed, with some sense of urgency—was to develop even sounder, more systematic ways to reduce school casualty rates, or, put more positively, to increase the probability of effective, rewarding school outcomes for young children. The search for ways to meet this challenge was the motor force that launched the project's second major evolutionary phase, that is, developing and exploring the use of the child associate as the principal direct help agent in PMHP's still evolving, preventively oriented, school-based program model.

STAGE 2: ENTER THE CHILD ASSOCIATE (1963–1968)

Rationale

At the time PMHP's child-associate venture started in 1963, the step was a bold leap forward in the sense of "entrusting" noncredentialed, nontraditionally trained personnel with roles and activities in the heretofore closed guild-world of the mental health professional. Although happenings on the then-current scene provided a clear rationale for this new thrust, because it flew in the face of standard operating procedures for the mental health fields, caution pervaded PMHP's first probes in this direction. However, given the extent and magnitude of the school adjustment problems identified in PMHP's initial period, and the fact that ignoring those problems was not an acceptable option, we concluded that exploring the child-associate role was a step that needed to be given a fair and open trial.

Thirty years after that first tentative probe, the child associate remains at the very core of PMHP. Moreover, at least in some small measure because of PMHP's experience, the use of nonprofessional help agents in diverse mental health roles is more widespread, and much less of an "eye-opener," today than it was 35 years ago, when glimmers of such a development first captured our interest.

The preceding, however, jumps ahead of the script. To understand how and why the child associate step got off the ground in the first place requires rolling the cameras back both to the findings of PMHP's initial exploratory period, and to realities of the social and mental health scenes at that time. In that earlier period, we had taken important first steps, both conceptually and practically, toward articulating a framework for systematic early identification of young children's school adjustment problems. One key discovery from that process, already noted, was that roughly one third of young urban children were experiencing moderate to serious early school adjustment problems. Left alone, those early difficulties often exacted a substantial toll by third grade and seriously reduced the likelihood of children's ultimate school success.

To the extent that the 1 in 3 at-risk figure that we had found was representative, schools faced a situation in which rampant, early school adjustment problems far overtaxed the limited school mental health resources that could be directed to their resolution. The later findings of the

Task Force of the Joint Commission on the Mental Health of Children (Glidewell & Swallow, 1969), based on a composite of 27 studies of the incidence of school maladjustment in American cities, reflected a similar (i.e., 3 in 10) early school maladjustment figure. These stark findings, our own and others', clearly suggested that viable proactive alternatives for arresting an otherwise likely downward spiral—one that is very difficult to reverse after a certain point in time—needed to be identified. This need was also reflected in Caplan's (1964) warning that even the most efficient screening and early detection procedures are of little value unless they are backed by a soundly functioning system that can correct the problems identified and prevent their escalation.

What happened next in the unfolding PMHP scenario was very much a by-product of emerging awarenesses and early corrective stirrings, of the late 1950s and early 1960s. One important happening of the time was the comprehensive report issued by the Joint Commission on Mental Illness and Health, *Action for Mental Health* (1961). That volume, a summary of the commission's findings and recommendations, detailed in 10 component subvolumes, carefully documented the current status (and lacunae) of the mental health system in America. On that basis, it offered a comprehensive blueprint for the coming decades, designed both to address existing problems and to build toward a farther-reaching, more effective national system of mental health services.

Several aspects of that high-impact report were especially pertinent to those involved in PMHP's start-up. One, clearly, was the work of the commission's Manpower Task Force, headed by George Albee. This project culminated in the publication of *Mental Health Manpower Trends* (Albee, 1959), one of the most influential of the commission's 10 reports. This report showed that professional manpower shortages in the core mental health fields ranged from 25% to 75% and that rising demand for mental health services from diverse sources, including prior nonusers, had created a situation that was already straining, and would strain even more in the future, that is, a finite pool of available mental health professionals.

These findings and projections for the future pushed the commission toward a more "liberalized" view about people or groups that might appropriately become involved in the business of interpersonal helping. The following quote from the commission's Final Report reflects this liberalized position (for *that* time) on the use of mental health personpower:

> psychiatry and the allied mental health professions should adopt and practice a broad liberal philosophy of what constitutes, and who can do treatment and... non-medical mental health workers with aptitude, sound training, practical experience and reasonable competence should be permitted to do general, short-term psychotherapy.... Such therapy containing some elements of psychiatric treatment, client counseling, 'someone to tell one's troubles to,' and love for one's fellow man, ob-

viously can be carried out in a variety of settings, by institutions, groups and individuals." (Joint Commission on Mental Illness and Health, 1961, pp. ix–x)

Viewed retrospectively, from a perch that offers 35 years of hindsight, the preceding view surely reflects a difference that has made a difference—indeed an enormous difference. The commission's statement challenged a heretofore sacred taboo and liberated what has developed from a slow trickle of tentative, semi-apologetic, exploratory probes to a major tide of change in the conceptualization and delivery of certain types of mental health services and their associated uses of personpower.

In effect the commission had dared to say that the restrictive rules by which the mental health game had always been played were not working so well and that there was need to explore a family of more natural, less guild-bound intervention alternatives. The orienting, licensing quality of that conclusion, and the unmet needs that it reflected led among other things to active exploration of new options in the use of mental health personpower. Several exciting and effective alternatives among the latter helped to shape the next steps in PMHP's evolution.

One such set of explorations involved the development of programs that used college students as companions and help agents with mental hospital patients (e.g., Holzberg, Knapp, & Turner, 1967; Rappaport, Chinsky, & Cowen, 1971; Sanders, 1967; Umbarger, Dalsimer, Morrison, & Breggin, 1962). Several research studies (e.g., Poser, 1966) documented the effectiveness of this approach both in its own right, and in comparison with what professionals could accomplish with such patients. Other innovative explorations in the use of personpower as help agents with seriously disturbed patients were also launched. For example, Project Re-Ed, (Hobbs, 1966, 1967; Lewis, 1967) created the effective new role of "teacher–therapist" in residential settings for children with serious emotional disturbances, including major problems of school maladaptation.

In a different arena, demonstrations were developing of the effectiveness of another new type of help agent, the indigenous nonprofessional, working out of storefronts located in chronically underserved, inner-city neighborhoods (Reiff, 1967; Reiff & Riessman, 1965; Riessman, 1967). This then-novel step combined the use of nonprofessional help agents with situationally adaptive changes in the locus and mode of delivery of helping services, in hopes of making such services more available to, and effective with, heretofore underserved groups. Within this development was embedded the notion of the *helper-therapy* principle (Riessman, 1965), which is the recognition that for some people the most therapeutic thing that could happen to them personally was to be genuinely helpful to another human being who needed help. Put within the framework of a concept that has since gained visibility and respect, the benefits that accrued to helpers through the process of helping others can be thought of as "empowering" (Rappaport, 1981, 1987). In that regard, one can see in the early indigenous neighborhood help-agent movement, vestigial precursors of elements that have since become central to the flowering of self-help programs (Gartner & Riessman, 1993). Many of the latter actively avoid the involvement of mental health professionals.

Two other developments of the time introduced another new type of nonprofessional help agent: homemakers. In one such program, conceptually similar to Project Re-Ed, housewives were recruited and trained to work individually in a special setting outside of school, with severely disturbed (e.g., schizophrenic) children who had been excluded from the regular school system. Over time, this program enabled a significant proportion of child participants to return to school and function adequately within the regular class framework (Donahue, 1967; Donahue & Nichtern, 1965).

A second widely publicized and influential program was developed at the National Institute of Mental Health by Rioch et al. (Rioch, 1967; Rioch, Elkes, & Flint, 1965) to train housewives as psychotherapists, in the face of prior contrary tradition and exclusionary practice. Three years after their training ended, these women were functioning effectively in several mental health–related settings, including clinics, hospitals, and schools (Magoon, Golann, & Freeman, 1969). Further evidence of the knowledge and skills they had acquired came from the fact that they outscored psychiatry residents on the Psychiatric Board Examination.

Although we were much impressed with Rioch's demonstration, its potential applicability to schools, our primary area of focus, was limited in several ways. First, Rioch's housewives were highly educated women with university degrees. Second, training in her program stretched out over a 2-year period, approximating master's level training. Finally, and importantly, the primary role for which those women were being prepared was as psychotherapists with adults. Our planned focus, by contrast, was on helping interactions with young children in schools.

We remained closely attuned to these innovative projects exploring new uses of nontraditional personnel in mental health roles, as they were developed and described in the professional literature. Indeed, in 1965 we sponsored a major national conference in this domain, followed by the publication of a volume summarizing its proceedings: *Emergent Approaches to Mental Health Problems* (Cowen et al., 1967). Thus, by the early 1960s, we realized that evolving explorations of innovative personpower uses in mental-health-related roles had much potential applicability to issues (i.e., starting school-based prevention programs) with which we were grappling.

What could be said globally at that time was that diverse new types of help agents (e.g., students, indigenous neighborhood residents, housewives) not previously thought of as potential mental health personpower had been shown to be effective interpersonal helpers with different, hitherto underserved target groups in need (e.g., inner city residents, school children, children with major emotional disturbances) in different, sometimes unorthodox delivery settings (e.g., neighborhood storefronts, schools).

These demonstrations opened our eyes to the possibility that one's ability to genuinely help a child in need did not necessarily depend on formal professional background, training, and experience, as had always been assumed, and might, instead, be a product of the helper's personal qualities, experiential background, and/or prior life experiences. Although we weren't yet ready to "bet the ranch" on that assumption, the combination of substantial, nonrepressible need (i.e., large numbers of underserved children) and encouraging findings from the "cutting-edge" programs described above moved us toward serious exploration of the use of nonprofessional helpers with primary graders experiencing early school adjustment problems.

Selection and Training

Once that decision was made, concrete "who" and "how" questions rose to the surface. Given that the targets of our programmatic effort were to be primary grade school children, it made good sense to consider homemakers as the nonprofessional help agents in the emergent project's new helpgiving role. Several convictions fed that decision. The first was that many such women had had relevant, prior "battle-line" experience as mothers, that could be readily harnessed and applied in work with young children experiencing school adjustment problems. Within such a large hypothetical helper pool, we reasoned that it would be possible to find many women with considerable free time on their hands because their own children had become more independent, and that some of those women, with amply honed helping reflexes and talents, might be looking for new ways in which to direct their energies gainfully. For many such women providing meaningful help to young school children in need seemed, in principle, to be a "natural."

Even so, we were not so naive as to assume that all women with grown children and an expressed interest in the child-aide role would automatically qualify for this new role. To the contrary, because we fully realized that the "bold" step planned flew in the face of tradition and established professional "rules of the road" for intervention, we were duly nervous about the undertaking and anxious to maximize the likelihood that the new approach would work smoothly and effectively. Accordingly, we built into the emergent system the two strongest safeguards we could imagine. The first was to select women who, in the light of all known research data, and the field's regnant convictions, seemed to have the essential qualities (e.g., warmth, empathy, compassion, effective interpersonal relationships, psychological mindedness, strong interest in children) needed to be genuinely helpful to young children experiencing early school adjustment difficulties. The second, also a quality-control step, was to provide careful training and close supervision, both of which we viewed as essential to the new system's effective functioning.

Although the steps we were about to take were heavily influenced by new personpower explorations of the time, particularly Rioch's work on training housewives as psychotherapists, they differed from that work in three key respects. The first was the decision to select women for their personal and experiential qualities rather than advanced education and prior degrees. The second was to prepare these carefully selected women to work as help agents with young school children, rather than as psychotherapists with adults. And finally, given the assumption that the motor force in the helping process would be the aide's natural reflexes and acquired battle-line wisdoms, we counted on the sufficiency of a finite, time-limited training experience, which would not compete with professional training in depth or complexity. Rather, the training we had in mind had only two simple goals: (a) to provide a finite corpus of starter knowledge and information, and a way of viewing children's problems that associates would find useful in this new role and (b) cutting the keen edge of anxiety that some associates were feeling about entering a mysterious, indeed sacrosanct, world heretofore peopled exclusively by mental health professionals.

Consistent with a belief that has been basic to PMHP's way of operating since Day 1, two principles guided the start of the child-associate program: (a) think small at first and (b) emphasize quality control. PMHP has always assumed that a sound, effective, operating starter model is a program's best selling point. Thinking small, in this case, meant confining our initial efforts to the primary grades of only one elementary school and working with a manageable group of six carefully selected child associates who seemed to possess qualities essential to the new role. The next section describes the recruitment and training of these first child associates and their early functioning in the program.

The recruitment process began with a markup of our still-fuzzy vision of the new child associate role, and a somewhat clearer description of the qualities we were looking for in the ideal child associate. This first vision was based on the assumptions that (a) associates would be stationed *in the* classroom and (b) when problems arose they would somehow interact with children, on the spot, either individually or in small groups. How that imaginary script would unfold in actual practice was something we hadn't completely thought through. Soon enough, however, we began to get educated in the "school of hard knocks!"

In any case, the vague initial job description we used appeared as a help-wanted flyer, which said that women were being sought a for new school-based early detection and prevention program for primary graders. The semiprojective phrase in the announcement that came closest to approximating a role description was "to serve as an extra pair of hands to help teachers provide hyperactive, withdrawn, periodically upset, or underachieving children with the extra help they needed to adjust better in school." The announcement also said that associates would work 5 half-days a week, and that they would be paid the not-so-munificent sum (even in 1963) of $25/week for this work.

These first recruiting steps were built around a search for highly promising women who we thought would have a "real shot" at meeting the imposing ideals we had established. Also, to minimize the pitfalls and potentially negative fallout sometimes inherent in open announcements and mass-screening procedures, we limited circulation of the help-wanted flyer, accompanied by a description of the qualities of the ideal child associate, to a small group of mental health colleagues at the university and in the school district. The flyer used the following description:

> The woman we would like to recruit should possess a personal warmth and liking for children, in connection with which the experience of having successfully reared children of her own would seem to be an important prerequisite. In addition, flexibility, genuine commitment to the type of work we describe, a life situation which would permit her to devote the necessary time to the project, and an interest in the school situation would also be important. Hopefully, the person would herself be relatively free of major personal problems. These attributes would be valued above formal education. (Cowen, Trost, et al., 1975, p. 81)

We hoped that this demanding description would both (a) "end-run" the major pitfalls and time investments associated with open announcements and (b) build into the selection process a serious, albeit informal, prescreening step that would increase the likelihood of finding truly well-qualified candidates.

The use of these procedures generated a starter group of 11 strong applicants. Each applicant completed a detailed preliminary application form that included (a) a self-description and a description of one's family, education, and employment history; (b) information about interests, hobbies, skills, health, and personal goals; (c) reasons for interest in the new position; and (d) perceived personal assets and limitations in relation to such work. This background information was available to interviewers during the ensuing multistage selection process. In retrospect, it seems as if this process rivaled, in depth and breadth, the process of selecting astronauts for space travel.

An initial "hour-plus" selection interview was conducted jointly by a university professor of clinical psychology associated with PMHP and an advanced clinical graduate student. That interview yielded applicant ratings on a set of 21 personal, social, intellectual, and attitudinal qualities thought to be relevant to the new job role (Cowen, Dorr, & Pokracki, 1972). Interviewers also rated the extent to which they liked the candidate personally and the likelihood that she would do well on the job and listed what they saw as her prime assets and limitations. One contraindicant to selection was the belief, sometimes expressed by an applicant with a Carrie Nation fervor, that many teachers were incompetent and most schools needed to be reformed. Accompanying this conviction was the implication that it was the associate's job to cure those putative ills.

Candidates who survived this initial "trial-by-fire" advanced to a second, in-depth interview with the professionals in the designated project schools. If the school interviewers concurred with the positive initial ratings, the applicant was accepted. If they had reservations, for whatever reason, the applicant was not considered further. This comprehensive screening process identified six women, ranging in age from 26 to 58, for the new child-associate role. All were mothers who had reared their own children successfully; none had a visible "axe to grind" about teachers or schools; and all gave clear evidence of a primary motivation and strong desire to work with and bring help to young children in need.

A 6-week, part-time training program for the newly recruited associates, conducted in an informal, discussion-oriented way, featured several substantive components. It sought first to establish a framework within which to view the new program (i.e., its "place in the cosmos"), by talking about traditional mental health roles, current personpower shortages, and the pressing need to expand the reach of meaningful helping services for children. Next, background information was provided in the areas of parent–child relationships, children's personality development, and child behavior problems. Time was also spent orienting the "trainees" to the school, class routines and practices, and the teacher's role and providing some rudimentary teaching skills.

A second, more practical aspect of the training involved the use of clinical materials (e.g., films, classroom observations), followed by discussions of what had been seen and the issues they presented. During the later phases of training, associates participated directly in classroom activities, followed by meetings with supervisors to discuss things seen, problems encountered, and helpful steps that might be taken in their wake.

First Trial Run

In the period when associates were being selected and trained, staff met often with principals and primary grade teachers both to orient them to the new program and to invite their inputs in identifying maximally useful ways of functioning. Although participation in this orienting process, by all parties, was good and the program concept well accepted as an abstraction, the preceding speaks only to what the situation seemed to be like before the program actually moved into a concrete, operational stage.

Again, without dotting all relevant *i*s or crossing all relevant *t*s, it is fair to say that although some aspects of the initial trial run (e.g., on-the-job training, supervision) went as well as could have been hoped, the overall pilot program fell far short of being a smash hit in everyone's book. A key stumbling block on that first round was the lack of role clarity for all players in the classroom's dramatis personnae (i.e., teachers, children, and associates). For example, the vagueness in the description of the associate's role noted above, came home to roost. The six new associates were assigned to the six primary grade classrooms under an insufficiently clear "game-plan," that is, that teachers would use associates in ways that seemed most helpful to them, and associates would do their darndest to interact with children in ways that would be most helpful educationally and interpersonally. However, there were many different ways in which those vague roles might have been implemented, and different views of each role by different players in a classroom. Indeed, in most classrooms, the children developed their own perceptions of the new associate and her roles.

Thus, de facto problems of role definition, territoriality, and belongingness came up often for teachers and child associates during the initial trial run. At the core of these tensions was a concern expressed by several teachers that, in their efforts to maintain order in the classroom and go about the business of educating, children were likely to see them as the "bad guys," whereas by contrast, they typecast associates (whose role was to aid, abet, and comfort children in distress) as the "good guys"—all-loving, all-embracing mothers. Even stronger manifestations of this basal tension came up when certain teacher actions raised eyebrows of, or were questioned by, associates, or conversely when teachers put a damper on the occurrence (more often, timing) of associate–child interactions. Through these tense moments, the core underlying issue, put metaphorically, was "Who is chief cook in this kitchen?" Whereas we had hoped, ideally, to create a cohesive team, working closely together to advance young children's educational and personal development, the initial system, as it unfolded, turned out in several cases to be a power struggle or, if not that, then at least a difficult exercise in role definition that created de facto tensions, stumbling blocks, and inefficiencies. The system, in other words, was not operating automatically in ways that optimally met the needs of children.

Because the processes of recruiting and training child associates and preparing school personnel for the new program were time consuming, the initial PMHP "dry run" didn't start until early March. All involved parties had agreed beforehand to take stock of the new program's accomplishments and pitfalls at the end of the school year. This was to be done through individual conferences with program teachers and child associates.

Teacher reactions, anticipatably, focused around (a) the need to maintain order in the class, (b) competition that had developed for the children's attention, and (c) concerns about another person in the room "looking over one's shoulder." Although the associates reported having experienced interesting challenges and major satisfactions in their new work, they too had no trouble identifying areas that presented problems for them. For one thing they did not clearly understand the extent to which they were supposed to be a mental health aide, a tutor, or, as one of them put it, a baby-sitter. Most associates felt that teachers wanted them, most of all, to be tutors and baby-sitters. They, by contrast, were cathected primarily to the perceived mental health component of the new role. At the very best, role understandings were unclear and tensions surrounding differential understandings were often close to the surface.

The paradox of this situation was that even though associates were "fired up," challenged by, and very much enjoying their contacts with children, they felt less than 100% welcome in the classroom, indeed often felt like a "5th wheel on the wagon." A final pertinent observation by associates was that although they were presumably available to all children in the class, in practice most of their time and efforts were directed to a very few children (i.e., 3 or 4) with the most visible and strongly expressed needs for contact.

Although we were taken off guard by the scenario that unfolded during this 3-month "dry run," our observations and feedback, clarified during the end-of-year program assessments with participants, added up, post hoc, to a "blinding glimpse of the obvious." Although most parties retained warm thoughts about the program's underlying rationale and objectives, few were keen about its initial defining mechanisms. At the core of these reservations, in the eyes of both teachers and child associates, was the belief that the program would not fly *in the classroom.*

What came out of this pilot experience, and the ensuing dialogue, was a new blueprint for PMHP—a blueprint that included several crucial changes in the initial script. One such change was the decision that teachers would first identify specific children who they thought could profit from early preventive intervention. (Project staff later developed several assessment tools to facilitate that process.) Once these children were identified as candidates for referral, the locus for ongoing associate–child contacts would be outside the classroom, at a time and in a place that made mutual good sense to the teacher and the associate. The possibility was left open for associates to do brief observations of children in the classroom before starting to work individually with them.

The need for a third, somewhat more subtle, change also became apparent in these discussions. All the fanfare and glitter associated with the new program had clearly pivoted around the groundbreaking role of the child associate. Both in the Hollywood sense, and in terms of how we had focused our training efforts, the associate had gotten top billing by a wide margin, in program discussion, "hype," and public representation. Although teachers had been given some background about the program, that input, in comparison to the investments made in associates, came through as something of an afterthought. In any case, it was clear that we had, at least to some extent, unintentionally set up opposing camps. We concluded that the recast program had to be built around the notion of coequal contributions of concerned parties, working closely together as a team to enhance young children's sound academic and personal development. That cherished goal is difficult enough to reach when everyone is pulling in the same direction; when that is not the case, it is impossible to reach.

Although the preceding changes were hit upon within PMHP's first 4 months, they were critical to the project's later unfolding and success. The modified program model that evolved then, with continuing embellishments and role broadenings to be sure, has pretty much remained in effect ever since. Certainly the revised model for the child associate's location and activities remains today as a core defining feature of PMHP.

Revised Program: Pilot Demonstration Period

The learnings (and bruises) of the initial run of the child associate program provided the raw materials needed to refashion it. With the cooperation and support of the principal, several unused classrooms were converted into a project headquarters area with space for the program's professional and secretarial staff and for group meetings, plus several small play areas in which associates could work individually with children. At the request of teachers, a delay period of at least a month was built into project start-up time at the beginning of the school year to permit the "dust of battle" to settle in the classroom and to allow teachers to get to know children well enough to make knowledgeable referrals.

Thus, a plan evolved whereby the teacher initially identified children of concern and discussed the suitability of referring them with the school mental health team. When all parties, including parents, agreed that a PMHP referral was the pathway of choice, professionals, teachers, and associates came together in an assignment conference to formulate an intervention plan to advance agreed-upon educational and socioemotional objectives for the child. Then, regular associate–child contacts began, with the goal of advancing team-established behavioral and educational objectives for the child.

The hope was that these structural and organizational modifications in project procedures would bring teachers and associates together as a more closely knit team, working toward the shared goal of children's optimal school development. In further support of this ideal of "teamness," two-way communication between teachers and associates about the child's progress both in the class and the playroom was encouraged, and periodic team meetings (e.g., progress and termination conferences) were established to take stock of the child's status and continuing needs in the program. Several mechanical changes were also introduced to further strengthen the program's image and ways of functioning. For one thing, the term *teacher-aide*, chosen originally to reflect the classroom base of PMHP's nonprofessional help agent, was replaced by the now more accurate term "*child*-aide" (later to be replaced by child associate). This was a welcome change for all parties—one that more accurately reflected the role we had hoped to develop. Second, substitute teacher time was provided to permit regular classroom teachers to participate in assignment, progress, and termination conferences and to underscore PMHP's view of the importance of those conferences.

With these basic changes in project definition and practices, the program model began to jell in ways that made better sense to participants and seemed, at least impressionistically, to be working better for children. These changes can be seen as a victory for practice and "battle-line experience" over armchair speculation.

Five of the six original child associates remained with the project in its second year. Indeed four remained with the project for 20 years or more. One associate was not invited to return in Year 2; a second dropped from the program because she was the wife of the educator who, by coincidence, was appointed as the new principal of the project school.

The next 3 years were good and productive ones. The evolving program model continued to be debugged and strengthened. Teachers and associates came to work and communicate better with each other. Teachers who had previously been "gun shy" about referring, now started to refer children. Project personnel, at all levels, became clearer about, and more confident in, their roles. The availability of attractive new project space and easy access lines improved communication and fostered a sense of teamness. And the processes of identifying and bringing early help to children in need were made more efficient.

The initial idealized vision of the associate's role also moved closer to realization. Associates' confidence and their armamentaria of technology and experience grew steadily, and rough edges and knowledge gaps diminished. Thus, the acceptance of the child associate as part of the project team grew by leaps and bounds during this period and a team concept involving many building people, working closely together to serve children's needs, jelled increasingly.

Accomplishments of the child-associate program, in this early period, proved to be documentable beyond the positive clinical impressions about it that had formed in the schools. Several formal outcome studies were done to evaluate its effectiveness, and other studies were done to pin down information about child associates' personal qualities, job activities, ways of functioning, and satisfactions. The latter information is reported in chapter 6.

In one early outcome study (Cowen, 1968), referred children were assigned randomly to groups seen by child associates, trained college student volunteers, or as controls. The two active groups were seen individually for an average of 4 months. Using teacher behavior ratings as the main program outcome indicator, and help agents' ratings as secondary outcome criteria, this study found that (a) the combined "seen" groups did significantly better than matched, nonseen controls and (b) children seen by associates did significantly better interpersonally and academically than those seen by students. Those findings were not surprising given the careful selection of associates and their extensive supervised experience with children over a long time period, in comparison with the college student volunteers.

Although the preceding findings were informative, they reflected only immediate postprogram changes rather than potential longer term program benefit to child participants. Hence, a study was also done to track the later development of children seen by PMHP child associates (Cowen, Dorr, Trost, & Izzo, 1972). In this follow-up study, comprehensive (1½ hour) interviews were done with mothers of children seen by PMHP 2–5 years earlier. These largely open-ended interviews also probed specific areas if they did not come up spontaneously. The latter included reasons for the child's referral to PMHP; how helpful PMHP was seen to have been; the child's current physical, behavioral, and educational status; relationships with family members, teachers, peers, and neighbors; and level of happiness. At the end, mothers were asked to do nine objective ratings of perceived changes, for better or worse, over the follow-up period. Seven of these pertained, respectively, to the child's educational performance; attitude to school; and relationships with teachers, schoolmates, parents, siblings, and neighborhood children. They were also asked to rate the child's current happiness and the extent to which PMHP was seen to be responsible for the changes noted. While the parent was rating these items, the interviewer (a project-related person, *not* previously known to the parent) did the same nine ratings in another room. The key study finding was that both mothers and interviewers judged across-the-board significant gains to have taken place, over time, in PMHP-seen children. These findings were not due to interviewer bias; indeed mother-reported gains were directionally more positive than those judged by interviewers.

Backing off from these specific data trees to perceive a larger forest, the early findings reported above offered support for the efficacy of PMHP's approach—an approach born of obvious need and initially implemented in an atmosphere of mixed hope and uncertainty. Study data confirmed that the child-associate program resulted in short-, and intermediate-term gains along key educational and interpersonal dimensions, as assessed from the perspectives of teachers, parents, and interviewers. Globally, this early demonstration offered support for a then-germinating view in several mental health–related areas, that carefully selected, trained, supervised nonprofessional help agents had much to offer in addressing pressing problems facing the mental health system. Specifically, they showed that the child-associate model that PMHP had pioneered with simultaneous optimism and trepidation was more than just sensible theoretically, it was demonstrably effective when assessed empirically.

The period of initial development of the child-associate approach lasted 6 years (i.e., 1963–1969). Its demonstrations and findings (cf. above) wrote an end to the second major phase of PMHP's development. By then, PMHP had taken important forward strides in exploring and furthering systematic early detection and screening approaches and had piloted and documented the efficacy of the child associate intervention approach.

During the 12-year duration of these first two developmental stages, PMHP existed in only one Rochester school. It was a time of slow, cautious exploration, learning by trial and error, and piloting and evaluating under good quality control conditions. The ultimate goal of this effort was to arrive at a clearer understanding of the potential, and caution points, of a seemingly exciting new service-delivery system, still experiencing growing pains. At the end of this 12-year venture, we concluded that the program's developmental steps had been sound and sensible, and that its promising outcomes provided a framework to guide future program directions. Armed with the tools of a sharper early detection system and a seemingly effective, preventively oriented associate-intervention model, we were persuaded that the base for a viable service-expanding preventive approach in the schools had been laid down.

That conclusion structured our next set of challenges, that is, moving from a scope-limited pilot project in a single school to an alternative school mental health approach located in many schools and school districts, intended to increase greatly the reach of early effective helping services to young children in need. That PMHP today provides in-depth, preventive helping services for many tens of thousands of young children in thousands of schools across the country, indeed around the world, testifies to the extent to which that hope has been realized.

The sense of direction laid down by the end of Stage 2 translated into the concrete next missions expanding the program both in its geographic area of origin and other school districts around the country. The first formative steps in that part of the PMHP story were taken during the project's third (i.e., expansion) period, from 1969 to 1976.

STAGE 3: PROJECT EXPANSION (1969–1976)

Although project expansion, considered later under the banner of dissemination, has been an active process since 1969, only its first, tentative starter steps will be touched on here. Most of PMHP's complex expansion story is presented in chapter 7. The several steps described here represent an important aspect of PMHP's early metamorphosis, which laid a groundwork for later significant developments in this sphere.

Program expansion was not something that PMHP had in mind when the project first started. Rather, the notion grew on us over the years, sometimes when we hit a plateau in consolidating new knowledge and experience, and sometimes through serendipitous happenings. One such serendipitous event, toward the end of PMHP's second stage, proved to be crucial in the project's local area expansion. At that time, our area's prime mental health planning body, the Rochester Mental Health Council, appointed a subcommittee to review current school mental health services and to formulate recommendations to strengthen such services for the future in this geographic region.

The committee's work was extensive. Its scope was nationwide. The committee met with many school superintendents, pupil personnel directors, and school and community mental health professionals and gathered extensive information about school mental health programs around the country. While doing this homework, the committee heard, only incidentally, about the PMHP pilot project. That discovery led to several meetings during which PMHP staff provided information about the project's origins, objectives, ways of operating, and findings to date. Committee members reacted sympathetically to the abstract goals of early detection and prevention and saw PMHP as a sensible and effective model for future school mental health programming. The committee's final report to the area Mental Health Council, distributed to all area school districts, included the strong recommendation that the PMHP model be adopted more widely by school districts in the local geographic area.

Thus, by the end of PMHP's second developmental stage, two important new impetuses to expansion had developed. The first consisted of program evaluation studies documenting the efficacy of the new model, and the second was the advocacy of an impartial review body charged with making recommendations for future school mental health services in the Rochester area.

Several outcomes, some anticipatable, others not, followed the committee's review process. An anticipatable one was the committee's strong endorsement of the PMHP program model in its final report. A second outcome was more surprising. Unlike most committees, which do their work, file their reports, and disband, this committee got "hooked" on PMHP and decided, on its own, to remain active as a voice for program implementation and follow-through on its recommendations. And therein lies the beginning of a "story within a story"—one that has continued actively and influentially right up to the present moment. Thus, shortly after the committee's report was accepted by the local area Mental Health Council, committee members formed a not-for-profit agency, incorporated in New York State as PMHP Inc. The corporation continues to exist today; indeed, in the metaphor of chapter 1, it is the third "master" to which the project reports—the first two being the participating school districts and the University of Rochester. Members of PMHP, Inc. have worked diligently to support PMHP's programmatic efforts; this includes fund-raising and public information activities that have strengthened the project's base and facilitated its survival and expansion.

Early Expansion Steps

The immediate task at hand for PMHP staff and the newly established PMHP, Inc. was to promote program implementation in the local geographic area. That was not easy given both the newness of the program model for schools that had long lived within the framework of traditional school mental health services, and fiscal crises of the time in school districts. (The latter, in retrospect, seem to have continued with no loss in intensity for the ensuing 27 years.) The ups and downs of this early venture in program expansion were described in the prior PMHP volume (Cowen, Trost, et al., 1975) and will not be repeated here. The long and short of the matter is that after lots of hard work by many people, PMHP programs were successfully started, in 1969, in 11 schools—6 in the RCSD and 5 in several nearby suburban districts under the administrative aegis of the Monroe County Board of Educational Services (BOCES I). These 11 schools were diverse in terms of location (inner city to affluent suburbs); size (from small K–3 neighborhood schools with total enrollments of about 150 to a very large K–3 school with more than 1,100 children); ethnicity (from 100% white to 97% minority); and the grade levels they included (i.e., K–3 vs. K–6). It was truly to be a test of the emergent program model's versatility because of the range of applications that could be fit under the program umbrella.

During this program expansion period, PMHP Inc. was able to attract monies needed for the new program to come into being—most particularly dollars to support the new child-associate role, unfamiliar to most school districts. From the start, however, costs for mental health professionals in PMHP have been borne by school districts. The critical issue at that level was not to hire more mental health professionals, but rather to reconceptualize professional roles and, on that basis, to reallocate existing professional hours in ways that could best support core PMHP goals and activities.

After program schools were chosen came the nitty-gritty challenges of moving from the drawing-board to a smoothly operating entity in the field. That agenda included readying space, materials, and equipment in schools; providing relevant program information to school staff and parents; and preparing program professionals for new roles, including particularly the selection and training of child associates. The school year 1969–1970 was consecrated to these tasks, using the September–February period to prepare project space, orient school personnel and families to the new program, and provide training for project professionals, and March–June, for an initial "dry run" involving the child associates seeing children. Following that step-stage format, we hoped that the program would be operational and functioning smoothly when schools reopened in September 1970. A brief abstract of how these preparatory steps unfolded follows; more detail is provided in the prior PMHP volume (Cowen, Trost, et al., 1975).

Program professionals in the new schools were not hand picked. Rather they were the professionals already assigned to those schools. PMHP's goal, at this level, was not to seek out particularly talented, sympathetic professionals but rather to better align professional roles with the ecology and thrust of an emergent program model that differed substantially from the then-dominant repair model of school mental health services.

With that as our goal and preferred method of operation, professionals (psychologists and social workers) in project schools participated in weekly training and discussion sessions, over a 6-month period, to prepare for the start of the new program. Foci for these meetings ranged from relatively abstract matters of program rationale (e.g., pressing current problems in mental health, the need for early intervention and prevention with children) to earthy, concrete matters (e.g., aims, methods, and findings of the pilot PMHP program, alternative ways of professional functioning in the schools).

At its core, however, the training was intended to provide information and resources that would ease the impending role transition for PMHP professionals. Concretely, this meant considering essential steps needed for the program to take hold and proceed smoothly (e.g., staff meetings, parent meetings, preparing and equipping space, record keeping, relationships with school personnel, the place of research) and, importantly, establishing a framework for selecting, training, and supervising the new child associates.

Since the latter activities were likely to be (a) the most uncharted, for professionals; (b) a backbone element in the program; and (c) central to its effective functioning, they were seen as key steps in the complex retooling process.

Initial steps toward recruiting child associates for the expanded program began while professional training was still underway. As a result of several radio, TV, and newspaper stories about the new project, some women contacted project headquarters spontaneously to inquire about position openings. Others were identified via contacts with colleagues in the professional community and several inner-city antipoverty agencies. To that end we prepared an overall description of attributes we were looking for in child associates and requested that colleagues who knew such women refer them to us. Collectively, these steps produced a number of applicants for child associate positions. Although the initial applicant pool ranged in age (from 19 to 67) and in ethnicity (15% Black or Latina women with inner-city backgrounds), the modal applicant was a white, middle-class woman, in her 40s, with three children.

Although we had spoken abstractly during professional training about personal attributes we considered important in child associates (e.g., warmth, caring about children, evidence of effective child-rearing histories, psychological mindedness, openness to new learning, likability), we recognized that final decisions about a candidate's acceptability also had to reflect the "druthers" of the school professionals with whom associates would be working closely every day. That awareness structured the procedure used in selecting the project's first big wave of child associates.

Specifically, each applicant was given a list of the 11 project schools and was asked to identify the site in which she preferred to work. Candidates were then interviewed jointly by the school psychologist and social worker in this preferred work site. For this purpose, a detailed 1½ hour interview outline was presented and discussed during professional training. The interview dealt focally with such topics as the applicant's background and prior employment history, current family situation, and interests and skills pertinent to the role of being a PMHP child associate. On the basis of this searching interview process, 56 child associates were hired to staff the program in the 11 new schools.

Several studies were conducted to clarify aspects of the new child-associate development. In one study, all candidates interviewed for associate positions were rated on 18 scales, reflecting characteristics of the ideal associate (e.g., warmth, interest in children), by the interviewing psychologist and social worker (Cowen, Dorr, & Pokracki, 1972). The selected women had significantly higher ratings on all 18 scales than those not selected.

Several other studies sought to pinpoint distinguishing qualities of the selected associates. Based on an extensive test battery that associates took during the 10-day waiting period between the time of hiring and start of training, Sandler (1972) compared the selected group with 89 demographically comparable volunteers for diverse community programs on a set of personality, interest, and attitude measures. PMHP associates scored as more affiliative, nurturant, and empathic than the comparison group and were less inclined to be either aggressive or "loners." They had stronger interests in teaching and social service occupations, and weaker interests in technical–scientific and mathematical–clerical roles. A related study, using Sandler's measures, identified six factors on those tests, and found that associates significantly exceeded comparison women in social interests, positive school attitudes, and overall helping orientation (Dorr, Cowen, Sandler, & Pratt, 1973). The preceding findings confirmed that this initial wave of PMHP associates consisted, as we had intended, of women with the qualities of natural helpers. Hence there was reason to hope that they would succeed in bringing meaningful preventively oriented help to young children evidencing early signs of school maladaption.

A next challenge was to train the new associates. Although project staff had developed a model for such training in the pilot period, we recognized that most of this training would, for several reasons, have to be done by the professional teams in the 11 new project schools. One practical reason for this was that it made better sense (in terms of fostering close personal contact and discussion) to do training in subgroups of 10 than to train 56 people en masse. A second, even more important, reason was that the professional teams had selected their associates, knew their needs, backgrounds, and styles best, and were in the best position by far to know the special needs, resources, and operating styles of the particular school in which the associate would be working.

On the other hand, because project staff had had lots of experience on the pilot round in developing training guidelines, conducting training, and monitoring the posttraining project in action, a decision was made to package the wisdom of that experience in a training manual for the school professionals. Although we did that, we also stressed that the materials provided were to offer options, not to constrain, and that the teams would be the ultimate arbiters of what, in the training package, would and would not fly for their trainees, and the modifications that made best sense to them.

In the end, this "fence was straddled" as follows: Project staff prepared an extensive (100+ pages) training manual, calibrated to fourteen, 2-hour training sessions. The manual was written for a hypothetical new school professional, for someone who had never before led a training group and had little idea of how to do so. Thus, the curriculum outline for each session provided a set of goals, format suggestions, and detailed information about relevant content areas, including several suggested readings. We highlighted throughout, however, that the manual was only a resource option and that professionals could use, not use, revise, or add to it as they saw fit.

For several reasons, project staff opted to conduct the first two sessions. The first was to show support for, and be involved at some level in, the actual "nitty-gritty" of the training. The second was to provide associates with specific information about PMHP that they were better positioned to do than school-based professionals. Session 1 thus sought to anchor PMHP's "place in the cosmos" by reviewing the origins of the mental hygiene movement, mental health's accomplishments and still unresolved problems, current professional roles, and the need for the use of carefully selected, trained nonprofessional help agents in school-based early detection and prevention programs. Session 2 presented a summary of PMHP's rationale and accomplishments to date and described all key project roles and activities.

The remaining 12 training sessions were conducted by school-based mental health teams, for the 10 or so associates who would be working in their two assigned schools. (Here we provide only a telescoped summary of that early training. Associate training has, understandably, changed and evolved in the ensuing 25 years. The reasons for, and nature of, those changes are considered in later chapters.) These sessions focused on a range of topics. The first several considered the special characteristics and operating styles of the schools in which the associates would be working, their community "surrounds," and the types of problems that children in those settings were experiencing. Other school personnel (e.g., principal, teachers) participated in these initial sessions designed to orient associates to their new work sites. The next several meetings were built around the topics of personality development, parent–child relationships, and children's behavior problems, using clinical materials, films, and brief classroom observations of children, followed by discussion.

Later training sessions focused more specifically on the child associate's role. These sessions drew upon the presence and involvements of the four senior associates from the original child associate group. These now-veteran associates shared their own program experiences and served as resource people for the incoming associates. This proved to be a real plus. New associates identified readily with veteran peers and found them very credible. Their presence and natural, comfortable ways of handling questions (e.g., "Oh, remember how we felt the same way when we first started—really worried about whether we could handle this mysterious, complex professional role?") acted to cut some of the anxiety new associates were experiencing at this point in time. These initial steps in charting out the associate role were followed by several joint meetings of teachers and associates to get to know each other better, clarify roles and activities of teachers and other school personnel, and establish communication and feedback mechanisms for project personnel.

Thus, this telescoped training experience was intended mostly to provide new associates with an understanding of the project and schools in which they'd be working and an orienting lens for the challenging work they were about to start. Given that our "game plan" was first to identify and recruit outstanding natural helpers and then to harness their existing skills, relevant prior experience, strong interest in kids, and natural helping reflexes, training was focused and time-limited.

As a group, the associates navigated training with a mix of excitement and anxiety. When it was over they were ready to get started—appropriately edgy about the uncertainty of the new role and keenly aware of the imminence of major new responsibilities and challenges. On the other side of the coin, project schools, which in one or another way had gone through a half year of preparing for the new program, were by this time ready for the phantom to materialize. Though we had all along nourished the fantasy of a slow and easy program start, schools had more than done their homework and were poised "at the ready" for the program's launch date. Within a month of starting, new associates were seeing an average of 6+ primary graders each.

During the new program's 4-month debugging period (i.e., March–June), associates tried out new approaches in an effort to identify ways of interacting that came naturally and comfortably to them and seemed most useful to the children they were seeing. School-based project staff encouraged such exploration. In parallel, professionals explored the goodness of fit and efficacy of different supervisory approaches and sought to strengthen patterns of cooperation and communication among PMHP team members. The ultimate goal behind all this exploration was to maximize program benefits to children.

Outcomes of this pilot period were tracked closely as harbingers of things to come. Concerned parties were anxious to discover what was working well and what was broken and needed fixing. Surprisingly to us, even in the short 13-week pilot period, the project brought an average of 20 or more preventively oriented contacts to 330 children—nearly 10% of the primary grade enrollment in the 11 new project schools (Cowen, Dorr, Sandler, & McWilliams, 1971). This brief trial run was informative in several other ways: First, a substantial, heretofore unmet need for early program services was shown. Second, school personnel at different levels reacted positively to the trial run. What PMHP was doing made sense to teachers and other school personnel, who felt a strong need to do something promptly about evident or incipient child problems. Child associates also felt at home in the new role and enthusiastic about it. Both the associates and the supervising professionals felt, clinically, that they were being helpful to children. In sum, the model evidenced real promise for expanding significantly the availability of prompt, effective, preventive services for young children.

Once past the rosy glow of the preceding positive impressions, how-ever, it was not difficult to identify less than ideal program domains that needed some rethinking and problem solving. For example, moving from the idyllic, well-staffed, "hot-house" setting that PMHP had been in a single school, to 11 scattered school buildings was accompanied by a drop-off in communication. Because there were so many more players in the new project scenario, communication lines were more complex, and break-downs occurred more often. The latter included some frustrations and mis-understandings on the part of people (e.g., teachers) who lacked a suffi-ciently clear picture of the project's goals or working procedures. It is but one short step from less than ideal communication and a lack of clear understanding of project procedures to feelings of alienation. Some of the latter were apparent in the early expansion period. Relatedly, setting up the new project in a school imposed a new set of demands on school personnel (e.g., for project meetings, formal and informal contacts with parents and teachers, supervising child associates) that crowded already taxed schedules, and, some professionals, in candor, experienced discom-forts (growing pains) in adapting to the requirements of unfamiliar new roles in training and supervising child associates.

So we carried important but mixed messages away from the frenetic debugging period. First, and most basically, our experience with the pro-gram and the early outcome-research data suggested that the new program would fly well and meet the needs to which it was addressed. At the same time we realized that some problems remained that would have to be solved in order for maximal program benefits to accrue to children.

SUMMARY

The developments thus far described reflect PMHP's first two periods, and the start of a third stage, that is, up to the early 1970s when we "came up for air" and wrote the initial PMHP book. The review provided in this chapter covers most of what we plan to say about PMHP's early history. Later evolutionary steps addressed three sets of issues and goals, each of which grew naturally and sequentially out of the earlier project experiences. Set 1 concerns modifications in the basic PMHP approach, most reflecting field perceptions of unmet needs or new issues. At their core these modi-fications sought to strengthen the efficacy and expand the reach of basic PMHP services.

A second set of steps involved developing procedures and mechanisms for sharing PMHP's hard-come-by, battle-line experience with others to promote effective early detection and prevention services for dramatically increased numbers of children. A third major thrust was to develop and document new (i.e., beyond PMHP) primary prevention program models for children, either to be implemented independently or to be grafted onto the basic PMHP model by schools. The goal of these latter developments is to enhance children's wellness from the start and increase the likelihood that they will have successful and rewarding life experiences. In one or another form, these directional themes have attracted increasing amounts of our program development and research time in the past 20 years.

The chapters that follow provide a fuller picture of the practices that characterize PMHP's operation today in many school settings and extensions of those practices that enhance the array of options that PMHP can offer. They also describe how PMHP's program base has been expanded structurally, through systematic program dissemination and substantive steps to develop and evaluate true primary prevention program modules for young school children.

4

SETTING UP AND CONDUCTING A PMHP[1]

The first several chapters of this book described PMHP's rationale, development, and early format. This chapter describes PMHP's current approach, including a nuts-and-bolts account of how its major components work. The chapter is intended to be user friendly, that is, to give the reader a clearer sense of how PMHP conducts its daily business.

The chapter consists of three major sections. It begins with an overview of how to start a new PMHP program, covering entry issues, readying a school for the program, space, staffing, and equipment considerations. Next, it describes PMHP's core defining elements: (a) the screening and referral processes; (b) assignment, progress, and end-of-program clinical conferences; (c) child associates—who they are and what they do; (d) supervision of child associates; and (e) professional roles and activities. These descriptions include some comments, reflecting extensive experience in the "school of hard knocks," about how these elements may best be implemented. Although these observations will not perfectly fit all situations, we offer them in the spirit of what one PMHP consultant once called "throw-away dialogue." The chapter ends with a hypothetical case history,

[1]Thanks to Deborah Johnson for her substantive and editorial contribution to this chapter.

taking a "composite" child on a walking tour through PMHP. That account is intended to vivify and concretize the prior abstract description of PMHP.

STARTING A NEW PMHP

It takes considerable effort to start a new PMHP. How that start-up process unfolds is important to the program's success. An aphorism that well describes this situation is "As you sow, so shall you reap!" Starting a new program, among other things, calls for careful planning. Concerned parties must be given essential information about the program and its ways of operating. Relevant school personnel, including administrators, mental health professionals, and teachers need to participate in planning and start-up steps, both to educate them about how PMHP works and to get their inputs in adapting it to the new setting. Such involvement increases participants' sense of program ownership.

A first step in starting a new PMHP is for school personnel to learn enough about the project's rationale, goals, and ways of functioning to enable them to form a preliminary judgment about its "goodness of fit" in a given setting. These judgments must reflect a setting's needs, resources, styles, and predilections. Because schools differ in these regards, as well as in their due-process decision-making mechanisms, gestation time between initial exposure to the PMHP approach and a program's start may range from months to years.

School personnel learn about PMHP in several ways. One is through the printed word. There are scores of articles in the professional and scientific literature about PMHP overall, specific aspects of the program, and project research findings. Also, three book-sized accounts offer comprehensive, integrated views of PMHP: (a) the initial PMHP volume (Cowen, Trost, et al., 1975); (b) a detailed "how-to-do-it" manual that describes all aspects of PMHP concretely (Johnson, Carlson, & Couick, 1992); and (c) this volume. These sources can be very helpful both in making decisions about implementing a PMHP and fleshing out details of PMHP practice for users.

Although such printed documents are indeed helpful, experience over the years has shown that direct, firsthand exposure to the program and its personnel is the single most important factor in getting new PMHPs started. Such firsthand exposure both breathes life into the approach and provides a format within which prospective users can get information about start-up issues that pertain specifically to them and their schools. These meaningful, direct, experiential contacts can come about in several ways. One, where geography permits, is to visit an active PMHP program to see how it works and talk with the people who staff it. A second option is to attend a PMHP training workshop (See chapter 7). The Rochester PMHP,

Regional PMHP Dissemination Centers, and states involved in systematic program dissemination now all conduct annual workshops for that purpose. Participation in such workshops has greatly facilitated the start of new programs. Many (self-selected) people who attend these workshops come with an already established interest in the possibility of starting a new PMHP.

Readiness on the part of some school personnel who have become familiar with PMHP is a necessary but not sufficient condition for starting a new program. Important others, including those in a decision-making position in the school and those who will be significantly involved in the program, must concur in that judgment.

Although we would like to think that a district's decision about starting a PMHP is based solely on the program's obvious (to us) good sense and demonstrated merit, we are not so naive as to believe that that's always the case. Although most districts are, to be sure, interested in a program's effectiveness, for some that's second in importance to information about program *costs*. Relevant cost information can be found in several sources (Dorr, 1972; National Mental Health Association, 1995). Because PMHP does not tamper with a school's professional staffing, most new program costs stem from the child associate program. A recent estimate (National Mental Health Association, 1995) notes that the average cost of seeing a PMHP child through the school year is less than $500. Although PMHP program costs vary across schools, particularly as a function of program size, an average per year cost of $4,000–$5,000 for the child associate program is a reasonable estimate. This figure translates into a persuasive economic argument for school districts thinking about starting a PMHP. The argument is this: A program that averts (prevents) just one special education placement in a school year more than pays for itself; averting a single costly long-term residential placement could well cover program costs for 6–10 schools in a district.

Such rational arguments notwithstanding, fiscal concerns in some school districts work against starting a PMHP. And, in reality, there are other reasons why a PMHP may *not* be for all districts at all times. Some districts, for example, may have stronger needs and pressures for other types of programs (e.g., academic preparedness, violence control). Others may be going through power struggles in which any new program would become a pawn. Put positively, it is important that a PMHP fall within, and be connected to, a district or school's goals, priorities, and resources.

The obvious point in this discussion is that a school district or school must be ready for a PMHP before the program can be implemented. If that is not the case, time may be better invested in steps directed to enhance a system's readiness to start this type of prevention program. Thus, the key objective of an initial (preentry) system analysis is to establish that a

PMHP is feasible within a district or a school. In parallel, clear delineation of a system's needs, problems, and pressure points helps to shape the particulars of a new program.

PROGRAM ENTRY

Once it has been established that a new district can, and is ready to, start a PMHP, several concrete entry steps follow. These steps go more smoothly when several realities are kept in focus: (a) a school's de facto way of functioning may differ considerably from its de jure table of organization; (b) knowledge of and respect for de facto ways of functioning can facilitate a new PMHP start-up; (c) time, sometimes many months, may be needed to navigate a district's normal procedural and due-process mechanisms; (d) patience, persistence, and sensitivity to the needs of relevant school constituencies are needed to build a solid program foundation; and (e) support from multiple levels within a school district or school increases the likelihood that a new program will root well. With these orienting caveats in mind, we next describe several useful early steps that can be taken to acquaint school personnel and parents with PMHP.

Initial School Organizational Meetings

Several months before program services are scheduled to start, meetings involving key school personnel (e.g., principal, mental health professionals, teachers) and a PMHP program consultant should be held to clarify how PMHP will actually be conducted in a building—its procedures, time lines, and the roles and responsibilities of different school personnel in the program. It is also important to clarify how PMHP's procedures may affect other school programs. This is essential because, as noted, PMHP works best when connected to a school's mission, philosophy, and other services—in other words, when it blends smoothly into a school's natural fabric.

By design, PMHP changes the role of the school professionals. This change, crucial to a program's success, must also be clarified at these initial planning meetings. Moreover, there is a need to discuss how such change can best be integrated into overall building procedures. These early organizational meetings are also used to formulate plans for obtaining and preparing program space, equipment, and materials and, importantly, for selecting and training new child associates.

Faculty Meetings

Soon after deciding to start a new program, a meeting is needed to describe PMHP to the full school faculty, allowing for questions and discussion. The goal of such a meeting is to get essential program-launching steps started in a way that is task oriented and keeps relevant parties informed. If that goal cannot be met in a single meeting, another meeting should be scheduled.

Between the time of the initial faculty meeting and the start of program services, other meetings are needed for the teachers who will be most directly involved in PMHP. The exact composition of that group varies as a function of a school's specific implementation plan. Most will be primary grade teachers since the majority of all PMHP referrals come from that level. However, if a school decides, as PMHP recommends, to "start small and go slow," the new program may be limited initially to only the first grade; in that case only first grade teachers would participate in these preparatory meetings.

These additional in-depth meetings serve several purposes. They keep communication lines open and provide an open forum for discussing and dealing with concerns about the program. They also enable participants to learn more about specific program procedures (e.g., screening and referral steps) and to sharpen initially fuzzy program understandings. Concerns that come up with some frequency at meetings of this type include how does PMHP interface with other school programs; how much of my time will be needed for screening; and who should parents call if they have questions about the program. However, the most important purpose of these meetings is to communicate interest in, and respect for, faculty inputs and thus enhance faculty's sense of program ownership and involvement.

Informing Parents

Parallel informational meetings should also be held for parents during the start-up period. The program will significantly change a school's way of operating in the mental health area and will introduce new helping personnel (e.g., child associates), about whom parents will know little beforehand. Like the teacher meetings, parent meetings should describe the new program's rationale and explain what it can offer to children and families, how it actually works, and options for parent involvement. Parent meetings are important for several reasons. One, obviously, is to inform parents about the new approach before the fact, rather than having them stumble into it by accident. A second is to provide concrete information about how PMHP will actually work, and how they can avail themselves of the options it offers. In this context, we note that at least a small proportion of requests for PMHP services originate with parents.

Informing parents and community groups about PMHP is very helpful. This can be done in several ways beyond the parent meetings described above. Examples include (a) describing PMHP at a parent meeting, (b) an article about the program in the school newsletter, and (c) a program brochure given to parents at the time of kindergarten registration. Each of these mechanisms can serve the useful purpose of elevating parent and community consciousness about PMHP and, in so doing, facilitate access to its services, when needed.

Space

Typically, the principal designates an area for PMHP in the building. The setting should be a safe, comfortable place for children. It should be inviting and have adequate lighting, heating, and ventilation. Carpeting is not essential, though its presence makes for a more welcoming environment. Throw-rugs can be used effectively for that purpose. It is desirable, if feasible, for associates and children to have small individual areas, often partitions in a larger room, they can call "their own," where they can set up shop semipermanently. Such space eliminates the need for associates to carry equipment and materials from place to place and offers a kind of privacy needed to work effectively. Empty classrooms can be converted to meet PMHP space needs through the use of dividers to create individual work areas and of bookshelves and storage bins for play materials. The goal, in any case, is to carve out a play environment that is comfortable and engaging for young children.

Sometimes, space options in a building are very limited. An alternative in such cases is to share rooms used by part-time staff (e.g., music, art, and speech teachers). If this is done, it is important to minimize disruptions caused by the comings and goings of others while sessions are in progress. Privacy adds to the child's sense of security; it helps to establish the play area as a special and safe environment. In addition to play areas, the project also needs conference space for meetings with teachers and parents, supervisory sessions with associates, and program and clinical consultation meetings.

Figure 1a illustrates one type of space arrangement that has worked well in some PMHP schools. In this arrangement, an available classroom is sectioned off to provide each associate with her own small work space (8 × 8 ft). Each small work area has a table, several chairs, and a storage place for essential materials and supplies; some also have a sandbox, dollhouse, painting easel, and bobo doll. The overall space arrangement includes a larger communal area that doubles as a conference room, place to write reports, and coffee/kitchen area. That larger area also provides room for storing office supplies, crafts materials, and books and games that associates use in their contacts with children. Figure 1b is a photo of a small area of such a larger space layout (clutter and all) in a PMHP school. Usually, PMHP professionals have nearby office space that can also be used for supervising associates and meeting with parents.

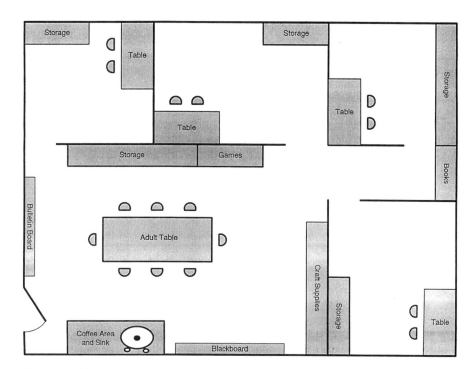

Figure 1a. PMHP representative space arrangement.

Figure 1b. PMHP play area.

In terms of play areas, child associates have been eager, imaginative, and creative in "prettying up," and making appealing, some initially dismal looking areas. In one school, for example, the only available space was an unused basement locker room. From a dim, musty, dungeonlike chamber, with faded, cracked brown-tiled walls, associates fashioned a most attractive set of play areas by using throw-rugs, brightly colored bean bags, patterned cloth stretched over 2 × 3-foot picture frames, and hanging children's drawings on the walls. In this area, painting was wonderfully experiential, and clean up was rarely a problem.

Playroom Equipment

Playrooms are like snowflakes; no two are alike. On the other hand, some materials that engage children naturally in play and expressive behavior can be found in most playrooms. The latter include a furnished doll house with small human figures, puppets, crayons, clay, paints, paper, dolls, stuffed animals, a sandbox with associated tools, and different games. Playroom materials need not be expensive. Many playrooms, in fact, are equipped using donated materials and rummage-sale items. Indeed, charitable organizations often respond favorably to requests to provide PMHP playroom items. Appendix A lists some equipment, materials, and supplies that merit consideration in furnishing a PMHP play area.

The final stocking and arrangement of a playroom is often deferred until associates are hired. This makes it possible for areas to include materials that associates would like to have and gives them a chance to put their imprimatur on the area and develop a greater sense of ownership of it.

PERSONNEL

Learning about a school's functioning, needs, styles, and readiness for PMHP, preparing teachers and parents for the program, and developing suitable space and equipment are all, to be sure, essential aspects of the start-up process. Two other crucial steps in that process involve the personnel who are central to the program's operation: school mental health professionals and child associates. Although those two roles can be extended and made more effective by support from school staff and outside consultants, they are always *the* central elements in a PMHP program. Depending on a school's resources and staffing patterns, different professional groups such as school psychologists and social workers, or elementary counselors, both full time and part time, have served as program professionals. These people both have the professional skills needed to conduct

PMHP and are familiar with the school's ecology, needs, personnel, and operating styles.

Some larger PMHP programs have a named "coordinator," in central administration, in charge. Whether or not there is such a designated title, it is important that someone (e.g., a school mental health professional, principal, Pupil Personnel Services Coordinator) be able to assume the role of program spokesperson. The person who functions in that role must have a clear understanding of the PMHP model and be able to describe it at multiple levels (e.g., school board, central administration, school administration, faculty, parents).

Child Associates: The Heart and Soul of PMHP

Child associates are unquestionably central in PMHP. Indeed, viewed over the project's 38-year history, the development and refinement of that role may be PMHP's single most significant, innovative contribution. By way of backdrop for the account that follows, Appendix B1 presents a job description for the child associate role that some PMHP schools use in the hiring process.

Selection

Selecting child associates is a crucial step in starting a PMHP. The program's success depends squarely on the wisdom of those decisions. Accordingly, hiring associates has always been a deeply invested step in PMHP; bringing that step off successfully more than justifies the extensive effort that goes into it. Although the principle of hiring maximally able child associates in PMHP is nonnegotiable, the hiring process itself can proceed in several different ways, reflecting a system's due-process mechanisms and natural operating styles. The description to follow reflects the step-stage process *we* have used in hiring child associates.

The process starts with a formal written application soliciting information about the applicant's prior experience with children. Prospective applicants are first interviewed in depth by the program coordinator (WGH). Interview questions assess the candidate's (a) interest and commitment (e.g., "Why do you want this position?" "How does it fit your life at this time?"); (b) relevant prior experience (e.g., "Tell me about your past experience working with children and/or adults"); (c) attitudes and experiences with school (e.g., "What was school like for you?" "What do you think about teacher roles in the school?"); and (d) personal resources (e.g., "What do you see as your strong points for this role? Any weaknesses or concerns?"). Johnson et al. (1992) list other questions that have yielded useful information in interviewing prospective associates.

Based on such questions, the interviewer forms initial judgments about the extent to which interviewees have the qualities considered to be basic to the child associate role (Cowen, Dorr, & Pokracki, 1972). These include being child oriented; a history of enjoying, and working well with, children; warmth, empathy, and the ability to relate comfortably to children and adults; an openness to new learning and experiences; flexibility and adaptability; and reliability. Appendix B2 presents a rating form used to provide such judgments. In some settings, other selection requisites are important, such as an ethnic–cultural match between the associate and the program's target children.

Candidates who surmount this tough initial interview hurdle are next interviewed by school-based mental health professionals. Because they are the people with whom associates would be working daily, the fit between professionals and associates must be good. This second interview is oriented toward specific work-match issues such as liking the applicant at a "gut level," judging her amenability to training and supervision, and judging her fit with school personnel and the school's ways of operating. Some schools pursue these issues in a third interview involving the principal and teachers.

We clearly recognize that this "trial-by-fire" interview sequence is tough for an applicant to get past. It is so intended! But the safeguards and benefits it offers more than justify the effort. Hiring associates who have been carefully screened by several people, and using high standards in so doing, is the most important step that can be taken to ensure a program's sound start and ongoing success. That, in a nutshell, is why the process of recruiting associates warrants a major investment of time and energy. As that particular twig gets bent so will the program's bough grow. Child associates who have gone through this rigorous selection process are keenly aware of what it entails. As one newly hired associate put it, "It's like being interviewed for a job at the White House and then getting paid minimum wage."

Initial Child Associate Training

Great care is taken to hire child associates with skills and qualities that make for effective help giving with children. Training is intended to build on these positive qualities. Trainers do not "tinker" with the natural caring reflexes and effective interpersonal skills for which associates were hired; rather they strive to orient those skills to the context and challenges of work with young children in schools. A second goal of the training process is to reduce the anxiety some associates may feel about taking on this "awesome" new role.

Associate training in PMHP is an open, ongoing process. It includes initial formal training and continuing on-the-job training for all associates, and later, more advanced training options that associates are offered to broaden their skills. This section covers only the initial training; chapter 5 describes advanced training options for associates. Again, we note that there is leeway in what the initial associate training covers, and we recognize that such training must be "in sync" with a district's needs and styles. In describing PMHP's approach to initial associate training, we weigh heavily on things that have worked for us.

Initial training may either precede, or run concurrently with, the associate's first several months on the job. This training is designed to impart information and skills that facilitate work with children in a school environment and to clarify basic PMHP procedures and intervention strategies. In recent years, most initial associate training cycles have been conducted in eight 3-hour sessions. Although such training, by preference or necessity, sometimes has to be done in concentrated blocks (e.g., 2–3 full days), most PMHP trainers have found a distributed training pace to be less wearing on all parties and more likely to avoid information overload. In any case, the training summary provided here is based on eight 3-hour sessions each with specific topical foci.

Within such a format, Session 1 considers PMHP's history, rationale, and purposes; identifies characteristics of children who are most appropriate for referral; and overviews the program's basic operating practices. Strategies for building relationships with children are introduced and the need for confidentiality is stressed. Finally, a school's policies and procedures (e.g., reporting responsibilities in instances of child abuse) are reviewed in relation to the child associate role.

Session 2 focuses on the school context in which the associate will be working, and PMHP's screening process. Associates need to understand roles and relationships pertinent to their new work environment. Clarification of the school's de facto operating practices facilitates the development of open, effective communication lines between associates and school personnel—from secretaries to the principal. Associates' understandings of the nature of the school environment, personnel, and basic operating practices are important to PMHP's success in a school. Session 2 also reviews PMHP's early detection and screening procedures. Because that information provides a base on which intervention goals are built, and approaches with children mapped out, associates need to understand the rationale, purpose, and mechanics of these processes.

Sessions 3 and 4 cover topics that are important to the associate–child interaction. These topics range in content and level of abstractness. One example is the information provided about developmental stages in young children. Such information helps associates better understand behavioral norms and expectations for children of different ages and to use technology appropriate to a child's developmental level. A second example is the extensive consideration given to the nature of an effective helping relationship, its importance to children, how it sets the stage for the child's growth and progress in the program, and what can be done to promote a good relationship. In the latter context, time is spent on techniques, including listening skills, sensitivity to nonverbal communication cues, and responding strategies such as simple acceptance, reflecting feelings, and limit setting. These sessions thus offer associates how-to-do-it tools.

Sessions 5 and 6 further develop prior themes, including those involving intervention skills. One objective is to enhance associates' understanding of children's play. Play is depicted as a natural means of expression and communication for children, and its developmental stages are considered. The associate's roles as an observer and facilitator of children's play are considered, as are concrete matters such as equipping and organizing a playroom, helping children to select materials and activities that facilitate the achievement of established goals, and practical issues such as how to handle "gifts" or projects the child completes in the playroom. In brief, then, having established that the core of PMHP rests on the associate–child relationship, these sessions focus on how play can best be used to enhance that relationship.

Sessions 7 and 8 are integrative. They include further discussion of PMHP strategies and procedures, and information about handling some difficult situations such as hitting, and other types of physical contact, that come up in the playroom. The topic of termination is also discussed. Termination is a difficult process in most helping interactions, certainly so for child associates with strong, natural, parenting reflexes. These final sessions also address questions associates have in anticipation of starting to work with children, or, in some cases, about experiences they've already had. Later training options for associates may also be discussed and, in some cases, introductions to advanced specialty training options may be provided.

Associate training sometimes involves activities beyond the content coverage described above. Associates, like other people, have different learning styles. Some learn well by reading, others by listening and watching; most learn through firsthand experience. Activities such as "modeling" by the trainer, role-plays, videotapes, and active group discussion help to enliven training and make it more enjoyable. Relatedly, although major portions of associate training are done by the project coordinator and/or a school mental health professional, it is often helpful to involve relevant others such as veteran child associates with extensive front-line experience with children, in the initial training cycle. Indeed, it is not unusual for veteran associates—people with backgrounds and starting points very similar to those of the "trainees"—to be more credible than professionals to fledgling associates.

Finally, we note that the very process of training new child associates is an important team-building element in a PMHP school (Johnson et al.,

1992). Those involved in this process as trainers and trainees will be working closely with each other and with pupils, teachers, and other school personnel as part of a cohesive child-serving team for some time to come.

Associates' activities with children are more fully described later in the chapter. Here, we add only a few comments beyond the material already presented. First, the associates' primary responsibility is to the children they serve. Associates work under the school mental health professionals who guide their work and provide supervision. A first, universal goal for child associates is to establish rapport and a sound working relationship with a child. A caring, positive relationship helps to create a facilitative framework within which efforts to meet established goals (e.g., reduction of school adjustment problems and promotion of school-related competencies) can gainfully develop.

Child associates are integral to the PMHP team. They are also part of the larger school team. They are involved in many aspects of PMHP, including screening, training activities, and program conferences. They meet with teachers to confer and exchange information about individual students. With additional training (see chapter 5), many come later to work with children in small groups and with parents. The child associate's most important role, however, is to meet with referred children and, based on a caring relationship established, help them through conversation and play to deal effectively with problems and develop adaptive skills and competencies. In discharging this primary role, associates keep progress notes on children and participate in training and supervision.

The PMHP Team

In addition to the central roles of child associates and school professionals, the PMHP team includes the principal and teachers. A principal's positive cathexes and involvements put a stamp of approval on the program and set a tone for it to function effectively. Primary grade teachers are central to PMHP. For one thing, they are the prime source of referrals. Moreover, their efforts as part of a team approach contribute to positive program outcomes for children. In some schools, other people, such as a consultant or school nurse, have viable program roles. The team, in any case, has responsibility for all aspects of a building's PMHP. In that context, teams often hold weekly, or biweekly, meetings to review program progress and issues and plan for the future.

This chapter has thus far overviewed several key steps that prepare a school to start a new PMHP and to carry it through an initial year's operation. Although schools must follow individualized time lines in carrying out these steps, Figure 2 presents one reasonable sequence and time line for the start-up process. This is at best a rough guideline, not a rigidly bound schedule; we know from experience that the timing and sequencing of start-up steps necessarily vary across schools, sometimes appreciably so.

BASIC PMHP PRACTICES

Children Served by PMHP

PMHP's guiding strategy has been to intervene with children as soon as possible in seeking to optimize their school functioning. In pursuing this goal, PMHP is targeted primarily to children with already evident or incipient school adjustment problems in the mild to moderate range, not to children with already crystallized, serious dysfunction who need professional help.

This intended focus is depicted schematically in Figure 3. Although the figure appears to represent three "discrete" levels of adjustment, those levels are, in fact, more continuous than discrete. Distinctions between them are particularly fuzzy at their joining points. That limitation notwithstanding, the figure helps to clarify the intent of program targeting. It first conveys the notion that most children are adequately adjusted and do not need PMHP services. It also depicts a smaller group of children in whom mild to moderate school adjustment problems are already established, or incipient. Those are the youngsters to whom most PMHP services are targeted. The top, and by far the smallest, level of the pyramid depicts already identified children with specific diagnoses (e.g., seriously emotionally disturbed, major conduct disorder, major depression), who are, or should be, receiving professional help through a school's special education system or from mental health professionals outside the school. These "identified" children fall outside PMHP's prime intended orbit. Although the same may be true for some children at the upper end of the "at-risk" category, district practices for those youngsters vary more than for the already-identified children, sometimes as a function of the availability of other helping resources in a community. Thus, the proportions of children falling into these three "categories" will vary some across schools.

Early Detection and Screening

Early detection, screening, and referral are focal in PMHP because they form the base on which the program's early preventive intervention steps rest. Screening in PMHP is an "open" process that extends over time and reflects informal, as well as formal, components. Although these in-

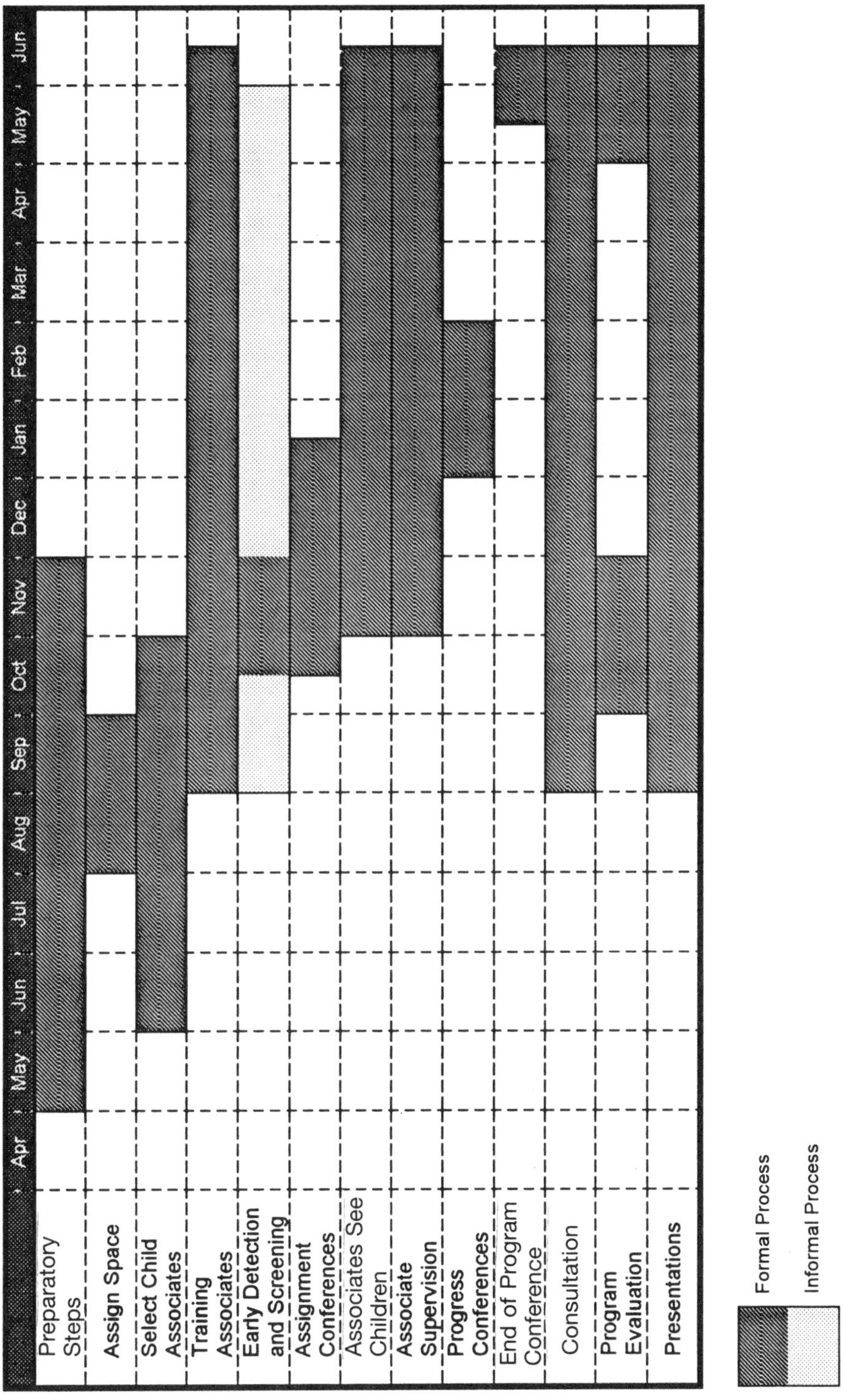

Figure 2. PMHP time line for new projects.

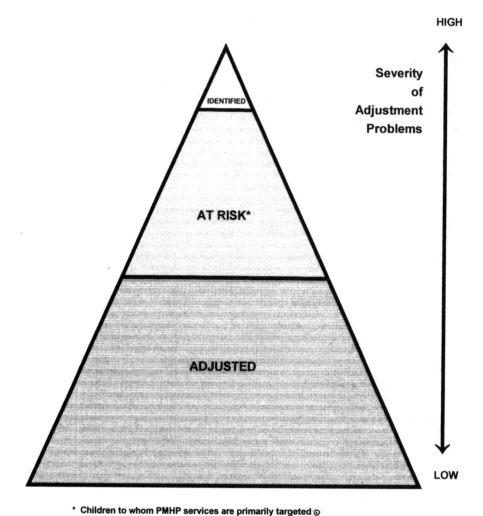

HIGH

Severity
of
Adjustment
Problems

IDENTIFIED

AT RISK*

ADJUSTED

LOW

* Children to whom PMHP services are primarily targeted ©

Figure 3. Children served by a PMHP.

formal elements are important in PMHP's way of operating, they tend to get lost in compartmentalized descriptions of "*the*" formal screening and referral process. Hence, although the descriptions to follow are built around formal screening and referral components, informal aspects of that process are also reflected.

Screening

Although this section focuses on PMHP's early mass-screening steps, we emphasize that screening in PMHP schools is an ongoing process. This is so because personnel in PMHP schools are keenly aware of the program's presence, scope, and ways of functioning and are attuned to the importance of early identification and effective early intervention. As in any school, personnel in PMHP schools are witness to a running stream of daily behavior samples from all children. If and when their concerns about a child reach a certain threshold, they have ready access to the PMHP team, for raising such concerns, discussing them, and getting informal feedback about next possible steps. Hence, there is ongoing observational vigilance (informal screening) in PMHP schools and a mechanism (i.e., team contact) for addressing concerns that arise spontaneously at any time, in any class.

The goal of the PMHP screening process is to develop an accurate representation of all children's early school adjustment. The purpose of the initial mass-screening step is to launch a process, early on, of identifying children who stand to benefit most from PMHP. This step also provides a low-cost mechanism by which the PMHP team can review the early school adjustment of all children. It is recognized, however, that not all pertinent emotional and social dimensions can be assessed in this first screening step. A more realistic goal is to develop a composite sketch of each child's current adjustment situation. The utility of these sketches is enhanced to the extent that they reflect multiple methods, characteristics, input sources, and time points.

The PMHP screening process begins with the collection of information as soon as school starts. Informally, teachers and other members of the PMHP team observe students in various settings in the school (e.g., classrooms, halls, cafeteria, playground). Child associates often arrange times with teachers to observe children in the classroom. Team members review school records and, where pertinent, screening information from prior years. Some teams also do structured observations when standardized testing is being done in class. Although many of these "informal" processes are school or district specific, the overall PMHP screening process strives to be systematic, multidimensional, and outreaching. Its prime goal, at least in a preliminary way, is to identify existing problems and competencies in several relevant domains of school functioning, for all children, early in their school careers.

In most PMHP schools, teachers become involved in formal aspects of the screening process about 4–6 weeks after the start of the school year. That delay allows time for children to settle down in their classes and thus provides a more representative picture of their behavior. For similar reasons, we recommend that kindergarten screening be done at the end of the first semester. Most PMHP schools conduct formal screening with primary graders. Teachers complete rating scales for kindergarten–first grade students. Teachers, and sometimes also children, complete such ratings at the second and third grade levels. This formal, mass-screening step is intended as an X ray that can identify children for whom later, more extensive review and action is indicated.

The first formal mass-screening step is built around a brief (12-item) objective measure, called the AML Behavior Rating Scale—Revised (AML-R; see Appendix C1), that teachers complete for all children in their class (Primary Mental Health Project, 1995). Before doing these ratings, the team will have briefed teachers on the use of this measure so that they are familiar with its purpose and mechanics. The AML-R takes less than 1 minute per child to complete—perhaps a half hour for an entire class. Its 12 items consist of three 4-item factors: Acting Out ("disrupts class discipline"), Moody ("is moody"), and Learning Difficulties ("needs help with school work"). All items are rated on a 5-point frequency of occurrence scale (1 = never; 5 = most or all of the time). Item ratings are summed to yield subscale and total scores. Detailed norms (by grade level, gender, and place of residence) are available for the AML-R; hence, children's scores can be related to an appropriate reference group to provide a rough initial index of their adjustment status. The AML-R is easy to score, reliable, and valid; large numbers of these measures can be processed very quickly by machine. The quick and easy processing of AML-R scores facilitates prompt feedback and follow-through with teachers.

In many PMHP schools, second and third graders and older children complete the 24-item Child Rating Scale (CRS; see Appendix C2) as part of the formal screening process. On average, this measure takes 15–25 minutes for a class to complete. The CRS has four empirically derived scales: Rule Compliance/Acting Out ("I behave in school"; "I get in trouble"); Anxiety ("I worry about things"); Peer Social Skills ("My classmates like me"); and School Interest ("School is fun"). Each item is rated by the child on a 3-point scale (1 = usually no, 2 = sometimes, and 3 = usually yes). Like the AML-R, the CRS can be scored by hand or machine and detailed norms are available. Psychometric data for this measure are reported elsewhere (Hightower et al., 1987).

Systematic use of the AML-R, CRS, or similar measures comprises one key element in PMHP's mass-screening procedures. But even though mass screening is a focused, important early-on step, screening does not end with that step in PMHP schools To the contrary, screening, as noted earlier, is an ongoing, open process, in which teachers and other school personnel function throughout the year and across school years as observers and reactors whose concerns about children can be raised any time with a sympathetic, help-oriented PMHP team.

Assignment Conference

Most PMHP-seen children first become candidates for intervention as a result of findings from the screening process. After formal and informal screening steps have been taken, all relevant information is brought together at an assignment conference. The PMHP team meets, reviews this assembled information, creates composite sketches of children's school adjustment, identifies children who seem most appropriate for in-depth PMHP services, and for those children, begins to formulate an intervention plan. At that point, the referral process starts for children who appear to need PMHP services. Establishing the likelihood of a PMHP referral activates a more extensive information-gathering process.

Although assignment conferences can occur any time during the school year, most take place early in the year for both full-year and semester programs. For the latter, a second set of conferences is needed at the start of Semester 2. The assignment conference formulates decisions about which children will be referred and how most of the program's child-serving resources for the year will be allocated. Depending on a school's size, and the number of referrals generated, it may take several days to complete a round of assignment conferences.

Although schools structure assignment conferences differently, the teacher's presence is needed both to provide pertinent information about a child's behavior and performance in class and to participate in the referral and goal-setting processes. Teachers' involvement in those important processes is facilitated by hiring a substitute teacher, who moves from class to class freeing up a block of time for each referring teacher to participate in these conferences. This practice highlights the importance of the assignment conference and avoids imposing the burden of lunch-hour or after-school meetings on teachers.

Discussion time at these meetings is not allocated evenly across children. More typically, in a class of 25, most children will quickly get a clean bill of health, and 90% of the discussion time will focus on a small fraction of children who appear, on the basis of available information, to be at some risk. For the latter, the focal issue is what makes best sense as a next step. Although the answer for a few children may lie in a suggested change in the teacher's classroom management style or perhaps a referral to an outside source, for most, referral to PMHP is likely to be the logical next step.

In some schools, the team discusses potential referrals informally with teachers, before the assignment conference, to be sure that the teacher's current views are known. During such meetings, teachers may add names of children not listed, or ask to hold off on one or more potential candidates, because they now seem to be functioning reasonably well in class.

Sometimes, parents or other school personnel (e.g., nurse, lunchroom monitor, reading, music, or gym teacher) make referrals to PMHP or have pertinent information about a child's school adjustment. In such situations these people may also be invited to participate in the assignment conference. The full exchange of information that takes place at this conference helps participants to reach a clear understanding of the child's strengths and problems, which in turn facilitates development of an intervention plan that best fits the child.

As with many PMHP procedures, schools vary in how they conduct assignment conferences. One way that has worked for us is to start by having the teacher describe the child, including his or her problems and resources. If the child has been observed in class, that information is presented next. After that, the school professional summarizes pertinent information gathered from multiple sources (e.g., teacher and self-ratings of adjustment, test data, the child's cumulative school record). If the parent was interviewed by the social worker or the senior associate, impressions from that contact are also reported.

There is nothing sacred about the above procedure; indeed, assignment conferences proceed perfectly well in other ways. At bedrock, however, this conference seeks to assess the child's current situation (problems and competencies) from pertinent perspectives and, on that basis, to develop a sensible, mutually agreed-upon plan to address the child's needs. Sometimes the data available converge and an intervention plan falls neatly into place. In more complex cases (i.e., where views of the child diverge), the review process takes longer. On average, a 1-hour assignment conference, involving a single teacher, can cover an entire class, including more in-depth planning for three to four children. For children selected to participate in PMHP, time is also spent establishing goals, based on available information. In this process, teachers are asked to specify changes they would like to see in a child's classroom behavior.

By the end of the assignment conference period, children from all classes will have been reviewed, and those appropriate for PMHP referred. As part of this process, some children may be put on a "watch" list and others referred for further evaluation, or outside services. In the ideal, agreed-upon goals will have been established for children to be seen through PMHP.

Although this mass-screening process identifies most children who are referred to PMHP, referrals also come from other sources. For some children, initial problems that slipped through the mass-screening "net," or did not "flower" until later, become apparent. Other children with problems transfer into a school after the formal screening process has ended. Sometimes children who were doing well initially experience buffetings that adversely affect their school adjustment. And sometimes parents initiate referrals.

These realities highlight several points. Referrals to PMHP can, and do, come from many sources, and for many reasons. One of those sources, an important one early on, is the screening process. Referral, however, is always an open option in a PMHP school; it can come up for any child at any time.

Parent Consent

For children identified as potential candidates for PMHP, written parent consent is required before further steps are taken. Schools use different procedures to obtain such consent. In some schools, an explanatory letter with a consent form is mailed to the parent after the assignment conference. Other schools have teachers make the initial contact, since they already know the parent and may be less threatening than a mental health professional. In this initial contact, which can be done face to face or by phone, the teacher describes the program briefly and explains why the child was referred and how the program may help the child. If the parent agrees with the referral recommendation, a program description and permission form are sent home with the child, or by mail. In some schools, permission for the child's participation is obtained during a parent conference.

Referral

Preliminary identification of children who may be appropriate for PMHP, and receipt of parental consent, activates a more complex, in-depth referral process designed to better understand the child's needs, verify his or her suitability for PMHP, and finalize an appropriate intervention plan. The referral process builds on information already available and gathers additional information from multiple sources, so as to formulate an optimal intervention plan for the child. Although schools differ some in the exact nature of the information they gather, as a generalization it is fair to say that such information is substantial and reflects multiple strands of a child's behavior, occurring in multiple settings, as provided by multiple informants.

The teacher is an important source of additional information because he or she is most familiar with the child's current school behavior and performance. For referred children, teachers are asked, almost universally, to complete the Teacher Child Rating Scale (T-CRS; see Appendix C3), a two-part, 36-item measure of children's school problem behaviors and competencies (Hightower et al., 1986). Factor analysis has shown the T-CRS to consist of three 6-item problem factors: Acting Out (overly aggressive with peers, fights); Shy–Anxious (shy, timid); and Learning Problems (poor work habits)—and four 5-item competence dimensions: Frustration Tolerance (copes well with failure); Assertive Social Skills (defends own views under group pressure); Task-Orientation (a self-starter); and Peer Social Skills (well-liked by classmates). The T-CRS thus yields three problem factor scores and a sum problem score, as well as four competence factor scores and a sum competence score. The T-CRS has been shown to be psychometrically sound in terms of reliability and concurrent and discriminant validity (Hightower et al., 1986). Like the AML-R and CRS, the availability of extensive T-CRS norms by place of residence, gender, and grade level makes it possible to compare any child's profile with an appropriate reference group.

Peaks and troughs on T-CRS dimensions, and specific items that stand out, can help to frame goals for the ensuing PMHP intervention. Indeed, in some settings teachers are invited to list specific intervention goals and objectives for a child after filling out the T-CRS. At the end of the school year, teachers complete a second T-CRS, which is used both for progress assessment to date and next steps, and for program evaluation purposes.

A second instrument often used in the referral process, the Background Information Form (BIF), also requires teacher inputs. The BIF provides demographic and educational information used to clarify the child's background situation and formulate intervention plans. Appendix C4 presents a copy of the five-part BIF. Parts 1 and 2 consist of background information (e.g., child's name, address, teacher, school, student ID number) and demographic data (e.g., gender, date of birth). Part 3 describes the child's parenting situation (e.g., single-parent family, both natural parents, foster placement). These three parts can usually be completed by a child associate or mental health professional from school records. Parts 4 and 5, however, are ordinarily completed by the teacher. Part 4 consists of 11 items relating to the child's educational experience (e.g., has repeated a grade; has transferred schools), and Part 5 lists six child characteristics that may inform the referral process (e.g., visits school nurse often; ongoing medical problems; frequent illegal absences). The BIF provides helpful information in formulating intervention plans and goals for the child.

Other sources of school data, if not previously available, also become part of the pool of referral materials. One potentially useful source is the child's cumulative school record, which includes information such as report card grades, ratings of a child's behavior and work habits, anecdotal descriptions of the child's school experiences, copies of reports to parents, and standardized test information. Systematic review of such data can help to establish meaningful, realistic, intervention goals and facilitate planning on the child's behalf.

Some schools have used other information to clarify referrals, including classroom observations of children, child self-report measures, and contacts with parents. Parent contacts in the referral process, either in face-to-face interviews or by phone, can help to inform PMHP staff about the child's school situation and apprise the team of relevant family information.

Because parents can provide pertinent information not available from other sources, some schools now ask parents to complete a Parent–Child Rating Scale (P-CRS), a recently developed PMHP assessment tool. The P-CRS parallels the T-CRS in coverage, format, and factor structure, though several T-CRS items (e.g., "participates in class discussions"; "disruptive in class") have been modified to make them more appropriate to the home situation. Appendix C5 presents a copy of the P-CRS. Because this measure is still in an early developmental stage, it lacks the extensive normative data available for the other PMHP assessment devices.

It is always possible to modify the initial tentative intervention plan formulated for a child. Because children usually start in PMHP as soon as parent permission is received, associates' early impressions and inputs can be used in that context as an additional planning source. To that end, after associates have seen children four times, they are asked to report their impressions on the 20-item Associate–Child Rating Scale (A-CRS; Primary Mental Health Project, 1995). Following a format and structure similar to the CRS, T-CRS, and P-CRS, the A-CRS (see Appendix C6) includes four empirically derived scales: Participation ("looks forward to coming"), Acting Out/Limits ("tests limits"), Shy–Anxious ("is fearful"), and Self-Confidence ("copes well with failure"). Child associates rate each A-CRS item on a 5-point scale in terms of how well it describes the child (1 = not at all, to 5 = very well). A-CRS subscales have a median alpha coefficient of .86. A-CRS norms are available for a sample of PMHP referred children.

Detailed information about all PMHP assessment measures has been assembled in a single comprehensive source document called *Screening and Evaluation Measures and Forms* (Primary Mental Health Project, 1995). This set of guidelines includes a copy of each measure; information about its purposes and scope; a description of its scoring procedures; explanations of the meaning of scores and how to interpret them; cautions in test usage; sources of additional information including literature cites; and, where available, test norms.[2]

DIRECT PMHP SERVICES

The essence and uniqueness of the PMHP approach lies in its blending of four key structural components. Perhaps the most basic of those is the ongoing interaction between child associate and child. No matter how smooth a PMHP program looks otherwise, the single determinant that most centrally shapes child outcomes is the associate–child interaction in the playroom. Two words, *relationship* and *play*, that are crucial to the associate–child interaction process, and what happens as a result of it, must be front-and-center in the description of PMHP services.

In PMHP's normal sequence, after parent permissions have been received and the referral process completed, teachers and associates agree on a mutually convenient time for the child to be seen. Associates then begin

---

[2]This set of guidelines may be ordered from PMHP Measures and Manuals Division, 685 South Avenue, Rochester, New York 14620.

to see children in regularly scheduled individual or group contacts, as established at the assignment conference. The associate, known popularly to many PMHP children as "my lady" or "special friend," picks up the child in the classroom before each session starts and returns him or her after it ends. Most children look forward to meeting with their lady. Indeed, non-referred classmates sometimes ask if they too can go and, on special occasions, when it fits the course of the intervention to do so, a child may be allowed to bring a friend to the playroom. Associate–child meetings, on average, last 25–45 minutes, somewhat longer for older children. Although schools also vary in frequency and total number of contacts per child, 20–25 sessions is typical for full-year programs and 12–15 sessions for semester programs.

The associate's initial task, an important ongoing one as well, is to develop a sound relationship with the child. There is no single formula for doing this. Associates, like other people, are individuals with different experiential histories, interaction styles, and comfort zones. Children also differ in needs, styles, and what makes them feel comfortable or uncomfortable. Each associate–child dyad is thus unique and may call for somewhat different steps to build and maintain an effective relationship. The point to stress is that the royal road to an effective relationship must reflect the uniqueness of any given dyad. That is why PMHP's recruiting practices place heavy emphasis on an associate's history of effective contacts with children and skills for establishing warm relationships with them. If those qualities are present, an associate will get off to a good start with most youngsters.

Often an associate–child relationship falls quickly and neatly into place. But that doesn't always happen, sometimes because the right entry path can't be found and sometimes because children have been so badly bruised in past relationships that they are mistrustful of new ones. The existence of a warm, trusting associate–child relationship is the foundation on which significant attitudinal and behavioral change in children rests. Its presence enables the associate to apply her natural skills and sensitivities as a supportive listener, a special friend, and a caring adult who can help the child to deal with existing problems and develop adaptive skills. Many, but not all, instances of restricted child progress in PMHP reflect some limitation in the associate–child relationship.

Several built-in aspects of the PMHP system offer checkpoints for considering the associate–child relationship. The most important is the regularly scheduled weekly or biweekly supervisory meeting, which offers a natural forum for reviewing relational and other matters. PMHP's midyear progress conference (cf. below) provides another forum for reviewing a child's status in the program, including the nature of the associate–child relationship.

The associate–child interaction is set in a playroom because play is intrinsically engaging and a natural medium of expression for children. The child's play, and the words exchanged between associates and children, are PMHP's main currencies of interaction. A trusting relationship between the associate and the child makes the playroom a place where the child feels secure, comfortable, and in control—a place where the child can feel safe being him- or herself. Beyond such a relationship, the playroom, as noted earlier, should be set up to create a context and set of materials (e.g., bright colorful decorations, posters, books, games) that are intrinsically appealing to young children and encourage them to explore and express a range of feelings and emotions.

From the start, associates encourage children to take the initiative in choosing playroom activities, that is, to lead rather than follow. This is done both to encourage development of the child's autonomous decision making and to respect the child's internal barometer of what is safe and comfortable at any point in time. On the other hand, the associate's awareness of goals and objectives for specific children sometimes leads her to ease the child toward certain playroom activities. Doll play, for example, might be gently encouraged for a child experiencing problems at home, and a very shy child may find the bobo doll to be a good outlet for feelings that are otherwise difficult to express.

Thus, through play, in the context of an accepting relationship with a caring adult, children in PMHP come to express and work through thoughts and feelings about matters that are important to them in, and outside of, school—matters that significantly affect what they can derive from the school experience. Otherwise put, play provides young children opportunities to explore their world in a way that simultaneously offers a language for communicating needs and desires and a window to their emotional lives. Many young children can express much more through play than through words.

A child's play is thus central in PMHP. It is encouraged, in the first place, by a playroom setting that engages the child and offers a range of appealing, age-appropriate activities, and it is further catalyzed by a relationship with a special adult that makes it possible for the child to explore and express thoughts and feelings safely and securely. The specific media of exploration and expression range widely across associate–child pairs as a function of such variables as the child's developmental level and interests, and, to some extent, the activities with which an associate feels most comfortable and adept.

The associate is an active participant in the events of the playroom, not just a passive observer. Her actions and words strive to create a climate of unconditional acceptance for the child and his or her feelings. The preceding is not to say that *all* behaviors are acceptable in the playroom.

Some actions (hitting, cursing, spitting) are out of bounds. An approach of choice in dealing with such instances is to distinguish between a behavior that is not acceptable and the feelings behind it, which are always acceptable, and to provide acceptable alternatives for the latter (e.g., "I can see you're angry with me and would like to hit me, but people aren't for hitting. But you can hit the bobo doll if you like.").

Throughout, the associate is active and responsive; hence playroom activities unfold in a context of running exchanges of conversation between associate and child. The associate may simply describe what a child is doing to communicate understanding and acceptance. And, as feelings move to the surface of the child's play activities, associates may gently reflect those feelings in ways that can lead to productive exploration of meaningful aspects of the child's current situation and problems. And indeed, when the associate "reads" both a need and readiness in the child, she may suggest an activity that offers an entry point to the domain in question.

Some playroom activities involving associate and child have instrumental value. For example, reading to the child, or playing a game (cards, checkers, board game) may help to build or solidify a trusting relationship. Relatedly, typical playroom interactions between associates and children (e.g., games, stories) provide a framework within which children can comfortably and nonthreateningly learn important childhood "lessons of life" (e.g., taking turns, following rules, paying attention to the task at hand, winning or losing graciously, tolerating frustration). In summary, a child's playroom experience in PMHP unfolds in the presence of a caring, supportive child associate, who provides a secure relationship, acceptance, realistic limits, and verbal inputs, in response to the child's words and play, that help the child better to understand and deal with important feelings and to acquire stage salient skills and competencies.

In PMHP, the child associate is never a solo performer. Rather, she is backed by the full resources of the PMHP team, which are at her disposal. Moreover, PMHP has built-in check points and quality-control mechanisms to ensure that those resources are well used. Those include both regularly scheduled supervision of associates and periodic clinical (review) conferences.

Senior Associates

Relatively early in PMHP's evolution, as the project grew in larger districts, it became clear that (a) program management, communication, and quality control needs were mounting more rapidly than the resources available to meet them; and (b) additional professional time for these purposes was not to be found. To address this problem in a manner consistent with the personpower solutions previously developed by PMHP, the role of senior associate was created and explored (Cowen, Trost, & Izzo, 1973). As initially conceived and piloted with four women who had functioned effectively as child associates for 6 years, the new role involved five different sets of activities, designed both to provide relief for harried professionals and support the program's quality control standards. These activities were associate-serving, child-serving, team-serving, administrative, and research roles.

Over the ensuing years, the senior associate role has developed and blossomed; it is now an important element in the effective functioning of some PMHPs—particularly larger programs with many associates in multiple schools. Senior associates typically divide their week among several schools, where they work with different professional teams and child associate groups.

Senior associate roles can be grouped as clinical roles, featuring associate- and child-serving activities, and program management roles, reflecting team-serving, administrative, and research-related activities. In the former sphere, senior associates have participated actively in orienting new associates to the program and the associate's role. They have also functioned as first-line sounding boards for associates on management issues that come up in the playroom and as providers of information about the use of materials and equipment and practical matters (e.g., program procedures, time lines) involved in seeing children. In some settings, senior associates conduct mini skill-training sessions, as for example in the use of arts and crafts materials, finger paints, or puppet play, depending on their expertise. On request, they observe associates actually working with children and share impressions and suggestions with them afterwards. Also in the clinical context, senior associates sometimes function as program spokespersons and contact persons with school personnel (principals and teachers) and parents. These clinical roles are enjoyable for senior associates, useful and meaningful for child associates, and helpful to the program's effective functioning.

Senior associates' management roles include (a) scheduling program meetings and conferences and informing pertinent parties about them; (b) setting up and maintaining project folders; (c) coordinating space arrangements; (d) procuring program materials and supplies; and (e) "riding shotgun" on questionnaires and research instruments by getting materials to respondents and following up to ensure they are completed and returned on time.

The preceding "sampler" of senior associate functions makes it clear that these roles range from secretarial and clerical at one extreme, to activities that border on what is construed as "professional" (e.g., serving as an on-the-spot resource person for child associates, meeting with parents to discuss children). As a rough, de facto, rule of thumb, the latter roles tend to be more frequent in professionally underresourced programs.

The senior associate role is diverse; it embraces many different mini-roles. The combination of this role diversity and the importance of these roles to a program's well-being have moved observers to describe senior associates as key members of the PMHP team, indeed sometimes as the glue that holds the program together. Although senior associates are very much individuals in terms of the things that they most enjoy doing, as a generalization, it is fair to say that the clinical roles, those for which their training and experience most directly prepared them, are enjoyed more than the managerial roles in which they do in fact function more as an extra pair of hands. The point to highlight, however, is that the senior associate role has grown and evolved in PMHP over the years. In larger programs, it is a role that adds appreciably to PMHP's smooth functioning and effective child serving.

Supervision

In addition to their child-serving contacts, associates meet regularly with school professionals for supervision, and with teachers to exchange information about the children being seen. These meetings are designed to enhance the program's quality control and to promote communication among relevant parties about the child's functioning in the playroom and classroom, to maximally coordinate the school's helping efforts on the child's behalf. Supervision in PMHP is an ongoing process that rests on an established relationship between school professionals and child associates. It serves several purposes, the most important of which is to optimize services to children.

Associates usually come to supervision with notes about what has been happening with the children they are seeing and a set of questions and issues to be discussed. Examples of such issues include the following: What is the nature of the associate–child relationship and how can it be strengthened? Which approaches seem to be working well or not so well with a given child? What changes in tactics might better help to meet established goals? What special issues and problems have come up in the associate's mind, and are there issues, or stumbling blocks, that the supervisor believes bear consideration?

Supervision enriches associates' understanding of children and broadens the range of technical skills they bring to the playroom. Thus, both in an immediate and long-range sense, supervision contributes to PMHP's bedrock objective of improving services to children. Supervision also offers a continuing window for viewing the associates' activities and growth. For all those reasons, the principle of regular supervision for associates is basic in PMHP. What can and does vary, as a function of a program's operating style and resources, is the specific nature of the supervisory framework used (i.e., the frequency, duration, and form of supervisory contacts). Some programs, for example, supervise associates individually, whereas others prefer group supervision to capitalize on the potential of learning from peer experiences. Still others mix both supervisory modalities. A supervisory pattern we have found to work well, given our situation and resources, involves 2 hours of individual supervision and one and a half hours of group supervision, per month. The importance of supervision is affirmed by establishing regularly scheduled times for that purpose and protecting those times from interruptions.

The preceding account refers to a program's formal supervisory procedures. Supervision also proceeds informally in PMHP—sometimes necessarily so when issues come up that must be addressed before a next regularly scheduled supervisory meeting. For that reason, most PMHP supervisors also make themselves available to associates on an "as-needed" basis. Associates find this informal, "availability supervision" to be necessary at times, and very helpful. It adds to their sense of security and contributes to the efficacy of their work with children.

Although there are common elements in all forms of supervision, supervisory formats vary a good deal as a function of time and resources available and the supervisor's professional training. Most supervision in PMHP is done by school mental health professionals (social workers, psychologists, and elementary counselors). The presence of the same supervisors and associates on a PMHP team for some years builds a framework of common views, a common vocabulary, and importantly a close, mutually respectful working relationship—attributes that are all helpful to the supervisory process.

Notwithstanding common elements in the supervisory process, supervisors have different styles (e.g., degree of activeness) and theoretical orientations (e.g., cognitive–behavioral, nondirective, psychoanalytic). Each theoretical framework tends to have its own special vocabulary and foci of emphasis. We have not found any one supervisory framework (theoretical approach) to be better than others in PMHP. To the contrary, our experience suggests that a program can proceed smoothly within multiple supervisory frameworks and, for that reason, there is an advantage for it to be conducted within a framework in which the professional supervisor feels most knowledgeable and comfortable.

The training of school mental health professionals does not always prepare them for supervisory roles. Hence, over the years, PMHP professionals have often requested additional information and training in this area. To that end, Mijangos and Farie (1992), based on a review of literature on supervision in the schools and interviews with seasoned PMHP professionals, prepared a *PMHP Supervision Manual* that describes in more detail what this section has overviewed only briefly.

Progress Conferences

About half way through the PMHP intervention cycle (i.e., January–February for full-year programs), a conference is held to take stock of all children's progress in the program to that point. Although most PMHP programs conduct a full set of these midyear progress conferences, this type of review can be initiated any time to assess what is happening with a given child.

The main purpose of the formal progress conference is to learn about what has been happening with children in the playroom and classroom. The conference format permits key players to update each other on the child's status; judge the extent to which initially established goals are being met; and, if they are not, plan changes in course. Progress conferences are typically attended by the same people who were at the initial assignment conference. They tend, however, to be shorter and more focused than the latter, because most participants, by then, know the children and their backgrounds well.

Typically, the two main "reporters" in the progress conference are the teacher, who sees the child's classroom behavior and academic performance every day, and the child associate, who has seen the child in the playroom for 8–10 weeks. Specific questions around which progress conferences are structured include the following: How well is the child doing? Have there been improvements in areas that were seen as central at referral? What changes in strategy or intervention practices might better help to better meet established goals?

Sometimes team members agree that the child has met his or her goals and should be terminated following several wind-down sessions. Other scenarios, however, also come up. One such scenario is the consensus that things are moving in sound directions and that the best plan is to continue on the same course. Another scenario is one in which few, if any, visible signs of progress can be seen either in the classroom or playroom. This may happen either because positive change requires more time than originally anticipated or because the initial intervention plan was inadequate and needs overhaul. Yet another scenario is when key observers report discrepant views of the child's behavior or progress. Sometimes those disagreements reflect the fact that different environments "pull" for different behaviors. An example is the child whose behavior in class, when he or she competes for attention with 25 other children, is disruptive and difficult to handle, but whose behavior in a nonthreatening, free choice, one-on-one playroom situation, where he or she has the undivided attention of a warm, caring adult, is seen as at least angelic. Such diametrically opposite views can be so firmly held that a neutral observer is hard pressed to believe that the two accounts are about the same child.

Although discrepancies of the type noted are vexing when they come up, they can also be instructive when they stimulate discussion that clarifies situational determinants of a child's behavior and illuminate the tasks different players face in a larger common scenario. Illustratively, for a teacher such discussion can potentially illuminate promising approaches with the child not heretofore perceived or considered, and for the associate it can serve as a stark reminder that there's more to life than the playroom, and that the most meaningful playroom gains are those that generalize to important other realities of the child's life. Finally, for the team, such sharply discrepant views suggest that more work, and further coordination of effort in the child's behalf, lie ahead.

Thus, the midyear progress conference provides a formal channel for team members to communicate about children being seen and take stock of their progress. Relevant information is shared. Instances of success or lack of progress are noted and, for the latter, corrective steps are planned.

End-of-Program Conferences

End-of-program conferences are held during the last several weeks of the school year (or semester). As with assignment and progress conferences, all PMHP team members participate. These conferences assess children's overall progress in the program and their current level of functioning and, on that basis, make disposition decisions for each child. The main input data come from teachers and child associates, who provide information about what has been happening in these two crucial areas and the extent to which initially established goals for a child have been met. When pertinent, other information about the child's current adjustment status (e.g., from other school personnel, parents) also enters the end-of-year conference.

Although most PMHP-seen children are judged at this time to have made significant progress toward originally established goals, and thus no longer to need PMHP services, that is not always the case. Indeed there are always children who evidence anywhere from little or no, to at most modest, progress toward initially established goals. Whereas PMHP tended initially to see these children for a second year, there is little research evidence to show that it is helpful to do so. Now, children seen for a second round are primarily those who have shown some progress and for whom further PMHP contact, including some changes in handling strategies, is seen as a promising option.

Parent Involvement

In principle, open communication with parents and their involvement in the PMHP process make for better child outcomes. Indeed, recognizing that point, during the period when PMHP was first developed as a pilot project in a single school, the social worker routinely did in-depth interviews with parents of all first grade children. That practice was helpful in several respects, including the obvious ones of informing parents about the project and obtaining relevant information about the child's early development and family situation, and the less obvious ones of opening home–school communication lines and evidencing the school's active interest in the family and child's well-being.

Over the years this important contact step has lost ground, not because it was not helpful, but because it was time consuming and costly for schools to take. Although most PMHP programs today still recognize the importance of parent involvement and most try to do all they can to advance that objective, they differ greatly in what they actually *do* in this sphere. Some programs have sufficient resources to arrange for one or more individual parent contacts during the year. Others can only conduct several large-group parent meetings. To enhance resources available for home contacts, PMHP developed a program in which associates were trained for work with parents, including home visits to learn more about the child and family and to exchange information about the child's situation at home and school, as these relate to the child's PMHP involvements. This "parent–associate" program, described in chapter 5, has proven to be one helpful way of solidifying home–school contacts in PMHP.

Professional Roles and Activities

PMHP professionals are intimately involved in most aspects of program implementation. The professional role in PMHP differs substantially from the traditional school mental health professional role. The essence of that difference is that the PMHP professional's time, rather than going to in-depth diagnostic and therapeutic activities with a few of the school's most troubled children, seeks to promote effective early detection and prevention for many more children than traditional approaches can reach.

One important professional activity (i.e., supervising child associates) was described earlier in this chapter. Five other roles and activities of the PMHP professional bear mention here: (a) team leadership and decision making, (b) consultation with teachers and school staff, (c) recruitment and training of child associates, (d) evaluation-related activities, and (e) public relations and presentations.

The professional role in PMHP was once described using the metaphor "mental health quarterbacking" (Cowen, Trost, et al., 1975). This term highlights the fact that the PMHP professional is the program's lead, and key decision-making, person; its prime representative in the school and community; and accountable for the program's well-being. This role is reflected in decisions about (a) who should be hired as child associates;

(b) when to conduct clinical conferences, which children to review, and what formats to follow; (c) end-of-year termination or continuation of project children; and (d) initiating contacts with parents and/or teachers, and shaping the substance of such interactions. PMHP professionals frame all such decisions and are accountable for them, though others may actually conduct the activity. A case in point is that senior associates do most of the arranging and scheduling of PMHP clinical conferences with participating parties, and also schedule parent and teacher meetings. Those activities, however, are carried out on the professionals' behalf and with the professional's knowledge and approval.

Within-school consultation is another important activity of the PMHP professional. In this context we note again that a PMHP program serves an entire school, not just individual children; that is, it is an integral part of a school's ecology. Thus, PMHP professionals are often called upon to provide help to teachers, the principal, and other school staff. One previously cited example of this is the opportunity that the early detection, screening, and assignment cycle creates for mental health professionals to provide systematic information to teachers about all children in their classes. Not infrequently, as part of this review process, they can helpfully address problems teachers are having in class management, or with individual children. Effectively done, that starter step builds bridges to continuing future use of the professional as a consultant. To the extent that this consultative role upgrades the sensitivity and skills of school personnel, it enhances PMHP's preventive efficacy.

Another key role for PMHP professionals involves selection and training activities. When PMHP started, the child associate role was unique. As conceived, the new role did not make sense in isolation; its meaning and effectiveness depended on cognate changes in the school mental health professional role. One obvious change was the professional's heavy involvement in selecting child associates. This called for in-depth interviews with candidates to ensure they (a) had the qualities needed to be genuinely helpful to young children and (b) were people with whom the professionals could work comfortably and productively over long time periods.

After associates are selected, PMHP professionals take on new roles in training and supervision. This includes heavy involvement in initial associate training and a more peripheral role in later training exercises (see chapter 5) designed to enhance associates' skills and versatility. The PMHP professional's training role also extends to supervision of child associates, as described earlier in this chapter.

PMHP offers child associates a rich, continuing smorgasbord of training options that serve both to promote growth in the associates and to enhance services for children. In this context, a recent set of interviews with experienced associates identified the combination of the training opportunities that PMHP provides and the intrinsic satisfaction of helping young children in need as key reasons for which associates continue to work for PMHP, skimpy remuneration notwithstanding. The points to highlight are that PMHP's commitment to new learning for associates adds greatly to the attractiveness of that role, and that PMHP professionals are crucial lead figures, formally and informally, in this rewarding educational process. Finally, it should be noted that the professional's training role in PMHP goes beyond his or her activities with child associates to include training meetings and educational exercises provided for teachers, other school personnel, and parents. Thus, training is a central activity for the PMHP professional.

The PMHP professional also plays several important roles in evaluation and research. These include (a) involvements in planning and setting up school-based program evaluations; (b) knowing research measures well enough to be able to explain and answer questions about them; (c) monitoring the cooperation of respondents (e.g., teachers) on research measures, and ensuring that appropriate procedures and time lines are followed in conducting a research study; and (d) presenting and interpreting pertinent research findings to school personnel and school district administrators.

The PMHP professional is also more directly involved in program evaluation. As part of the termination process, professionals complete a Professional Summary Report (PSR), a one-page, two-part objective summary of the child's experience in PMHP, based on all currently available information (see Appendix C7). Typically, this is done around the time of the end-of-year termination conference, following consultation with all pertinent players (e.g., teacher, child associate) in the child's PMHP scenario. Part 1 of the PSR includes 13 objective items (e.g., interest in school, academic performance, overall school behavior) each rated on a 5-point scale (1 = much worse; 5 = much better) to reflect the child's judged progress during the year. Part 2 consists of two "disposition" items, the first indicating the child's status at the end of the year (e.g., has met goals, moving, has moved) and the second, a recommendation for the next year (e.g., terminate from project, reevaluate in fall as basis for deciding). The PSR thus serves as a concise summary of the child's PMHP experience; it is widely used both in making decisions about the future and in research and as one index of child outcome.

Although the term *public relations activities* may seem foreign to most school mental health professionals, such involvement is often important in starting and maintaining a PMHP program. In general, prevention programs such as PMHP are not as well understood as "damage-control" programs. They are relatively new on the school mental health scene, rarely mandated, and at best, only minimally supported. And, because they do not focus primarily on visibly troublesome problems, they often lack a vocal constituency. Nor can it be assumed that school board members, administrators, or faculty have a clear grasp of what prevention programs seek to accomplish and how, in fact, they work. Relatedly, even after prevention programs are established, when lean times come up they are among the first to be susceptible to termination. The point to stress is that PMHP professionals must be prepared to devote time to meetings and presentations explaining the program's goals and defining nature to relevant individuals and groups, as part of the process of maximizing chances for a PMHP to start and be maintained.

A CONCRETE EXAMPLE

The chapter, to this point, has described PMHP's major components and processes at an abstract level. This final section, by contrast, takes a composite child, step by step, through the entire PMHP cycle. Our goal in doing so is to concretize and vivify PMHP procedures and processes that have thus far been described in a relatively objective, impersonal way.

The hypothetical child we focus on is a first grade boy named Gregory. His teacher, Jean Fox, referred Gregory to PMHP about a month after the school year started. In Gregory's school, first grade children are screened with the AML-R. Although Gregory's AML problem scores were not as high as several other children in Ms. Fox's class, in reviewing those test findings with the school psychologist, she expressed genuine concern about him. Although he was completing his academic work and achieving fairly adequately, he seemed emotionally detached and sad and had no close friends in the classroom. Ms. Fox was concerned that if those problems were not dealt with, Gregory would be susceptible to later more serious difficulties in peer relationships, and that his learning would ultimately be impaired.

Ms. Fox raised these concerns at a PMHP assignment conference in late October. Before then, she had mentioned the same concerns to Mr. Brown, the school social worker, who had made it a point to observe Gregory in class prior to the conference. What he saw clearly supported Ms. Fox's concerns. Based on two separate classroom observations, Mr. Brown described Gregory as withdrawn, emotionally "flat," and not involved with other children.

Thus, based on converging reports from the teacher and school social worker, as well as evidence from the AML-R suggesting that Gregory was at risk, he was referred to PMHP. His participation was contingent on parental consent. Because Ms. Fox had met Gregory's mother, she agreed to call her to explain the reason for the referral and purpose of the proposed intervention. After that contact, the PMHP team sent a follow-up letter and consent form to Gregory's mother, who agreed that he should be seen by PMHP.

Beyond the recommendation that Gregory be seen in PMHP, the assignment conference reached several other decisions about how to proceed. One concerned the preferred mode of intervention for Gregory (i.e., being seen individually by a child associate, or in a small group). Although small groups are often an approach of choice for socially isolated children, and Gregory did indeed have seriously inadequate peer relationships, a group approach was not chosen because Gregory's poor social relationships were seen as secondary to a more basic emotional constriction and sadness. Accordingly, weekly individual contacts with a child associate was selected as the intervention mode, in the hope that this approach could provide an environment in which Gregory would develop a trusting relationship and come to express feelings in ways that would enhance his adaptation and development.

Based on his knowledge of Gregory's background and situation, Mr. Brown, the social worker and supervisor, recommended that he be seen by Diane Rogers, a child associate with 8 years' experience. In his prior supervision of Diane, Mr. Brown had noted that she was particularly adept in establishing rapport with withdrawn children. Also at the assignment conference, the team decided that both Diane's work with Gregory and the teacher's understanding of his classroom behavior could be facilitated by obtaining more information about his family situation. The school's senior associate, who had had additional training in parent work, was asked to contact Gregory's parents to obtain more background information and to provide whatever support seemed needed and appropriate.

At the time Gregory's mother agreed to his being seen by PMHP, she asked for more information about why he was being referred. Such information was provided for several reasons. One, obviously, is that she had the right to know. A second is that the very process of providing such information sometimes helps parents to better understand the family situation. A third, importantly, is that having interested, involved parents facilitates home–school collaboration around the shared goal of helping a child.

In any case, after parent consent was received, Diane set up an initial meeting with Gregory. He came to this meeting willingly. The initial contact, however, was uneventful; although Gregory played quietly with several games, he scarcely spoke to Diane. In her first supervisory session with Mr. Brown, Diane shared her initial impressions of Gregory. She described him as polite and cooperative, but aloof, inexpressive, and almost robotic. This depiction helped Diane and Mr. Brown develop a plan for understanding the meaning of Gregory's behavior and, on that basis, to establish appropriate goals in working with him. A first goal was to establish a relationship in which Gregory would feel safe and come to trust Diane. Although this relational goal is a "given" for all PMHP children, actually establishing such a relationship entails different approaches for different children. Whereas it is important for an aggressive, externalizing child to feel that his or her behavior can be contained, and that both he or she and the associate are safe in the playroom, the need for a withdrawn child, such as Gregory, is to feel welcome without being overwhelmed by demands. The latter conditions make it easier for a frightened child to express feelings and thoughts. Diane and Mr. Brown also agreed that even though a warm, welcoming attitude was important for Gregory, she should follow his lead as much as possible so as to give him room to establish his own "footings."

A second technique goal that Diane and Mr. Brown agreed was important was to encourage Gregory's use of play as a means of expressing feelings. This goal was based on two tenets that guide associates' work: (a) play is a child's natural medium of communication and expression and (b) through play children can work through, and find resolutions for, their adaptive problems. To this end, Diane encouraged Gregory's symbolic, expressive play (such as playing with human figures and puppets rather than board games) and reflected meaningful themes she perceived in his play. By conveying such understanding, she hoped to help him feel less isolated and encourage his further expression of feelings.

During the first several supervision sessions, Diane reported to Mr. Brown that although Gregory still came to the playroom willingly and was cooperative, he remained withdrawn and communicated only minimally. Although Diane was at times frustrated by this seeming lack of progress, she maintained a patient, accepting stance and continued to encourage Gregory's expressive play.

Shortly thereafter she and Mr. Brown learned from the senior associate, who had met with Gregory's mother, that the parents had separated the previous spring. This was followed by a bitter custody struggle, still not resolved. This information helped Diane understand one likely source of Gregory's sadness: the loss of his family, as it had been, and the fear of further loss stemming from the continuing conflict between his parents.

At the midyear progress conference in January, Ms. Fox and the PMHP team reviewed Gregory's situation. Although he was still quiet and interacted little with the other children in class, several small, encouraging signs had surfaced. For one thing, he had started to talk more with Diane. For example, he mentioned spontaneously that his parents did not live together any more. The combination of some signs of progress and a continuing awareness of the need for further change, prompted the team to recommend that Gregory continue in the program for the rest of the school year. They also recommended a follow-up contact with Gregory's mother, by the senior associate, to help clarify developments in the changing, and potentially volatile, family situation.

In the next several supervisory meetings, Diane reported signs of changes in her relationship with Gregory. With her subtle encouragement, he continued to play with a group of human figures. And, at least in the interactions he created among those human figures, he came to express a wider range of feelings. One day, for example, he built a high tower and had a figure career down from the top of the tower to the table. He repeated this routine several times and, as he did, expressed an anger that he had not previously shown. Although the ensuing meetings were less dramatic, Diane noted that Gregory seemed to be more comfortable in the playroom and was expressing more feelings in his play.

At the end-of-year conference in mid May, Diane reported other changes she had seen in Gregory. He interacted more with her and he seemed much less sad. Ms. Fox reported improvements in the same areas. She also noted significant academic progress. She was now quite confident that he would succeed in his second grade work. Although Ms. Fox was still concerned that he had few peer relationships, he had at least be-friended one quiet boy in the class. Based on these reports, the team decided that the goals established for Gregory in October had, in the main, been met.

This conclusion was reinforced by the senior associate's report of her follow-up meeting with Gregory's mother, who described similar positive changes in him at home. Although the family situation was relatively stable at the time of follow-up, the custody situation had not been resolved. For that reason, the team decided that if the custody issue reemerged as a problem, Gregory would be reevaluated and decisions about further intervention made on that basis.

The preceding account of one child's experience through the PMHP cycle highlights aspects of the approach that may be easier to palpate via "real world" examples. The point to stress in this account is that PMHP's effectiveness is enhanced when the intervention is built around a collaboration involving teacher, school mental professional, child and senior associates, and parents; that is, when all relevant parties work together on the child's behalf, rather than in isolation. In this case, Diane's ability to work effectively with Gregory was enhanced by the understanding she and her supervisor had about Gregory's family and classroom situations. An associate who works in isolation with a child has less of a chance to be effective both because pertinent knowledge about a child's life circumstances and factors that influence his or her behavior is missing and because she may be working, if not at cross-purposes, then in less than additive ways, with teachers or parents.

Gregory's experience in PMHP also illustrates how a sound relationship between a child associate and a child can facilitate the child's adaptation and development. For young children, such a relationship develops in the context of play activities, the child's natural medium of expression and communication.

5

PMHP MINIPROGRAMS: EXTENDING AND REFINING THE BASIC OFFERINGS

At several earlier points in this volume, PMHP was depicted as an ever-changing, ever-evolving program, rather than a static, "stand-on-your-laurels" one. Modifications and/or extensions in basic PMHP practices, and there have been many, have been fueled both by research findings and the direct clinical observations of those who work closely with the school-based program. Collectively, these two sources provide information about (a) project components that seem to be working well or not so well and (b) relevant child problem situations that PMHP is not reaching because technology for doing so has not yet been developed.

The change issues that PMHP has addressed pivot around practical matters such as (a) How can we do better in the future those things that PMHP has always sought centrally to do? and (b) How can the program's reach and scope be extended to deal with real problems of young school children that the project has not yet been able to address?

Beyond these immediate challenges lies a more complex, deeper issue raised in the closing chapter of the prior PMHP volume (Cowen, Trost, et al., 1975): Given that PMHP is fundamentally a program in ontogenetically early secondary prevention, even if it functioned 100% perfectly, which it surely does not, there would still be a need to develop more basic primary prevention program models designed both to forestall maladaptation before it takes hold and to build strength and competencies (wellness) in children proactively.

As a project, PMHP has always been carefully self-scrutinizing, and sometimes harshly self-critical. This underlying orientation has fueled ongoing, deeply invested efforts, as noted above, both to fine-tune and buttress PMHP's basic practices and develop new "add-ons" of a more primary preventive nature. All those change efforts—how and why they came about, what we actually did and found, and how those findings became part of an expanded PMHP mainstream—are part of the story to be narrated in this volume. This chapter, however, focuses only on one aspect of that narrative: program extensions that refined and broadened the scope of the basic PMHP approach.

Most of these new program developments have unfolded in the last two decades. They did not come into focus until after the original house of PMHP had been set in order. By that we mean that (a) the program's core defining practices had been reasonably well honed, (b) key PMHP players had become practiced and comfortable in their new roles, and (c) the program had been extensively field tested and shown to be effective. Understandably the preceding "bread and butter" challenges framed PMHP's agenda in the project's early years. Only after those challenges had been met were energies freed to refine and extend PMHP's offerings.

The success of early PMHP solidifying steps was gratifying indeed. Those forward steps, however, did not occur in a vacuum. Thus, even as project basics were being nailed down, observant, reactive PMHP personnel with daily exposure to the school scene and its issues could perceive unresolved problems and ways in which more realistic, scope-extending PMHP services might be developed. These observations became part of a things-to-be-explored agenda and, as time and resources permitted, they were indeed explored, sometimes successfully, sometimes less so.

All extension programs evolved in much the same way structurally. All have elasticized the child-associate role and enhanced the associates' versatility, while in parallel, providing a broader range of services for children. As noted earlier, each program began when direct clinical feedback or research findings identified a problem, or a way in which the project's scope might be gainfully expanded. Based on such inputs, a program designed to address the issue in question was prepared and a training curriculum developed. Once those early steps were taken, a pilot program involving only a few associates was conducted, and clinical impressions about its effectiveness were formed. If those impressions were positive, other associates were trained in the approach and a larger scale field trial was conducted that included a formal program evaluation study. If findings from the latter were again positive, the new program was incorporated increasingly into PMHP's mainstream as resources permitted.

This chapter focuses on five such "miniprograms," each a survivor of the preceding "trial-by-fire" sequence, that came eventually to expand PMHP's offerings. These were not the only programs that were field tested; other similarly conceived programs simply failed to pass muster. An example of the latter was a miniprogram in which associates were trained to teach PMHP children social problem-solving skills in a one-on-one context (Flores de Apodaca, 1979). That program faltered because (a) associates found the structured, didactic role the program called for to be "out of sync" with their more familiar and comfortable playroom role and (b) the program's (individual) context precluded the use of important skill-enhancing exercises (e.g., discussion, role play) that require interaction with, and feedback from, peers.

The sections that follow focus on five surviving PMHP extension programs: training child associates for (a) seeing children in small groups, (b) crisis intervention, (c) work with acting-out children, (d) conducting planned short-term interventions, and (e) work as parent associates.

WORKING WITH CHILDREN IN GROUPS

Over time, two salient considerations—one structural, the other substantive—merged to suggest the potential value of developing a program to train associates for work with small groups of children. The structural input was the awareness that children's need for PMHP services exceeded the project's ability to provide such services. In many implementing districts with limited resources, supply shortages relative to need and demand for services were considerable. The group modality thus offered a theoretically appealing option for extending the reach of existing services. Even more important, however, was the substantive consideration that for some youngsters, with shy–anxious problems and deficits in social skills and interaction patterns, the group modality involving kindred peers seemed, in principle, to offer an intervention option that was in tune with their needs and realities.

These were the main considerations that led to the development of a training program in group work for child associates. First, the broad contour of such a program was drawn up; this plan emphasized the goals of providing child associates with a knowledge base about group work and firsthand experience in applying the approach with young referred children who might profit from it. All 57 PMHP associates at that time were given a brief program overview and invited to participate. It was emphasized, however, that participation was voluntary. Thirty-one associates opted to participate; of those, 24 actually ran one or more groups in their home schools.

The program had three main components: (a) four 1½-hour training sessions led by two advanced clinical psychology graduate students; (b) further experiential training while groups were in progress; and (c) consultation and program follow-up. The program's cornerstone was a specially developed curriculum covering basic principles of group work with children (Terrell, McWilliams, & Cowen, 1972). Focal topics included a rationale for using the group modality; principal goals of the group approach; problems encountered in working with groups; effective limit-setting strategies; selection, composition, preparation, and termination of groups; and group process and facilitation skills. During training, associates were encouraged to ask questions, offer comments, and express feelings and concerns about the still unfamiliar role leading a group. This open format helped to forge bonds among the associates, which in turn acted to reduce apprehension about the new role.

In the second phase of the program, associates participated in plans to form and conduct groups. Guidelines for identifying and selecting appropriate children were prepared. An emphasis was placed on including shy, undersocialized youngsters and excluding children with major acting-out problems. That exclusion was intended to minimize (a) interaction problems within the group and (b) the possibility that group meetings might become disruptive in the school.

Children were prepared for the group experience in an individual contact with a child associate before the first meeting. At that time the associate described what the group experience would be like and answered children's questions. Associates were responsible for scheduling suitable meeting times and arranging for a suitable meeting place. Information provided in the early didactic training sessions came alive when the program got under way. Starting then, associates faced many practical challenges, including instances of verbal and/or physical aggression, competition among members for the leader's attention, questions of how to stimulate the involvement of withdrawn children, and having to modify strategies when progress was slow.

Program leaders, who served both as trainers and consultants, worked in several different ways with the 24 associates who ran groups. In some cases, they observed associates while they were conducting a meeting and followed these observations with feedback, suggestions, and discussion of how things were going. They also led regular consultation–supervisory meetings with all group leaders in each school.

Program evaluation (Terrell, 1973) was based both on associates' impressions along several dimensions and on a formal objective evaluation of program effects for participating children. With regard to the latter, the total of 132 primary graders seen by the 24 child associates who had group training, included 32, 56, and 44 seen in group, individually, and group plus individual, respectively. All groups were small ($n = 3$). Outcome measures included child adjustment ratings reflecting the perspectives of parents, teachers, children, and child associates, as well as report card grades and ratings. Study findings showed that children improved evenly (i.e., no outcome differences in adjustment) across the three intervention modes.

Associates' qualitative reactions to the program and their ratings of several aspects of it helped to round out the outcome picture. A questionnaire was developed specifically to assess associates' relative preference for the individual or group modality along six dimensions: personal enjoyment, being challenged, providing insights about and understanding children, helping children improve, and numbers of children served. Associates' relative preference for the individual versus the group modality was summed across items to get a total preference index. The latter yielded several interesting findings. Overall, associates preferred to see children individually rather than in a group, but there were individual differences in the direction and strength of that preference. Second, a significant relationship was found between the associate's preference for a given mode, and positiveness of outcome in that, compared with the less preferred, mode.

The preceding findings suggest that although the group approach was per se effective it was neither a "cure-all" nor more effective than the individual approach. Quite a few associates were neither fully comfortable nor pleased with the group approach, citing as drawbacks the management problems it created and a feeling of loss of in-depth contact with a child, so often seen as a hallmark of the individual approach. Those realities notwithstanding, associates who preferred the group approach had better child outcomes in that modality than in individual contacts.

Several comments follow about the subsequent course of group work in PMHP. The group approach was never seen as a panacea, and history confirms that it has not been. Associates, initially trained and practiced in the individual mode, are more at home and comfortable in that mode than with a group. Hence, associates' receptivity to the group approach is at best modest. A related issue is that many school-based PMHP professionals are also uncomfortable with, and unschooled in, the group approach and feel shaky as supervisors in that mode. For that reason we have offered periodic minicourses for professionals to raise their level of comfort with the group approach.

Over the years, we have continued to offer group training to associates and supervisors to maintain a pool of school-based PMHP people who have background in the approach. Although group work remains very much alive in PMHP, it serves more as an available option on a smorgasbord than one that has taken the project by storm. Currently, about 10% of all PMHP children are seen in groups, with substantial variation (i.e., 0–40%) across schools.

Across the full range of PMHP program implementations in other communities there is even more variation in the extent to which groups are used. In some districts and in one state program (see chapter 7) up to two thirds of all contacts are conducted in groups, with good results. Pond-ecology factors are important in this regard. Where program professionals are experienced and comfortable in the group approach, where associates receive early training in this mode, and where the system is geared naturally from the start to include group work, it works quite well. By contrast, when the group approach is introduced into a system that has always featured individual contacts, and in which program professionals are more at home in the individual modality (as in the parent PMHP), the group approach is likely to become one option in a larger system, used only by help agents who find it congenial and comfortable.

CRISIS INTERVENTION

Crisis intervention, a second major addition to PMHP's tool kit, came about in a different way than group training and has had a different subsequent history. By the mid 1970s, school-based PMHP personnel had become more aware of, and concerned about, the effects of stress on children's school behavior and adjustment. Divorce rates, for example, had begun to rise sharply and the negative fallout of divorce for young children was clearly visible to school personnel.

At that time, the existing PMHP intervention model was, so to speak, unidimensional. Although associates, to be sure, sought to adapt their foci and intervention methods to children's particular situations and needs, systematic technology had not yet been developed for dealing with the special adaptive problems confronting children who experienced different life crises.

PMHP's efforts to engage such issues over the past two decades have been diverse and extensive. The first preprogrammatic steps taken in this direction were research steps that sought to understand more clearly the effects of certain stressors on young children. That research quest, which continues up to the present time, is reviewed in chapter 6. From among those studies, several early ones "pointed our noses" toward developing a prototypic model for crisis intervention with young children.

The first study in this series (Felner, Stolberg, & Cowen, 1975) showed that children who experienced parental divorce or death of a close family member had more serious school adjustment problems than referred, noncrisis peers. Moreover, different types of adaptive problems were associated with specific crisis situations. Whereas children with histories of parental death were significantly more anxious, depressed, and withdrawn than matched noncrisis controls, those who experienced parental separation or divorce evidenced significantly more acting-out problems than comparison children. These differences were also evident when the two crisis groups (death and divorce) were compared directly with each other. Similar findings were shown in a replication study (Felner, Ginter, Boike, & Cowen, 1981).

These early PMHP studies, along with other research findings of the time, showed that stressful life events place children at risk for adjustment problems, including specific problems associated with specific stressors. In so doing, they paved the way for an initial, preventively oriented crisis-intervention model within PMHP designed specifically for children who experienced major life crises.

Crisis, as an ancient Chinese wisdom suggests, is both danger and opportunity. The dangers are obvious. Crisis fallout can disrupt normal functioning in the short term and, if not adequately dealt with, can pre-dispose longer term maladaptation (e.g., a girl who is angry at her father for initiating a divorce may come eventually to generalize that anger to many people, especially men). On the other hand, crisis need not lead automatically to negative outcomes. Rather it represents a crossroad and, depending on how the turns in that crossroad are negotiated, good or not so good outcomes may ensue. That is why crisis is also seen by some as opportunity—opportunity to deal effectively with strong feelings, enhance strengths, find adaptive new ways to cope, and in so doing, shed maladaptive, self-defeating behaviors.

Hence, PMHP came increasingly to see the need for crisis-related preventive interventions designed to help children cope effectively with the adjustment demands that a crisis poses before associated problems become chronic and entrenched. Simply sitting back and watching the negative sequelae of a crisis take hold was not an appealing alternative. Based on this thinking, an initial pilot prevention model was developed for children who had experienced any of four stressful life events in the past 2 months: (a) parent separation or divorce, (b) death or a life-threatening illness in the family, (c) hospitalization or surgery, or (d) birth of a new sibling. The model called for veteran PMHP child associates to receive special crisis intervention training and then to meet with children who had recently experienced one of these crises, using a time-limited (i.e., 12 sessions in 6 weeks) format.

Associates who volunteered for this program participated in special training for this purpose, based on a detailed curriculum written by PMHP staff. The first four training sessions sought to help associates better understand the meaning of certain crises for children, the problems they posed, and effective methods for working with children in crisis. Later sessions provided information about specific ways in which targeted stressors (e.g., parent divorce, death of a close family member) impacted children and appropriate intervention goals in such cases. Training emphasized that crisis intervention was to be a time-limited, goal-oriented, problem-solving approach. The program's main goals were preventive; that is, to restore "normal" children who had been buffeted by a major life crisis to their prior levels of functioning and to teach adaptive skills that could help them cope more effectively with future stress.

With those as focal program goals, the associate's role was seen as more goal oriented and directive than in the traditional PMHP model. Associates were trained with that view in mind. The associate's most basic functions in this program were to (a) encourage expression of, and abreaction to, crisis-related feelings; (b) provide emotional support; (c) give accurate information to help reduce children's anxiety; and (d) foster active coping. After training ended, associates began to see children who had experienced any of the targeted crises. Trainers and associates continued to meet for six weekly, small-group supervisory sessions while the program was in progress.

Felner, Norton, Cowen, and Farber (1981) reported an evaluation study with 57 primary graders seen in the new crisis intervention program. Study findings showed that the program succeeded in reducing target children's behavior problems. Specifically, program children decreased significantly in trait-anxiety and teacher-rated shy–anxious behaviors and increased significantly in teacher-rated adaptive assertiveness. In addition to findings from the formal program evaluation, both parents and school personnel reported that the program effectively addressed important needs of children in crisis.

This early work testifying to the potential fruitfulness of a preventively oriented crisis intervention thrust within PMHP was very influential, not because it offered a final pat answer to the problems of children in crisis but rather because it offered an early, heuristic preventive model that has since been effectively developed in several directions.

Even though early findings (cf. above) were positive, several factors limited the potential of the initial program model. For one thing, it was an individual child approach when, in principle, a group intervention for children who experience comparable crises had much to offer by way of credible support from peers. A second limiting factor was that although some aspects of the approach were indeed targeted specifically to children in crisis (e.g., focus on expressing crisis-related feelings) in contrast to standard PMHP intervention technology, the intervention was not yet well adapted to the defining attributes of specific crisis situations. Third, and perhaps most important, the model's focus was limited to four largely acute, circumscribed crisis situations. By contrast day-to-day experience with PMHP was coming more and more to highlight fallout from a different type of stress-related problem situation: growing up in the shadow of chronic, ongoing stressful processes. The latter problems were increasingly evident both in referrals and as factors to be considered in planning intervention goals and strategies.

Over the years, PMHP's interest in the effects of crises and stressful life events has grown both at the research and programmatic intervention levels. Importantly, however, for the reasons noted above, the focus of this work has also shifted in several directions: (a) developing preventive interventions specifically for children who have experienced common stressful events (e.g., parental divorce) and (b) shifting focus toward children, particularly inner-city children, who grow up under conditions of chronic exposure to major life stress. These two kinds of involvements, both in research and intervention, have grown so much in recent years and have become so central to PMHP's overall portfolio that they constitute the prime focus of two later chapters (9 and 11). The early crisis intervention work reported in this section is an important historical predecessor of later, much expanded efforts to intervene preventively with children who experience early major life stress.

AN INTERVENTION FOR ACTING-OUT CHILDREN

As with the crisis intervention program, PMHP's efforts to develop an effective intervention for acting-out children were shaped both by clinical and research inputs. Quite independent of PMHP, it had long been recognized that children's acting-out problems are especially troublesome to deal with and that they endure, indeed often pick up steam, over time (Robins, 1966; Tremblay, Pihl, Vitaro, & Dobkin, 1994). A related body of research showed that child psychotherapy is less effective with children experiencing acting-out problems than with virtually any other group (Levitt, 1971). PMHP's early clinical experiences were consistent with those observations and findings; that is, children with significant acting-out problems at referral presented the most vexing difficulties for child associates to handle and had the least positive outcomes.

These recurrent observations fueled a two-stage methodological–substantive study within PMHP. Step 1 was to develop an objective system for classifying the predominant nature of children's school adjustment problems at referral (Lorion, Cowen, & Caldwell, 1974). Although we recognized that referral problems came in diverse (including mixed) forms, we also suspected that for some substantial fraction of children, those problems centered predominantly in one area. To that end, a mathematical algorithm was generated to assess density of saturation of a child's referral problems in a specific factor area (e.g., Acting Out, Shy–Anxious, Learning Problems) in relation to all other areas. If a given area's problem density exceeded chance, according to the algorithm, the child was classified as a "pure type" for that area.

This system classified about 60% of all referred children as pure types; the remaining 40% were mixed problem types. Pre–post comparisons of three demographically matched pure-type groups on teacher-rated adjustment measures showed that acting-out children profited significantly less from the PMHP intervention than shy–anxious children. This finding prompted several further studies (Cowen, Gesten, & DeStefano, 1977; DeStefano, Gesten, & Cowen, 1977), which showed that child associates, PMHP professionals, and teachers perceived acting-out children as the least enjoyable of all types to work with and, clearly, as the most difficult to handle (Sarason, 1995).

These findings stimulated development of a PMHP program-extending model designed specifically for acting-out children. This new model was built within Ginott's (1959) framework for work with acting-out children, predicated on the belief that a help agent can maintain empathy for these challenging, often provocative, children only in a context of appropriate limit setting. A slightly modified version of this approach (Orgel, 1980) was used as the basis for a 10-week, 1½ hour-per-week training program for PMHP associates to prepare them specifically to work with acting-out children.

The new training model highlighted Ginott's distinction between a child's feelings, which deserve unconditional empathy, and actions which require only conditional empathy. When a child's behavior conforms to safe, socially appropriate standards, it is accepted and reflected. However, when it is unsafe or inappropriate, limits are set and the impulse or feelings behind the behavior are redirected into acceptable, symbolic outlets for expression. Within that broad framework, associates were taught a four-step Ginottian approach for working with acting-out children:

1. The adult recognizes and reflects the child's feelings and wishes.
2. When needed, the adult intervenes to prevent or interrupt unacceptable behavior, differentiating between the child's feelings and actions and focusing attention on the behavior, not the child's personality.
3. The adult actively teaches the child to sublimate unacceptable behaviors through symbolic activity.
4. The adult recognizes and reflects the child's feelings about the limits.

Beyond emphasizing these four fundamental guidelines, training also considered the following topics: the nature of the therapeutic relationship, reflective techniques, and characteristics of acting-out children and their behavioral consequences. A detailed curriculum outline was developed for training purposes. Training was conducted by Arthur Orgel, a former colleague of Ginott's and a highly skilled, experienced child-clinical psychologist. Most topics in the curriculum were illuminated by video excerpts from actual child therapy sessions conducted by the trainer. Ten initial didactic training sessions were followed by 10 weekly, 1½ hour group supervisory meetings to review videotapes of associates actually working with referred children.

Associates responded enthusiastically to the new program, because it added skills to their repertoires in an area in which they most felt the need for help. Videotapes of actual sessions with children showed that associates were every bit as adept in picking up and applying this new body of knowledge and technology as advanced professional trainees.

An evaluation study involving 15 child associates trained in the approach and the 234 children they saw over a 2-year period was conducted to determine whether its application resulted in positive changes for acting-out children (Cowen, Orgel, Gesten, & Wilson, 1979). Program efficacy was assessed using pre–post teacher ratings of children's classroom problems and competencies, associates' ratings of children's problem behaviors, and estimates of behavioral change in children made by school mental health professionals. The principal study finding, an important one indeed, was that children seen by program-trained associates showed significantly greater reductions both in acting out and in overall adjustment problems than matched peers seen for similar periods of time by otherwise comparable associates who had not received the new training. In summary, findings from this study offered important evidence that a training program to prepare associates to work specifically with young acting-out children led to significant reductions in those children's acting-out behaviors and overall maladjustment.

A small parallel study (Gesten, Cowen, Orgel, & Schwartz, 1979) shed additional light on those findings. Based on a scale developed specifically for that purpose, associates who were, and were not, trained and experienced in the Ginottian approach were compared along several dimensions relating to work with acting-out children. Trained associates felt more comfortable with those children and believed that they had a richer repertoire of limit-setting skills and technology for handling overtly aggressive behaviors. They also felt more positively about working with these difficult children and reported that their playroom approaches with them did, in fact, change in ways that left them feeling more in control. Those changes may explain why associates trained in the Ginottian approach were significantly more effective with acting-out children.

These research findings, especially in the light of the major problems that acting-out children present to would-be helpers, provided a strong validation for this miniprogram. Accordingly, training in the Ginottian limit-setting approach has continued annually ever since and has, by now, been taken by almost all PMHP child associates. Clearly, it has strengthened their skills and confidence for working with youngsters often considered to be vexing by parents, teachers, and help agents alike. Hence, the approach stands as another crucial element in an expanded PMHP tool kit.

PLANNED SHORT-TERM INTERVENTION

Planned short-term intervention (PSI), is another PMHP scope-expanding miniprogram. This influential development began in the early 1980s, stimulated both by external happenings of the time and developments that were largely internal to PMHP.

One key external impetus to this development was the report of the President's Commission on Mental Health (1978), which highlighted shortages in mental health services for several groups, including children, and the need to develop effective new reach-expanding ways. The challenge the Commission sounded stimulated exploration of alternatives ranging from prevention to new parsimonious treatment options including planned short-term targeted intervention (Bloom, 1980; Pardes & Pincus, 1981). Such exploration was also stimulated by the conclusion of an influential review of the time (Casey & Berman, 1985) that children's gains in short-term psychotherapy appeared to be as stable and robust as those made in longer term treatment.

In parallel, PMHP findings at that time were also moving us to consider exploration of planned short-term approaches. One such finding noted both in annual PMHP service-utilization data and several PMHP program outcome studies (e.g., Lorion, Cowen, & Kraus, 1974) was that most PMHP children were seen for the entire school year. Although year-long contact may well be appropriate, indeed even necessary, for some children, the fact that this practice was typical for the great majority of PMHP-seen children suggested that it may have been based, at least in part, on factors other than the child's need for help. Otherwise put, it seemed that year-long contact had somehow become an inadvertent, hidden program "regularity" (Sarason, 1971), that is an unquestioned program practice that operated independently of children's needs.

If some children were indeed being seen longer than they needed to be, because PMHP was a finite resource system, that meant that other children who might profit from the program were being excluded. This was a serious concern, especially in the light of then-current reports of major shortages in mental health services for many children, particularly poor children (President's Commission on Mental Health, 1978).

Another relevant, if serendipitous, PMHP input source that stimulated exploration of planned short-term intervention came from our early crisis intervention work. The seeming success of that time-limited (12-session) intervention with specific, targeted goals led us to think that short-term approaches could profitably be explored further. The preceding, in any case, was the route by which we came to explore PSI as an alternative to PMHP's traditional non-time-limited intervention model.

To that end, an initial pilot program was developed to test a model of planned short-term intervention within PMHP's broader framework. This model explored an individually tailored, goal-oriented intervention with a small number of kindergarten–fifth grade children, seen for either 6 or 12 sessions. Clinical impressions about the new program from teachers, mental health professionals, and child associates were positive; that is, the program seemed to be helpful to the children. Two further impressions shaped the ensuing larger scale, more formal PSI program: (a) older children appeared to benefit a little more from the approach than younger ones, perhaps because they were better able developmentally to consider and deal with the targeted behaviors, and (b) 12 sessions appeared to work better than 6 sessions.

The ensuing larger scale study of the efficacy of the model included a PSI intervention group and two demographically matched comparison groups: (a) children seen in traditional PMHP interventions and (b) children with similar school adjustment problems, who received no services. Selection of PSI children proceeded structurally within PMHP's standard framework (i.e., an assignment conference with input from team members). The two main criteria used to select those children were (a) the absence of long-standing, serious adaptive problems and (b) the presence of a teacher-identified focal target problem (e.g., child cries when teased by others) in one of three areas: acting out, shy–anxious, or learning problems.

PSI children were seen twice weekly for 6 weeks in 40-minute sessions. Fourteen experienced child associates, five of whom had participated in the pilot project, volunteered to serve as help agents in PSI. Before actually starting to see children, associates participated in six 2-hour training sessions to familiarize them with the main features of the PSI model. In parallel, eight supervisory sessions were provided for the associates while the program was in progress.

Although the PSI model was not a standardized intervention in the same sense as a social problem-solving program (with common training procedures and exercises for all children), it did follow a common structural format within which specific intervention steps were tailored to a child's needs. Thus, the first two sessions were built around support-enhancing and information-gathering activities. These sessions sought to (a) assess the child's understanding of, and ability to express, feelings and (b) stimulate exploration of feelings and experiences. Session 3 was crucial. Using information gathered in the first two sessions as well as teacher referral data (i.e., identification of a specific target problem), an intervention focus, including the child's role and involvement in working on the targeted problem, was established. This focus was presented positively to the child as the goal of the work to be done with the associate (e.g., "We'll be talking about different things you can do to make friends.").

Work on the focal problem proceeded actively through the remaining sessions, using techniques such as drawing, role-playing, and dialoguing to keep session content relevant to the target problem. Children were encouraged throughout to consider all aspects of behaviors relevant to the focal goal, including reasons for the behavior, its consequences, and alternative strategies for coping with situations that precipitated the targeted behavior. To highlight the program's goals and time frame, children were informed of its 12-session limit from the start. They kept track of that time frame actively by crossing off each session on a calendar kept in the playroom for that purpose. Children were reminded of termination time starting in Session 10. The last three sessions focused on consolidating skills acquired, reinforcing positive attitudes and behaviors shown by the child, and dealing with feelings about termination and sources of help after the program ended. Throughout the program, associates met with teachers to keep them informed about the child's progress. Those meetings were part of a concerted team effort to engage the child's targeted problem consistently on several fronts.

A program evaluation study (Winer-Elkin, Weissberg, & Cowen, 1988) compared PSI-seen children with two demographically matched groups: (a) regularly seen PMHP children who averaged twenty-five 40-minute sessions over a 5–6 month period and (b) comparison children with similar initial adjustment status identified in non-PMHP schools. Study findings confirmed the efficacy of the PSI intervention; PSI children were rated by teachers, at post, as having improved significantly in classroom competencies and decreased in problem behaviors. Those gains were comparable to gains shown by PMHP children. Because of the selection procedures used however, PSI children tended to be somewhat less maladjusted than PMHP children at referral. Both PSI- and PMHP-seen children improved significantly more in classroom adjustment than comparison children who received no services. Follow-up, 6 weeks after the program ended, showed that PSI children maintained their postprogram adjustment gains whereas the adjustment of control children remained unchanged.

These findings were encouraging. Leastwise for children with relatively focal, targeted problems, they suggested that past decisions, often made by default, to see PMHP children for an entire year, might not reflect optimal utilization of limited program resources. Information from the PSI development study (Winer-Elkin et al., 1988) has been applied to encourage the use of time-limited intervention, wherever appropriate and feasible, and has increased wariness about seeing referred children "automatically" in a year-long intervention. On a broader scale, findings from the PSI program evaluation study also helped to shape California's adaptation of PMHP (see chapter 7). The entire state program in California is based on a short-term intervention model designed to allocate finite program resources to benefit the greatest number of children.

PARENT ASSOCIATE PROGRAM

The last program to be considered, the Parent Associate Program, differs from others thus far described. The obvious differentiating feature of this program, as its name implies, is that it is directed to parents, not children. One factor that stimulated development of this program was the limited resources available to some schools at the time PMHP moved from its initial location in a single school district to a model applied under real-world conditions to many school districts and schools, reflecting diverse program formats and resources.

In its early developmental years, PMHP had extensive contact with parents (Cowen, Trost, et al., 1975). Most of those contacts came about through the activities of PMHP social workers. Indeed, one of PMHP's important "liberating" features was the time that social workers gained for parent contacts because direct service needs with young children were being met by child associates.

Although that was a sensible and effective scenario for its time, changing times and PMHP's spread to many new, differently resourced districts put that way of functioning to some serious challenges. For one thing, some newly implementing districts had little or no social work time. Moreover, escalating demands on the time of school social workers, even in more amply staffed districts, limited their ability to meet with *all* parents and to provide them with the support that could best help children profit from their PMHP involvements.

These shifting realities, in the face of continuing respect for the importance of meaningful contacts with parents, led to the development of a program to train child associates for work with parents of PMHP children, functioning, in effect, as social work assistants in several specific roles (e.g., fostering two-way home–school communication, helping parents to manage everyday crises). This program was fueled by the belief that enhancing home–school contacts would benefit PMHP children. A description of the new program was prepared and distributed to child associates and, based on that description, a number of associates volunteered to participate.

A second, less obvious objective of the Parent Associate Program was to harness the parents' interest and involvement in the PMHP process (e.g., help them to help their own children). Thus, just as PMHP's original child associate program was a way of extending the reach of school mental health professionals to many more children, so was the Parent Associate Program an attempt to extend that same reach to parents.

The Parent Associate Program went through several training rounds that involved extensions of focus and changes in format. Currently led by PMHP's Chief Social Worker, the program includes five 1½-hour training sessions designed to facilitate parent associates' functioning in three areas. The first is information gathering; that is, obtaining information from parents about the child and his or her background that can help the PMHP team better to understand the child and family and thus formulate intervention plans. Relevant information may include significant family events, ongoing processes to which the child and family are adjusting, and developmental information that helps to clarify the child's adaptation. A second purpose of these home contacts is to provide parents with information about PMHP and the child's participation in it. Parents who feel included in the program and understand its goals and mechanisms are more likely to identify with and support PMHP's efforts and less likely to feel threatened. A final important area of functioning that training addresses is to help parents in their efforts to function effectively in the many, sometimes trying roles that are part and parcel of being the parent of a young child. This latter area includes helping parents to deal with both specific parenting dilemmas such as appropriate discipline practices and broader matters such as how and where parents can find needed help and resources for their family.

Unlike PMHP's fixed schedule of contacts with children, parent associates meet with parents on a flexible, less preordained schedule. A typical contact pattern might entail three or four meetings spread out over the school year. However, in a few cases, where parent needs have been urgent, as for example during a family crisis, associates have met weekly with parents over a period of time.

Some qualities that make for a good child associate also make for a good parent associate (e.g., caring and compassion, warmth, good listening skills, and empathy) although the essential qualities for these two roles are not necessarily identical all the way down the line. Attributes that are additionally important for the parent associate role include the abilities to establish good rapport with adults and to be accepting and nonjudgmental about a parent's life situation and his or her relationship with the child. These are qualities we at least look for in selecting associates for the parent training program. Experience over the years has shown that some associates are more comfortable working with children whereas others seem more at home in the parent associate role.

There has been no formal research evaluation of the parent associate program for several reasons. One is that program activities range broadly from one parent to another, reflecting, in the process, the associate's judgment of what is useful, timely, and important with a given parent. Second, PMHP's concern in the final reckoning is with how the program ultimately benefits children. Hence, the Parent Associate Program, which has been running for nearly 15 years and has trained many scores of associates, is sustained and nourished by the strong, supportive inputs of those who are touched most directly by it: associates, parents, and school professionals. Feedback about the program at those levels has been consistently positive.

SUMMARY AND IMPLICATIONS

This chapter, as much as any other in the volume, vivifies the assertion that PMHP has been an ever-evolving, self-correcting entity rather than a stand-pat, "cook-book" program. The chapter has reviewed five programmatic extensions of PMHP's initial unidimensional model. These five programs, culled from an even broader set of PMHP-sponsored new program explorations undertaken over the years, collectively reflect a substantial effort in program development. The result of this effort has been to add real, palpable, and enduring extensions to the smorgasbord of PMHP service options.

The programmatic variations on a theme described here have come about at different times and for somewhat different reasons. Each, however, is a product of PMHP's continuing effort to do better those basics that the project set out to accomplish in the first place. Several of these add-ons (e.g., programs for acting-out children and groups) stemmed from the conviction that certain child problems could better be served by an approach that modified the standard PMHP intervention in some key respect. Others (e.g., PSI, parent associate, and, to some extent, groups) resulted from the changing resource situations that PMHP encountered as the project spread to new and different school situations—many with considerably fewer resources than the original amply staffed PMHP model. And indeed at least one miniprogram (i.e., crisis intervention) came about because of ongoing social changes that made such problems a matter of increasing visibility and concern to schools.

Each add-on program developed slowly and carefully over time. Defining curricula were written for each, and the programs were evaluated first on a pilot basis and then on a larger scale. Ultimately, those shown to be viable were incorporated into the mainstream of available PMHP options. Although not all of these new programs have been adopted by all PMHP-implementing school districts, the potential for doing so (e.g., detailed program descriptions and training manuals) is there. For that reason a substantial number of implementing districts have, in fact, been able to incorporate one or more of these offshoot programs into their offerings.

Taken collectively, these program variants make PMHP a more versatile, farther reaching, and more efficient child-serving model. What brings them together is that each is a scope-enhancing variant, or fine-tuning, of PMHP's initial program-defining model. Later chapters describe other scope-enhancing options that differ even more basically (i.e., qualitatively) from PMHP's original program model.

6

EVALUATING THE EFFECTIVENESS
OF PMHP

In the prior volume on the Primary Mental Health Project (Cowen, Trost, et al., 1975), PMHP's research story fit handily in a single chapter. Subsequent growth in the size and scope of PMHP's research activities dictates a different approach here. One change, in the interest of internal cohesiveness, is that research on specific PMHP offshoot and extension programs is blended in with the description of those programs, as in chapter 5 and in later primary prevention chapters.

Also, this chapter touches only briefly on several highlights of pre-1975 research. Interested readers will find details of that early research in the prior volume. Although the chapter provides examples of different types of more recent PMHP research, it emphasizes "bread-and-butter" program evaluation studies relevant to practitioners and aspiring implementers.

The chapter first overviews the place of research in PMHP, including some good and not so good experiences we have had in that domain. Next, it considers several pre-1975 lines of research that played key, stage-setting roles in PMHP's development. The largest section of the chapter, however, reviews PMHP research thrusts in the past two decades, emphasizing major program evaluation studies we have done and several large-scale, independently conducted, state-level program evaluations.

RESEARCH–SERVICE INTERFACES

From its inception PMHP has operated as an open system that uses a research–service blend to examine key features of its programs. The term *open system* is used to convey several emphases. First, it means that all key PMHP components have been carefully researched and significant findings from that research have shaped program changes. These areas include (a) assessing adjustment and educational outcomes of PMHP-seen children; (b) documenting types of child problems referred to PMHP and comparing outcomes across problem types; (c) studying the selection, characteristics, and performance of child associates; (d) documenting the nature of the associate–child and associate–supervisor interaction processes and their relationship to child outcomes; and (e) enhancing understandings of diverse factors (e.g., home and life experiences) that relate to a child's school adjustment and performance. Each of these domains, central to PMHP's operation, has been studied extensively with the dual goals of ensuring program quality and providing the grist needed to fine-tune program services and maximize their impact and reach.

Another factor that feeds into PMHP's open system service–research blend is the realization that both microsystems (e.g., the family) and broader mesosystems and exosystems (Bronfenbrenner, 1979) importantly shape children's school adjustment. For example, both research on social indicators and PMHP's direct experience suggest that phenomena such as parental divorce, exposure to violence, and substance abuse that adversely affect children's school performance and behaviors are on the rise. Optimally, preventive interventions should be attuned, and responsive, to shifting social realities and, on the basis of such data, include features that are maximally helpful to children who experience these "heavy" stressors.

A third important element in the open system service–research blend is the search for factors that strengthen competencies in children and families and thus build toward wellness (Cowen, 1994). Central to a child-oriented prevention framework is the need to promote competencies that act to protect the child against failure and adjustment problems (Strayhorn, 1988) and provide a base on which long-term adaptive strengths and wellness can rest. Hence the enhancement of competence has long been a service goal for PMHP, as well as an important focus for its research.

At many points in this volume, the hand-in-glove relationship between service and research in PMHP is evident, including concrete demonstrations of how PMHP research findings have paved the way toward the initial development and/or enhancement of PMHP's service elements. Unlike many service programs, PMHP has always viewed the service–research relationship as synergistic. In our view, much about PMHP's success reflects its solid research substrate. PMHP's emphasis on research, particularly program evaluation research, is consistent with a growing call from national and state-level planning bodies for empirically validated prevention programs (Mrazek & Haggerty, 1994; Price, Cowen, Lorion, & Ramos-McKay, 1988). Indeed, PMHP's citation as an exemplary prevention program, through receipt of the National Mental Health Association's Lela Rowland Prevention Award, surely in some measure reflects its solid program-justifying empirical substrate.

The needs for accountability and credibility have fueled PMHP's program evaluation research. Accountability addresses the questions: Does the program work? and Does its prevention focus help children in the short and long term? Affirmative answers to those questions license a search for specific factors that facilitate such positive change. A later challenge, after an approach has been shown to work, is for program developers to communicate its feasibility in ways that are useful to those interested in implementation. The presence of a solid supporting research base documenting a program's efficacy is a great asset in the dissemination process.

Credibility is an extension of accountability. As PMHP has evolved many promising ideas for improving its helping strategies with young children and families have come up and been explored. Some of those explorations have succeeded, others have failed. Initially promising options gain in credibility from ongoing refinement and research documentation. Continuing program evaluation research is also needed because of the ever-changing ecology and structure of families, schools, and communities. The key point for us, however, is that PMHP's unflagging research emphasis over the years has been an important force in the project's survival, strengthening, and dissemination.

Although we have highlighted the research–service marriage in PMHP throughout, we did not say that the marriage was always a bed of roses. Whereas PMHP staff, from the start, has seen the project's basic and applied research as integral to program services, that view and the enthusiasm that goes with it is not always shared by PMHP school personnel. In part, this is because the intrinsic demands of research and field programs often differ and indeed sometimes clash (Cowen, 1978; Cowen, Lorion, & Dorr, 1974; Price & Smith, 1985). A concrete case in point: Most teachers have more than enough to do each day and not enough time to do it. Small wonder then, if some are less than enthralled with a request to complete 30 child-adjustment rating forms, the results of which will not, in their view, solve today's class management challenges or provide tomorrow's lesson plan. Taking this concern one step further, some school personnel feel that service and research are competing, rather than mutually enhancing endeavors and that investments of time and energy in research take resources away from needed services. These, in any case, are realities that must be anticipated and addressed.

Because input sources for PMHP research studies include both central project staff and school personnel, it is understandable that PMHP research foci have ranged widely across basic and applied issues. Within that diverse range, the largest single focus has consisted of program evaluation studies that PMHP staff has done both of its own and other PMHP programs, as well as program evaluations conducted independently by implementing school districts.

There have been several different types of PMHP outcome studies. Although most have been global outcome studies based on all project-seen children, some have focused on the efficacy of program modifications for children (a) with specific problems (e.g., acting-out children, children who have experienced parent death or divorce) and (b) who received time-limited PMHP services for specific targeted behaviors. More recently, there have been evaluations of several new primary prevention programs (e.g., class-based competence training, interventions for children of divorce).

Although program outcome studies have been the largest single item in PMHP's research portfolio, there have been other research initiatives as well. The latter include (a) scale development and refinement work, (b) studies of the associate–child and associate–supervisor interaction processes, (c) research identifying early predictors of school adjustment, and (d) studies of the effects of stressful life events on children.

EARLY PMHP RESEARCH FINDINGS: A BRIEF REVIEW

As noted above, only a few highlights of pre-1975 research are cited here: those that illuminate primarily natural progressions from early studies to more recent ones. Most early PMHP research focused on practical matters such as scale development, program effectiveness, paraprofessionals as help agents, and "consumer" views of the project.

Scale Development

Scale development research was important to PMHP from Day 1. It still is. This time-consuming work, often unnoticed or underappreciated, sought to develop objective assessment frameworks to be used in two domains: (a) referring children, identifying their focal problems, and establishing intervention goals, and (b) evaluating program outcomes.

The prior PMHP volume reported scale development work for two teacher-completed measures: the AML, an 11-item screening or X-ray device, and the Teacher Rating Form (TRF), a lengthier measure of young children's school adjustment problems. Over the years, those two measures have been refined and strengthened and their descendants remain in active use today.

The AML was first developed within the California State Department of Education (Bower, 1960; Van Vleet & Kannegieter, 1969) to screen young school children for acting out, shy–anxious, and learning problems. Our early research confirmed the AML's factor structure, documented its reliability and validity, and established age, gender, and place of residence (i.e., urban, suburban, rural) norms for the measure (Cowen, Dorr, et al., 1973).

The 41-item TRF (Clarfield, 1974) was a more comprehensive measure of children's school adjustment problems that, like the AML, assessed the domains of acting out, shy–anxious, and learning problems. The TRF was used both in planning interventions for children and assessing program outcomes. Around the time the 1975 volume appeared, the TRF was modified, refactored (confirming the original three-factor solution), and renamed the Classroom Adjustment Rating Scale (CARS; Lorion, Cowen, & Caldwell, 1975).

Early PMHP assessment tools focused exclusively on children's problem behaviors. Over time, on both conceptual and pragmatic grounds, the need became clear also to have a picture of children's competencies. On conceptual grounds, PMHP, as a prevention program, was committed to the goal of strengthening children's resources; moreover, strengthening resources often provided a meaningful path to reducing problem behaviors (Strayhorn, 1988). At a practical level, we also noted over time that (a) at any level of problem severity, there were major differences in children's resources and (b) early interventions could be planned more sensibly with knowledge of a child's resources, not just problems. These considerations prompted Gesten (1976) to develop a multifactor measure of children's resources, which, in one or another form, has been an important element in PMHP's early detection and program evaluation frameworks ever since.

Recent years have witnessed continuing significant modifications in PMHP measures. These efforts, described later in the chapter, were shaped by an awareness of heavy demands on teachers' scarce time and the need to be maximally parsimonious in assessment.

Early PMHP Outcomes Studies: A Brief Overview

A central question for PMHP, or any other intervention, is Does the program work? A positive answer to that question justifies exploration of other program-relevant questions. Because answers to initial global outcome questions are often gray rather than black or white, ongoing, refined program outcome studies are needed to address more specific questions such as, Does the program work better for some children than others? What are weak points in its scope or effectiveness? How can those be shored up? The latter questions have also been central PMHP research foci.

Two early PMHP program evaluation studies (Cowen et al., 1963, 1966), noted in chapter 3, helped to justify the program's rationale and shape its course. Both studies began by identifying two matched, but contrasting, cohorts of first grade children: those already experiencing, or seemingly at risk for school adjustment problems, called red tag (RT); and those adapting well early on, called non-red tag (NRT). Both studies used outcome measures reflecting academic, health, attendance, and adjustment indicators, and both measured child adjustment from the perspectives of teachers, peers, and the children themselves.

By the end of third grade, NRTs consistently exceeded RTs on measures of health status, educational achievement, and teacher, professional, peer, and self-ratings of adjustment (Cowen, 1971). The clear message from these studies was that many early detected problems did not remit spontaneously in the first three school years. To the contrary, by then there were increasingly menacing signs of ineffective school functioning and problem behaviors. Moreover, longer term follow-up of these early findings confirmed that initially classified RT children continued, at seventh grade, to struggle and lag significantly behind their NRT peers on measures of school achievement, peer acceptability, and school adjustment (Zax, Cowen, Rappaport, Beach, & Laird, 1968).

A subset of children from these early study cohorts was also tracked for entries, over an 11–13 year period, in a Cumulative Psychiatric Register for the Rochester–Monroe County area (Cowen, Pedersen, et al., 1973). The register included recorded contacts with area clinics, hospitals, and private practitioners serving mental health needs. In the initial classification of these children, 11–13 years earlier, one in three had been red tagged. Roughly 33% of the initial RT, versus 5% of the initial NRT, sample had register entries. These figures were highly disproportional. This same study also explored which of many school performance and adjustment measures, collected when these children were primary graders, predicted later register entry. A comparison of 60 tightly matched pairs of children who did versus did not later appear in the register, showed third grade peer sociometric ratings to be the most sensitive predictor of that outcome (Cowen, Pedersen, et al., 1973). Thus, findings from the register study confirmed that children whose early school adjustment problems are ignored or inadequately served are at risk for long-term negative outcomes.

In addition to tracking the courses of initially classified RT and NRT children in the first three school years, several primitive preventive intervention trials were conducted during that same period (Cowen et al., 1963, 1966). These pilot interventions antedated the child associate program and differed substantially from the PMHP format that later evolved. Their main components included identifying first grade children at risk; social work interviews with all mothers; a consultative role for the school mental health professionals in relation to other school personnel; parent and teacher discussion groups; and an after-school activities program for identified children (Cowen et al., 1966). The program was conducted in the primary grades of a single elementary school, with demographically comparable children from two adjacent, nonprogram schools constituting a comparison group.

This early preventive intervention yielded modestly positive outcomes. Program children, compared with controls, had fewer visits to the school nurse, better report card grades and achievement test scores, and more positive adjustment ratings by teachers (Cowen et al., 1966). These findings testified preliminarily to the promise of a school-based prevention approach and led to the idea of extending, and individualizing the reach of, preventive services to young children through a new child associate program.

Several other early program outcome studies were conducted after the child associate program started. Although these studies varied in design (e.g., use of comparison groups), data sources (parent, child associate, child, or teacher) and time periods covered (e.g., postprogram only vs. follow-up) they continued to show positive outcomes for PMHP-seen children. One such study (Cowen, 1968), for example, compared adjustment changes among children seen by child associates, by college students in an after-school program, or not at all. Both seen groups gained significantly on a teacher adjustment rating scale, with stronger gains for children seen by associates. Child associates' ratings also showed significant gains for these children (Cowen, 1968).

Other, less adequately controlled studies, found significant adjustment gains for PMHP-seen children as judged by child associates (Dorr & Cowen, 1973), and both teachers and associates (Cowen, Lorion, Dorr, Clarfield, & Wilson, 1975). A follow-up interview study with parents documented continuing school and interpersonal success of children seen by PMHP 2–5 years earlier (Cowen, Dorr, Trost, & Izzo, 1972). Although some of the studies cited presented problems of methodology and design, their cumulative findings supported the efficacy of early PMHP intervention efforts.

Other Narrow Outcome Studies

After these early studies established PMHP's efficacy, several finer grained studies were done to clarify the intervention's effectiveness for different groups and to evaluate program modifications for specific subgroups of children. Cowen and Schochet (1973), for example, compared teacher adjustment ratings for children who did versus did not terminate in PMHP at the end of the school year. Terminators were found to be less maladjusted than at preintervention and to have gained more from participating in PMHP. Follow-up showed that these terminators were not referred back to the project by their next year's teachers and were seen to be adjusting well by the latter (Lorion, Caldwell, & Cowen, 1976). These findings suggested that there may be programmatic advantage in focusing PMHP services on relatively less troubled children.

Several early, theory-guided, outcome studies illustrate how research data were harnessed to modify program practices. A study by Lorion, Cowen, and Kraus (1974) compared demographically matched children seen once versus twice a week, on referral and outcome measures. Frequency of contact did not relate either to seriousness of referral problems or to outcome benefit. Indeed, with respect to the latter, children seen less often (i.e., once, rather than several times, per week) tended directionally to improve more. These findings led to the conclusion that limited program resources could better be used by seeing more children less often.

Another study compared outcomes of children whose predominant referral patterns involved acting out, versus shy–anxious, versus learning problems (Lorion, Cowen, & Caldwell, 1974). Shy–anxious children had the best, and acting-out children the poorest, outcomes. This finding led to the development of a specialized program (chapter 5) that trained associates to work with acting-out children (Cowen et al., 1979). A third study sought to identify child and program attributes that discriminated between more and less successful PMHP outcomes (Lorion & Cowen, 1976). In general, older children, lower socioeconomic status urban children, and initially more maladjusted children had less positive outcomes than their opposites. These findings too led to concrete suggestions both for selecting PMHP children and for program refinements (Cowen & Lorion, 1974).

PMHP's strong interest in the sequelae of children's early school adjustment problems made follow-up a natural part of its research agenda. Several studies, for example, examined relationships among personality, behavioral, achievement, and performance measures, as children got older. Data from these studies provided evidence of important relationships between a child's early (i.e., primary grade) self-perceptions, and peer, teacher, and parent ratings of adjustment on the one side, and indicators of school adjustment and achievement at the intermediate level (Cowen, Huser, Beach, & Rappaport, 1970; Liem, Yellott, Cowen, Trost, & Izzo, 1969; Yellott, Liem, & Cowen, 1969; Zax, Cowen, Beach, & Rappaport, 1972; Zax, Cowen, Izzo, & Trost, 1964). These findings reinforced the sensibility of an early, preventively oriented intervention strategy.

Early Research on the Helping Process

The child associate is a central figure in PMHP. Several early research studies sought to pinpoint distinguishing characteristics of PMHP associates and document the key role they played in the project. Data from selection interviews showed that associates scored very high on interviewer-rated dimensions of interpersonal styles and skills (Cowen, Dorr, & Pokracki, 1972). A study comparing new child associates and demographically matched women involved in other community volunteer activities (Sandler, 1972) showed that the two groups differed in style of interpersonal relationships, interests, and attitudes. Illustratively, associates had significantly higher empathy, affiliation, and nurturance scores and lower aggression scores than comparison volunteer women. Dorr, Cowen, and Sandler (1973) again compared associates and volunteer controls after associates had worked with children for a semester. Based on a vignette measure that described several hypothetical child problem dilemmas, associates, compared with volunteers, gave significantly more understanding and fewer rejecting responses.

An early process study (McWilliams, 1972) documented the nature of the associate–child intervention and relationships between intervention practices and outcomes. Associate–child interactions differed for different presenting problems (e.g., acting out, versus shy–anxious, versus learning), and attributes of associates. Overall, associates spent most of their time in play activity with children and lesser amounts of time in problem-oriented conversation and tutoring. Frequently cited goals for these activities included helping children to make independent choices, strengthening their academic abilities, and building their close friendships and confidence.

One other early research probe assessed teachers' views of the project's utility (Dorr & Cowen, 1972). In this study, PMHP was rated positively in terms of access to professional staff and being able to get help in working with children. The project also compared favorably with other school mental health programs teachers had known.

PMHP RESEARCH—THE MODERN ERA (1975–CURRENT)

The preceding overview sets the stage for a review of PMHP research in the last 20 years. Several research foci remained central during this period, although ways of studying them changed. These continuing areas include methodological and scale development studies, program evaluation research, and research on "consumer" views of PMHP. Also during this period, new areas (e.g., studies of the effects of stressful life events on children's school adjustment, and relationships between class environment variables and children's adjustment and learning) became part of PMHP's research focus.

Scale Development and Refinements

Assessment measures are used clinically in PMHP to establish a clear picture of a child's presenting problems and for planning intervention goals. In research they provide an objective matrix within which to assess the achievement of relevant program outcomes. Hence, developing and refining assessment devices has remained a continuing central challenge. However, because PMHP is set in a bustling school world, where teachers and other school personnel have limited time for research projects, such measures must be brief, clear, and objective and reflect behavior domains that are important to teachers. Although PMHP's earliest assessment tools (cf. above) were developed in the image of those needs, field experience shaped further streamlining changes in them in the past 20 years.

PMHP's first screening tool was the 11-item AML, designed to provide a quick X ray of children's acting-out, shy–anxious, and learning problems (Cowen et al., 1963). The original 11-item AML had five acting-out, five shy–anxious, and one learning item. PMHP later revised the AML, both to expand the learning factor and refine several items. This resulted in a revised 12-item AML-R (4 items per subscale), with strong reliability and validity, and norms for kindergarteners–third graders (PMHP Screening and Evaluation Measures, 1995).

Another important step was the development of the Health Resources Inventory (HRI), a 54-item teacher-rated measure of children's school competencies (Gesten, 1976). Factor analysis identified five HRI competence dimensions: Good Student, Adaptive Assertiveness, Peer Sociability, Follows Rules, and Frustration Tolerance. The HRI had a test–retest reliability of .87, significantly discriminated normal and disturbed children, and, as expected, correlated negatively with school adjustment problems (Gesten, 1976). The HRI's development first made it possible to include competence dimensions in PMHP's assessment and planning processes and, later, to measure competence gains in prevention programs designed to enhance wellness. Otherwise put, the HRI broadened the scope and focus of PMHP's "measurement field," by objectifying the assessment of children's adaptive strengths.

The development of the T-CRS (Hightower et al., 1986), PMHP's most basic current assessment device, was an ambitious undertaking. In effect, the T-CRS fused the 41-item CARS and the 54-item HRI, previously used to assess problem behaviors and competencies. Although both these measures had been carefully developed and successfully used, given the realities of the school environment, their major "sin" was that they were too long. Thus, the main purpose in developing the T-CRS was to combine and sharply reduce the number of items in the two scales.

This work was done via a step-stage process. First, redundant and weak-loading CARS and HRI items were dropped, resulting in a provisional 46-item scale. Several studies were done to refine this scale, establish its psychometric properties, and test its utility with diverse child samples (e.g., normal and referred; urban, suburban, and rural). That pilot work led ultimately to the final, now widely used, 38-item T-CRS (18 problem behaviors, 20 competencies).

Several factor analyses showed this measure to consist of three 6-item problem factors (Acting-Out, Shy–Anxious, and Learning Problems), and four 5-item competence factors (Task Orientation, Frustration Tolerance, Assertive Social Skills, and Peer Social Skills). These abbreviated factors resembled their respective, lengthier CARS and HRI factor predecessors. The new T-CRS was internally consistent and reliable and sensitively differentiated between referred and nonreferred children (Hightower et al., 1986). Thus, the T-CRS scale development effort yielded a lean, compact 38-item assessment tool that was as sensitive as, but much more parsimonious than, the two scales (95 items) it replaced.

A recent second-order T-CRS factor analysis showed that its problem and competence factors merge into conceptually meaningful, more global units, that is, two cohesive "superfactors" that seem useful for research purposes. The first, Engaged–Disengaged, unites the Acting Out and Learning Problem factors with the Frustration Tolerance and Task Orientation competence factors. The second, Socioemotional Adjustment, includes the Shy–Anxious factor and Peer Social Skills and Assertive Social Skills competencies. Although these superfactors offer a compact way to view research outcomes that should be useful in future program evaluation studies, they do not replace the use of first-order factors in PMHP's clinical assessment goal setting processes.[1]

We are now developing a Parent–Child Rating Scale (P-CRS) to parallel the T-CRS. This step was undertaken because existing, psychometrically sound parent measures of child adjustment are lengthy and problem focused (Achenbach & Edelbrock, 1983). Since those are both limiting factors for PMHP, we began to explore new parent rating scale options (McKim & Cowen, 1988). In so doing, it became clear that a parent rating measure tapping the same domains as the T-CRS would facilitate cross-source comparisons of child adjustment ratings. Hence, the P-CRS was

---

[1]Given recent rapid sociodemographic shifts in the urban school population, a major renorming of the T-CRS is under way as this volume goes to press.

developed to parallel the T-CRS, rewording some items to remove their content from the school context.

An initial P-CRS factor analysis yielded a factor structure that parallels the T-CRS, that is, three 6-item problem scales (Acting Out, Shy–Anxious, and Learning Problems) and four 5-item competence scales (Frustration Tolerance, Assertive Social Skills, Task Orientation, and Peer Social Skills). Alphas for these factors range from .85 to .92. Substantial correlations (range, .5–.6) were found between parallel scales (e.g., Acting Out, Shy–Anxious) on the two measures (Hightower, 1994). Those correlations are similar to ones reported modally, between teacher and parent ratings of children's adjustment (Achenbach, McConaughy, & Howell, 1987). Additional research is needed to solidify the P-CRS's psychometric base and provide normative information about parent judgments of child adjustment by gender, age, and ethnic and sociodemographic groups.

Another basic PMHP assessment tool, the CRS was developed to assess school adjustment from the child's perspective (Hightower et al., 1987). CRS items were written to be clear, developmentally appropriate, and assess school adjustment domains that are relevant for young children. They include both problems (Acting Out and Shy–Anxious) and competencies (School Interest and Peer Social Skills) assessed by other PMHP measures.

An initial pool of 75 items was developed with those objectives in mind. Pilot testing with first–fourth graders, plus feedback from school personnel, reduced this pool to 35 items. The latter were administered to several thousand first–sixth graders in 34 urban and suburban schools. This process established a final 24-item scale consisting of six items for each of four factors: Rule Compliance, Anxiety–Withdrawal, Peer Social Skills, and School Interest. Alphas and test–retest reliabilities for these factors range from .69–.74. Several different types of validity were shown for the CRS. Referred children reported more problems than demographically matched nonreferred peers, and scores on the CRS Shy–Anxious subscale related to scores on the Spielberger's (1973) Trait Anxiety Subscale. Significant relationships were also shown between child and teacher ratings of similar adjustment dimensions (e.g., CRS rule compliance with T-CRS acting out). The CRS enhances PMHP's measurement matrix by assessing key domains of school adjustment from the child's perspective. This provides another comparison point for reports of child adjustment status by significant figures (e.g., peers, teacher, parents) in the child's life.

Other PMHP scale development work unfolded in the context of PMHP offshoot projects. Several examples follow. Our research on child resilience (chapter 11) pointed up the need to assess children's sense of efficacy. Although experts in the field (Rutter, 1987; Werner & Smith, 1992) considered the child's sense of efficacy to be important in shaping resilient outcomes, at the time there was no assessment tool for that purpose. For that reason, and because self-efficacy gain may also be a potentially important PMHP outcome, we developed a measure of perceived self-efficacy (PSE) for young children (Cowen et al., 1991). This 20-item measure was an extension of a set of 10 self-efficacy items, used in the child-interview portion of the resilience study, that were shown to sensitively differentiate stress-resilient and stress-affected children (Wyman et al., 1992).

All 20 PSE scale items followed a common stem: "How sure are you that things will work out well for you when . . . ?" The child's task was to rate these items (e.g., "You have to work out a problem with a friend"; "You have to get something done right under pressure") on a 5-point scale (1 = not at all sure, 5 = very sure). Factor analysis of the test responses of fourth and fifth graders identified three efficacy dimensions: difficult situations, new experiences, and problems with people. PSE factor reliabilities ranged from .65 to .78; the full scale had a reliability of .81. Cowen et al. (1991) also found relationships between PSE responses and scores on other child adjustment indicators (e.g., internal locus of control, low anxiety level, peer sociometric acceptance).

There have been parallel scale development steps in the context of our evolving primary prevention programs. One example is a measure of children's interpersonal problem-solving strategies that relates to teacher, peer, parent, and self-ratings of child adjustment (Work, 1986) and discriminates between highly stressed urban children with stress-affected and stress-resilient outcomes (Cowen et al., 1992). Another is the development of a measure of children's coping styles, consisting of two positive (i.e., seeking support and self-reliance) and three negative (i.e., wishful thinking, distancing/denial, and "no cope") dimensions. These styles also related to child adjustment indicators and differentiated stress-resilient and stress-affected children (Work, Levinson, & Hightower, 1995).

Program Evaluation Research: 1975–Current

PMHP program evaluation research has grown enormously in the last 20 years. Several factors have contributed to that growth. One is the large number of PMHP programs that started in New York State. In parallel, PMHP's dissemination activities (see chapter 7) resulted in rapid program growth in several states with strong interest in program evaluation research. Thus, by the early 1980s, there had been an explosion of new school districts implementing PMHP and seeking feedback on program success. Accountability based on program outcome data had become a more visible concern both at the school district and state levels.

Another development that accelerated the pace of program evaluation research was the emergence of computer-related technologies such as optical mark scanners that facilitated rapid, large-scale information processing. By the late 1980s, statewide PMHP program outcome information was being collected systematically in New York, California, and Washington involving data inputs from teachers and program mental health professionals and sometimes (especially in New York) additional data from children and child associates. The availability of this new technology made it possible to process screening data and provide feedback to districts within a few days. Moreover, by late summer or early fall of each new year, we were able to provide district-level program evaluation data from the prior school year.

As a result of these technological advances, it is not an exaggeration to say that PMHP conducts hundreds of miniprogram evaluations for individual school districts each year. Most of these "studies," done primarily for local feedback purposes, use a simple pre–post design, do not include a comparison group, but do include multiple data sources (teachers, child associates, mental health professionals, and children) in evaluating changes in child behavior.

A review of that work on a study-by-study basis could fill the pages of a large urban phone directory, without establishing much beyond the platitude that the program seems to be working well in most districts. Hence, consideration of PMHP program evaluation research here focuses on large-scale, cross-district, including state-level, program evaluations[2] and several studies with special design features that illuminate particular outcome issues.

LARGE-SCALE PROGRAM EVALUATION STUDIES

One constraint to keep in mind in considering multidistrict, and certainly state-level, program evaluations is that although there are important common program features across districts, districts also vary in the specifics of their program implementations and sometimes in the design, format, and focal questions for their program evaluations. Hence, to the extent that cross-district and state-level program evaluations yield positive findings, such findings highlight the utility of the program's core defining features, even in the face of variation in the exact ways in which those features are implemented.

New York

Two large-scale program evaluations, cutting across New York State school districts, were conducted in the 1980s. The first was a multiyear

---

[2]Descriptions of these state programs and how they developed are presented in chapter 7. Here we touch only on their program evaluation components.

study involving 20 schools from five urban and suburban districts in the greater Rochester area (Weissberg, Cowen, Lotyczewski, & Gesten, 1983). Program evaluation data collected over a 7-year period (1974–1981) demonstrated consistently positive outcome findings across these sites.

This study included many thousands of kindergarten–third grade children seen, on average, for 21–24 sessions. Teachers, child associates, and professionals provided pre and post ratings of children's competencies and problem behaviors. Significant reductions in shy–anxious and learning problems, and significant increases in competence (e.g., being a good student, adaptive assertiveness, peer sociability, follows rules, frustration tolerance) were found consistently across districts and program years. Although changes in acting-out behaviors reported by teachers and child associates were less consistent, such changes did occur in some program years and in the pooled sample across years. A modest correlation (.3–.4) in behavior change estimates across rater sources suggested that (a) there was indeed some cross-observer consistency in judged change and (b) the ratings obtained may reflect real cross-setting differences in child behaviors. Although these findings offer evidence of the program's efficacy across multiple sites and substantial time periods, their interpretability is restricted by the lack of a comparison group.

During the period of PMHP's major expansion in New York State, new districts were encouraged to evaluate their programs. A number of districts did so. This made possible a study of program efficacy involving six school districts ranging from Western New York State to Long Island, that had recently started programs (Cowen et al., 1983). At the time, these programs were 1–3 years old, had 6–12 hours per week of professional time, and were staffed by 2–11 associates. Collectively, they provided intensive helping services (M = 23 sessions) to nearly 400 primary graders. Although there were some differences in the outcome measures districts used, all districts had CARS and HRI data for problem behaviors and competencies. Outcome data were analyzed both individually by district and pooled across districts. Four districts showed significant improvement on at least six CARS and HRI factors; the other two showed such gains on three or four factors, respectively. Because sample sizes were small in some districts, the data were tested for overall effects. In these analyses, PMHP-seen children evidenced significant pre-to-post gain on all ten CARS and HRI factors and total scores. These findings supported the feasibility of disseminating the PMHP model to other sites, in a way that preserved the program's defining essences.

Several other program evaluation studies in New York State speak to PMHP's applicability to districts with special features. One such evaluation was based on an extension of the PMHP model to a consortium of six small, geographically separated, rural school districts in the northeast corner of the state, each with insufficient resources to conduct the program independently (Farie, Cowen, & Smith, 1986). The consortium arrangement, coordinated by the Executive Director of the County Mental Health Association, enabled participating districts to use a common resource pool for recruiting, training, and supervising child associates; consultation; inservice training; and research. It was designed to (a) expand, and upgrade the quality of, program services, (b) enhance cross-district communication and sources of stimulation, and (c) reduce the sense of isolation and loneliness that people often experience in rural settings. Program outcome data, based on pre–post teacher ratings of children's school behaviors, demonstrated that child participants improved significantly. These positive findings, and the good sense that the program made to participants, made this approach a model that other rural districts have emulated.

A second very different program application involved extending PMHP to a prototypic urban, inner-city school district, Community School District 4 (CSD 4) in the East Harlem barrio section of New York City. This district, consisting of two thirds Hispanic and one third Black children is characterized by very high rates of poverty, unemployment (>40%), health problems, infant mortality, teenage pregnancy, and drug use. PMHP began on a small scale in CSD 4 in 1985. Since then, the project has expanded to eight schools that provide services to some 500 children annually. Several schools had concurrent access to either a social problem-solving or a parent information program.

CSD 4's program was evaluated over a 4-year period. All annual evaluations and the combined 4-year evaluation yielded positive findings on all principal outcome criteria (Meller, Laboy, Rothwax, Fritton, & Mangual, 1994). Specifically, teachers rated program children as having significantly fewer problems and more competencies on the T-CRS postintervention, both overall and on all problem and competence factor subscales. Associates judged PMHP-seen children to have improved significantly in initiative and participation, observing behavioral limits, reductions in shyness, and increases in self-confidence. Similarly, the children judged significant improvement to have occurred on all CRS subscales and total scores. Finally, program-seen children evidenced significant pre–post improvements in self-efficacy ratings, social problem solving, and participation in clubs and activities (Meller et al., 1994).

Findings from the rural consortium and CSD 4 program evaluations testify to the applicability of the PMHP model in diverse settings. The fact that both of these extensions reflect areas in which children's needs have been chronically underserved (President's Commission on Mental Health, 1978) highlights the utility of the model for chronically neglected, underresourced settings.

California

California's version of PMHP is called the Primary Intervention Program (PIP). Although PIP implementations include all of PMHP's defining structural features, the program differs from PMHP in two key respects. Based on a PMHP research finding demonstrating the efficacy of planned short-term intervention (Winer-Elkin et al., 1988), PIP interventions are limited to one semester (12–15 contacts). This decision extends the program's reach substantially. Second, each implementation, by law, has to be jointly planned and conducted by a school district and a geographically proximal mental health center.

Comprehensive statewide program evaluations conducted for 5 consecutive years (1989–1994) in California, provided a unique opportunity to assess the impact of an extensive, state-level implementation program. These evaluations were designed to provide maximally useful information to the state. To facilitate the conduct of these studies, PMHP's computer feedback system was used to return screening data to schools promptly each fall, and to provide end-of-year summary information about each program's effectiveness to districts. PMHP was also responsible for preparing annual reports summarizing the effectiveness of the statewide program.

Table 1 summarizes findings from these five PIP program evaluations. Before considering details of the findings, we note overall that, by using multiple criteria, the program was shown to be very effective in delivering early, cost-effective preventive services. The scope of the statewide program, as the table shows, was substantial; over the 5-year study period, some 47,000 children from 700 schools in nearly 200 school districts were seen. Consonant with PIP's mandate, children were seen short term, averaging 12 contacts. Although program growth during the 5-year period was rapid (from 45 districts serving 4,500 children in 1989–1990 to 184 districts serving 24,000 children in 1993–1994), positive outcome findings were maintained.

Using the T-CRS as the study's main outcome measure, a four-level coding system was developed to aggregate findings across districts and years. The most positive outcome, indicating significant pre–post gain on at least eight of nine T-CRS scales, was coded very strong (VS). The next level, strong (S) was used to indicate significant gain on five to seven scales. The last two levels, moderate (M) and inconclusive (I), reflected two to four and zero to one subscale gains, respectively. Based on this framework, over the 5-year study period 83–90% of the districts had either VS or S outcomes—a very high proportion of "successful" programs. Unsuccessful programs ranged from only 3% to 7%, per year.

TABLE 1
California Statewide Primary Intervention Program: 5-Year Summary of Program Outcomes

Program year	Number of districts	Number of children	Mean contacts	% T-CRS classification				Effect size		% repeaters	% goals met
				VS	S	M	I	Prob.	Comp.		
1989–1990	45	4,500	12.1	63	27	5	5	.37	.43	0	52
1990–1991	63	5,700	12.6	65	22	10	3	.43	.49	9.5	56
1991–1992	72	6,000	12.2	72	17	7	4	.43	.48	9.2	62
1992–1993	93	7,300	11.7	63	23	10	4	.43	.45	4.5	60
1993–1994	184	24,000	11.4	60	23	11	7	.40	.44	7	58

Note. T-CRS = Teacher–Child Rating Scale; VS = very strong (8 or 9 factors); S = strong (5 to 7 factors); M = moderate (2 to 4 factors); I = inconclusive (0 or 1 factor); Prob. = T-CRS problem total; Comp. = T-CRS competence total.

Next, using teacher ratings of total problems and competencies as outcome criteria, an annual effect-size for the state program was calculated depicting the extent of overall gain among seen children. These 10 effect sizes (i.e., 2 for each of 5 years) ranged from .37 to .49, with a median of .43. Effect sizes in the .3 to .5 range are considered to depict "moderate" positive change (Cohen, 1988; Rosnow & Rosenthal, 1993). Otherwise put, on the basis of hundreds of district programs and of over 47,000 children seen in California over a 5-year period, statistically meaningful improvements were demonstrated in children's school adjustment based on teacher ratings of problem behaviors and competencies. The table's last two columns reflect similarly positive outcomes based on other data sources. On average, only 6% of the children seen were program "repeaters"—a very low proportion for this at-risk group. At another level, mental health professionals judged that 60% of PIP children seen in this 5-year period (range 52–66%) met the goals established for them.

In addition to the preceding findings, outcomes for specific subgroups were studied as were several issues pertaining to program regularities and nuances of program implementation. For the 5-year period, gains made were similar for boys and girls, by grade level, by school location, and across diverse family situations (e.g., two-parent vs. one-parent families). Several other findings of interest emerged from these supplemental analyses. In Year 1, success rates were compared for 437 children whose screening (AML) data classified them as relatively pure acting-out, shy–anxious, or learning-problem types. Defining successful PIP children as those who both met goals and were recommended for termination by program professionals postintervention, success figures for the Acting-Out, Shy–Anxious, and Learning-Problem groups were 38%, 54%, and 63%, respectively. These findings, like earlier ones from PMHP (Lorion, Cowen, & Kraus, 1974), confirmed that acting-out problems were the most difficult to modify.

Although the California project had few repeaters overall, starting in Year 2, outcomes for repeaters and nonrepeaters were compared. Non-repeaters were found to do better than repeaters. Younger children (kindergarten–second grade) also tended to profit more from the program than older children, thus pointing to the usefulness of providing PMHP services as soon as possible. Children who were less at risk preintervention had better outcomes than those who were more at risk. The 5-year California program evaluation study is among the most comprehensive of its type ever done; its findings offer strong evidence of PIP's efficacy.

Washington

PMHP (PIP) program evaluation studies in Washington have sought both to evaluate the efficacy of the overall state program and to explore the role that definable program elements (e.g., types of children seen, duration, frequency of contacts) play in program outcomes. Starting in 1989, evaluations of Washington's program were conducted for 4 successive years, using four data sources. Two, the Background Information Form and the Child Contact Log, provided descriptive information; the other two, the T-CRS and (except for Year 1) the Professional Summary Report, were used to assess children's change in the program.

The first evaluation was marred by several problems (e.g., late start-ups for most programs, incomplete data). Although 17 of 24 then-implementing districts (9 continuing, 8 new) participated in the evaluation, because of data gaps among the latter, evaluations of the two types of programs were done separately. The 700+ children seen by continuing programs averaged 9 individual and 15 group contacts during the year. For those youngsters, significant pre–post gains were found on all T-CRS factor and total scores. The eight new districts saw only 192 children due to late program starts, averaging only 8 individual, and 6 group, contacts. Even so these children also improved significantly on all T-CRS subscales except peer sociability.

A more extensive Year 2 evaluation was conducted with 33 implementing districts: 12 multiyear programs serving 1,100 children, 12 first or second year programs serving 500 children, and 9 new programs serving 600 children. Outcome data were analyzed both overall, and separately for the three naturally occurring groupings. Significant positive changes were found on all T-CRS total and subscale scores for all three types of programs. Within this overall framework of positive findings there was a tendency for established programs to show more reductions in problem behaviors and increases in competencies. As in California, program gains were similar by gender, grade level, and location.

The Year 3 and 4 Washington state program evaluations were based on a subset of districts approximating the state's overall proportions of urban, suburban, and rural school districts. Year 3's evaluation involved 12 districts with 850 program children. Significant pre-post gains were again found on all T-CRS scales with comparable gains by gender, grade level, and location of school districts. There were similar positive findings on the professionals' post-only behavior change ratings. Findings from the Year 4 study, done in 8 districts with nearly 600 children, closely paralleled those for Year 3. Specifically, both teachers and professionals judged positive changes, across the board, to have taken place in PIP-seen children.

Several other findings from this study bear mention. First, successful terminators showed two to three times more positive change than unsuccessful ones. Second, contrary to the expectation generated by a regression-to-the-mean explanation, children with fewer risk indicators preintervention improved more than peers with higher initial risk scores. This finding has implications for selecting children who may benefit most from PMHP's early preventive focus.

The two unique, large-scale evaluations of state-level programs described provide strong support for the efficacy of the PMHP program model. Such confirmatory data facilitate the task of dissemination and suggest that the integrity of the program model can be maintained despite the complexities inherent in a comprehensive state dissemination program.

OTHER PMHP OUTCOME STUDIES

This section reviews post-1975 PMHP program outcome studies that differ from the large-scale state program evaluations described. These include several follow-up studies and several with nonprogram comparison groups.

Chandler, Weissberg, Cowen, and Guare (1984) followed up a sample of 61 urban children, seen 2–5 years earlier in PMHP, to assess their current adjustment. All PMHP children met the dual criteria of (a) having been seen for at least 3 months, at least 2 years earlier and (b) still attending the school in which the initial PMHP services were provided. A comparison group consisted of 61 non-seen youngsters from the same schools, matched to the PMHP sample by gender, grade level, and current classroom teacher. A third study group ($n = 38$) consisted of same-grade children identified by 19 current teachers as among the two least well adjusted children in their classes. Because the latter nominations came from teachers who had no knowledge of children's prior status, it turned out that of the 38 selected, 27 were new, 8 were former PMHP children, and 3 were comparison children. In the final cross-group comparisons, the latter 11 children remained with their initial placement groups.

Adjustment ratings by current classroom teachers confirmed that PMHP children had maintained their initial gains, 2–5 years later. Indeed, on several specific problem and competence subscales, as well as overall problem and competence scores, they had registered significant further gains. Thus, PMHP children, as hypothesized, fell between the never-seen and least-adjusted groups on all adjustment indicators. The fact that current teachers were unaware of children's prior status, or the purpose of the follow-up, lends greater import to the findings. It was also of interest to note that PMHP children were comparable to never-seen children on all child-completed measures of perceived competence and achievement, except perceived social competence, on which never-seen children had higher self-ratings. To summarize, although PMHP children were still differentiable from never-seen children at follow-up, they had clearly moved back into a "normal" range by then.

Work, Lotyczewski, and Raymond (1995) did a follow-up study comparing 2nd–5th grade rural children seen in PMHP 1–4 years earlier with demographically matched classmates, using T-CRS ratings by current teachers and child self-ratings on the CRS. Teachers were not told about children's PMHP involvement; rather the study was done as a general follow-up of all special services offered by the school. Pre- and postteacher ratings were available for 59 PMHP-seen children both in the year they were first seen (T_1) and at the 1–4-year follow-up point (T_2). As a group, these youngsters showed significant adjustment gains both in the years in which they were initially seen and again at T_2 as judged by new teachers. As in Chandler et al.'s (1984) study, those initially at-risk PMHP-seen children were found to be in the 40th–50th percentile in adjustment at T_2, and indistinguishable from classmates on teacher and self-reports of adjustment. Controlling for predifferences in adjustment, PMHP children also gained more than the matched comparison group over the follow-up period.

Two other, non–statewide outcome studies in California provide additional support for PMHP's efficacy. The first, conducted by the Southwest Regional Educational Laboratory (SWRL), was based on a request by the state for an outside impartial program evaluation (Thomas, 1989). Within districts, this study compared children from schools with and without PIP. The latter were all schools that had expressed interest in having PIP. The PIP and comparison samples were similar initially in adjustment, report card grades, and absences. Postprogram comparisons of these two groups showed that PIP children significantly exceeded comparison children on six of seven T-CRS factors and both T-CRS sum scores. In absolute terms, their gains ranged from 3% to 7%. The author concluded:

> the results uniformly favored students participating in the treatment group and were almost always highly significant. Translating these results into less statistical language, these findings indicate that about two-thirds (64%) of the PIP students will demonstrate levels of social adjustment equal to, or better than, the average student who does not participate in PIP. This is a significant advantage for students in their social adjustment who participate in PIP as opposed to students who do not participate in PIP. (Thomas, 1989, p. 17)

Thomas acknowledged two limitations of the study: (a) the lack of a within school and/or class comparison group and (b) not being able to assign children randomly to PIP and non-PIP conditions as in a true experimental design. These two issues were addressed in a recent broad evaluation of PIP's effectiveness that was part of an even larger study of the effectiveness of several types of early preventive programs for young children (Duerr, 1993). This study used a sophisticated delayed-treatment control group design, with initial random assignment of children to intervention or comparison groups. This design offered the advantages of consistent selection criteria for the two groups and close matching, including motivation for the child to be seen. Eighteen school sites involving 379 PIP children and 290 delayed controls participated in this study. Several important findings emerged. First, PIP children improved significantly more than the delayed controls in T-CRS problem reduction and competence gain. Second, the magnitude of gain for PIP children was substantial, averaging about 5 points in both problem and competence totals.

The PMHP outcome studies cited in this chapter by no means exhaust that category. Chapter 5 for example reported evaluations of PMHP offshoot programs such as those for acting-out children and planned short-term intervention. Similarly, later chapters describing primary prevention program developments include program outcome research findings.

Overviewing PMHP's many outcome studies, including studies of the whole project, studies of specific components, studies we ourselves have done, and independent studies by others, several conclusions stand out. The design of these studies runs the gamut from the primitive to the fairly sophisticated. No single study, by itself, provides definitive confirmation of PMHP's short- or long-term efficacy. Taken together, however, the results of these studies provide a considerable weight of evidence in support of the program's effectiveness. This body of evidence has helped establish a credibility base that has contributed importantly to PMHP's survival and expansion.

CLASS ENVIRONMENT STUDIES

PMHP's longstanding search for factors that relate to children's school adjustment focused first on child and family variables of potential relevance (e.g., stress experienced). A next natural step was to study aspects of class environment in relation to children's school adaptation. Several converging strands shaped this development. One was prior research documenting the importance of structural aspects of school environments (e.g., going to a small or large school) in shaping children's school-related views (e.g., sense of satisfaction or belonging) and behaviors (Barker & Gump, 1964; Willems, 1967). One instrumental facet of that research was the development of measures such as the Classroom Environment Scale (CES) to assess salient aspects of class environments (Moos & Trickett, 1974; Trickett & Moos, 1974). These objective measures helped to define key dimensions of class environments and to explore relationships between variations on those dimensions and student outcomes (Moos, 1979).

The emergence of this way of thinking and the development of relevant measurement technology stimulated PMHP's interest in exploring the impact of class environments on children's behavior and school performance. Behind that interest was the longer term ideal of constructive modification of class environments in ways informed by such generative data. This section describes several studies that illustrate early PMHP efforts in this area. More recent programmatic steps in this direction are summarized in chapter 10.

Two related studies (Wright & Cowen, 1982; Wright, Cowen, & Kaplan, 1982) examined student and teacher perceptions of class environments and their relationship to children's mood, achievement, popularity, and adjustment. Subjects in these studies included 511 fifth and sixth graders and their teachers, from 23 classes in four suburban schools. Children completed a short form of the CES developed for this age group. Study outcome measures included a Mood Adjective Checklist, an academic performance index, a peer rating scale, and teacher ratings of children's classroom adjustment. The main study findings revealed that student perceptions of class environments as high in order and organization, affiliation, and involvement related to positive student mood, greater peer popularity, greater self-control, and more positive teacher ratings of pupil adjustment (Wright & Cowen, 1982; Wright et al., 1982). These results, linking perceived class environment variables and student outcomes, were consistent with Moos's (1979) findings with high school students. The challenging practical (prevention-oriented) question they raised was how to foster student affiliation and involvement in ways that might improve class adjustment.

To that end, an intervention was designed to enhance student affiliation through peer teaching. This program was based on the "jigsaw" teaching method used successfully in fifth grade social studies classes in Texas to reduce racial tensions (Aronson, Blaney, Stefan, Sykes, & Snapp, 1978). In the jigsaw approach pupils work in small ($n = 5$), independent learning groups made up of children at different ability levels. Each team member is responsible for mastering one segment of an overall topic and teaching it to other group members. Cooperation is essential in the jigsaw framework, because assignments cannot be finished without collaboration and pooling of information.

Wright and Cowen (1985) developed a 10-week jigsaw curriculum for fifth grade social studies classes. First, two curricular units (36 lessons over an 8-week period), covering the South Central States and the Civil War, were written in a jigsaw format. Two classes used the new format, while two comparison classes used a standard curriculum and learning format. Outcome measures included the CES, self-esteem and sociometric measures, and teacher ratings of children's adjustment and academic performance.

At the end of the 10-week program, jigsaw children perceived their class environment as more involved, orderly, and organized than controls; evidenced stronger interest in science and social studies; were judged to be better adjusted by teachers; and, importantly, did better academically. Interestingly, children who gained most from the program academically were those who were functioning at the lower levels initially (Wright & Cowen,

1985). These findings pointed up the proactive potential of a class-based cooperative learning strategy, also reflected in the later Study Buddy program (see chapter 10).

LIFE STRESSORS AND ADJUSTMENT: IMPLICATIONS FOR PREVENTION

In the past 20 years, PMHP has been extensively involved in studying relationships between life stress and children's school adjustment (Cowen & Hightower, 1986). This work was stimulated both by direct observation of serious negative effects of stress on children in school and by research studies documenting this same relationship. Our research in this area has contributed importantly to the development of prevention interventions such as those for children of divorce and children who experience chronic and profound life stress (chapters 9 and 11). In this section, we present highlights of this generative research and consider the implications of its findings for preventive intervention.

One early study (Felner et al., 1975) assessed the effects of two major stressors (parental divorce and death of a close family member) on children's school adjustment. Although both stress groups had more serious school adjustment problems than matched controls, they experienced different types of problems. Whereas children of divorce had elevated acting-out problems, also reported by others (e.g., Emery, 1982), children who experienced the death of a close family member were more likely to show withdrawal and anxiety problems. Such specific information can be used in developing preventive interventions to minimize the negative effects of particular stressors.

Several later PMHP studies examined relationships between risk and resource factors and school adjustment. The first (Cowen, Lotyczewski, & Weissberg, 1984) focused on the interplay of risk and resources in shaping young children's adjustment. This study grew out of a larger PMHP test-norming project with more than 1,100 urban and suburban first–fourth graders. Teacher-completed CARS and HRIs were available for 123 PMHP children in this sample, plus 152 PMHP children not in the norming sample. Teachers provided background information for all children on 40 items in four domains: (a) physical and health characteristics, (b) recent stressful events, (c) special school services and activities, and (d) family background information. These 40 items were grouped as either risk (e.g., parental divorce) or resource (e.g., father employed) factors. The total risk and resource indices correlated −.57. High risk scores related to more serious adjustment problems and fewer competencies; conversely, high resource scores related to few problems and greater competence.

This study also compared three demographically matched groups with different risk–resource profiles: (a) low risk–high resources, (b) high risk–high resources, and (c) high risk–low resources. The low risk–high resource group significantly exceeded both other groups on all problem and competence dimensions. On several dimensions (e.g., good student), high risk–high resource children significantly exceeded high risk–low resource peers.

The further evidence of a link between stress and maladjustment in these findings underscores the theoretical appeal of developing interventions designed to reduce the negative effects of major life stressors. That the presence of competencies can help to mitigate negative effects of stress, points to the potential utility of competence training in preventive interventions for children who experience stress.

A related study (Cowen, Weissberg, & Guare, 1984) compared PMHP referred and matched nonreferred children on (a) current family status, (b) physical and health characteristics, (c) recent stressful events, and (d) concurrent school activities and special services. Nonreferred children, as anticipated, were significantly better adjusted than referred children on all adjustment measures. They also exceeded referred children on such physical characteristics as judged attractiveness, fine and gross motor coordination, and fewer illnesses. Conversely, referred children had experienced more recent stressors such as death or serious illness in the family, parent separation or divorce, economic difficulty, or new person in the home. They also had more referrals to special services including remedial education, nurse visits, formal disciplinary actions, and being sent to the principal, and more reported problems at home, including the absence of a father and lack of educational stimulation.

These findings documented a broad array of problems among referred children. Moreover, because the two groups were closely matched, study findings appear to identify life differences that co-occur with referral, rather than potential confound variables such as gender, grade, ethnicity, or place of residence. Most importantly, however, the findings again highlight the negative effects of life and family stressors on children's school adjustment.

Sterling, Cowen, Weissberg, Lotyczewski, and Boike (1985) compared the school adjustment of demographically matched samples of first–fourth grade children who had, or had not, experienced one or more stressful life events in the past 6 months. Teachers judged children who had experienced recent stressors to have significantly more problems and fewer competencies than those who did not. The study also compared the adjustment of children who had experienced one, two, or three or more stressors. As in prior studies (Rutter, Cox, Tupling, Berger, & Yule, 1975), children who experienced three or more stressors were judged to have significantly more serious adjustment problems than non- or less-stressed peers on all teacher-rated adjustment indicators. A related study (Lotyczewski, Cowen, & Weissberg, 1986) focused on a subset of health-related stressors (e.g., prolonged illness, hospitalization). Children who experienced health-related stressors had more serious school adjustment problems than those who did not and, as in the Sterling et al. (1985) study, the more stressors experienced, the more serious were the school adjustment problems.

Several parallel studies were conducted using children, rather than parents or teachers, as reporters of stress experienced. Brown and Cowen (1988) found that children who reported having experienced stressful events had more serious teacher- and self-rated school adjustment problems than demographically matched nonstressed peers. On the positive side, the presence of resources (e.g., support) for children who experienced stress moderated the negative effects of stress on adjustment (Brown & Cowen, 1989).

Two main conclusions from these studies were that life stress adversely affects children's school adjustment and these negative effects mount under the onslaught of multiple stressors. Other findings from these studies suggested that different stressors predisposed different types of problems and that the presence of competencies and resources (e.g., social support) moderated otherwise anticipatable adjustment decrements for children who experienced stress.

These findings had relevance for establishing goals and foci in individual PMHP interventions. But they were even more important, as we shall see in later chapters, for planning and conducting primary prevention programs designed to short-circuit the negative effects of major life stress on children.

SUMMARY

Research has been a major part of PMHP's fabric from Day 1. Research findings have contributed significantly to the project's evolution and growth. Even so, because research needs do not always mesh well with a program's immediate service pressures, doing research in PMHP has sometimes involved juggling acts that ended in compromise. Those realities led us once to describe PMHP research as being set in a "community cauldron" (Cowen, 1978; Cowen et al., 1974; Cowen & Gesten, 1980).

Since our prior PMHP book (Cowen, Trost, et al., 1975), impediments to research in the schools have grown and the challenges of doing research have increased. At one level, pressures for scarce teacher time have mounted along with the growing pressures to account academically. At a different level, the need to obtain informed consent for research is much more salient today (appropriately so) than it was 20 years ago. Although these changes are palpable and can usually be managed, they sometimes act to undermine the purity of a research design. Perhaps more serious is the tendency for many school people to polarize research and service, to the point where some believe that resources invested in research are, ipso facto, resources subtracted from service.

These are obstacles that the PMHP research operation has faced and, for the most part, surmounted. Leastwise, it is fair to say that the extent of PMHP's research effort has not diminished in the face of them. Several factors have made this research continuity possible, even in the face of contrary concerns that many school people have. The most important is that PMHP offers schools a meaningful, concrete service that, in several key respects, entails a close working partnership. The operation of such partnerships and the program's ability to meet important needs help to establish a climate of trust and respect, which, in turn, gets a "first foot in the door" for PMHP research team members.

A second factor that has facilitated PMHP research is that the project has always sought to conduct research on a partnership, rather than an "imposed," basis (Sarason, 1982). This means several things: Many PMHP research studies grow out of school-identified needs and they focus on matters of practical relevance to the schools. In parallel, outcomes from PMHP research studies are fed back promptly to schools in digestible forms, with an emphasis on how study findings can be used to modify program practices constructively.

For purposes of accountability, credibility, and future planning, PMHP has always relied heavily on its research base. The latter provides a framework needed both to judge program success and to identify areas for constructive program change. Hence, even after 38 years of relentless research activity, it is still timely to restate a resolve to continue empirical study of basic PMHP practices, and the effectiveness and utility of new program innovations.

PMHP could not have evolved as it did without a fully committed, persistent research component. In our view, a blend of basic (generative) and applied research is needed both to keep sound prevention programs such as PMHP "alive and well" and to provide information to shape the midcourse corrections needed to maintain and enhance their effectiveness.

II

NEWER DIRECTIONS

INTRODUCTION

To this point, the narrative has focused on aspects of PMHP's early development and the refinement of its core program elements. We first considered the social context in which PMHP emerged, with special emphasis on unresolved mental health and educational problems of the time. Embedded in that analysis was a formulation of PMHP's underlying rationale and how the project might address the problems identified.

On that base, we provided an X ray of PMHP's main defining elements and described its early evolution. The chapters that followed put more meat on those bare bones by providing in-depth information about how PMHP elements operate in current practice. Those chapters, cast in a practical, "how-to-do-it" framework, included most of the "name-rank-serial-number" information needed by aspiring implementers to start a school-based project of this type.

Through a process of continued tracking of program issues in PMHP's early history, strengths and weaknesses of the program inevitably came to our attention. Over time, we were able to identify issues that the original program had either failed to address or had not addressed satisfactorily. Cases in point included (a) the special problems that "acting-out" children presented in the playroom, (b) circumstances for seeing children in groups, and (c) problems growing out of life crises that children experienced. As such gaps were perceived, new PMHP service-expanding modules were conceptualized, piloted, and evaluated, with the goal of enhancing the program's reach and efficacy. And, as new workable approaches were found, they were incorporated into the project's mainstream. Those program-broadening steps were also described in the earlier chapters, as were PMHP's extensive research activities and accomplishments. Collectively then, the material presented in chapters 1–6 can be seen as "the basic PMHP story." With a summary and comments about future needs and directions, that story could stand as a complete, internally cohesive unit.

But, that's not how the "cookie crumbled" in real life. The more deeply immersed we got in PMHP, and the more field experience we accumulated with the program, the more we recognized the need to take major new program-expanding steps that could not have been anticipated during PMHP's early developmental period. These changing perceptions identified new domains in which to develop early school-based prevention programming.

As a result of this natural evolutionary process, the prevention agenda that began with the original PMHP has gotten more complex and diversified since the 1975 volume. This second major chrysalis is the main focus of Part 2. Put globally, the period from 1957, when PMHP first started, to the mid 1970s was an extended "proving and credentializing" period. Basic project mechanisms were carved out, field tested, set in place, and fine-tuned. The program was small and intimate, communication and feedback were good, and all facets of PMHP were accorded careful research scrutiny.

The accomplishments of that developmental period brought us slowly but surely to a new vision of prevention challenges. By then, we had come to believe that PMHP's innovative program model, though well short of perfection, offered a feasible, heuristic alternative for school mental health services that made good sense to schools and better matched their needs and realities than past traditional approaches. As that conclusion crystallized, our attention shifted to two new areas that, in H. G. Wells' "Things-to-Come" idiom, were to have major shaping impact on the project's future course.

The first grew out of the (Socratic) question of how PMHP's hard-come-by knowledge might best be shared with "interested others" in ways that could ultimately extend the program's preventive benefits to many thousands of young children in diverse school districts beyond Rochester, New York. This was the challenge of knowledge utilization, or dissemination. A second challenge noted in the last chapter of the prior PMHP volume (Cowen, Trost, et al., 1975) was to extend the PMHP's ontogenetically early secondary prevention model in more basic, primary prevention directions.

Despite the many gratifications of the early PMHP experience, and the reflex to "stand pat with a winner," by the early 1970s the abstract challenges of dissemination and primary prevention were already well formed in our minds. Since then, those activities have become increasingly important as investments in a broadened prevention portfolio and have attracted more of our energies, resources, and time deployments.

This gradual, but very real, change process is depicted schematically in Figure 1. Although the latter may look official and precise, it is little more than a crude attempt to depict how our operation has changed in recent years. Several of the figure's features bear highlighting. One thing it shows is that the basic PMHP program model has always been the single largest component in our total effort, and still is. In the absolute sense, that component has grown at least 20-fold in scope and magnitude since PMHP began. Until the mid 1970s it represented 100% of our operation. When the new dissemination and primary prevention thrusts first surfaced, around 1976, each was only a tiny "blip" in our total effort. Since then, however these two components have grown steadily, and more rapidly than the basic PMHP. At this time, we estimate, as Figure 1 shows, that roughly 50% of our total effort goes into basic PMHP and about 25% into each of the two newer strands.

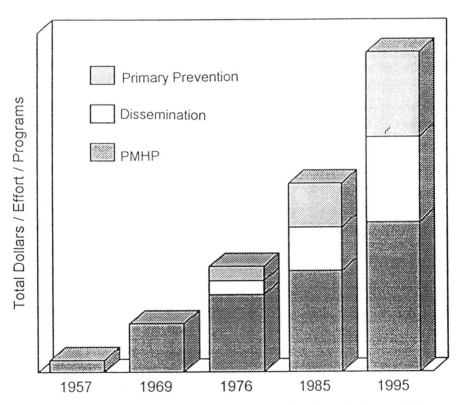

Figure 1. Primary Mental Health Project (PMHP), program dissemination, and primary prevention involvements, 1957–1995.

The point to stress is that dissemination and primary prevention activities have become major investments in our building's overall prevention portfolio. These investments account for much of the uniqueness of our development in the past two decades and, insofar as we can read tea leaves, they are likely to be key aspects of future program development.

The next five chapters write that part of the story. Chapter 7 describes PMHP's extensive dissemination efforts. Chapters 8–11 consider four prevention thrusts that have been or are still being developed, in the order in which they emerged: (a) social problem solving (1975); (b) the Children of Divorce Intervention Project (CODIP; 1982); (c) Study Buddy cooperative peer learning (1985); and (d) resilience in urban children experiencing major life stress (1987).

These new primary prevention probes are not part of the basic PMHP. They are conceptually kindred, albeit qualitatively different, developments that can be grafted onto an existing PMHP or stand free as program entities in their own right. Collectively, however, they have moved our total operation several significant steps toward before-the-fact, intentional, mass-oriented efforts to promote wellness in the many (Cowen, 1980). Vintage PMHP has not been forsaken in pursuing these new directions; rather the two approaches have developed side by side. Our long-time guiding deities of prevention, young children, and the schools remain entirely central to the objectives and operations of these approaches, though they embody important changes in program strategies, including their timing, targeting, and formats.

The shift in emphasis of these new programs toward being mass oriented and before the fact of maladjustment was justified abstractly, but marked up only fuzzily, at the end of the initial PMHP volume (Cowen, et al., 1975). Although we had done virtually nothing at that time to develop the approach, we recognized that it differed qualitatively from PMHP's defining ways; that is, using systematic early detection and screening procedures to identify children experiencing early school adjustment problems, or at risk for such problems, and taking active early steps to strengthen such adjustment.

We highlight this difference in strategies because it corresponds roughly to a point of demarcation between ontogenetically early secondary, and primary, prevention and as such, helps to clarify subtle conceptual distinctions between the original PMHP and the four newer primary prevention thrusts. Although the latter as a group differ importantly from ontogenetically early secondary prevention, they also differ from each other in their defining scope, content, and basic operating mechanisms. A second difference among the four is the amount of time and effort thus far invested in program development, conduct, and evaluation (e.g., a great deal for

CODIP, relatively little for interventions to enhance resilience among highly stressed urban children). And finally, the programs also differ in the extent to which they are truly mass-oriented, before-the-fact programs (i.e., social problem solving, Study Buddy) as opposed to developments for children at specific risk for maladjustment (i.e., CODIP and resilience).

7

DISSEMINATING THE PMHP
PROGRAM MODEL

A central challenge for a viable program model is whether its defining procedures and outcomes can be replicated across settings and over time. If that can happen, it greatly enhances the model's likelihood of surviving and of contributing to constructive social change. Dissemination is best undertaken after a program model has evolved to a point of clear internal satisfaction and its efficacy has been documented empirically. This, in any case, was the pathway that PMHP followed in pursuing systematic program dissemination.

PMHP's expansion, in 1969, from a pilot–experimental program in a single school to a program located in 11 urban and suburban schools in the local geographic area (chapter 3), was an unplanned precursor to larger scale dissemination, by bringing to our attention several realities that were to be relevant to such work. Examples of these stage-setting "blinding glimpses of the obvious" included the awarenesses that (a) individual schools differed greatly in needs, concrete problems faced, day-to-day operating styles, and decisions made about how to allocate resources; (b) program personnel, both professionals and nonprofessionals, differed in skills, interests, beliefs, preferred work styles, and cathexes to PMHP; and (c) depth, and to some extent effectiveness, of communication diminished as the overall program grew larger.

163

These realities hinted at several possible hazards that might be encountered in large-scale program dissemination, stemming from loss of control over the specific operations of many, and diverse, new program implementations. One near certainty was that a heretofore closely monitored, "pure" PMHP program would operate differently and with different degrees of effectiveness in different settings. It also seemed likely that idiosyncratic versions, or perhaps mutations, of the program would develop as necessary conditions for survival in different school environments.

Notwithstanding these reality constraints and warning signs, research findings confirmed that the program continued to operate effectively during PMHP's initial expansion period (i.e., 1969–1972). In parallel during that period, there was a growing concern, at the national level, about how successful, innovative, federally funded programs could be implemented systematically to serve constructive social change. Thus, convergence between PMHP's direct experience during its initial expansion period and an evolving focus on knowledge utilization at the national level, created conditions that were conducive to PMHP dissemination.

EARLY STEPS IN NATIONAL DISSEMINATION

Fund-granting agencies in the early 1970s were aware that monies allocated to aspiring new programs had to be viewed as *risk capital*, that is, that only a small number of funded projects would prove to be genuinely successful. That much they understood and accepted as part of the defining fabric of the funding game. What concerned them more was that the most likely end product, even for the relatively few successful pilot-demonstration projects, was a thick final report destined to do little more than yellow in the archives. This latter awareness was a key factor in catalyzing an emphasis by funding agencies on the application and utilization of hard come-by new knowledge. Moreover, granting agencies became more vocal in communicating this new emphasis to grantees, including PMHP, and to prospective applicants.

The message we heard, directly and indirectly, had both flattering and scary aspects. The flattering element was that objective outsiders perceived PMHP's accomplishments and findings to date to be important enough to warrant systematic dissemination. The scary part was that we were rank amateurs about what effective program dissemination entailed. There were, however, several things that we did know. The first was that change in established, rutted practice would not happen easily (Cowen, Davidson, & Gesten, 1980). A second was that only a small fraction (i.e., less than 10%) of innovative change in mental health was known to have come about through the printed word alone (Shore, 1972). Rather, opportunities for direct, personal exposure to program activities increased the likelihood both of undertaking, and succeeding in, implementation (Fairweather, 1972; Fairweather, Sanders, & Tornatzky, 1974). Hence, the strategy that shaped PMHP's early dissemination efforts, and continued over the years, was to provide firsthand, "involving" opportunities for relevant people to learn about the program, rather than relying primarily on passive approaches such as program descriptions or manuals.

Based on that strategy, we set into motion a three-tiered program to promote new PMHP program implementations. At its core was an intensive, week-long workshop for highly placed representatives from school districts that had evidenced preliminary interest in implementing PMHP. These orienting workshops sought to (a) elevate people's awarenesses of the PMHP approach, (b) describe all concrete program elements in detail, and (c) provide practical information, and address questions about how best to launch a school-based PMHP. In sum, the workshop's goal was to lay as solid as possible a foundation for starting a new program. We recognized, however, that helpful things beyond an initial workshop could be done to stimulate the start of new programs, that is, that the workshop was only a first step in an ongoing process that needed, as follow-up ingredients, open communication and concrete sources of help and support during a new program's emergent phase.

Accordingly, three other program-catalyzing options were offered to workshop alumni districts that moved toward implementation. These included (a) consultation to support a district's efforts during the program-planning period; (b) having a PMHP staff member do an on-site visit to the district to meet and talk with program personnel about salient start-up and program conduct issues; and (c) short-term (i.e., 2–5 days) internships in PMHP laboratory–training–demonstration schools to give personnel from new districts a chance to see the program in action and talk with PMHP professionals and child associates about project roles, activities, joys, and heartaches.

This same set of options was provided for four years, with continuing "fine-tunings" based on what we learned through experience. For example, we soon realized that the initial supersaturated (6 days, 10 hours a day) workshop experience we had offered was so intense that it violated virtually every law of human motivation. In our well-intended surge to provide prospective users with "everything they could possibly want to know about PMHP and more," we had repressed several bedrock motivational realities. Eventually, we realized that (a) it was not necessarily sinful to allow participants a few hours of fun and relaxation several times during a training week; and (b) net relevant learning from 50 hours of highly concentrated class time might well be less (and certainly was much less satisfying) than what might be achieved in half that time.

Early on then, we cut back on the intensity of the initial workshop format, a change further warranted by the difficulty that school personnel had in obtaining a week of release time in the middle of the busy school year. On the other hand, because we recognized the catalyzing value of an initial program-explicating contact, we have continued to provide some form of workshop experience, less intense than the original, in each of the past 22 years. (The current version of this workshop is described later in the chapter.) The point to stress is that a prospective implementer's first-hand involvement in a practically oriented (i.e., how-to-do-it) starter workshop has, in our experience, been a key factor in getting new programs started—qualified only by the realization that a more intense initial exposure is not necessarily better than a less intense one.

At the end of this initial 4-year dissemination effort in 1977, we conducted a survey to determine how many new PMHP programs had started and what their defining attributes were. Because this survey and its findings have been reported elsewhere (Cowen et al., 1980), only a brief summary is provided here. One key finding was that 30 or more new PMHP program implementations had developed and were still in operation at the end of this period. Each of these implementations reflected PMHP's defining structural features, with some modifications dictated by local needs. They were located in demographically diverse schools with a range of issues and problems.

Thus, PMHP's first "shot-in-the-dark" dissemination effort seemed to have met with at least moderate success and, although we were still far from expert in the labyrinthian, challenging dissemination "jungle," we (Cowen et al., 1980) were brazen enough to venture a few speculations about active ingredients in PMHP's dissemination success to that point. These included

> direct experiential involvement by consumers, an action orientation by disseminators, perseverance, providing continuous support for local change-agents, developing materials and experiences that simplify and demystify program conduct; a credibility base through research, and the program's adaptability to multiple realities. (p. 45)

NATIONAL CENTERS

Although we were pleased with the modest success of this early dissemination effort, it was clear that progress would be slow if we continued to follow this limited route. Hence, the question we came to ponder more and more was how to accelerate the pace of dissemination. Two realizations shaped the next steps: (a) that we ourselves could not serve forever as direct consultants and resource persons for large numbers of developing programs across the country, and (b) that there were some well-conceived and -conducted programs that faithfully reflected PMHP's guiding structural principles among the 30 or more new programs that had rooted. This awareness shaped PMHP's second major dissemination phase (1977–1981). During this period, four new Regional PMHP Dissemination Centers (RCs) were established, each located in a school district that, from the initial dissemination round, had gone on to establish its own viable program. Backed by inputs and support from the parent PMHP, each was thought to have the capability of taking a lead role in program dissemination within a specific geographic region. The four RCs were located in Ft. Worth, Texas (Southwest); Cincinnati, Ohio (Midwest); Huntington Beach/Ocean View, California (Far West); and Charlotte–Mecklenburg, North Carolina (Southeast).

PMHP maintained close contact with all four RCs during this period and provided them with continuing consultation and support. Efforts were also made to encourage communication and feedback among RCs so as to create a viable RC network. With coparticipation by PMHP staff members, each RC conducted at least one, annual regional training workshop. Collectively, the four RCs also conducted more than 125 site visits to school districts actually implementing or seeking to implement the program in their regions, and also provided short-term internships to more than 150 line personnel from those districts during this 4-year period.

A new implementation survey was conducted at the end of this second period (Cowen, Spinell, Wright, & Weissberg, 1983). This survey identified 87 implementing school districts, which collectively screened 33,000 children and provided intensive (child associate) helping services to 7,500 children annually. As in the prior survey, implementing districts were diverse in location, size, population demographics, and staffing patterns. Most new programs well embodied PMHP's basic structural principles.

This assessment of Round 2's accomplishments identified both plusses and new awareness of intrinsic limitations in the dissemination approach taken so far. The most obvious plus was that new program implementations had grown rapidly, with accompanying evidence of sound program operation under a range of conditions. Although that gratifying finding helped to underscore further several key elements in effective dissemination, experience during this period also made us aware of things that the RC's basic dissemination approach had not been able to accomplish and probably could not accomplish in the future.

Specifically, the best combined effort of the parent PMHP and the RCs had succeeded in rooting new programs only in a small number of favorable, socially sensitive school districts. We called this useful but limited outcome *demonstrational innovation*. On the flip side of the coin, the dissemination path that we had followed had not, and could not, bring about wholesale program dissemination that could serve millions of young children in thousands of school districts around the country. Achieving the latter important goal, it seemed to us, would require systematic, rather than just demonstrational, dissemination.

Thus, notwithstanding the important accomplishments of this second dissemination period, we concluded that neither PMHP alone, nor PMHP in concert with its established RC network, had the wherewithal (i.e., mandate, resources, requisite administrative structures, or follow-through mechanisms) needed for systematic program dissemination that held promise for widespread, positive social change. The nub of the matter was that a school district-based RC, no matter how outstanding its program, was neither a logical nor natural locus for spearheading such a development. Hence, the central challenge that our experience on this second round framed was how to advance more systematic dissemination of the PMHP model. Visibly shifting federal funding policies at that time, along with a small but important set of experiences in New York in the later phases of the second dissemination period, provided the cues needed to move the PMHP dissemination process to a next, more systematic level.

STATE-LEVEL DISSEMINATION

Changes that were unfolding at the end of the second dissemination period significantly shaped the nature of PMHP's dissemination activities for the following decade. Also around this time, the National Institute of Mental Health (NIMH), PMHP's major support source for the prior 15 years, began to shift support away from the local (Rochester area) PMHP toward application of knowledge gained from that experience to the national arena. This changing focus for federal support, resulted in several lean, indeed trying, years for the local PMHP and moved us to seek alternative funding sources for that aspect of our operation. As a result of that process, the State of New York (first, briefly, through the Department of Mental Hygiene and later through the State Education Department) became PMHP's main funding source. It has remained in that role ever since. State support, however, was provided not solely, or even primarily, for the local PMHP, but rather to promote systematic, within-state program dissemination and the development of new primary prevention program models.

Those aspects of the dissemination story are discussed later. The point to stress here is that the locus of responsibility for planning and funding in mental health, including school mental health, was shifting rapidly at that time from the federal to the state level (Swift, 1980; Tableman, 1980). This real and keenly felt change suggested that future systematic PMHP dissemination steps would require an informed partnership between those who were experts in the approach and duly empowered personnel from relevant state agencies. The latter reality, reinforced by our recent experiences in New York state, strongly shaped PMHP's dissemination objectives and activities for many years to come. Some details of this process, and its accomplishments during the 1980s, have been presented elsewhere (Cowen, Hightower, Johnson, Sarno, & Weissberg, 1989).

The wisdom of hindsight identifies four factors that nourished the development of a state dissemination program and accounted for much of its success. Two of those four factors reflect important realities of the time; the other two involve the specific dissemination mechanisms that we used. The two reality factors that helped to catalyze PMHP program dissemination were (a) a growing interest in the need for and appeal of prevention as opposed to repair approaches in the schools; and (b) an awareness, for reasons noted above, that the state was likely to be the "action" level for all new programming efforts for a long time to come. These conditions supported the good sense of the dissemination direction that we were planning. Moreover, at a practical level, we had by then cumulated enough knowledge and experience with PMHP in diverse settings to be able to be responsive to those developments.

Although the two preceding background conditions spoke favorably to the principle of targeting PMHP program dissemination to the state level, mechanisms and procedures were needed to catalyze that readiness and convert it to positive action. Two such expediting mechanisms developed. The first, reflecting the shift in interest noted above, was a small seed-grant that NIMH gave to PMHP, in the early 1980s, specifically to explore the feasibility of state-level program dissemination. The second was a detailed state-level dissemination manual that PMHP staff prepared to create a concrete framework within which state dissemination could proceed smoothly. These two developments are discussed next.

Convocation of State Leaders

By the time it became clear that federal support for education and mental health programs would be decentralized, the notion of state-level program dissemination was already prominent in our thinking. In that climate of shrinking federal support, we asked for, and were awarded, a small ($9,000) grant to be used specifically for a pilot project in state-level program dissemination. A first step was to contact 15 states known to have possible interest in dissemination, to call our evolving dissemination plan to their attention, and to assess their interest in participating. Specifically, we provided information packets describing how PMHP worked, and offered to state representatives opportunities to discuss dissemination options and how those options could best be adapted to a state's specific needs and resources. To that end, states were invited to apply for PMHP's next training workshop, a segment of which was to be devoted to state implementation steps. These applications required supporting letters from an appropriate state office expressing interest in state-level dissemination. We recognized that the specific office of relevance would vary from state to state, depending on a state's operating styles and local conditions.

The key steps and sequencing we envisioned for the state dissemination process were as follows:

1. elevate awareness of relevant state agencies about school-based early detection and prevention programming;
2. identify states with the strongest interests in and potential for systematic dissemination;
3. work out realistic plans for such programming in ways that best fit a state's needs, styles, resources, and follow-through mechanisms;
4. train state personnel in the "nitty-gritty" of program conduct;
5. help states to plan and conduct state-level training workshops;
6. help states to establish their own laboratory-demonstration program sites; and
7. provide the information, materials, guidelines, as well as modeling and consultation, needed to support the development of new programs.

Of the 15 states contacted, 12 expressed interest in participating in this initial state-training workshop, although the level of support from relevant state offices varied across states. In the end, limited budget and resources restricted us to nine awards to applicant states. Representatives from those states participated in PMHP's basic annual training workshop as well as in additional ad hoc sessions to provide specific information about state dissemination requirements and issues and address questions that state people had about that process. Although this form of state-level convocation was both ad hoc and short lived, this initial meeting was crucial in laying the groundwork for some comprehensive, enduring state dissemination steps that followed.

Guidelines for State Level Dissemination

The steps described above pertain to what we saw as being necessary preconditions for state program dissemination, that is, educating state personnel about PMHP and identifying states that seemed to have the best potential for program implementation. Subsequent dissemination steps had more of a "how-to-do-it" quality. To that end, we developed a detailed set of guidelines (i.e., a manual) for within-state PMHP program dissemination. The manual first presented a brief rationale for school-based early detection and prevention programs and indicated why such a development could best proceed at the state level. The following overview of the manual's scope and purposes was provided:

> This document is written for state agencies with some knowledge of PMHP's history, operating procedures and accomplishments, and interest in within-state program implementation. . . . Its main purpose is to provide a rough set of guidelines to facilitate within-state program dissemination. Those guidelines evolve from our own (sometimes hard come-by) experience over the years. They are presented as best "guesstimates" and, hopefully, constructive suggestions, not as immutables. We recognize that states have their own (sometimes idiosyncratic) organizational structures and ways of operating, which must necessarily shape specific approaches to dissemination.

The rest of the guidelines document sought to establish a clear, quasi-contractual base on which the ensuing dissemination process would rest. The document described things that PMHP staff would provide, cost-free, in support of a state's dissemination effort, and things that states were expected to bring to this development. Specifically, PMHP committed itself to provide

1. program descriptive information, evaluation reports, and clinical materials, including screening measures and guidelines for selecting and training child associates;
2. consultation visits, backed by mail and telephone support from PMHP staff members, to implementing states and visits by state personnel to school-based PMHP sites around issues of how best to set up and evaluate programs; PMHP staff was also available to states as consultants in writing program-enabling legislation and establishing procedures (e.g., requests for proposals) for soliciting and evaluating school-district proposals for new programs;
3. opportunities for line program personnel from implementing states to attend PMHP workshops and complete short-term internships in PMHP dissemination schools so as to have firsthand contact with the program;
4. help in conducting state training workshops describing the program's objectives and defining practices for personnel from districts considering implementation;
5. help in planning a model demonstration-training site for the state program;
6. training for school personnel in how to start and maintain quality control standards for new programs;
7. consultation on planning and actual coparticipation in site visits by state personnel to new programs and on planning

internship activities at the state's program demonstration site;

8. help for state leaders in setting up effective ways of monitoring and evaluating the effectiveness of new programs.

In summary, PMHP's main commitments were to provide the information packages, hands-on training experiences, and support needed to get state dissemination programs off to a sound start. We assumed, correctly, that the need for those inputs would be greatest in the early phases of dissemination and would diminish appreciably as state personnel became more familiar and comfortable with the new program activities. The ultimate goal, shared by all, was the autonomous conduct of effective state programs by state personnel.

The dissemination coin also had an important other side: commitments that states had to make with regard to their roles in the dissemination process. A state's first task was to learn enough about the requirements of a dissemination program to decide whether it wanted to undertake it and, if so, where it would best fit in a state's administrative hierarchy. We recognized that the latter decision had to be made at the state level, and that it would differ across states. After the preceding issues were resolved, the next recommended step was to appoint a state program coordinator. Beyond the leadership role, the coordinator was seen as having administrative responsibility for planning, expediting, and conducting all facets of the state program including training, establishing a program laboratory, developing site visit and internship options, maintaining communication with the parent PMHP, monitoring progress, and ensuring quality control. The coordinator was also to be responsible for assembling relevant program materials; establishing a program library for the implementing districts; maintaining a liaison with other state offices about the program's nature, progress, and needs; gathering and summarizing information about the program's actual functioning; and making such information available to relevant agencies and responsible administrators through periodic progress reports.

The state was also responsible for establishing a training–demonstration site in a district having a program that met high quality-control standards. The guidelines manual listed criteria for judging the effectiveness of field programs to help states select demonstration sites. These included amount and quality of available mental health professional time; care given to selecting, training, and supervising child associates; adequacy of program space, equipment, and materials; effective use of assignment, progress, and termination conference formats; the extent of a program's acceptance in the school; and the adequacy of communication patterns between program staff and other school personnel.

Recognizing the potential value that prior hands-on involvements of program personnel had for sound early program development, the guidelines recommended that states provide at least one annual training workshop, regular on-site consultation to new programs, and internship options at established training sites for personnel from districts starting new programs. Detailed explanations were provided about the purposes of each of these mechanisms, and how, concretely, they might best operate.

States were also responsible for tracking the program's overall progress, including information about numbers of implementing program sites; workshops conducted (e.g., format used, content covered, numbers and types of participants); and the use of site visit and internship options. They were also encouraged to collect information about defining features of district programs: main program elements, time available from professionals and child associates, number of children seen by grade and gender, and number of contacts provided. Such information, summed across all implementing districts, provided the data needed to sketch an overall program profile for a final annual report. Although school districts were not required to prepare a formal program evaluation study, states were encouraged to support districts interested in doing so. For the latter, PMHP offered support in setting up program evaluation studies and data analysis.

The guidelines document included a section explaining how relatively small amounts of seed money could help in the launching and rooting of new programs. For example, because school district budgets are often finalized long in advance, we realized that some aspiring new programs might not have the resources needed (e.g., travel and living costs) for their personnel to participate in training workshops or internships. The guidelines therefore noted that small early investments in such preparatory activities could help appreciably in launching a district's program. We also knew, from prior experience in New York, that some districts with strong interest in and some resources for implementing might be blocked from proceeding because they lacked money for one or more essential program ingredients (e.g., child associates, a part-time consultant–trainer). In that respect too, we had found that small, short-term (i.e., less than 3 years) seed grants could serve an important catalytic function in helping a new program to root soundly, demonstrate its efficacy, and establish a base for continuing support by the school district. At least that has been a typical scenario for many programs in New York. Although most started with small, short-term seed grants, about 70% of all currently active programs in the state are now self-funded and operating effectively on their own.

The preceding bilateral set of understandings established an overall framework within which PMHP's state dissemination program developed. The verb "developed" in the preceding sentence bears further comment, if only because ensuing events did not follow a predictable course. For one thing, formal grant support for the state dissemination program was short lived—a victim of the changing political climate of the early 1980s. For another, our initial hunches about which states would or would not establish enduring within-state dissemination programs proved to be less than Nostradamic.

Thus, time and reality together have shown that several states that emitted only weak early signals of dissemination promise, actually turned out to have mounted and maintained sound and enduring dissemination programs. By contrast, other states that seemed to be outstanding early prospects for dissemination, including several that got off to fast starts, faltered and eventually fell. The reasons for faltering were varied and usually beyond anyone's control. Examples included a critical program figure (e.g., state coordinator) strongly cathected to dissemination, with whom PMHP had worked closely for several years, who left to take another job and no one else in the system could or would pick up the program torch and carry it with conviction; fiscal crises or changes in the political leadership in a state resulted in the loss of program support dollars. Conversely, different conditions and reasons, some quite unanticipated (cf. below), led to the solid rooting and long-term stability of several very effective state dissemination programs.

Given diverse de facto realities (cf. above) that worked against 100% success in rooting state dissemination programs, this step has not truly realized the initially fantasized goal of full and systematic program dissemination. Even so, its accomplishments in places where it did take hold, bespeak greater potential for this development than might be inferred on the basis of the few states that have been involved. In effect, four states, New York, California, Washington, and Connecticut, formed a vanguard for formal, systematic, enduring state dissemination, followed by several other states that have taken noteworthy, but less systematic or extensive, strides in this direction.

The following sections focus individually on each of those four state developments: how they came about, their place in the state's administrative hierarchy, and the program's scope and service patterns. Then, we report less formal program dissemination activities in several other states. Finally, several conclusions are drawn about factors that have facilitated state-level dissemination and the implications of this development for the future.

NEW YORK

Given PMHP's roots and early history, it is understandable that the first, and for many years most extensive, state dissemination program unfolded in New York state. This program began in the late 1970s. By then, it had become clear that PMHP's future depended importantly on developing a strong state dissemination component. That reality fueled an application to the New York State Education Department (SED) to support PMHP's within-state dissemination. This request was approved and funded, and this source of support has continued ever since.

The New York state award has four main components, two of which relate directly, and two indirectly, to dissemination. First, the award provides support for the parent PMHP in Rochester to serve both as the program's leadership site and as the prime laboratory, training, and demonstration base for the entire state. A second component supports PMHP's development and evaluation of new primary prevention program modules. Examples of such programming, described in later chapters, include social problem solving (SPS), study buddy (peer teaching), and the Children of Divorce Intervention Program (CODIP). The other two award components relate even more directly to dissemination: conducting an annual PMHP training workshop for the state of New York, and providing newly implementing New York school districts with small seed grants to start a program.

PMHP has conducted a training workshop annually, since 1973. The workshop's main purpose is to bring the PMHP model and its ways of operating to the attention of potential New York implementing districts. Although the workshop has gone through natural evolutionary changes over the years, the most basic information it conveys (i.e., PMHP's goals and technologies) has been largely constant. The workshop is conducted in the fall, usually in late October or early November, as an intensive, 2-day learning experience built around how PMHP actually works. The workshop cycle starts with a mailing of announcement brochures (to all New York school districts) that include a brief description of PMHP and provide basic workshop information (e.g., dates, location, costs). Consonant with the state grant's prime dissemination thrust, districts with interest in, and potential for, implementation are invited to apply for workshop tuition scholarships by completing a form, included for that purpose, in the workshop announcement packet. In recent years, an average of 200 people, most from New York school districts, have attended these workshops.

The workshop's two most basic goals are to provide a clear picture of PMHP's "nuts and bolts" and the model's adaptability to diverse settings, and opportunities for participants to learn about the requisite steps for program implementation. The first morning of the workshop typically includes three main segments: (a) an in-depth overview of PMHP's essential components and operating ways; (b) a movie (built around one child) depicting, in softer more human ways, how basic project elements unfold in practice; and (c) a panel presentation by a PMHP action team consisting of individuals from a single school representing each major project role (e.g., principal, psychologist, social worker, teacher, senior associate, child associate). Each panelist first describes his or her role and how it interfaces with other project roles, after which the panel fields questions from the audience. This mechanism offers an important window for viewing all basic project elements.

The first afternoon and second morning are built around a series of 1½ hour topical seminars, each of which offers an in-depth view of a key project component identified but touched on only lightly in prior sessions. The content of these topical seminars has evolved over the years. Whereas initially attendees could take only two topical seminars out of a total of four or five offered, they can now take four seminars from a rotating smorgasbord of 12–15 offered each year. Several topical seminars, covering core project procedures such as early detection and screening, professional roles and consultation, and selection and training of child associates, are offered—and heavily attended—in at least three different time slots per workshop. Others, less basic but nevertheless of substantial interest (e.g., PMHP research, children of divorce, resilience, supervision), are offered in one or two slots per workshop. Still other more specialized topics (e.g., bibliotherapy) are offered only occasionally.

A plenary session, in late morning of Day 2, seeks to provide a cohesive program summary and to sketch out subsequent steps for districts to take in the implementation process. A final, optional afternoon session on Day 2 offers in-depth (2½ hour) seminars on a specific project component (e.g., children's play, intervention techniques with acting-out children).

During the workshop, dialogue among participants from different districts, and between participants and PMHP staff members, is encouraged. Such exchanges provide useful information for individuals, and help to establish meaningful cross-fertilization, support, and communication lines for districts starting new programs. Relatedly, workshops have benefited from the presence, and representation on the program, of personnel from other implementing groups. Thus, the workshop mechanism has provided opportunities for constructive exchange of ideas and experiences among people with kindred interests and program backgrounds.

People from implementing New York programs are often workshop repeaters who return to learn about new program developments, solidify contacts with colleagues from other programs, and take in seminars they missed earlier. Indeed, the widespread nature of this "recidivism" syndrome led to one change in workshop format, that is, conducting parallel sessions the first morning. Whereas first-time participants attend the basic PMHP orientation described above, the parallel sessions are attended by professionals and child associates from implementing districts who have attended prior workshops. Led by senior PMHP staff members, these sessions deal specifically with program issues of relevance to the respective repeater groups (e.g., exchange of information and discussion among program peers from different settings of things that are working well or presenting problems in their respective programs). These parallel sessions have been valuable both for the information they provide and the help and support they offer to those in comparable program roles who have lived with and well understand the concrete program issues brought up for discussion.

Another key component of the SED award, from the start, is the seed money it offers for new programs. These awards, which are small (less than $5,000/year) and require matching district dollars, have helped to get district programs off the ground and moving in wholesome directions. For some districts, such support is crucial during the start-up period when a program must establish its viability to gain programmatic and fiscal support from the host district.

Most new programs in the state have evolved following initial participation in the annual PMHP training workshop. Districts that go on to request new program start-up monies, complete an application that calls for (a) background information about the district and its school population, and district resources and needs; (b) a plan describing how the proposed program will operate; and (c) a budget request. All such requests are reviewed by a PMHP staff team, headed by the New York State program coordinator. Insofar as a given year's program funds permit, seed grants are awarded to meritorious applicant districts.

A senior PMHP staff member is assigned to each new district as a program consultant. The consultant's main goals are to support the program's sound early development and maximize its quality by (a) providing relevant information and materials, (b) being available as a resource person via mail or telephone, (c) conducting on-site visits; and (d) providing feedback and suggestions on ways to strengthen the program.

The New York state dissemination program started small. In its first years, only five (geographically and sociodemographically diverse) districts were part of it. Things worked well, and relatively simply, during that period. Consumer satisfaction was high. Both word-of-mouth from active programs and the growth of the program's visibility through the workshop mechanism heightened interest in PMHP around the state and quickly escalated the number of new program starts. Several other developments also helped to catalyze this process. Thus in 1987, PMHP was validated as an exemplary program through the New York Transfer for Success program, a state-level analog of the National Diffusion Network (NDN). Shortly thereafter, the New York State Division of Substance Abuse provided funds for 15 new district programs, in exploring the possibility that effective early intervention can help to avert later substance abuse problems. For similar reasons, other new monies came to the statewide program through New York's Youth-at-Risk Initiative.

Thus, by the mid-80s, the New York PMHP dissemination program was growing considerably in scope and services provided. As this process unfolded, it became clear that, although the basic dissemination principles being followed were sound, the mechanisms and resources needed to extend the application of these principles from an initial five to potentially hundreds of implementing districts did not exist. This obliged us to consider other, more realistic ways of advancing effective statewide dissemination.

The solution we opted for, and time has shown it to be a good one, was to establish a state network of Regional PMHP Dissemination Centers (RCs). Beyond the goal of having a geographically representative RC network, the two main criteria used to select RCs were the presence of an effective PMHP program in the district and the availability of competent, experienced program personnel with the skills and commitment needed to carry out dissemination activities. It was anticipated that each RC would have prime responsibility for rooting and supporting the activities of new programs within an approximate 50-mile radius. Within such circumscribed geographic regions, RCs were expected to replicate the parent PMHP's activities (i.e., provide relevant program information and materials as well as training, site visit, and internship opportunities, and maintain quality-control standards for implementing districts).

As the RC development unfolded, the parent PMHP began to move away from a "do-it-all" operation with all implementing districts, toward meta-training and consultation with personnel from a limited number of other trainer districts (i.e., RCs). This role shift was intended both to accelerate the pace of program dissemination and to enable the parent program to use more of its energies and resources to pilot useful new ways of service delivery for the state. One example was the establishment of several effective rural consortia, made up of 6–7 districts that shared resources for associate training, supervision, and consultation (Farie et al., 1986). This modus operandi both expands the reach of services in those districts and provides sources of interchange and stimulation that serve as antidotes to the discouragement and burnout that have long plagued personnel in isolated systems with few resources. A second important development was to root PMHP in some truly high-risk areas of New York City, where the program is now working effectively. Each of these new program steps also became grist for the mill of RC dissemination activities.

The state RC development, like most other new PMHP "wrinkles," started modestly in the mid 1980s, with an emphasis on quality rather than quantity. Initially, there were only two such centers: Herkimer, for upstate, and Island Park, outside of New York City, for downstate. Early effectiveness indicators for these centers were positive both from the standpoint of direct feedback from the centers and their implementing districts and, importantly, from the rapid growth in new PMHPs in their regions. This positive initial experience paved the way for developing a larger network of geographically and sociodemographically diverse RCs around the state. Currently, there are seven RCs—the two mentioned above plus five established later: Hyde Park (downstate), North Tonawanda (western New

York), New York City, Plattsburgh (rural northeast New York), and Binghamton (central New York).

A close, effective, working relationship involving PMHP and state RCs has developed over the years. A PMHP staff member serves as program consultant to each RC and stays in regular telephone and mail contact with the RC's director. Because communication at that level has been good, there is a clear awareness all around of each RC's current issues, needs, and accomplishments. The program consultant also visits the RC at least once a year, thereby getting to know RC program personnel better over time and benefiting from firsthand observation of a program's flavor and ambiance.

RC personnel often attend, and participate actively in, PMHP's annual workshop. Also, three 2-day meetings involving parent PMHP staff members and RC personnel are held annually. Agendas for these meetings are full and diverse. Exchange of information among RC people provides a good snapshot, at any point in time, of procedures that are working well or not so well. Because participants at these meetings overlap in goals, activities, and interests, they are attuned to similar issues and speak a similar language. Hence, support, useful information, and advice are all readily shared.

At these meetings, PMHP staff members also present information on new program developments and research findings, and their implications. Common program problems are discussed in the context of searching for new and better ways to conduct the program and importantly, visions about new directions for PMHP to explore evolve from these discussions. Sometimes, this happens because RC personnel have taken a venturesome new program step (e.g., increasing parent involvements in PMHP) with encouraging early returns. Such exchanges of information stimulate exploration of ways to develop budding initiatives more systematically and when these explorations identify useful new ways, how best to infuse that information into the dissemination mainstream.

Having worked together for some time, the RC team is now well integrated and closely attuned to PMHP's workings and intricacies. Members know each other well, respect each other's wisdom and experience, and share a strong commitment to the project's goals and ways of operating. Otherwise put, the state RC group functions as a closely knit family, with the shared goal of promoting preventively oriented, school-based programs for young children.

Although the New York RC thrust has, from the start, seemed sensible and effective, more palpable outcome data (e.g., number of new programs started, the combined service impact of those programs) is needed to confirm those impressions. One very relevant fact is that state district implementations grew rapidly, during a period in which overall program budget increments were small, in ways that paralleled the growth of the

RC initiative. Information about program scope comes to PMHP twice a year, via midyear and end-of-year utilization of services reports that implementing districts and RCs submit. These, in turn, are integrated into semiannual reports of the program's operation and accomplishments that PMHP submits to the SED.

Recent program information for New York identified 134 PMHP implementing school districts. Of those, 48 were receiving short-term seed grants from the state; the remaining 86 (most districts that at one time had seed money support) were now functioning with school district dollars or other specific program support awards.

Semiannual, utilization of service reports are required only for currently funded districts. Although we also ask for and welcome comparable data from nonfunded districts, their response is optional. In fact, some nonfunded districts have not provided such information (in our most recent survey, 50 of 86 nonfunded districts provided utilization information). Given that constraint, our overall service figures for the state program involve some modest guesswork. On the basis of extrapolations of information obtained from reporting districts, plus some firsthand (albeit slightly "rough-around-the-edges") knowledge we have about the scope of nonreporting programs, we estimate the following profile to exist for the overall state program:

1. PMHP programs are now situated in roughly 300 schools in 134 New York school districts;
2. these schools, collectively, screen many tens of thousands of children annually; and
3. they provide extensive, early preventively oriented helping contacts, averaging 20 or more contacts per child, for roughly 7,000 young New York school children of whom more than 90% are primary graders (kindergarten–third grade).

Given evidence testifying to the program's efficacy, these figures reflect a major expansion of early effective school-based preventive services for young children. Additionally, the New York program has actively pioneered new school-based prevention options and has made the fruits of such efforts available to implementing districts around the state and elsewhere.

CALIFORNIA

California's version of PMHP, called the Primary Intervention Program (PIP), was among the first state dissemination programs. PIP has been in continuous operation since 1982, with major expansion in the past few years. The program's roots go back to 1980 when, following several prior PMHP contacts with school personnel in California, PMHP received a request from a state legislator with long-standing interest in mental health issues (the Hon. Thomas Bates of Alameda County), to attend PMHP's annual workshop. Assemblyman Bates stayed in Rochester for several days after the workshop to meet with PMHP staff members to discuss procedures, strategies, and timetables by which program implementation in California might proceed best and most realistically.

When he returned to California, Assemblyman Bates explored the interest of several state agencies in the planned dissemination program. He also set up a team to formulate PMHP program-enabling legislation in California. As part of this process, PMHP staff members (a) provided extensive telephone and mail consultation to relevant state personnel, while basic program defining mechanisms were being articulated and requirements for district level programs were being clarified; and (b) conducted an in-depth workshop (spring 1981) to introduce PMHP to state administrators and school district personnel in California. Following these preparatory steps, a legislative act (AB 1639) was written to establish a 3-year PIP demonstration project under the administrative aegis of the California Department of Mental Health (CDMH), the state agency designated to sponsor and support this development. The bill, with a provision to allocate $250,000 annually to support the dissemination effort, was passed by the legislature and signed by the Governor in September 1981.

After that key step was accomplished, CDMH and PMHP staff members worked together closely to establish specific mechanisms and procedures by which AB 1639 would operate. This entailed developing a set of program-defining guidelines, and criteria for their use, and creating formal application procedures and review frameworks to guide the allocation of program awards.

To catalyze sound program start-ups, PMHP staff conducted several additional workshops in California before the actual programs got underway. The first (3/82), was an informational meeting for aspiring applicant districts; the second (8/82), after initial grant award decisions had been made, was an in-depth training seminar for personnel from newly funded programs. Also, four CDMH staff members attended PMHP's fall 1982 training workshop.

Officially, PIP began in California schools in September 1982. At that time, the program was legally authorized only for a 3-year pilot-demonstration period. PIP's initial success and seeming good sense provided a base for steps designed to stabilize and broaden the program's base. With those objectives in mind, follow-up legislation in 1983 intended to ensure the program's continuity and growth, allocated to PIP monies accruing to the state from the sale of property confiscated in the context of prosecutions for controlled substance abuse (e.g., a yacht seized in a "drug bust"). A subsequent legislative act, in 1985, established PIP as a permanent program in California.

Although California's program closely resembles PMHP philosophically, goal-wise, and in its basic operating procedures, it is not a clone. To the contrary, it clearly has features that reflect California's special needs and pond-ecology. Thus, all California programs supported by CDMH must include a de facto working partnership between a county mental health center and a school district. Relatedly, direct state support for a program is limited to 50% of its total costs, with the remainder to come from the two local program-related entities. Another difference is that PIP placed limitations on its core program services. The program was set up with the expectancy that relatively short-term (12–15 sessions) preventively oriented services would be provided for at-risk but not already seriously disturbed children. Over the years, PIP has adhered to that guideline, with some flexibility in cases in which small time extensions seemed compellingly to be warranted. Given that 12–15 sessions can readily be completed in one semester, that guideline enabled PIP programs to reallocate resources to a second wave of children in Semester 2.

The CDMH monitors PIP's implementations across the state. It provides monies for a full-time state program coordinator and for training and consultation services at the state, regional, and local levels. These services include visits to districts by the coordinator to review a program's status, provide technical consultation on program procedures, and provide information, as needed, about funding sources and public relations strategies. Statewide training workshops are offered at least once a year. Periodic regional meetings are also held to enable program personnel to exchange information, develop support mechanisms and other forms of networking activities, and address program issues of common interest. As the state program has expanded, effective district programs have come more to be used as visitation sites for new, and about-to-start, districts. Also, experienced program personnel from effective sites have been used (as in New York state) as regional consultants who provide start-up, maintenance, and quality-control inputs to new programs.

By 1987, PIP was active in 88 schools in 50 California school districts in a cross section of California communities (Cowen et al., 1989). Roughly two thirds of these programs were state funded; the rest were locally funded. Child associates, called Special Friends in most California districts, were seeing an average of 12 children in an 18-hour work week. The program's local community (CDMH) professional provided weekly consultation. All programs, by law, had to be integrated with both other school programs and the continuum of local mental health services. District awards averaged $22,000, much more than in New York. Programs were providing to 3,800 referred children (90% primary graders) an average of 12–15 contacts each.

An early program evaluation study, based on 2,700 children from 33 districts, showed PIP to be working well.

Several recent developments have accelerated the pace of California's dissemination program. One was the commissioning by the CDMH and completion by the Southwest Regional Educational Laboratory (SWRL), of a comprehensive *Primary Intervention Program: Program Development Manual* (Thomas & Brock, 1987), later revised and updated (Johnson et al., 1992). This major undertaking began with a visit to Rochester by the SWRL writing team to assemble sets of basic PMHP materials, test forms, and procedure manuals and to talk with PMHP staff members about all aspects of the program. The SWRL team also met with CDMH staff members and staff in active programs. From this process, an initial draft of a program articulating manual ("how-to-do-it kit") evolved and, after extensive feedback from PMHP staff and administrative and school personnel in California, a final version was readied for distribution in fall 1987. This 250-page manual included major units overviewing the project's goals and rationale, history, modus operandi, and cost estimates, and provided detailed, concrete information about recruitment of program personnel, screening and identification of program children, basic program services, training and supervision of child associates, program evaluation, and public relations and funding.

The PIP manual is a practical, useful compilation of information on how to start and conduct a program of this type. It is well written, clear, to the point, and down to earth. All basic project procedures are described in detail. Copies of essential project measures and instruments are reproduced and their uses clearly described. An appendix includes some 40 transparencies ready to be used "as is" in training sessions and workshops. The availability of this manual and several informative program videotapes have facilitated the start of new programs in California. Such materials help to demystify the program's launching process.

Another development also facilitated major recent program growth in California. Prompted by a commitment to the goal of prevention of school maladaptation in children, Governor Wilson recommended a quantum expansion of PIP's state budget, in 1991. The legislature approved this recommendation and major program expansion (e.g., starting programs with parent components) has taken place in the past few years. This adolescent growth spurt in California's program has complicated the state coordinator's monitoring, training, and supervisory responsibilities and made even more important the role and inputs of regional consultants (i.e., experienced professionals from successful district programs).

A census following these major changes (1993–1994) revealed that PIP programs were operating in about 600 schools in 180 California school districts, providing in-depth services to about 24,000 primary grade children annually. This geometric program expansion means that California surpassed New York in total program budget ($11 million vs. $810,000) and in program reach (24,000 vs. 7,000 children seen annually). During the period between 1989 and 1993, comprehensive annual statewide program evaluation studies (see chapter 6, this volume), yielded consistently positive outcome findings both at the school district and state levels.

PIP's strengths, beyond its prime school-based preventive focus, include its strong emphases on training, frequent site visits, firsthand contacts with implementing programs, use of regional consultants, and quality control. The program has also built solid school–community bridges and has forged links among school district programs and between such programs and relevant state administrative and legislative offices.

WASHINGTON

Although Washington State's PMHP dissemination program overlaps with those of other states in several key ways, it too has its own special pond-ecology. The Washington program is a descendant of a prior federally funded Child Development Center (CDC) program that operated in Seattle from 1972 to 1980, when its federal funding ended. At that time, CDC board members began to explore alternative program options and funding sources. PMHP was one such option. In the context of that exploration, representatives from Washington participated in PMHP's 1982 state training workshop (Cowen et al., 1989). That involvement sharpened interest in a state dissemination program and led to a series of postworkshop explorations of the feasibility of such a program, involving personnel from Washington's Mental Health Department's (MHD) Education and Children's Services divisions. These discussions established an optimal profile for a state dissemination program in Washington (a program that should be centrally based within the MHD and started, as in California, by legislation).

Guided by these premises, CDC's former president, who later became the first state program coordinator, brought the program model to the attention of several influential legislators and won their support for establishing a state dissemination program. A bill modeled after that of California was written and passed in 1983 with special proviso language for school-based early intervention programs. The bill required that school districts provide in-kind funds matching at least 43% of any state award; authorized a biennial program budget of $436,000; and created a program oversight committee with representatives from public instruction, local school districts, and community mental health programs. After this bill was passed, a formal program announcement and a request for proposals were prepared with joint inputs from PMHP and relevant state officials. As had been done in California, PMHP staff took part in several preparatory workshops to clarify program elements and provide technical assistance to school districts in preparing applications for program support.

PMHP also participated in the review of district applications for an initial 2-year program grant. Of the 19 applications submitted, 10 were approved for funding in 1984. The MHD developed a specific program contract with each district delineating guidelines about the program's scope and its professional and nonprofessional staffing patterns, and describing the extent and types of preventive services that programs should provide for children and parents. All approved projects, as in California, required active collaboration between a school district and the community mental health center. Each award district was also required to form an advocacy board consisting of school and mental health agency representatives, as well as parents.

All 10 of the originally funded programs continued through a second biennium. A 50% increase in program funds that included contributions from other state agencies (e.g., Children's and Family Services) made it possible for five new programs to start at that time. Unlike the New York and California programs, which see relatively few (5%) children in groups, Washington's programs see many children in groups; however, they also provide individual contacts, crisis intervention, and consultation with teachers. Evaluations of the Washington program, noted in chapter 6; have confirmed its efficacy. Other state agencies have come to view this school-based program as an important preventive service; they have worked in close collaboration with it including the provision of additional program funds.

A recently completed program census for Washington revealed that the program was located in 53 elementary schools in 34 school districts (32 state funded) during the 1993–1994 school year. Supported by an annual state budget of $900,000, the program brought in-depth, preventively oriented helping services to about 2,500 children during that school year.

CONNECTICUT

Connecticut's dissemination program emerged via another route. By sheer coincidence, PMHP's then-Research Coordinator Roger Weissberg left in 1982 to join the psychology faculty at Yale University. Shortly thereafter, he began discussions with the Connecticut State Department of Education (C-SDE) about the evolving dissemination thrust. As a result, several C-SDE people attended PMHP's 1982 state training workshop. This involvement stimulated planning for a state program and, by spring 1983, several launching steps had been taken in that direction. Specifically, a state program coordinator was appointed; plans were completed for conducting a consciousness-elevating state workshop jointly with PMHP staff;

monies were allocated to permit several pilot PMHPs to begin in fall 1983; and explorations were started with other state agencies (e.g., Children and Youth Services, Justice Division) to obtain additional program support dollars.

An initial statewide PMHP workshop, attended by representatives from 100 Connecticut school districts, was held in Hartford in June 1983. By that time, with the help of small grants from several other state offices (cf. above), funds had been located to start four school district pilot projects. This important program launching step was followed by a legislative act in 1984 allocating $45,000 to support the development of additional PMHP projects in Connecticut. Similar to decisions made by other states, the Connecticut legislation limited these awards to 3 years and required that local school districts provide at least 25% in matching program dollars. By 1987–1988, program support grew to $70,000—enough to support 10 district implementations. As of then, four other districts were conducting programs with their own funds.

Several whole or part evaluations of Connecticut's program have been conducted. An early study with 250 PMHP-seen children from eight implementing school districts showed that these youngsters had improved significantly in social skills, interpersonal relationships, and educational performance. They also had fewer special education placements, discipline contacts, retentions in grade, and absences (Weissberg, Pike, & Bersoff, 1986). Parents reported that PMHP-seen children improved in self-confidence, school attitudes, and academic and social functioning. A later, related study, based on New Haven's PMHP (Krauss & Weissberg, 1988), showed that PMHP-seen children improved significantly on adjustment ratings made by teachers, school mental health professionals, and child associates and were less likely than comparison children to have been retained, referred to the principal for disciplinary action, or referred to special education.

By 1987, the state program was operating in 23 school buildings in 14 implementing districts, providing 9,000 helping contacts for about 500 referred children (95% primary graders). The program has since continued to grow in budget, scope, and services; in the 1993–1994 school year, 49 elementary schools in 23 school districts (21 state funded) were implementing PMHP and the C-SED's program support budget had grown to approximately $300,000. Collectively, these 23 implementing districts brought intensive, preventively oriented helping services to roughly 1,100 children.

OTHER STATES

The preceding account covers four states in which dissemination proceeded formally, under conditions of strong support and close monitoring.

Although that account reflects the largest element in PMHP's overall state dissemination activities, it does not tell the whole story. For reasons not fully clear, a modest amount of state dissemination activity has unfolded somewhat independently of the formal dissemination process described earlier. It is known, for example, that *multiple* (defined as five or more school districts) PMHP programs have been established, at one time or another, in the states of Arizona, Hawaii, and New Jersey, as well as in the province of Ontario in Canada. Collectively, these implementations add up to more than 50 school districts. Moreover, some 12–15 other states (e.g., Delaware, Oregon, Oklahoma, Pennsylvania) and foreign countries (e.g., Israel, Australia) are known to have established one, two, or three district program implementations.

One can only guess as to how and why these additional implementations have come about. For states or countries with only a few implementations, the combination of attending a PMHP workshop plus modest follow-up contact, catalyzed by the efforts of a single, committed individual, may explain how a given implementation scenario unfolded as it did. By contrast, in states in which quasi-systematic sets of implementations developed without the extensive formal processes of the "big four" states, something more was involved than just participating in an initial PMHP workshop. In those cases, short of the state's being able to commit fully to dissemination, an arrangement for a smaller, less formal, dissemination package was worked out involving such activities as PMHP staff members doing an on-site visit or conducting a mini-workshop in the state, or visits by state personnel to PMHP. Although program-facilitating activities of that type were less frequent or formal than they were in the big four states, they were nevertheless supported to some extent by communication lines that were kept open and by occasional consultation.

DISSEMINATION: OVERVIEW OF OUTCOMES

This review highlights the fact that although the state-led PMHP dissemination thrust had only limited funds and resources, it was most successful in states that followed a formal implementation process. Paced by New York, California, Washington, and Connecticut, the big four states in which dissemination proceeded both formally and continuously, but also enhanced by several other states with limited dissemination, PMHP programs are now believed to be located in about 1,500 schools in more than 700 school districts around the world. Collectively, these schools screen 150,000 or more primary-grade school children and provide early-intensive, preventively oriented helping services to at least 50,000 youngsters, annually. Program outcome data, coming from many diverse schools within this larger framework, provide substantial evidence of program efficacy as assessed by short- and long-term reductions in school problem behaviors and increases in socioemotional, behavioral, and academic competencies that enable children to profit more from the school experience.

There have been differences in how these dissemination programs unfolded and operated in the big four states. They are, for example, housed in different agencies in their state hierarchies—two in state education departments (New York and Connecticut) and two in state departments of mental health (California and Washington). Whereas two programs (New York and Connecticut) grew out of a special collaborative arrangement between an academic department and a state agency, the mandates of the other two (California and Washington) reflect a different common element—the requirement that programs include major, de facto inputs from both school district and community mental health center personnel. Whereas several programs function entirely within a single state agency, several others (Connecticut and Washington) have used and blended resources that cross agency lines. States have also largely gone their own ways with respect to the nature of their program articulating announcements and RFPs; funding procedures for applicant districts including their review processes; size and duration of program awards; and specific procedures used for training, program monitoring, and program evaluation. Although these differences understandably reflect the states' operating styles and resources, they also serve as reminders that there is no single, obligatory route by which all state dissemination programs must proceed. Otherwise put, the real variations in such program structures that we have seen suggest that, given interest and commitment, state dissemination can proceed effectively within a range of different administrative and procedural frameworks.

The preceding de facto differences in state programs notwithstanding, there are important common features as well. All participating states have sought to ensure fidelity of program implementation by providing detailed program-descriptive materials and training, reviewing program descriptions carefully when funding proposals are submitted, and conducting on-site visits to observe implementing programs in action and be sure that they reflect high standards.

Several structural features have also facilitated state dissemination. One, for sure, is the availability and effective use of detailed guidelines describing basic program steps and procedures. Such information is vital for program staff and helps immeasurably to demystify the implementation process. California's detailed program manual (Johnson et al., 1992) is a very useful codification of program procedures. Other important ingredients in effective state dissemination include the strong initial interest and commitment of a state coordinator, continuity of people in key program roles, and the availability of sound outcome data testifying to the program's efficacy.

One difference between states that have disseminated successfully and initially promising others that have not is that the former had basic program mechanisms reasonably in place before PMHP's federal dissemination grant ended. Given that kind of start, plus the additional good fortune of continuity of key program personnel, those states were able to maintain close contact with PMHP and move ahead on shared involvements in key program-expediting activities (e.g., training workshops, site visits). Otherwise put, momentum for those states was well established, essential program mechanisms were in place, and the necessary "skids" for program activities had been effectively greased. Other seemingly promising states that did not reach that level of emergence early on were at best able to proceed with dissemination in informal, scope-limited ways. Among those that did reach that early level, the most important reason for a program to falter was the loss of a key senior program figure.

Although the state program dissemination thrust has not been free of frustrations and disappointments, it has also logged some noteworthy successes and peak experiences. Indeed, there have been enough of the latter to justify escalating the state dissemination mode for PMHP. More intensive effort at that level seems to be one sensible path to follow in seeking to broaden applications of PMHP's early detection–prevention model. The hope and promise of such extension, beyond the constructive contrast that it offers to established school mental health approaches, is that it can significantly enrich the school and later life experiences of many young children at risk.

8

THE SOCIAL PROBLEM-SOLVING PROGRAM

Today, interpersonal or social problem-solving training for young children is a widely recognized and implemented primary prevention approach. Its proximal goals are to strengthen children's interpersonal problem-solving skills and reduce their use of inappropriate and ineffective strategies. A more basic distal goal is to enhance children's long-term adjustment. With the latter as the prospective "pot-of-gold at the end of the rainbow," it is not surprising that many social problem-solving (SPS) curricula have been developed and used in school settings. Indeed, the impact that the SPS development has had is reflected in the fact that many current, broad, school-based competence enhancement training programs, such as social competence training, drug and substance abuse prevention, conflict resolution, and delinquency prevention, include major subunits designed to teach SPS skills.

This approach, however, did not have widespread recognition or acceptance when we started to explore SPS programming options. Such programming, exemplified in the groundbreaking work of the Hahnemann group (Spivack, Platt, & Shure, 1976; Spivack & Shure, 1974) and other pioneering groups (e.g., Allen, Chinsky, Larcen, Lochman, & Selinger, 1976) was just getting under way then. Thinking back to that period, we can still identify some experiential, conceptual, and empirical inputs that contributed to our evolving views of the impact of interpersonal interactions on young children's social and emotional development and, with that, an appreciation of the potential value of early SPS training.

Several factors that led us initially to the SPS development were rooted in observations and clinical experiences both within PMHP and in the broader school context. These experiences highlighted the important shaping role that interpersonal problem-solving skills, or deficits in them, played in young children's adjustment. Two common, primary grade classroom scenarios can be used to illustrate the importance of early social skill development. The first involves children who are isolated from peers because they lack the concrete skills needed to engage and interact productively with their classmates. A second involves children whose acting-out or aggressive behaviors raise concern, if not fear, in other children and adults.

Socially inept children evidencing clear early signs of potential future difficulties in interpersonal relationships may be found in all schools. Such youngsters not only have problems of school adaptation that hurt them and spill over detrimentally to peers in the here and now, but they are children whose longer term future potential may remain unfulfilled. Left unattended, some early maladaptive social styles become more refractory over time and act to crystallize (adversely) children's identity in the peer group and with adults close to them (e.g., parents, teachers). These socially inept children tend increasingly to be typecast and, as a result, their range of social interactive behaviors, both displayed and expected, narrows maladaptively. SPS programs can help such youngsters to avert this downward spiral by providing a set of adaptive interpersonal skills and strategies that can be used to prevent maladaptive interpersonal styles from becoming prematurely fixed and change resistant.

The preceding school-based observations can be viewed in PMHP's more specific context. In actuality, many PMHP-referred children are youngsters with classroom scenarios much like the hypothetical ones described. When teachers see such difficulties as serious enough to restrict the child's academic progress or be disruptive to the class (and teachers vary in their perceptions of thresholds for such outcomes), referral to PMHP ensues. Thus, one aspect of the problem configuration that many children presented when referred to PMHP was a disturbance in interpersonal relationships, particularly aggressive, acting-out behaviors or anxious–withdrawn behaviors in relation to other children or adults. Otherwise put, a key common denominator cutting across many PMHP-referred children was the interpersonal nature of their difficulty.

These class-based and PMHP-related observations raised questions in our minds about alternative ways (i.e., reactive vs. proactive) of viewing and engaging the skill problems many young children have in their interpersonal relationships. PMHP's basic approach was always to detect such problems as soon and as sensitively as possible and to provide the children with the skills and self-views needed to correct them before they root, fan out, and adversely affect other important spheres of their lives. This strategy is not to be pooh-poohed! Indeed, it often works well because the PMHP approach allows it to come into play early in the child's life when it has a chance to do the most good. Even so, it remains a somewhat reactive strategy.

An appealing proactive alternative was to build adaptive interpersonal skills and competencies before the fact in all children, not just in those at risk for referral to PMHP. The rationale behind this strategy was that helping children to become more effective, interpersonal problem solvers would reduce the number of problems experienced and exhibited in class and increase the number and level of positive social interactions among children. Achieving the latter goal would testify to the efficacy of the alternative preventive strategy of strengthening the adaptive competencies of all children.

The preceding were among the clinical–observational considerations that led to the exploration of the SPS approach. Another set of inputs, from the empirical arena, pointed in the same direction. One strand, from the social development literature, documented linkages between positive, peer social interactions and later competencies and adaptive behaviors. For example, children shown early to be sociometric stars continued to evidence adaptive, prosocial behaviors across the school and adult years (Parker & Asher, 1987). Those findings lent support to the notion that a preventive approach based on teaching children positive instrumental skills (SPS skills) might provide a solid base for later adaptation and wholesome development. On the other side of the coin, there was strong evidence that early, chronically undersocialized or asocial child behaviors predicted diverse later maladaptive outcomes such as criminal behavior, delinquency, drug and alcohol problems, arrest, and mental health difficulties (Cowen, Pedersen, et al., 1973; Eron & Huesmann, 1990; Spivack & Shure, 1974). Thus, the later life courses of children with underdeveloped early interpersonal skills are often unnecessarily difficult. Some may drift along as loners; others may join dysfunctional peer groups characterized by high rates of maladaptive or antisocial behaviors. In such cases, the lost potential of the affected child or youth is a matter of serious concern both for the individual and for society.

A final important stimulus for starting the Rochester SPS (RSPS) program, as noted above, grew out of the seminal early work of Spivack and Shure (1974) in developing the ICPS approach. These investigators demonstrated the promise of the ICPS approach for young children in classroom settings and provided a format and body of content needed for an effective, sequential, curriculum-based approach. Research evaluations of this program showed that

1. ICPS skills were teachable in the classroom (i.e., children acquired those skills readily as a result of their participation in the program);
2. children's adjustment also improved following participation in the program;
3. there were linkages between skill and adjustment gains; and
4. these two sets of gains endured at least over the short-term.

These were important and influential findings.

Thus, input rivulets reflecting our own experiences in PMHP and in the schools, research on children's socialization and adaptation, and early ICPS training programs (Allen, et al., 1976; Spivack & Shure, 1974; Spivack, et al., 1976) converged to underscore the good sense and prospective usefulness of a class-based SPS approach. In the final analysis, it was the blend of these clinical experiences and research strands that crystallized the rationales, objectives, and procedures of the SPS training programs that we conducted and evaluated for more than a decade.

In summary, the following salient considerations guided our SPS program development work:

1. Interpersonal (social) problem-solving skills are one important family of skills within a broader social competence cluster.
2. Good, social problem solvers are better adjusted than poor, social problem solvers and, on the opposite side of the coin, people with major adjustment problems (e.g., substance abuse, delinquent–criminal behaviors, major DSM disorders) have underdeveloped SPS skills.
3. Children can learn SPS skills both in class (Ojemann, 1967; Spivack & Shure, 1974) and at home (Shure & Spivack, 1978).
4. SPS training programs must be adapted to the age and sociocultural realities of specific target groups to be maximally effective. Early acquisition of SPS skills can facilitate the acquisition of later adaptive competencies (e.g., group planning and conflict resolution) that can be used in diverse educational, vocational, and social contexts.
5. SPS skills are generic. Because they teach children how, rather than what, to think, they can be gainfully applied in many situations.

PROGRAM OVERVIEW

Because SPS training programs for children reflect a common underlying rationale and set of objectives, SPS curricula tend to cover similar bodies of content and use similar training formats. At their core, these curricula teach children a set of sequenced steps to facilitate effective interpersonal problem solving. These include being able to recognize feelings in oneself and others; formulating what a problem is and deciding on a goal; thinking, initially in a nonjudgmental way, of all the different solutions to an interpersonal problem that can be identified (i.e., alternative solution thinking); considering what might happen next if these solutions were tried (i.e., consequential thinking); and integrating and executing problem-solving behaviors by trying a solution that seems to be good, and if that does not work, by trying another.

Although the preceding are the core steps in the SPS training process, the specifics of an SPS program must reflect a situation's defining realities. One relevant variable is the age of the children in the program. Six-year-olds clearly do not have the same concepts, language skills, interests, or attention spans as 12-year-olds. Effective programs for young children must reflect those differences, such as briefer sessions, greater use of involving activities rather than just words, more limited program scope and goals. That is why the SPS program we developed for kindergarten children (Winer, Hilpert, Gesten, Cowen, & Schubin, 1982) was limited to three steps: (a) saying what the problem is; (b) thinking of lots of different things to do; and (c) thinking of what might happen next. Similarly, the substance, style, language usage, and formats of SPS training programs have (appropriately) been modified to reflect sociocultural differences among target groups by tailoring the program to fit the experience and styles of the children participating in it so that they can relate meaningfully to and profit maximally from it.

Our SPS program model, as noted above, was built on the base of Spivack and Shure's (1974) comprehensive ICPS curriculum for young children. These investigators used the word *cognitive* in the program's name to highlight the importance of cognitive mediation in children's responses to interpersonal problems. The backbone technologies of these SPS training curricula involve teaching children to develop first a broad range of potential responses to interpersonal problem situations and then strategies for evaluating the likely consequences of these solutions. Clear consequential thinking enables children to identify the most promising alternative before acting.

As with the development of other PMHP offshoot programs, the SPS curriculum evolved gradually through several stages as the product of a set of iterative and interactive processes. Inputs from teachers and other relevant school personnel were actively sought both in the early stages of curriculum development and later, when curriculum changes came up for consideration. Much thought went into the decisions about how to present SPS lessons to children in ways that would maximize learning and application of basic program skills, and develop the clearest, most meaningful training materials and formats to enhance program outcomes for specific groups.

Important field-based learnings that emerged from these early steps in primary prevention program development (also applicable to later primary prevention programs we developed) include sound curriculum development that requires both considerable work and ongoing communication between curriculum developers and school personnel whose daily lives are affected by the program. Such communication is important for several reasons: (a) ecological realities require that curricula and program materials be well adapted to the operating ways of the classroom and the developmental abilities of the children; (b) ongoing feedback is needed about a program's de facto operation as a basis for making needed curriculum changes and, ultimately, as part of the process of evaluating the program's impact on the skill development and adjustment of participants; and (c) program developers must work closely with school personnel (i.e., must seek and respect their inputs) to foster a sense of ownership and involvement ("our" program, rather than "your" program) that this way of proceeding conveys (Sarason, 1982).

Although documenting the many twists and turns in the complex process of new program development and evaluation is beyond the scope of this chapter, the sections that follow touch on several factors that helped to shape the emergence and later modifications of the SPS programs that we developed.

THE CORE SPS CURRICULUM

A 34-lesson, second to fourth grade RSPS curriculum with 6 supplemental lessons is the forerunner of later SPS curricula we developed for elementary age children (Weissberg, Gesten, Liebenstein, Schmid, & Hutton, 1980). It provides both a framework for the sequencing of SPS lessons and details of the content and exercises that comprise each individual lesson.

The core curriculum consisted of five main units or clusters of sessions: Understanding Feelings in Ourselves and Others (4 lessons); Problem Sensing and Identification (5 lessons); Generation of Alternative Solutions (5 lessons); Consideration of Consequences (5 lessons); Integration of Problem-Solving Behavior (15 lessons). Six optional lessons, bringing the total curriculum to 40 lessons, provided additional opportunities to review SPS skills. Most lessons were built on participant activities and engaging learning exercises that included role-playing, modeling, and small-group discussions. As training progressed, "live" problems from the classroom were more often incorporated into the lesson formats. Throughout, posters and charts were used to summarize key program steps and highlight basic SPS principles.

Unit 1 teaches children what feelings are, and how to recognize feelings in themselves and in others. Those skills are prerequisites for effective interpersonal relationships. Young children vary considerably in their initial understandings of feelings. Teachers, for example, observed that when SPS training programs started, some children not only lacked a clear understanding of feeling words but also, importantly, did not realize that different people often have different feelings in the same interpersonal situation. Hence, the main goals of the early training segments are to enhance children's feeling vocabulary, ability to recognize feelings, and sensitivity to the feelings of others. This early affectively oriented curriculum unit provides a base for later SPS training, because emotional upset by one or both involved parties is a key defining feature of interpersonal problem situations. Moreover, if an interpersonal conflict cannot be resolved, emotional upset is likely to continue. Relatedly, if a child is insensitive to, or inept in, identifying emotional upset in others, it is difficult for him or her to be an effective interpersonal problem solver. Thus, an effective early feeling-training component is essential to later elements in SPS training for young children.

Unit 2 teaches children to identify both the nature of interpersonal problems, and the desired goals and outcomes in the face of such problems. Many young children find it hard to establish links between a clear problem definition and setting personal goals in a situation. Acquiring that skill may require lots of practice. Accordingly, lessons in this unit are designed to provide clear examples of problem definition and rationales for goal setting.

A problem in teaching this unit was that children, and sometimes even teachers, had trouble formulating clear problem definitions. Although Unit 2's lessons were not troublesome in themselves, the spontaneous examples brought up in trying to formulate problem and goal statements often stumped children. This difficulty is best addressed by training program leaders, usually teachers, to stress the importance of using clear examples and of highlighting concrete ways to help children formulate clear problem statements. Also emphasized in teacher training is the notion that poor examples sometimes have to be "let go!"

Because the steps of problem identification and goal setting are necessary preconditions for effective problem solving, training must consider how these steps can best be taken. One helpful way to facilitate such learning is to clarify carefully the definition of an interpersonal problem with children beforehand. This definition has two main components: an interpersonal problem (a) happens *between people*, and (b) gives someone an *upset* (emotional) *feeling*. For young children, visual displays may be used to reinforce the learning of these two definitional elements.

Once an interpersonal problem has been identified and isolated successfully, a clear goal definition is needed. Here, the most important challenge is to establish a goal that will be satisfactory to both parties in a conflict situation. To do that, children must be able to take the role of the other in the problem situation. Role-playing, including building in role-reversal steps, helps to establish mutually agreeable goals.

Unit 3 trains children to generate alternative solutions to interpersonal problems. In so doing, it begins to engage the basic program issue of what can be done to resolve problem situations and achieve the protagonist's prime goal. Accordingly, the unit's main goal is to teach children, experientially and in a nonjudgmental way, how to generate alternative potential solutions to interpersonal problems. This skill is an essential prerequisite for becoming an effective problem solver. Mastering it requires that the children and adults involved in the SPS program surmount several de facto challenges. Thus, teachers must encourage children to generate as many alternative solutions as possible without judging how good or bad these may be. In that context, when role-playing is used to concretize earlier training elements, children are reminded that the options proposed are only being discussed, not acted on. To highlight the provisional nature of the problem-solving process, the curriculum includes verbal and visual cues to remind children to "Stop and Think" before they act—a reminder intended to reinforce the preceding point.

This part of the training can get touchy when children, spontaneously (and sometimes adamantly) propose physically or verbally aggressive solutions to interpersonal problems. Rather than turning off such solutions, the trainer's challenge is to maintain a clear focus on children's active generation of a range of alternative solutions to interpersonal problems. To elicit different solutions, a trainer can note, nonjudgmentally, that only one type of solution has so far been proposed and can encourage children to think of other types. Involving a full mix of children in this process adds to the richness and diversity of the solution-generating process.

Clearly, alternative solution thinking is a key element in effective social problem solving. Children develop such skills through practice, repetition, role-playing, and small-group exercises. Throughout this unit the greatest challenge for teachers, because it runs against the natural grain of their teaching reflexes, is to avoid correcting seeming errors and to refrain from judging the quality of the solutions children offer. Training for this unit strongly emphasizes the need for teachers to encourage children consistently to expand the range of solutions they offer. One way teachers accomplish this is through use of the specific prompt: "What else might you do?" It is a simple, comprehensible question with good catalyzing value for promoting alternative solution thinking.

Unit 4, on consequential thinking, teaches children to examine the potential consequences of alternative solutions. Solution alternatives identified for interpersonal problem situations in Unit 3 can be considered further in Unit 4 because they are already familiar to the children. The points emphasized by trainers in this unit are that a problem solution works best when one takes into account specific aspects of the solution such as (a) *when* the problem solver might most appropriately speak or act; (b) how others are likely to react to *what* the problem solver says or does and *how* she or he does it; and (c) the types of interpersonal actions that are likely to yield the best results in seeking to realize one's goals.

One aspect of sound consequential thinking is the ability to understand the long-term as well as the immediate consequences of one's actions. Once children can understand and find ways to achieve this aspect of good problem solving, the quality of their solutions and ensuing interpersonal interactions improve substantially. Teachers are often pleasantly surprised to discover how thorough children can be in considering ways to resolve interpersonal dilemmas, when given the chance to ponder behavioral consequences on their own.

Unit 5, the final program unit, is designed to facilitate integration and incorporation of problem-solving skills because it gives children a chance to put all the pieces together. Situations are presented to simulate everyday problems that children experience. Both individually and in small groups, the children are given opportunities to apply recently learned SPS skills to resolve these problems. One useful technique for helping children to achieve these integrative, application-oriented goals is to have small groups work together, first trying to resolve a common problem internally and then going across groups to discuss and compare the types of solutions developed. This technique helps children realize that there can be more than one good solution to a problem; it also allows initially less effective problem solvers to learn from the modeling that more effective problem-solving peers offer.

In this final unit, children are given a chance to bring in their own interpersonal problems for consideration. Although this approach can be quite ego-involving because of its personal significance, it also entails some judgment calls by teachers about the appropriateness of certain problems for general class discussion. One way in which teachers have dealt with this issue is to have children talk privately with them about their problem situations beforehand and, if the problem seems to be nonintrusive, of general interest, and resolvable, to use it in the session.

At the end of this unit, there is a wrap-up for the entire program reviewing its major precepts. In this segment, teachers remind children that informal problem-solving activities will continue in the classroom throughout the year. In this latter context, a technique called *dialoguing* is widely used after the formal program ends. Dialoguing involves direct, natural applications of program learnings by teachers in dealing with everyday problems that come up in the classroom between children. For example, when children get into spirited and sometimes disruptive arguments about such everyday matters as who was playing first with a game, or who will get to take the class pet hamster home for the weekend, the teacher gently but firmly leads them through the problem-solving sequence as it unfolds by using problem identification and goal setting, and generating alternative solutions and thinking of their potential consequences. Doing this reminds children that their SPS training was not a distant abstraction and that such training applies meaningfully to everyday, real-life conflict situations. It also sharpens children's newly acquired SPS skills, both as participants and observers, to see those skills in continuing fruitful application; furthermore, it helps to move the teacher's role away from that of disciplinarian or "heavy" toward being a benevolent mediator who strives to catalyze application of effective interpersonal problem-solving skills in class, in ways that allow children to arrive at mutually agreeable problem resolutions on their own.

PROGRAM EVALUATION

Social problem-solving programs for young children are justified by data showing that SPS skill deficits are associated with adverse adaptive outcomes and, conversely, that the presence of such skills is associated with positive adjustment. Ultimately, however, it must be shown that SPS (or any other competence training program designed to strengthen children's adaptive skills) does in fact yield adjustment gains for participants (Cowen, 1980). Hence, evaluations of SPS training programs have pivoted around three key questions:

1. Did children's SPS skills increase following participation?
2. Did their behavior and adjustment improve?
3. Were linkages found between these two sets of gains?

Most RSPS program outcome studies were conducted between 1975 and 1985. During that period, several training curricula were developed, implemented, and evaluated with urban and suburban children from kindergarten to fourth grade. Follow-up studies were also conducted with program alumni, and the usefulness of several versions of the SPS curriculum was evaluated.

One early study compared the efficacy of an exploratory, full 17-lesson SPS curriculum (E_1); an abbreviated, 5-lesson modeling, videotape-only curriculum (E_2); and a no-treatment control group (C) for 201 suburban second and third grade children (Gesten, Flores de Apodaca, Rains Weissberg, & Cowen, 1979). All children were tested before the program started, at the end of the 9-week program period, and again at a 1-year follow-up point. The study's key outcome indicators included several problem-solving skill measures, a teacher-rated measure of children's school problem behaviors and competencies, and measures of children's self-rated adjustment, self-esteem, locus of control, and sociometric status. IQ scores were also available from record data.

Data collected just after the program ended documented significant gains in alternative and consequential thinking for the full-curriculum group, compared with both the videotape-only and control groups. These gains also showed up in a later, simulated behavioral problem-solving test. Comparable gains, however, were not found either on the teacher-rated measures of adjustment or on the child-rated measures of self-esteem or locus of control. Although there was some evidence of modest linkages between SPS skill and adjustment gains among Es, this finding was clouded by the failure of Es to exceed the other groups in adjustment at the end of the program.

At follow-up (Gesten et al., 1982), the full-implementation E group continued to show better consequential thinking skills than either of the other two comparison groups. They also exceeded the C group on 7 of 10 teacher-rated competence and problem indicators and on two peer-rated sociometric indices. These findings, suggesting delayed positive carry-over from the initial training, gain in credibility because all follow-up ratings were done by 16 teachers blind to the children's initial program–nonprogram status. Indeed, the classes these 16 teachers were teaching were made up of mixes of children from the several different groups in the original study. These follow-up findings highlighted the needs to study the potential positive effects of SPS training in a longitudinal framework, and consider ways in which curriculum changes might advance realization of the program's goals.

A further study evaluated the efficacy of an expanded, 52-lesson version of the SPS training program for 243 suburban and inner-city third grade children (Weissberg, Gesten, Rapkin, et al., 1981). Both urban and suburban children improved on measures of alternative solution thinking and solution effectiveness. Although suburban children also improved significantly on adjustment measures, no linkages were found between skill and adjustment gains. Moreover, the groups did not differ on measures of self-perception, perspective taking, or feeling identification. Thus, some findings from this study (SPS skill gains) were encouraging and others (adjustment change) were not.

In taking stock of the accomplishments and disappointments of these early SPS program development efforts, several unresolved issues came prominently to mind:

1. Which other SPS-related skills (e.g., perspective-taking) might gainfully be added to the curriculum, and at what age could children master these skills?

2. What program modifications were needed to adapt the program better to the experiences and realities of urban, inner-city children and their school settings?
3. What kinds of developmentally responsive program changes were needed for younger children?

These "open" issues fueled several later SPS program development and research explorations.

On the basis of the preceding thinking and empirical findings, an updated 42-lesson training curriculum, with a supporting 143-page user's manual, was developed (Weissberg et al., 1980). This curriculum was used as the basis for conducting a 14-week (3 lessons/week) SPS training program with 563 suburban and urban second–fourth grade children. A study to evaluate the efficacy of this program was built around the same questions that guided earlier SPS program evaluations:

1. Do the SPS skills of program children improve?
2. Does their adjustment improve?
3. Are there linkages between these two sets of gains?

Program children improved more than control children on all key problem-solving skill measures. These included standard paper-and-pencil measures of alternative solution thinking, solution effectiveness, and general problem-solving abilities. Program children also did significantly better than comparison children on a simulated real-life, behavioral problem-solving task involving strategies actually used by children to obtain a magic marker that an age peer, who was a confederate, was drawing with at the time. In terms of adjustment changes, Es exceeded Cs in reductions on overall problem behaviors and specific shy–anxious behaviors and improved more on competencies, global adjustment, and global likability. Although these gains in SPS skills and behaviors were found for both urban and suburban children, linkages between these two sets of gains were weak in both groups.

That findings from this new study were stronger than those from earlier SPS program evaluations may reflect two things: (a) curriculum refinement sought to separate wheat from chaff and to enhance wheat; and (b) the modified program began and ended earlier in the school year than prior programs. This created a block of postprogram time, during which teacher dialoguing (cf. above) was used in handling everyday classroom problems.

Having had some success in refining an SPS curriculum for second–fourth grade children, a next challenge was to develop a similar program for kindergarten children (Winer et al., 1982). Recognizing that the new curriculum would need to reflect important differences in cognitive development between 5- and 10-year olds, we built it around a simplified three-step training strategy, each expressed as an imperative:

1. Say the problem!
2. Think of lots of different things you can do about it!
3. Think of what might happen next!

The new curriculum also took into account attentional and motivational attributes of kindergarten children. Thus, training sessions were much briefer (15–20 minutes) than those used with older children and were built around activities and exercises that were intrinsically interesting and ego-involving for 5-year-olds. The curriculum's 42 lessons were taught over a 10-week period.

A program evaluation study compared outcomes for 63 suburban participants and 46 matched control children. Participants exceeded comparison children on several SPS skill measures (e.g., number of solutions offered, higher quality solutions, fewer irrelevant responses) and several teacher-rated adjustment measures (e.g., fewer problem behaviors, higher overall rated competence, greater frustration tolerance). Once again, no relationship was found between SPS skill gains and adjustment gains.

In the years following these early program development and evaluation steps, a number of teachers who had been involved in them did further SPS training on their own or with the support of occasional base-touches by consultants. Although these teachers continued to find the program useful both for children and for more effective classroom management, as districts added new educational activities and programs to the curriculum, some teachers began to express concerns about the time demands of an SPS training program in a context of shrinking time availability.

This feedback prompted the development, in the mid-1980s, of a streamlined (20-session) version (Work & Olsen, 1990) of the earlier, successful SPS curriculum for fourth graders. The new curriculum sought to distill essences from the Hahnemann and RSPS curricula in ways that were responsive to the ecological reality of the limited class time available for this type of training. Two suburban classes with 37 children were given SPS training based on the new version of the program; 45 children in two comparable no-training classes served as controls. Postprogram comparisons showed that Es exceeded Cs on measures of alternative solution thinking and teacher-rated adjustment (i.e., fewer problem behaviors and more competencies).

Although direct linkages were not found between SPS and adjustment gains, one facet of this research explored this issue from a somewhat different angle by investigating the role of empathy as a potential mediator of SPS skill acquisition. This line of inquiry was based on the possibility that having at least a minimal level of interpersonal empathy might be a prerequisite for investing effort in learning SPS skills. We thus considered it possible that the failure of some prior studies to show linkages between SPS and adjustment gains may have been due to overlooking the role of key moderator variables such as empathy. Regression findings showed that empathy at preintervention did, in fact, mediate adjustment gain in the presence of SPS skill acquisition. Much the same may hold for other important relational variables. If so, such findings will help to clarify the place of essential components in SPS curricula and how they can best be staged and sequenced.

Thus, findings from outcome studies based on several versions of RSPS training, including Weissberg et al.'s (1980) 40-lesson SPS curriculum for second–fourth graders, conducted in many urban and suburban schools, showed consistently that children acquired the program's targeted SPS skills. Although these studies also showed some adjustment gains for participants, they failed, in the main, to establish linkages between these cognitive and adaptive gains (Gesten, Flores de Apodaca, et al., 1979; Gesten et al., 1982; Weissberg, Gesten, Carnrike, et al., 1981; Weissberg, Gesten, Rapkin, et al., 1981). Work and Olsen's (1990) program evaluation study, noted earlier, shed light on the latter issue by showing that children with high, compared with low, initial empathy scores were more likely to acquire SPS skills, and that among the former group, there were clear linkages between skill and adjustment gains following SPS training.

IMPLICATIONS AND FUTURE DIRECTIONS

Even though our work in developing SPS training models is the earliest and among the more extensively traveled of our primary prevention projects, it is not an easy story to summarize or project to the future. Translating the preceding abstraction to a concrete behavioral level, it is fair to say that our SPS efforts since the mid-1980s have proceeded in limited ad hoc rather than persistent and systematic ways. To a considerable extent, this reduced pace of SPS inquiry reflects the combination of some equivocal SPS research findings and the parallel development in our shop of other primary prevention program ventures. Even more basically, however, it reflects gradual but significant evolutionary changes in how SPS training has come to be seen by the field at large, and how its major developments have unfolded in recent years. These complementary happenings bear further comment.

When we entered the SPS program development and research arena, the early Hahnemann (ICPS) program findings were first becoming visible to the field. For those with an interest in primary prevention programming for children, this new competence enhancement (health-building) strategy seemed to hold genuine promise for the future. At that early juncture, we were one of a very few groups actively exploring and evaluating this emergent type of primary prevention program model. In the ensuing decade, however, several things happened to change that situation. One was that many new individuals and groups joined the bandwagon of those seeking to carve out new and better versions of ICPS/SPS training programs. As a result, overlap developed in the approaches being explored, thus reducing the uniqueness and importance of the potential contributions of individual groups.

Another set of slowly unfolding discoveries was also influential. Although some findings from the early SPS thrust were, to be sure, exciting and promising, findings from other program outcome studies, several of our own included, were equivocal. Thus, although cumulative SPS findings from the first decade of this development were somewhat encouraging, they fell short of the very high promise initially held out for such programs, that is, they tended to be less robust or enduring than originally anticipated (Durlak, 1983).

Over time, several conclusions evolved about the impact of this early work that served significantly to shape the field's later development. One is that it is too much to expect that a circumscribed, time-limited SPS program could lead to robust, enduring skill acquisition with major long-term positive generalization to children's adjustment. More basically, a broad ideal of wholesome social competence development came to replace increasingly the laudable but substantially narrower goal of SPS training as a guiding objective toward which to target the field's efforts. Because social competence is an amalgam of several different families of skills that phase in at different developmental stages, it also became clear that no single scope- or time-limited training program could adequately embrace all essential social competence development components (Cowen, 1994).

The preceding considerations established a foundation on which more complex (i.e., greater depth, breadth, and temporal continuity) sets of second-generation, school-based competence training programs were built (Elias & Clabby, 1992; Elias, Gara, Schuyler, Branden-Muller, & Sayette, 1991; Weissberg, Caplan, & Harwood, 1991; Weissberg & Elias, 1993). These new programs seek to train multiple families of competencies, including those pertaining to physical, as well as psychological, well-being. Often, they extend over multiple school years and include efforts to create class or school environments that work actively to support and strengthen program learnings after the formal program ends.

This important shift in direction will not be considered further here, although its issues will resurface in a later chapter. The functional point to underscore now is that simple, isolated SPS training programs (including our own) have, for good and sufficient reasons, yielded place to more complex, time-consuming, and temporally extended social competence training packages in which early classic SPS training is one visible but limited element (Cowen, 1994).

Other factors that have shaped our more recent SPS-related activities, stem from our own observations and findings. For example, clinical observations involving many PMHP-seen children, over many years, brought home to us how solidly entrenched and difficult to deal with many school problems are by the time the child reaches third grade—especially among high-risk groups. This frequent, strong observation directed our thinking to the need for even earlier, preventive intervention foci, including social competence–oriented programs, and to issues concerning the optimal formats and defining mechanisms for such early intervention.

In this context, we note that our recent research on resilience among young, profoundly stressed urban children (see chapter 11) has documented the important protective function played by a favorable family milieu and a warm parent–child relationship in promoting felicitous adaptive outcomes in such at-risk populations. This finding hints that there may be real limits to the benefits that can accrue to young, profoundly stressed urban children from even the most benevolently intended, soundly conceived, and well executed preventive interventions, if those interventions are targeted exclusively to school-age children, independent of the home and family contexts in which they develop.

These clinical observations and research findings point in several directions with regard to SPS, and other primary prevention program thrusts for families that live under chronically stressful life conditions. First, they suggest the need to start such interventions much earlier than ages 6–10 years to which most first-generation SPS training programs were targeted. Such early starting programs must necessarily reflect a prime focus on parents. Although they may also include elements intended to nourish development of specific child competencies, they will require a significant parent component designed to promote sound attachments, caring parent–child relationships, wholesome child-rearing styles and discipline practices, and developmentally realistic expectations. Such formative ingredients collectively create a soil in which essential early child competencies (Strayhorn, 1988) can best grow. In families that experience chronic life stress, it may also be necessary to attend to and help relieve some oppressive burdens of day-to-day living and survival that parents face before positive substantive gains (e.g., competence acquisition, developing a sense of efficacy) can be promoted in children. In any venture of this type, it will be important to communicate training essences in culturally sensitive and relevant formats, if significant program benefits are to occur.

As noted earlier, we have not been extensively involved in SPS activities in recent years. We have, however, worked toward developing a simplified version of an SPS curriculum for 4-year-olds. This 34-lesson curriculum includes the training of preparatory skills, followed by exercises designed to strengthen the verbal reasoning skills that children use in seeking to resolve personal problems. Given the short attention span of 4-year-olds, lessons are limited to a maximum of 10–15 minutes and are built around intrinsically appealing games and exercises for children of this young age.

This new direction in program development, especially in urban settings, reflects the possibility that greater benefit may accrue to children from family-oriented, competence training programs that start when the children are very young (ages 2–3 years) than from programs targeted to children alone when they are 9–10 years old. In this context, the broader term "social competence training" seems to be preferable to the narrower notion of SPS training. Subject only to the limits in children's cognitive capabilities at various ages and people's ingenuity in engineering appropriate learning conditions and programs, there is reason to hope that early, well-conducted social competence enhancement programs can set the stage for subsequent training to enhance later, more complex, social competencies such as anger control, conflict resolution, and developing awarenesses of situations that one can and cannot control.

Social competence training, in various content and format packages, harbors important opportunities for positively shaping both educational and mental health outcomes during the childhood period. Any such thrust, however, must pay heed to two reality constraints. First, programs targeted to very young children, including preschoolers, must be simple in focus, engagingly crafted to capture their interest, and delivered in small parcels over brief time periods. Second, the younger the program's intended target group, the more important it is for significant adult figures in the child's life (e.g., parents, teachers) to be involved actively in the program's precepts and activities. Meaningful program involvements and participation by parents and teachers can both help to realize a program's prime didactic objectives and broaden the base of positive adult modeling experiences for children (e.g., in teacher use of dialoguing). There can also be important secondary benefits to adults from such program involvements. For example, the experiential learning that parents and teachers can gain from their involvement in competence training programs can radiate positively to other children at home (Seitz & Apfel, 1994) and future waves of children to be taught by participating teachers.

SUMMARY

Our SPS work to date has provided a structural model for developing and implementing programs to train young children in diverse adaptive skills and competencies. On the positive side, early SPS program evaluation studies showed that child participants did indeed acquire the program's targeted skills and sometimes also showed improved behavioral adjustment.

It was more difficult, however, to demonstrate linkages between SPS and adjustment gains.

Over time, reflecting both logical and empirical inputs, the field has come to see SPS less as an end unto itself and more as one of several families of skills that make up a broader, more inclusive construct (social competence). The field's subsequent programmatic efforts reflect this changing view (Elias & Clabby, 1992; Weissberg & Elias, 1993). Thus, competence-training curricula in the schools have gotten broader in scope, deeper in coverage, and more extended in time than first-generation SPS training programs such as ours. Specifically, emergent second-generation, social competence training programs extend over multiple school years, include "booster shots" for previously learned skills, and introduce new and more complex components as children mature cognitively. In parallel, greater emphasis is placed on creating school environments that are in sync with and support the substantive teachings of these class-based competence training programs (Elias & Clabby, 1992). Although these developments make good sense in their own right, as programs become more complex and extended in time, evaluating their outcomes becomes an increasingly complex, challenging task.

At another level, there have been efforts to move SPS and other forms of competence training back earlier in time for the child in hopes of maximizing the program's immediate and long-range benefits to children. As that moving back in time step is pursued, parents and teachers take on more important program roles in that they must necessarily be the ones to convey a program's substance to children.

Social competence training programs need to include interrelated families of competencies; SPS skills are but one type of those skills. Whatever their content foci, the specific procedures and styles of all competence training programs must reflect an awareness of and respect for the realities of the settings in which they are to be conducted and the natural and preferred styles of the people who inhabit those settings.

In a real sense, early SPS training program models now stand as ancestors to a range of current social competence training programs, including some complex ones developed in recent years. Although narrowly defined SPS training has given way, to a considerable extent, to more complex, ecologically valid social-competence training programs that extend over multiple school years, the import of the earlier SPS thrust remains visible as (a) a structural foundation on which taller edifices have been built, and (b) one specific component in evolving social competence training programs.

Clearly, early experiences with SPS training programs have helped to structure the emergence of a new, more complex generation of social competence program applications. The underlying preventive–wellness-oriented goals of these ambitious programs are similar to those that guided early SPS programs: to maximize the adaptation and effectiveness of young children. The difference is that the new generation of programs seeks to carve out more valid pathways to those crucial outcomes.

9

THE CHILDREN OF DIVORCE INTERVENTION PROGRAM

This chapter describes the Children of Divorce Intervention Program (CODIP), another of our primary prevention programs. Although CODIP is linked conceptually to SPS under the banner of primary prevention, the two approaches reflect different strategies and tactics for advancing that goal. Whereas SPS is a competence-training, wellness-enhancement program targeted to all children (Cowen, 1994), CODIP is targeted to children at risk for psychological difficulties by virtue of exposure to stressors associated with the termination of their parents' marriage (Bloom, Hodges, & Caldwell, 1982).

CODIP came into being as a result of both a growing body of literature (cf. below) identifying negative effects of parental divorce on children and, more concretely, the problems that many children of divorce were showing in schools. Divorce rates in America had skyrocketed in the 20-year period before CODIP. Whereas in the 1950s, 11% of children under age 18 experienced parental separation and divorce, the following two decades witnessed an unprecedented surge of broken marriages. Today, one of every two marriages ends in divorce, affecting nearly half the current generation of children.

After parental divorce, children on average spend 5 years in a single-parent family before another major transition occurs, that of entering a stepfamily. This poses another set of challenging adaptations, often entailing longer readjustment periods, especially for older children, than the initial divorce entailed (Hetherington & Clingempeel, 1992). About 75% of divorced mothers and 80% of divorced fathers remarry (Glick & Lin, 1986). Moreover, because divorce rates are higher for remarriages than for first marriages, one in four children experience two or more parental divorces before age 18. These stark realities highlight major changes in patterns of family living over the past 30 years and underscore ongoing change processes associated with marital disruption. The latter include a series of transitions and family reorganizations that modify many aspects of children's lives and development, ranging from emotional and behavioral changes to very different economic and living conditions.

Dramatic increases in divorce rates in the 1960s and 1970s were mirrored in referrals of children to PMHP. By 1980, more than half of all referred children came from single-parent families, most reflecting parental divorce. This reality highlighted the need for a school-based, preventively oriented program designed to help children cope with the stresses of divorce, and fueled an intensive effort in the early 1980s to develop such a model.

Although the acronym CODIP has thus far been used in a global, undifferentiated way, it is in reality a generic shorthand term for a family of six kindred programs for children of divorce that feature two common goals: (a) minimizing divorce's negative impact on children, and (b) teaching children skills and competencies to help them cope adaptively with the major problems they are likely to face following the breakup of their parents' marriage.

All CODIP programs are designed to establish a safe, secure, supportive group climate, and all strive to train in age-appropriate skills and competencies that help children cope effectively with problems associated with the dissolution of their parents' marriage. However, specific versions of CODIP for different age and sociocultural groups necessarily differ in operational detail and technology (e.g., number and length of sessions, group size, specific teaching formats, materials and exercises used, balance between games and activities vs. group discussion, ethnic identity of family figures and puppets used). Each new version of CODIP has been built onto the base of existing knowledge about developmental characteristics and sociocultural diversity, including family structure, that pertain to that particular target group.

This chapter first considers the effects of marital disruption on children's adjustment and factors that moderate outcomes over time. Such information constitutes the generative base on which CODIP is built. After that, the CODIP program is described in detail, including research findings bearing its efficacy.

THE EFFECTS OF MARITAL DISRUPTION ON CHILDREN'S ADJUSTMENT

When CODIP children are asked, "What comes to mind when you hear the word 'divorce'?" their responses typically reflect feelings of painful change and distress. Words often used to describe their reactions include: why, angry, weird, different, hopeless. At least initially, most children are very distressed by the news of their parents' separation, although they differ in how such distress is expressed. Common reactions include feelings of sadness, anxiety, anger, resentment, confusion, guilt, and somatic symptoms. Young children are apt to grieve openly over the news of parental separation. As one 7-year-old put it, "I pray every night that they won't get a divorce . . . that they'll get back together. . . ." Older children, who intellectually understand better the reasons for the breakup are nonetheless pained emotionally by the decision. Many children of divorce react to parental conflict and family disorganization with noncompliance and aggression (Emery 1982); others become confused by and apprehensive of changing relationships with their parents (Hetherington, Cox, & Cox, 1982; Peterson & Zill, 1986; Wallerstein & Kelly, 1980).

Thus, the major changes associated with divorce predispose stressful new adaptations both for adults and children. Illustratively, Holmes and Rahe (1967) found that, for adults, divorce was second only to death of a spouse in terms of the severity of the stressor and the amount of time needed to adapt to it. Research findings confirm that parental divorce is also highly stressful for children (Brown & Cowen, 1988; Yamamoto, 1979). Whereas for an adult, divorce may be an escape from an intolerable situation (Hetherington, 1989), for children divorce typically involves permanent changes over which they have little or no control. A comment by one CODIP child reflected this awareness: "I guess the divorce made things better for Mom and Dad, but not for me." At some level, nearly all children wish that their parents would not divorce; many continue to hope for a reconciliation for years.

Although most children experience some form of distress during the early stages of marital disruption, long-term outcomes are diverse. Some children show resilience and effective coping over time; others get derailed developmentally and struggle with ongoing adjustment problems. Still other children, who appear, on the surface, to be adapting well in the early stages of the family breakup, show important negative effects later, especially in adolescence (Hetherington, 1972; Wallerstein & Blakeslee, 1989).

Early studies of the effects of divorce on children, limited by flaws in design and methodology, may have overestimated such negative effects. Recent research on this topic has grown in extent and sophistication. Amato and Keith's (1991a) meta-analysis, reflecting many studies, showed that for 72% of uncontrolled studies and 70% of controlled studies, there were small but statistically significant negative effects for children of divorce of all ages in terms of parent–child relationships, psychological adjustment, academic achievement, self-concept, behavioral conduct, and social adjustment. The strongest of those effects were for conduct and parent–child relationships, followed by psychological adjustment and self-concept.

A parallel meta-analysis on the impact of divorce on adults (Amato & Keith, 1991b) yielded similar findings. Specifically, for adults, divorce was associated with a decline in socioeconomic status, poorer physical health, diminished psychological well-being including more depression and less life satisfaction, unhappier marriages, and more frequent future divorce. In summary, these two meta-analyses identified consistent negative effects of divorce on the adjustment of children and adults.

Similarly, several recent studies and surveys reported that children of divorce, compared with those from nondivorced families, evidenced more acting out and aggression, peer difficulties, learning problems, and school drop outs (Furstenberg, 1990). A study from the National Center for Health Statistics reported that children from single-parent and remarried families were two-to-three times more likely to have emotional and behavioral problems than children living with both parents (Zill & Schoenborn, 1990). Relatedly, a study by Hoyt, Cowen, Pedro-Carroll, and Alpert-Gillis (1990) found higher levels of depression, anxiety, and school adjustment problems among second and third grade children of divorce than demographically matched peers from nondivorced families.

Wallerstein and Blakeslee's (1989) 10–15-year follow-up of children from the California Children of Divorce Study identified a sleeper effect or adjustment problems not seen earlier in some young adults. They concluded that young people from divorced families are at a significant disadvantage in meeting the challenges of adult commitment and intimacy. Although this study had limitations (e.g., lack of a control group), its findings accord with those of other studies suggesting an intergenerational transmission of divorce. Thus, for children and youth, parental divorce is an enduring risk factor that may disrupt their own marriages. Children of divorce are also involved in more precocious sexual activity, more frequent out-of-wedlock childbirth, and earlier marriage (McLanahan & Bumpass, 1988); they also constitute a majority of all referrals to mental health services (Zill & Schoenborn, 1990).

Werner and Smith (1992) reported similar findings from the Kauai longitudinal study. This study followed the entire 1955 birth cohort on the island of Kauai, through age 32, monitoring regularly the impact of diverse biological and psychosocial risk factors and stressful life events. Parental divorce and remarriage in this study were found to create vulnerabilities in children that showed up as problems when they themselves became spouses and parents. Similar to Wallerstein and Blakeslee's (1989) finding for a clinical sample, Werner and Smith found, for an entire birth cohort, that the psychological effects of parental divorce often thwarted the establishment of commitment and intimacy in adulthood. Although such outcomes are unfortunate, they are neither universal nor inevitable. Rather, individual, family, and social factors play important mediating roles in shaping children's development over time.

Significant longitudinal data about the effects of the divorce process in children come from the National Survey of Children, a longitudinal study of a representative sample of 7–11-year-old children followed from middle childhood through adolescence and early adulthood (Zill, Morrison, & Coiro, 1993). Children of divorce were found, 8 years after the marital breakup, to have more school adjustment problems than children from intact families (i.e., 34% vs. 20%). However, the fact that 66% of these children were functioning reasonably well in school highlights the diversity of postdivorce outcomes. Whereas some children land deftly on their feet after the divorce, others face a life-long legacy of negative fallout.

The preceding reality poses the important challenge of identifying factors that shape, or mediate, children's adjustment to parental divorce over time—an important focus of recent research in this area. In brief overview, findings from this work suggest that a child's postdivorce adjustment is shaped less by the fact of parental divorce per se and more by the interplay of diverse risk and protective factors, including characteristics of the child (e.g., age, gender, temperament), coping strategies, additional cumulative stress that the child experiences, continuing qualities of the postdivorce family environment (e.g., parent conflict), and available resources and support beyond the family. The section that follows considers the role played by such factors in children's postdivorce adaptation and the implications of those findings for developing preventive interventions for children of divorce.

FACTORS PREDICTING RISK AND RESILIENCE IN CHILDREN OF DIVORCE

Historically, research on children of divorce has focused more on risk factors for negative outcomes than on protective factors that favor adaptive outcomes (Emery & Forehand, 1994). Although more research is needed identifying pathways to wellness following divorce, some child, family, and extrafamilial factors have been identified that provide clues for shaping preventive interventions.

On the plus side, family-related factors such as an authoritative, nurturant, effective parenting style; a sound parent–child relationship; parental cooperation in child-related matters; and encapsulated or minimal interparental conflict have been shown to be protective factors that enhance adjustment outcomes for children (Black & Pedro-Carroll, 1993; Emery & Forehand, 1994). Conversely, high interparental conflict has a negative impact on children's postdivorce adjustment (Emery, 1982).

Maladaptive coping styles, such as avoiding the reality of the divorce and attributions of self-blame, are child factors that increase the risk of psychological problems (Armistead et al., 1990; Kurdek & Berg, 1983, 1987). Research with middle school students highlights the importance of effective coping strategies in facilitating sound postdivorce adjustment (Grych & Fincham, 1992) and, hence, the need for preventive interventions to teach such strategies. At another level, extrafamilial support sources, including a warm, positive relationship with a teacher or other key adult outside the home, have been found to enhance child adjustment after the divorce (Cowen, Pedro-Carroll, & Alpert-Gillis, 1990; Hetherington, Cox, & Cox, 1979; Santrock & Warshak, 1979).

In any case, as divorce rates rose rapidly in the 1970s, the negative fallout of divorce for children presented more visible and vexing problems for schools. Indeed, by 1980 more than half of all PMHP referrals involved children from single-parent families. That reality fueled the need to develop a preventively oriented intervention for such youngsters.

The preceding review has highlighted several considerations that shaped the nature of that intervention. In our minds, the new intervention needed to feature two essential components: group support and training in adaptive coping skills. The section that follows describes the CODIP model—a by-product of this history and way of thinking. Development, implementation, evaluation, and dissemination of six different versions of CODIP, tailored to the specific needs of different sociocultural and age groups from kindergarten through eighth grade, has been a deeply invested effort in the past 15 years.

THE CHILDREN OF DIVORCE INTERVENTION PROGRAM: FOUNDATIONS

CODIP is a school-based program, built on the assumption that timely preventively oriented intervention for children of divorce can offer important short- and long-term benefits. CODIP's basic goals are to create a supportive group environment in which children can share experiences freely, establish common bonds, and clarify misconceptions; and to teach children skills that enhance their capacity to cope with the stressful changes that often follow divorce. Wallerstein's (1983) concept of specific psychological tasks confronting children of divorce is reflected in the program's defining features for different age groups.

The initial CODIP model was developed for fourth–sixth grade suburban children of divorce (Pedro-Carroll & Cowen, 1985). That program's success laid a solid foundation for adapting the model to children of different ages and sociocultural backgrounds. Through all these many changes, the program's basic goals of providing support and teaching effective coping skills remained constant, although its technologies were modified to reflect the needs and realities of specific age and sociodemographic groups. This evolutionary process led to both the refinement of the initial program and the development of separate versions of the program tailored specifically to younger (kindergarten–first grade; second–third grade) and older (fourth–sixth grade, seventh–eighth grade) urban and suburban youngsters. Detailed practitioner-oriented manuals have been written for each new version of the program.

Structural Model

CODIP meetings should be conducted on a regular schedule and in a school area that offers privacy. Confidentiality is essential. Although meeting times vary across schools, most CODIP groups convene during the school day. Decisions about optimal group size, session length, and duration of program depend on the developmental characteristics of the target group. For example, with older youngsters, weekly 1-hour sessions, for six-to-eight children balanced by gender, have worked well; with younger children, 40–45 minute weekly sessions with groups of four to five seem ideal.

Because children's predominant reactions to parent divorce vary by developmental level, CODIP content must also be geared to the attributes of different age groups. For example, whereas issues of loyalty conflicts, anger, stigmatization, and isolation are very salient for 9- to 12-year olds, sadness, confusion, guilt, and fear of abandonment are more prominent reactions for younger children (Wallerstein & Kelly, 1980).

Developmental factors also shape the methods used to facilitate group process. Older (fourth–eighth grade) children with more advanced cognitive development have a broader understanding of feelings, their own and others', and a clearer awareness of the causes and modes of expression of feelings. Consequently, they are more comfortable than younger children with a discussion format. Young children's action orientation and shorter attention span, by contrast, limit the effectiveness of lengthy discussion. Given the intrinsic appeal that play and concrete activities hold for young children, CODIP at that age level emphasizes engaging concrete activities, puppet play, games, and interesting books and filmstrips as vehicles for advancing key program goals and concepts.

Program Objectives

CODIP rests on knowledge of the stressors that divorce poses for children and the relationships between social support and children's adjustment. Although support from kindred peers can, in principle, provide a sense of comfort and a common bond for children of divorce, these youngsters often avoid peers precisely because they feel isolated and different. Also, they often lack the experience or skills needed to cope with family changes. These lacks can lead to frustration and withdrawal and subvert effective relationships with adults and peers. So viewed, CODIP's prime goals are to provide support and build skills that facilitate adaptive coping and reduce the inherent stresses of parental divorce. Within such a framework, CODIP's five basic objectives are built into a structured, sequential curriculum. Depth of involvement in these five areas and specific program formats and exercises used to advance them vary for different age and sociodemographic groups:

1. *Supportive group environment.* CODIP's format and exercises are designed to maximize support. Contact with peers who have had similar experiences helps to reduce children's feelings of isolation and promotes a sense of camaraderie and trust. From the very first session, a safe, accepting environment is established in which children can respond at their own pace.

2. *Identification and appropriate expression of feelings.* Parental divorce can trigger complex feelings in children that are difficult to cope with or even to understand. Young children especially can be overwhelmed by such feelings because they lack the cognitive understandings and coping skills of adults. Hence, CODIP seeks to enhance children's ability to identify and appropriately express a range of emotions. Leaders seek to create a safe group environment in which all feelings are accepted and to maintain a balance of emotionally laden and neutral experiences. The program curriculum is sequenced to consider the universality, diversity, and acceptability of feelings before focusing on divorce-related issues.

3. *Clarifying divorce-related misconceptions.* Because children's cognitive mastery depends on the accuracy of their perceptions, clarifying divorce-related misconceptions is an important aspect of the program. Over several sessions, CODIP strives to reduce children's fears of abandonment, feelings of responsibility for the divorce, and unrealistic fantasies about restoring an intact family. Children's ability to attribute the divorce to external realities, rather than to something they have done, helps to restore esteem and overcome feelings of responsibility for the parent's departure.

4. *Enhancing coping skills.* Enhancing children's coping skills is an essential program objective. Several program sessions seek to train social problem-solving and communication skills and appropriate ways to express

anger, using games and exercises to foster skill acquisition and generalization. These skills help children to cope better with many life changes associated with the divorce process (e.g., moving to a new school or neighborhood, being used as messengers or informants between parents, wanting to spend more time with a parent, being upset when a parent begins to date) and thus gain control over situations in which they might otherwise feel helpless. Specifically, children are taught to differentiate between problems they *can* and *cannot* control. This key distinction helps them to master the psychological task of disengaging from interparental conflicts and redirecting energies to age-appropriate pursuits.

5. *Enhance children's perceptions of self and family.* This final integrative unit emphasizes positive qualities of children and families. Children in the midst of stressful life changes often feel different and defective (i.e., "If I were a better kid, my parents would have stayed together."). Several esteem-building exercises are used to highlight positive qualities. For example, in the second- and third-grade curriculum, each child completes an *I Am Special* book detailing his or her characteristics, likes, feelings, wishes, and place in the group and family. Family esteem is also emphasized. Children often need help recognizing positive outcomes of the divorce (e.g., less conflict, more harmony). These sessions strive to heighten children's awareness and acceptance of nontraditional family structures and positive postdivorce family changes that may have occurred.

The Group Model

All CODIP programs are conducted in groups. Although limited professional resources in the schools is one reason for doing so, there are more basic and important justifications. Parental divorce alters children's lives profoundly. Many children of divorce, despite record-high divorce rates, still feel alone and different as a result of their family's dissolution. Hence, one important potential benefit of a group is that it offers children support and comfort by virtue of sharing feelings with peers who have been through similar experiences and learning that they are not alone at a time when it feels as if everything in their life is changing. The group format also provides natural opportunities for exchanging information on common divorce-related issues and clarifying common misconceptions about divorce.

An important thread in the preceding discussion is that children who have gone through common stressful experiences are more credible to peers than those who have not had that experience. Children who, deep down, fear that they are responsible for the breakup of their parents' marriage can find much comfort and relief in the words of a peer with exactly the same feelings—indeed more so than from the intellectual assurances of a noninvolved adult. Relatedly, in a group format, children who are further along in the process of adjusting to divorce can serve as credible, important coping models for those in the early stages of readjustment. Silverman (1988) highlighted this point:

> As children grow, they need to learn from peers who serve as role models and with whom they can explore their common dilemmas. Children who have role model peers do not feel alone, unusual, or isolated; they feel legitimated. (p. 182)

Also in CODIP's later, structured, skill-acquisition meetings, the group format offers children opportunities to learn about others' efforts to solve problems, deal with anger, disengage from loyalty conflicts, and other interpersonal skills. Peers in CODIP are a major source of support and comfort; additionally, the children learn from each other's successes and setbacks. The group format also provides good opportunities for discussion and role-playing. The latter engaging, ego-involving approach helps children practice and refine newly acquired program skills.

Group Leaders

CODIP's success depends on the interest and skills of group leaders. Children's groups may cohere slowly because some children are so absorbed with their own problems that they have difficulty taking the role of others. The leader's sensitivity, ability to establish a trusting climate, and ability to encourage children's involvement and expression of feelings, all promote group cohesion. Relatedly, the leader's ability to deal comfortably with emotionally laden issues sets a basic tone and climate for the group.

Usually, two leaders, a man and a woman, head the CODIP groups and share task and process roles. This arrangement helps children to observe first hand a positive, cooperative adult relationship. Also, because most CODIP groups are of mixed gender, it offers children a same-sex positive adult role model. Having two leaders also facilitates responses to sensitive and emotionally laden issues, nonverbal cues, and behavior management problems. What one leader may miss in the heat of the interaction, the other can pick up.

CODIP leaders are selected more for their interest, skills, and sensitivity than for their training in any specific discipline. In practice, leaders have included school psychologists, social workers, nurses, teachers, guidance counselors, principals, advanced mental health trainees, and a trained paraprofessional (teamed with a mental health professional). The leader selection process starts with a meeting for interested school personnel to describe the program, leader roles, and responsibilities. At this meeting, time commitments (about 3 hours/week) and role responsibilities are detailed to enable prospective leaders to judge their ability to participate.

Also, contact between potential leaders and CODIP staff helps to form two-way judgments about goodness of fit.

Leaders have four to five, 2-hour training sessions before the program starts and biweekly 1½-hour training and supervision meetings while it is in progress. The initial training sessions provide information about the impact of divorce on adults and children; children's cognitive and emotional growth including specific, age-related reactions of the target group to parental divorce; factors that shape children's adjustment to parental divorce over time; and group leadership and facilitation skills. Biweekly supervisory meetings review the prior week's meeting(s) including things that went well and problems experienced, provide opportunities to problem solve and modify curricular materials or management strategies, and overview the next week's curriculum. Occasionally, supervision meetings identify trouble spots involving questions about leader motivations and skills. Problems of that nature that cannot be dealt with comfortably in the group are followed up individually.

CODIP FOR FOURTH-TO-SIXTH GRADERS

The following session summary illustrates how CODIP program objectives are approached in the 12-session curriculum for fourth-to-sixth graders. At this age, many children react to divorce-related changes and tensions with anger and resentment. They know that divorce, unlike death, is not inevitable and may thus align themselves with one parent and blame the other. Also, children at this age often feel embarrassed and different from peers from nondivorced families. Some have lingering fears that they are to blame for their parents' marital strife.

The session outline below describes how the CODIP curriculum for 9–12-year-olds addresses these common reactions in a supportive environment that focuses on the five general program objectives.

Session 1: Foster a Supportive Group Environment

Support is a key underpinning of CODIP. It extends throughout the program. From the start, a safe, accepting environment is established in which children can respond at their own pace, share common feelings and experiences, increase awareness of diverse family forms, and reduce feelings of isolation. Confidentiality is explained and its importance highlighted, and discussion begins of the complex emotions related to parental divorce and things children find helpful in dealing with the problems it poses. Selecting a group name or symbol helps children to develop a common support bond.

Session 2: Understanding Changes in the Family

Session 2 focuses on divorce-related feelings and experiences and the clarification of commonly held misconceptions. Two activities—a filmstrip, *When Parents Separate* (Coronet Video, 1980) and a structured group discussion—stimulate children's involvement and expression of feelings about the divorce, often eliciting keenly felt but pent-up emotions. Other themes generated by the filmstrip and the group discussion include loyalty conflicts, custody and visitation disputes, and difficulties adjusting to parental dating and to blended families.

To help children realize that they are not alone and can find support and comfort from each other, we then pose the question: "What's been the hardest thing for you about your parents' divorce?" Most children are eager, indeed relieved, to respond to that lead, and the ensuing discussion paves the way to more involvement, shared experiences, and group cohesiveness.

Session 3: Coping With Changes

Session 3 strives to increase children's understanding of the impact of the divorce for them and their parents, encourages parent–child communication, and helps children identify appropriate coping strategies for their situation. The session is built around a filmstrip, *After the Divorce* (Coronet Video, 1980), focusing on ways to cope with the many family changes that divorce entails. Viewing the filmstrip is preceded by a discussion of why children behave in certain ways after divorce (e.g., lose their tempers more quickly, worry more, find it harder to talk with their parents). Those questions stimulate discussion of adaptive ways to cope with concrete postdivorce challenges that children face.

To increase child–parent communication, the idea of a group newsletter is introduced. The newsletter, initially conceived by children, offers a forum for creative writing, drawing, poetry, and humor that express feelings and reaches out to important others to enhance mutual understanding. It is one of several activities designed to strengthen bonds among children; moreover, the creative expression that it entails promotes a sense of competence and mastery.

Sessions 4, 5, and 6: Social Problem Solving

These meetings seek to build skills to enhance children's self-control and ability to solve interpersonal problems. Problem-solving steps and self-statements are taught to help children recognize that although some things, such as the divorce per se, cannot be controlled, they can control their own behavior and find adaptive solutions to problems. Role-playing is used in teaching children skills to cope with diverse real-life problems.

Specifically, Session 4 introduces a six-step procedure for resolving interpersonal problems:

1. identifying the problem,
2. generating alternative solutions,
3. analyzing consequences of the solutions generated,
4. choosing an alternative,
5. evaluating its consequences, and
6. implementing the chosen solution.

These steps are first applied to nondivorce-related problems with friends or family members. In this process, children are given a paper depicting the six problem-solving steps in cartoon format and take turns role-playing those steps. They are encouraged to take the cartoons home and go over them with their parents as a way of increasing parent–child communication. Finally, they are asked to bring a specific, real-life problem to the next session, to which the new problem-solving steps can be applied.

Leaders begin Session 5 by modeling application of the SPS steps to a personal problem of their own. Next, children apply these steps to the divorce-related interpersonal problems they brought in. After an alternative solution is chosen, children role-play its application in the sheltered group setting before trying it out in the real world. Typical problems brought in include negative reactions to news of the marital breakup, being used as a messenger or informant between parents, wanting to spend more time with a parent, feeling upset or angry when a parent begins to date, and concerns about peers.

Conducting coping-skills training in a group facilitates supportive interactions. Children become actively involved in generating alternative solutions to problems, considering their consequences, and providing feedback to peers engaged in problem solving. For many, the awareness that they are not alone with their problems is comforting. Involvement in these practice steps prepares them for testing out solutions to real-life problems with family or friends.

Session 6 seeks to consolidate and refine newly acquired problem-solving skills and, importantly, introduces a key distinction between problems children can and cannot solve. Many children, motivated (understandably) by the wish to restore interparental harmony and by their own feelings of helplessness, become enmeshed in trying to solve parental problems that are totally beyond their control. Sooner or later, they must come to recognize that some problems are beyond their control and therefore cannot be resolved.

With that reality in mind, Session 6 emphasizes the differences between solvable and unsolvable problems and explores ways of disengaging from the latter. Role-playing is used to dramatize solvable (e.g., whether to tell friends about the divorce) and unsolvable (e.g., the divorce itself) problems. Children are encouraged to disengage from problems they cannot control and to invest their energy instead in age-appropriate pursuits, such as spending time with friends and school activities.

Session 7: Panel of Experts on Divorce: WKID-TV

Session 7 provides an enjoyable way for children to consolidate problem-solving and coping skills thus far acquired and to clarify lingering misconceptions about the divorce. Children take turns as members of a panel of experts on divorce and field questions from the audience (the other group members). This activity (a) underscores common problems of children of divorce, (b) further clarifies misconceptions about divorce, (c) provides practice in solving personal problems, (d) highlights problems that can and cannot be controlled, (e) diversifies suggestions for coping with difficult problems, and (f) enhances children's sense of competence and self-esteem by concretizing the fact that they have indeed acquired skills for resolving problems and insights about divorcing families that can help others.

Sample questions from this activity include: "What are some things kids worry about when their parents separate?" and "My parents still fight even though they're divorced; what can I do to solve this terrible problem?" Children get very involved in WKID-TV; it is very real to them. They offer spontaneous solutions to the problems posed and sometimes debate the consequences of those solutions heatedly. The following examples of children's advice illustrate the wit, wisdom, and understanding that characterize these exchanges.

Advice for Parents

- "Don't give us everything we want just to get us to like you more than (the other parent)."
- "Don't use us as bullets. Don't fight in front of us. Don't say, 'Your Dad is an idiot.' Don't ask us if Mom is dating."
- "Let us know that it's okay to love both of you. Don't make us choose between the two of you."
- "Let us know that you love us. Even if we act like we already know, tell us again."

Advice for Other Kids

- "Remember, it's not your fault that your parents split up, even if you did laugh when your Dad told that joke about your Mom."
- "Find someone you can trust to talk to. Sometimes you just need to let it all out."

- "Remember there are some things, like your parents' divorce, that you can't change. Spend your time on things you can control instead."

Sessions 8 and 9: Understanding and Dealing with Anger

Sessions 8 and 9 deal with issues of anger, a frequent by-product of parental divorce for children. Emphasis is placed on understanding the causes of anger, how to identify it in ourselves and others, and appropriate and inappropriate ways to express it. For example, children are taught to express anger using "I" statements that communicate a feeling clearly without attacking the other person and intensifying the problem. Again, leaders actively model effective communication and appropriate methods for handling anger.

After basic methods of anger control have been considered, children choose anger-provoking scenarios from a "grab-bag" and practice adaptive ways of communicating about and dealing with anger. A sixth-grade girl who was upset about her father's late arrivals on visits, found the following formulation helpful: "Dad, I want to see you every week, but I feel hurt and angry when you're late. I wish you would let me know if you're going to be late." Direct expression of such feelings helps to reduce tensions otherwise expressed inappropriately through acting-out behaviors.

Session 9 consolidates skills introduced in the problem-solving sessions and deals with the evaluation of alternatives for controlling anger. Children are invited to suggest different ways of coping with the specific anger-provoking events raised in Session 8. The group evaluates the appropriateness of each suggestion. The latter are listed on the board under the headings: Good Control (makes things better) and Poor Control (makes things worse). Leaders also suggest coping strategies (e.g., writing or talking to the person with whom you're angry, talking to a friend, going to your room to cool off). Finally, children take turns role-playing in anger-provoking scenarios, applying the concepts of "I" statements, good control, and problem solving.

Session 10: Focus on Families

Session 10 seeks to help children understand the complex nature of family relationships, promote acceptance of diverse family forms, and learn how to deal with family problems within their control. Relevant book material (e.g., All Kinds of Families [Simon, 1976]) is used to stimulate this discussion. Points highlighted in the discussion are that (a) many different family forms exist, (b) most families, whatever their form, have some difficult times but there are ways to problem solve at those times, and (c) all family forms have potential for love and stability. Children then apply the skills learned to family problems by participating in a stage game called *Panel of Experts on Families*, structurally similar to Session 7's panel, but with a focus on issues of life in a single-parent family, parental dating and remarriage, and the challenges of blended families. Termination is discussed at the end of this session.

Session 11: "You're A Special Person" Exercise

This session's two main objectives are to bolster children's self-esteem and identify positive postdivorce changes. Leaders facilitate the discussion by highlighting the fact that although parental divorce is distressing and creates many family changes, some changes may be positive. This helps children to identify sources of hope for the future, often overlooked in the turmoil of marital disruption. Next comes an exercise designed to underscore children's self-worth and highlight their special strengths. In this activity, all children receive written feedback, from peers and leaders, about their unique qualities and special contributions to the group. Children enjoy this exercise; some keep their "special person" card long after the program ends.

Session 12: Termination

The last meeting deals primarily with termination. The group experience is overviewed with a focus on children's feelings about its ending. Both written comments and role-plays are used to help children express relevant feelings. Children are also encouraged to identify and seek out people (e.g., parents, friends, teachers) who can provide support after the program ends. After 12 weeks of sharing, learning, and, at times, crying together, children are open in talking about the group experience and their reactions to its ending. Several quotes convey their sense of the group experience:

1. "This group was a safe place where I could talk about things I've never told anyone before."
2. "My mom and I can talk to each other better now—not so much yelling."
3. "The group helped me see that divorce isn't my fault—I guess it's not really anyone's fault."

The session ends with a small party during which children are given certificates of achievement for "caring and sharing."

CODIP: KINDERGARTEN TO THIRD GRADE

The preceding section described the original CODIP model for the fourth-to-sixth graders. On the basis of positive results with that age group, a next step was to develop and evaluate a modified CODIP program for younger children. This section describes aspects of that modification that reflect age-appropriate changes in the CODIP curriculum. Basically, this downward program revision sought to preserve CODIP's goals and objectives within a framework better suited to the emotional and cognitive realities of younger children.

Although there are separate versions of CODIP for kindergarten and first, and for second and third grades, the two are considered as a unit here because of similarities in objectives and content. Program activities in each case, however, are tuned to the developmental realities of the targeted age group. Tailoring CODIP to kindergarten and first grade children was challenging. At this age, children are entering the concrete operations stage, their verbal skills and capacities for expressive language are limited, and their concepts of emotions do not stretch much beyond a gross good–bad polarity. They depend heavily on the family for security, stability, and meeting their physical and emotional needs. Although they need adult support at times of stress or major family change, their limited verbal and interpersonal skills restrict their ability to seek or obtain such support.

At this young age, most children are openly sad about family disruption and a parent leaving home. They hope and wish for family reunification. As one 6-year-old said: "When I blew out my birthday candles, my only wish was that they won't get a divorce. . . ." Misconceptions about the reasons for the marital conflict range from confusion (i.e., "because my Mom got up too early to clip coupons") to troublesome self-blame (i.e., "because I wet my bed . . . they were fighting over me . . ."). Themes of loss and sadness, fear of abandonment, deprivation, yearning for the noncustodial parent, and fantasies of reconciliation are prominent in this age group (Wallerstein & Kelly, 1980). Such strong feelings can overwhelm young children who lack the verbal skills or cognitive understandings needed to seek support or relevant information. The kindergarten-to-third grade programs address these issues by providing a safe, supportive environment in which children can express feelings and emotions; share experiences; seek needed information, help, and support; and deal effectively with everyday interpersonal problems.

The program's central support and skill-building components unfold in appealing, action-oriented contexts designed to capture young children's active involvement. Illustratively, puppet play is used throughout as one engaging, developmentally appropriate way to convey key program concepts and help children access their feelings. To that end, each group has an honorary member: a puppet named Tenderheart, who is introduced by the leader in Session 1. As the children are getting to know each other, Tenderheart explains timidly that this is also his first time in a group like this, so he is a little shy and not sure about what to expect. Leaders invite children to tell Tenderheart what they think the group is about, and how they can help him feel more comfortable.

Most children at this age respond enthusiastically to requests for help and are eager to suggest ways to help Tenderheart feel part of the group (e.g., "Let's all tell him our names"). Tenderheart soon becomes personified as a group member. He too is 6 years old and loves pizza and playing outside at recess. He too has just experienced the separation of his mom and dad. Gradually, he begins to talk about the feelings he has about changes in his family. This lead concretizes and models engagingly a way for children to identify, understand, and express their feelings. Tenderheart's role in the group illustrates one age-appropriate change in CODIP technology.

The curriculum for younger children also uses interactive games to teach coping skills. For example, one important communication skill for children of this age, especially children of divorce, is how to ask for what they need from parents and significant others. The program seeks to promote this skill through an age-appropriate game, Ask the Dinosaur, and the use of a Feelings Telegram that teaches children effective ways to ask for what they need (e.g., how to say "Mom, I need a hug" or "I feel sad when you fight over something; could you please leave me out of it?").

The program also seeks to expand young children's emotional vocabulary. As children acquire such vocabulary and learn about diverse emotions and how to put their feelings into words, they are less likely to somatize or act out in frustration. The program also includes several sessions designed to clarify misconceptions about the divorce, and the child's lack of control over reconciliation. Using age-appropriate technology, including structured puppet and doll play, simple discussion, and interactive books, the message is conveyed that divorce is a "grown-up" problem that children neither cause nor control.

Many CODIP children have limited or no contact with their fathers. For these children, missing dad and understanding his lack of involvement is a central concern. In searching for explanations, children often internalize the belief that they are not lovable enough to merit the absent parent's interest. With young children, puppet and doll play, books, and discussion are used to convey the notion that parents sometimes feel too guilty or upset to visit their children and that this in no way reflects on the child's worth or lovability. Being able to see nonvisitation by an absent parent as a product of external rather than internal factors is an important precondition for restoring self-esteem. The program also uses simple, age-appropriate methods for teaching young children to differentiate between problems they can and cannot control. This differentiation is crucial to mastering the psychological task of disengaging from interparental conflicts and redirecting energies into age-appropriate pursuits (Wallerstein, 1983).

The program for young children also uses games and activities extensively to teach and practice social problem-solving skills. Young children are taught to "stop and think" of various solutions when faced with diverse everyday problems. Puppet play is used to ease naturally into problem scenarios (e.g., you want to watch your favorite show on TV but your brother wants to watch something else . . . what can you do?), learn relevant problem-solving skills, and apply them to personal problems. Concrete age-appropriate games are used to reinforce these skills. The Red Light–Green Light game helps children differentiate between solvable (green light) and unsolvable (red light) problems, and a Tic-Tac-Toe game helps them learn to generate alternative solutions, evaluate their consequences, and choose the most appropriate solutions to problems. Semi-structured puppet play is used to depict common divorce-related problems and the children are asked to generate alternative solutions to help the puppets deal effectively with those problems.

The program for younger children also uses the *Kids Are Special People* game, a board-game designed to address specific divorce-related concerns and to reinforce coping skills and self-esteem. As with older children, termination issues figure prominently in the last few sessions. Leaders again promote discussion of children's feelings about ending. The final sessions also provide opportunities for children to review their experience focusing on special qualities of the group and its members. Concretely, each child is given an *All About Me* book with his or her drawings, feelings posters, problem-solving cartoons, and other program materials. Instant snapshots of each child, as well as an autograph and telephone number page, are distributed as mementos of the experience. Ways of identifying supportive adults to whom children can turn are considered. Finally, the group celebrates with a farewell party, and each child is given a certificate of successful participation.

CODIP FOR EARLY ADOLESCENTS

Clinical and empirical studies document risks that parental divorce poses for adolescents, such as problems in the areas of interpersonal relationships and trust (Franklin, Janoff-Bulman, & Roberts, 1990; Slater & Calhoun, 1988; Wallerstein & Blakeslee, 1989). Personal identity, trust in interpersonal relationships, intimacy, and emerging sexuality are all central issues in adolescence. Marital disruption and parental divorce add to the complexity of these developmental tasks and predispose reactions that challenge the adolescent's ability to cope and remain on task. Behind these challenges are feelings of being overwhelmed by loss, anger, betrayal, and loyalty conflicts in which the adolescent feels caught in the middle.

The CODIP program for seventh and eighth graders consists of 12 weekly sessions. The program features objectives that are important to all CODIP programs. These include a supportive group climate, appropriate ways to express feelings including anger, and problem-solving skills, as well as new age-relevant goals such as promoting realistic trust in future relationships.

Understandably, the approaches used to further program goals with seventh and eighth graders differ from those used with younger children. Interactive exercises that highlight unique features of the divorce experience for early adolescents are used to foster a sense of trust and support. One example is the showing of a video called *Tender Places*, written by a young adolescent whose parents divorced. The video vividly depicts feelings and conflicts that divorce poses for teens. It is used to catalyze discussions, extending across several sessions, of feelings and experiences about how parental divorce affects adolescents' perceptions of self, close relationships, hopes for the future, and willingness to trust others. Given the program's prime goals of promoting realistic hopes for future relationships and enhancing the capacity to trust, some exercises pivot around activities that seek to promote trust by taking small risks in a safe setting. One is the *Life-line* exercise, in which members chart the course of significant events in their lives and talk about those up and down times in the group. In a second such activity called the *Trust Roll*, members form a close circle and physically support each other as they lean back, eyes closed and roll gently around the circle. Members also bring in and talk about songs with lyrics conveying themes of trust in interpersonal relationships.

Although CODIP for adolescents centrally features the teaching of effective communication and social problem-solving and anger-control skills, it uses more sophisticated, age-appropriate technology for doing so. Group exercises such as *The One-Way, Two-Way Communication Experiment*, *The Great Stone Face Exercise*, *The Total Truth Letter*, and extensive use of role-playing and creative dramatics seek to provide realistic, enjoyable opportunities for skill acquisition and practice in these areas. A final program segment for this age group focuses specifically on feelings about future relationships, hopes, goals, and expectations. One approach used in this context is for group members to give advice to other teens whose parents have just divorced.

MODIFICATIONS FOR URBAN CHILDREN

The CODIP variants thus far described have been for different age groups. A second major set of program changes has sought to adapt CODIP to urban children who differ racially and socioeconomically from the initial suburban program targets. Several such changes are illustrated briefly here.

First, the criterion of what constitutes a divorce was elasticized to include functional disruptions in long-term couple structures, other than those based on formal marriage ceremonies (e.g., common-law marriages). Relatedly, program content placed greater emphasis on the existence and acceptability of diverse family structures and the special features of such structures.

At another more concrete level, diversified program materials (puppets, dolls, story books) were selected to provide all children with ready access to appropriate, comfortable identification figures. These changes were intended to maximize the likelihood that the CODIP environment, as well as its specific games, exercises, and materials, would be realistic and appropriate for all children, thus making it easier for them to relate to and profit from the program's basic substantive activities.

PROGRAM START-UP AND RECRUITMENT ISSUES

Guidelines for starting CODIP programs offer leeways that respect schools' idiosyncratic operating styles. Knowing about and respecting such ways is helpful (often essential) in getting a program started. Issues involved in starting CODIP differ for insiders and outsiders. CODIP began in PMHP schools in which long-standing, cordial working relationships existed (Cowen, Trost, et al., 1975). Although that history was helpful, start-up procedures still had to respect schools' different ecologies, needs, and realities.

We found it useful to introduce CODIP in new schools with a meeting to describe the program to relevant school mental health professionals. Because they are the ones most likely to be conducting the program, their interest and commitment is an essential precondition for starting. In schools where professionals expressed interest in CODIP, follow-up meetings were held with principals and other school personnel to obtain formal approval and establish preliminary contracts governing how the program would run.

After initial need and contract issues are resolved, recruiting of program participants can begin. To that end, letters, on school letterhead, describing the program are sent to all parents at the targeted grade levels. The letter includes a consent form. An information meeting is held at school for parents who want to learn more about the program. There, the coordinator describes the program's goals, reviews its activities, and responds to parent questions.

Occasionally, even with parent consent, a child may resist getting involved in CODIP. In such cases, we explain to the parent that the child's hesitation is understandable because not all children necessarily know what to expect from the program and request permission to meet with the child to explain how the program works. These steps are intended to give parents and children an accurate picture of the program and thus facilitate informed decisions about participating. Children are free to withdraw from the program at any time. Less than 1% choose to do so. Before the program starts, leaders meet individually with all children, to welcome them, provide further information about the program, and answer their questions.

To qualify for CODIP a child must (a) be within the targeted age range, (b) have parents who are separated or divorced, (c) have written parent consent, and (d) be capable of functioning adequately in a group by showing no evidence of serious acting out, aggressive behavior in groups, or severe emotional problems that require outside referral. These selection criteria are important. Sometimes, there is pressure to include children who are not appropriate for the group. Including such children can be frustrating for all parties if managing the child's inappropriate behavior, rather than the program's central divorce-related objectives, becomes the major focus. Otherwise put, CODIP is designed as a preventive intervention, not as an intensive group therapy experience.

Although we recognize, in principle, the merit of early intervention in seeking to forestall divorce-related adjustment problems, we have not limited CODIP only to children whose parents are recently separated or divorced. That decision was based on several considerations. One is that adjustment to divorce is a process that extends over time and poses different challenges for children at different times. Second, it can be helpful and realistic to include children at various time-points in the postdivorce cycle as potential coping models who have adjusted to some changes.

PROGRAM EVALUATION

Since CODIP began in 1982, it has been evaluated extensively to assess its efficacy with different groups. Research on the initial program with fourth-to-sixth grade suburban children using a delayed treatment control group design assessed CODIP's effects on the child's adjustment from four perspectives: parents, teachers, group leaders, and the children themselves. Program children, compared with matched control children assigned randomly to a delayed treatment condition, improved significantly more on teacher-rated problem behaviors and competencies. Their parents reported improved home adjustment (e.g., better communication, more open about feelings, more age-appropriate behavior, better able to deal with problem situations). Children reported significant decreases in anxiety and a greater acceptance and understanding of changes in their families. Group leaders reported similar positive outcomes (Pedro-Carroll & Cowen,

1985). A replication study with different group leaders and different schools confirmed these initial findings (Pedro-Carroll, Cowen, Hightower, & Guare, 1986).

Encouraging findings from those early studies fueled extensions of CODIP to children of different ages and sociodemographic backgrounds. Subsequent steps included adaptations of CODIP both for second and third, and fourth to sixth grade urban children. Evaluation of these new programs confirmed the adjustment gains previously reported for suburban samples (Alpert-Gillis, Pedro-Carroll, & Cowen, 1989; Pedro-Carroll, Alpert-Gillis, & Cowen, 1992). Overall, these data, involving multiple input sources, demonstrated improved home and school adjustment for CODIP children, reductions in their divorce-related concerns, and gains in their social competencies. Collectively, these data showed that the program model could be modified effectively for young children and low-income populations in which divorce is but one of many stressors.

An additional challenge for CODIP was to identify program components and practices that made for its positive outcome findings (Grych & Fincham, 1992). As noted earlier, CODIP rests on two key components: providing support and training coping skills. Others have also found these components to benefit children of divorce (Stolberg & Mahler, 1994). In seeking to disaggregate these components, Sterling's (1986) evaluation of CODIP for second and third graders, assessed the efficacy of a program with and without a social problem-solving (SPS) component. Sterling found that the support alone (i.e., no SPS) condition was less effective than the full program. She also found that 16 weekly sessions for this group yielded more positive outcomes than a twice weekly, 8-week program format. That information provided a useful foundation for the later adaptation of CODIP for very young children.

Evaluation of the CODIP program for kindergarten–first grade children provided multisource evidence of the program's efficacy (Pedro-Carroll & Alpert-Gillis, in press). Teachers reported gains in participants' school-related competencies and their ability to ask for help when needed, and decreases in their school-related problem behaviors, compared with a nonprogram, children-of-divorce control group. Similarly, leaders reported gains for participants in understanding the reasons for divorce (e.g., divorce is a grown-up problem and not children's fault), being able to talk about and deal with divorce-related feelings, getting along with peers, and thinking of ways to solve interpersonal problems. Parents reported similar improvements in participants' home adjustment (e.g., ability to deal with feelings, behave appropriately, and cope with problems). They also reported that their children were less moody and anxious, more open to sharing feelings, and that parent–child communication had improved. Finally, program children reported feeling more positively about themselves and their families, were less worried about the changes in their families, and said that they were talking more and enjoying talking more about their feelings with their parents (Pedro-Carroll & Alpert-Gillis, in press).

The positive findings cited reflect children's adjustment status when the program ends. Pedro-Carroll, Sutton, and Wyman (1996) assessed the stability of these outcomes over a 2-year follow-up period. New teachers, blind to children's initial group status, rated CODIP children as having significantly fewer school problems and more competencies than comparison children. Parent interview data showed that their improvements at home and in school lasted over the 2-year period. They also had fewer visits to the school health office than control children in the follow-up period. Spontaneous parent comments in the follow-up interview highlighted the value of the program's support and skill-training components. These findings suggest that CODIP gains had staying-power and helped children of divorce to cope more effectively over time.

A recent evaluation of the CODIP program for seventh and eighth graders (Pedro-Carroll, Sutton, & Black, 1993) again reflected the perspectives of parents, leaders, and children. Although findings from this study are tempered by relatively small sample sizes, agreement about important gains for participants was again found across diverse perspectives. Parents for example, reported improvements in children's overall adjustment and their ability to cope effectively with family changes. Leaders found program children better able to express feelings, manage anger, solve interpersonal problems, and differentiate between controllable and uncontrollable problems. In the latter context, children had acquired strategies for disengaging from parent conflict and refocusing on age-appropriate activities. Relatedly, children reported gains in friendship formation, anger control, and communication effectiveness.

Another finding of special interest for this age group was the significant improvement in participants' hopes and expectations for the future—a finding with implications for choices and decisions that shape their lives. Concretely, they saw themselves as having better futures in such areas as personal responsibility and interpersonal relationships, staying out of trouble, and having people who care about them. Such self-views facilitate responsible decision making and the formation of trusting, enduring, satisfying relationships. In this context, Wyman, Cowen, Work, and Kerley (1993) found that the presence of positive future expectations among 10–12-year-old, highly stressed urban children related to resilient outcomes 3 years later. Such views functioned as a protective factor in reducing the negative effects of major life stress.

SUMMARY

Significant stressors associated with marital disruption are experienced by millions of children annually. Although these stressors increase risk for psychological problems, research on risk and protective factors shows that long-term maladaptation is not an inevitable outcome for children of divorce. Sometimes, the protective elements needed to deflect maladaptive outcomes exist in the child's natural life situation. However, because that is not uniformly the case, prevention programs are needed to reduce the risk that stems from marital disruption. The CODIP thrust reflects a persistent effort to develop, field-test, and evaluate such a model over time. CODIP findings to date testify to the promise that preventive interventions hold for children of divorce of all ages and their parents.

All schools today have many children who have experienced family breakup following parental divorce. For many of these youngsters, this often protracted experience adversely affects school performance and adjustment. CODIP grew in the soil of these realities and the social changes that catalyzed them. It developed slowly and carefully over a 15-year period. During that period, a half-dozen variants of the program model were developed and field-tested. Each variant has its own detailed curriculum guide. Each offers supporting program efficacy data. Although the CODIP model stands well on its own and is now being implemented in many schools around the country, it has also become an additional option for PMHP programs because it offers an experience tailored specifically to the life situation and needs of children of divorce.

10

THE STUDY BUDDY PROGRAM[1]

This chapter describes the Study Buddy program, another primary prevention probe designed to go beyond PMHP's basic framework. Study Buddy differs from the primary prevention models described in the preceding two chapters in that it is based on a modification of everyday classroom practices. The program grew out of a set of convergent observations about the nature of traditional classroom structures, and the problems children have in cooperative work skills. The goal of the Study Buddy approach is to enhance wellness by creating a class structure that facilitates the development of cooperative work skills that children need to get along and work productively with peers.

Although the importance of good interpersonal working relationships is well documented, the development of such skills in schools has often been left to chance. In most traditional classrooms, children sit in separate rows and work independently; a common class rule is that children should not talk to each other. Rather than stimulating interpersonal skills or learning to work cooperatively, children often get the implicit message that working with other children is cheating or, if not that, at least against class rules.

---

[1]This chapter was coauthored by A. Dirk Hightower and Douglas B. Fagen.

Classrooms often do more to foster competition than cooperation. When children are permitted to work together, it is usually for brief time periods; such groups often involve four or more students and are subject to frequent changes. Thus, the message that many schools convey to children is, "Work by yourself and you'll stay out of trouble!" Whether overt or implicit, this view has important ramifications. By focusing on teaching children individually, we neglect the promotion of skills that children need to work effectively together. Such skills have immediate, instrumental, and long-term value.

In preindustrial America, families were larger and schools were structured so that children worked with and helped each other. Thus, children had ample opportunities to observe and learn cooperative work skills both at home and in school. By contrast, today's fast-paced, mobile, specialized society offers few opportunities outside of school for children to develop cooperative work skills.

Several defining features of an elementary school classroom (e.g., a place where peers share common goals) make that setting especially well suited to the task of teaching children how to work together. The importance of close working relationships for success in schools and society and the lack of opportunities for children to learn the skills needed to develop such relationships, together with a rapidly growing literature about the role of peer relationships in children's social development were the moving forces that led to the development of the Study Buddy program.

PEER RELATIONSHIPS AND SOCIAL DEVELOPMENT

Personality theorists have long recognized the key role that peer relationships play in healthy personality development. Sullivan (1953) wrote extensively about the importance of effective early peer relationships for later psychological health. Illustratively, he identified *chumship*, a close relationship between same-age, same-gender peers in middle childhood, as being critical both for healthy identity formation and the later capacity for intimacy in heterosexual relationships. Sullivan argued strongly that success begets success in peer relationships. His point has been affirmed by empirical findings showing that successful peer relationships in childhood do, in fact, facilitate future social success (Hartup, 1983; Hartup & Moore, 1990).

Sullivan also argued that successful peer experiences were especially important for children who experienced emotionally distant, neglectful, or abusive family relationships. For such children, the availability of an understanding, accepting peer is an important source of self-worth and offers needed practice in the interpersonal skills of mutuality, reciprocal communication, and compromise.

Others have discussed the importance of feeling socially connected for healthy personality development (Baumeister & Leary, 1995; Bowlby, 1982; Fromm-Reichmann, 1959; Kohut, 1984; Winnicott, 1965) and satisfying peer relationships throughout life (Damon, 1977; Isaacs, 1939; Rubin, 1974, 1980). Indeed, to a considerable extent, contemporary personality theorists have shifted their focus away from intrapsychic determinants to the central role of interpersonal relationships in the child's healthy development (Bowlby, 1982; Greenberg & Mitchell, 1983).

The importance of peer relationships for developing social competence has also been shown (Hartup, 1983). Children usually prefer and associate with same-sex peers. Such relationships play a formative role in a child's developing sense of self. The importance of same-sex relationships grows as the child's communication skills increase. Relatedly, the child's use of feedback increases with the development of empathy (i.e., the ability to take the perspective of another), a skill crucial for effective cooperative relationships.

When children work in dyads, as opposed to larger groups, they tend to be more task oriented and to like each other more (Hartup, 1983). Also, in small groups, consensus is reached more readily, the opinions of members are deemed to be more important, and there is more cooperation. At virtually all ages, the better children get to know each other, the more likely they are to see each other as friends. Whereas repeated experience with the same partner has been found to promote smooth, egalitarian interaction patterns, work groups that change are more susceptible to instances of dominance and coercion. Across all ages, proximity and participation in common activities are characteristics that make for close friendships. Although reciprocity and mutuality characterize all friendships, synchrony, smoothness, and cooperation become more evident by middle childhood (Hartup, 1983). The rationale for the Study Buddy program rests largely on empirical findings about peer relationships, cited above. Their importance in shaping key aspects of the Study Buddy approach will become clearer later in the chapter, when the program's details are described.

Research in the areas of peer tutoring and cooperative learning, which may be seen as special types of peer relationship programs, has produced consistent findings with regard to their academic and social impacts (Allen, 1976; Cotton & Cook, 1982; Hartup, 1983; Johnson & Johnson, 1974; Johnson, Maruyama, Johnson, Nelson, & Skon, 1981; Sharan, 1980, 1990; Slavin, 1983; Strain, 1981; Talmage, Pascarella, & Ford, 1984). This literature suggests that children can be very effective teachers of each other (Hartup, 1983), indeed, under some conditions, even more effective than teachers (Epstein, 1978; Jenkins, Mayhall, Peschyn, & Jenkins, 1974; Schunk & Hanson, 1985). The effectiveness of peer teachers has been found to increase when training and structure are provided for their activities (Talmage et al., 1984). Also, interdependent cooperative groups have been shown to have consistently higher academic achievement than competitive groups (Johnson et al., 1981) in reading (Talmage et al., 1984), mathematics (Schunk & Hanson, 1985), and social studies (Wright & Cowen, 1985). Peer behavioral management has been shown to be as effective as, or more effective than, behavioral management by the teacher (Carden-Smith & Fowler, 1984).

Benefits from peer teaching are more likely to occur with interventions that last over extended time periods (Hartup, 1983). At another level, Slavin (1983) concluded that the largest gains in academic achievement come from cooperative groups that work on the basis of group contingencies (i.e., shared rewards based on a single group product) and individual accountability (i.e., each student is responsible for a certain portion of the product).

Closely tied to the educational literature, work with group contingencies has been of special interest to behaviorally oriented psychologists. These techniques have been found to (a) be superior to individual contingency strategies when academic behaviors are targeted (McLaughlin, 1981; McLaughlin, Herb, & Davis, 1980); (b) encourage spontaneous, cooperative peer-tutoring behaviors (Hamblin, Hathaway, & Wodarski, 1971); and (c) be effective and generalize well when tied to reciprocal peer tutoring, in enhancing children's academic performance (Pigott, Fantuzzo, & Clement, 1986).

Several cooperative learning programs have targeted nonacademic goals, for example, improving relationships among children of different ethnic groups. Specifically, cross-racial cooperative learning groups have been shown to reduce racial stereotypes and tensions (Aronson et al., 1978; Hansell, 1984). Relatedly, educationally handicapped children grouped with nonhandicapped peers gained significantly in peer acceptance and academic achievement (Johnson, Johnson, Scott, & Ramolae, 1985).

Notwithstanding the considerable potential of cooperative learning formats, teachers use such formats infrequently (11% of the time; Lockheed & Harris, 1984). It should be noted that a class arrangement in which students work cooperatively significantly alters the teacher's role from a dispenser of knowledge to a consultant, available to work with groups when needed (Sharan, 1980). Teachers are more likely to develop a positive attitude to a cooperative learning format and to implement such a strategy more frequently when they are given prior training in its use (Talmage et al., 1984).

In sum, the literature reviewed documents the importance of peer relationships in childhood. Research has shown that children and youth who have difficulty relating to and working with peers are more likely to do poorly in school or drop out, have trouble getting and holding a job, eventually use drugs and alcohol, need more mental health services, and get involved more often with the criminal justice system (Cowen, Pedersen, et al., 1973; Ensminger et al., 1983; Hartup & Moore, 1990; Parker & Asher, 1987; Rolf 1972, 1976).

A related point is that peer acceptance and rejection patterns tend to remain stable over time. Thus, the popular child continues to be socially adept and to maintain successful social interactions, whereas the rejected child tends to remain outside the group mainstream, in the absence of intervention (Coie & Dodge, 1988; Hartup, 1983; Newcomb, Bukowski, & Pattee, 1993). Hence, interventions that promote effective peer interactions and work skills in young children can establish competencies to enhance interpersonal relationships and wellness outcomes both in the here and now, as well as distally. Such skills operate to protect children against adjustment problems.

AN ANTECEDENT TO STUDY BUDDY

As PMHP's interest in primary prevention alternatives began to develop, one appealing option was the health-building potential of cooperative learning formats. An influential demonstration of that era was Aronson et al.'s (1978) use of a particular cooperative learning format, called the jigsaw classroom, to reduce racial tensions among elementary-aged children in Texas. In the jigsaw format, cross-gender, cross-ethnic learning groups worked as cooperative units in fifth grade social studies classes. Aronson et al. (1978) found that this format both reduced racial tensions and enhanced participants' self-esteem.

Based on those findings, Wright and Cowen (1985) developed a similar cooperative learning format, also in fifth grade social studies classes. Cross-gender, cross-ability level groups, each with five children, were formed as cooperative learning units, for two large segments of a fifth grade social studies curriculum. The project extended over a 3-month period. Children in these jigsaw units had to learn one segment (one fifth) of a curricular unit, and teach that segment to their groupmates. Thus, in all groups, students had to function as both teacher and pupil in this vertical arrangement. Moreover, horizontally, across jigsaw groups, children responsible for each specific curricular segment met to ensure that they understood the segment fully and to exchange ideas about how best to teach it to classmates.

Children in the cooperative learning format judged their classes to be more involved, orderly, and organized and did better on report card and monthly social studies examination grades than children in the comparison group. Interestingly, the latter difference was due mostly to substantial improvements by initially weaker students (Wright & Cowen, 1985).

This experiential backdrop, along with an evolving cooperative learning literature with thought-provoking and encouraging findings, suggested several guidelines that shaped development of the initial Study Buddy program. To us, it seemed likely that children's ability to learn effective peer interactions and academic skills would benefit from the following program features:

1. a structured program;
2. small groups (primarily dyads) of same-age and same-gender peers;
3. long-term and frequent periods of close association, common activities, and shared experiences;
4. interdependent, cooperative work exercises;
5. group contingencies based on individual accountability;
6. situations that permit students to teach and help each other easily and naturally; and
7. teachers who facilitate the above conditions.

The Study Buddy program sought to create a structural model and set of conditions reflecting the above criteria. This entailed working with teachers, school mental health professionals, and administrators from the start to modify the classroom structure; working with entire classrooms rather than just with selected, at-risk children; and integrating teachers in the program development and evaluation processes.

Both short- and long-term goals were formulated for the program. Proximally, the program was intended to promote peer relationship skills and, in so doing, reduce classroom problems and the need for outside referrals. It was also thought that the program might help to identify children evidencing early signs of social difficulties. A longer term hope was that promoting children's peer interaction skills in childhood could reduce the social adjustment problems, in adolescence and adulthood, known to be associated with poor early peer relationships (Parker & Asher, 1987).

Given the challenges that children face, both in and out of school, we considered it appropriate to place the Study Buddy intervention in what Sarason (1986) called a "realistic time perspective." Sarason's point was that educators and psychologists often fail to recognize the complexities inherent in the tasks they undertake and, hence, do not allow enough time for programs to unfold. We mention this point to anchor the still emerging Study Buddy program in a longer term developmental framework.

PROGRAM DESCRIPTION

Study Buddy depends on the cooperation of program staff, school administrators, and teachers. From the initial contact through teacher training, program implementation, consultation, and program evaluation, Study Buddy is a collaborative program. The sections that follow discuss the components of a Study Buddy program and the roles of key players in such a program.

Study Buddy is a teacher-conducted, class-based, cooperative learning program. It involves pairing children, having them work together at least three times a week, in the same dyad, for the entire school year. Teachers play several pivotal roles in Study Buddy. These include helping to establish the initial Study Buddy pairings, creating program lessons, serving as resource persons for the children, and participating in the program evaluation. Conducting a Study Buddy program is facilitated for teachers by the existence of a support network that helps them to run the program smoothly in the classroom. Optimally, this program team includes teachers, a school-based mental health professional, and a Study Buddy program consultant who meet every few weeks to plan, discuss, and monitor the program. This network contributes to the program's success by providing inputs and support at multiple levels.

Training Sessions

The teachers' first in-depth contact with Study Buddy occurs in an initial set of two to four, 2-hour training sessions, conducted by a program consultant early in the school year. These meetings serve several purposes. The trainer first presents information about the program's theoretical underpinnings, including research findings on peer relationships and the effects of cooperative versus competitive learning environments. Teachers are also given a brief description of the program's structure that provides a base on which specific program goals are built. These goals are discussed and joint decisions are made about which goals and which program formats best meet teacher objectives. Teachers must be actively involved in this decision-making process because it increases the likelihood that program specifics (content, emphases, meeting times) will be in sync with classroom realities and because it empowers the teachers by increasing their sense of stake in and ownership of the program.

Even though teachers, understandably, vary some in how they prioritize program objectives, virtually all teachers support Study Buddy's most central goals of enhancing peer relationships and fostering effective cooperative work skills in the classroom. Other teacher-identified program objectives that have come up with some frequency include strengthening children's self-esteem and social skills, communication skills, and sense of responsibility. One fringe benefit of give-and-take dialogue about the program's objectives and format is that it helps to solidify a team working to achieve shared goals. Most basically, however, the approach described rests on the belief that Study Buddy works best when it is seen as addressing real classroom needs.

Once the program's objectives are agreed upon, training sessions familiarize teachers with Study Buddy's defining operations. Because the process of pairing children in dyads is central to the program's workings, pairing procedures are discussed with teachers, who work with the program consultant in the actual pairing process. Early training sessions also review structural changes that the program entails for teachers and students and covers such topics as planning and developing Study Buddy activities, introducing the program to the class, and coping with pairs that have trouble working together. These issues continue to be discussed throughout the year either in regularly scheduled program consultation meetings or whenever teachers encounter concrete problems in running the program.

Pairing

Because Study Buddy is designed to maximize all children's participation in a cooperative working relationship, it is built around the smallest, most manageable possible group, namely the dyad. Given that most selected dyads will be working together for the full school year, the process of pairing children is important. This is usually done during the second or third training session. Collaboration between teachers and program staff in this process is essential. Before the pairing session, teachers will have completed a T-CRS (a school adjustment rating scale described in chapter 4) for all children in their class. These rating scales are used to generate a profile of each child's school problems and competencies that, in turn, is the basis for pairings.

The pairing process rests on the assumption that each child has unique skills and abilities that can contribute to a Study Buddy pair. The most important objective of the pairing is to bring together children with complementary skills so that they can learn from each other. At the same time, Study Buddies need to have enough in common to feel compatible and be able to communicate comfortably with each other. Thus, a balance is sought in establishing Study Buddy pairings: partners should be different enough to benefit from their Study Buddy's strength, but their styles should not be so different as to create conflict. Experience has shown that certain types of pairings should be avoided. For example, two active, distractible children should not be paired. Such youngsters are better paired with secure, well-adjusted children with good interpersonal strengths and resources.

One good way to start the pairing process is for the consultant to demonstrate how it works, using T-CRS profiles from a single class. In doing this, profiles are coded so that children's identities are not initially known. This procedure ensures that only the child's teacher-rated qualities will be used at this stage. The goals of the pairing process are explained concretely as the consultant demonstrates these pairings. Teacher inputs are solicited during this demonstration. Often, classroom constraints ultimately force some less than ideal pairings. The process is most difficult at the end, when only a few children are left to chose from in forming pairs.

After teachers watch the consultant do pairings for a demonstration class, they in turn work in pairs to develop Study Buddy dyads for their own classes. Working in dyads gives them team experience, increases the level of thought and discussion that goes into the pairing process, and enables them to observe how others think through the issues at hand. Each teacher pair thus begins with one classroom and, together, they pair children into dyads following the guidelines established. The consultant monitors this process. All initial pairings are made anonymously and solely on the basis of T-CRS profiles. After that step has been completed, children's names are linked to profiles. At that point, teachers re-review the pairs and note any that include either best friends or worst enemies. Such pairs are reassigned to ensure that each selected dyad will have the opportunity to build a successful new relationship.

To recapitulate, collaboration between the program consultant and teachers in establishing Study Buddy pairs foreshadows the process of cooperation soon to unfold in the classroom. The actual pairing process pivots around teacher (T-CRS) ratings of multiple aspects of children's school adjustment. T-CRS derived profiles of children's strengths and weaknesses provide the basis for initial pairings of children. Teachers review these initial pairings and have the option of modifying any that seem to be nonviable on various grounds (e.g., friendship patterns, "bad chemistry"). Once Study Buddy dyads are established, the program's classroom component can begin.

Introduction to Students

Teachers can introduce the program to the class in several ways. The introduction is a key step, in that most children have had little prior experience working interactively with peers over extended time periods. Hence, the program may seem foreign, perhaps even a bit intimidating, to children who have not previously experienced a cooperative learning environment. Importantly, the teacher's introduction of Study Buddy sets the tone for the program.

Some teachers have found it helpful to move children's desks so that they are sitting next to their Study Buddy for a while before the program starts. Doing so gives children a chance to get to know their about-to-be Study Buddy and gives the teacher a glimpse of how pairs may work together. Other teachers have used the program introduction as an opportunity to talk to the class about social skills and to discuss the importance of working together. Still others have had students "discover" their Buddies, as part of some kind of fun, interactive activity.

A recently completed *Study Buddy Teacher's Manual* (Hightower et al., 1995) describes several ways for teachers to introduce Study Buddy to their class. Whichever way is chosen, the goal of the introduction is to highlight Study Buddy's cooperative nature and the need for children to learn how to work well, communicate, and problem solve together. In this context, the program is best represented as an opportunity to try something new, rather than an additional class requirement.

The program's first activity, after it has been introduced, is usually a structured, interactive exercise that helps children get to know their Study Buddy better. One activity used widely for that purpose is to have Study Buddies interview each other, using get-to-know questions such as "What's your family like?" "What's your favorite food? . . . TV show?" The first few Study Buddy activities can be challenging for teachers and students alike, as they try to redefine and get used to a new role in this exploratory period. Many teachers find it helpful to have a group discussion to process these early activities, build vocabulary around sharing and cooperating, discuss how it is sometimes difficult to work together, and continue to orient the class to program goals. Discussions can also be used to develop class-generated rules to be followed during Study Buddy time, such as agreeing on a place to do Study Buddy activities and deciding how projects can best be done jointly.

Program Maintenance

As noted, the Study Buddy program is structural rather than curricular. It functions as an overlay to a curriculum already in place. It does not require the teacher to develop a new curriculum; rather it reorganizes the classroom and provides a structure within which virtually any educational material can be made into a Study Buddy activity. Four structural components operate to advance the program's goals:

1. students work together in dyads;
2. the dyads work together at least three times per week, for 30 to 45 minutes (more or less, depending on grade level);
3. pairs remain together throughout the entire academic year; and
4. teachers are available as consultants at all Study Buddy sessions, but the prime impetus for learning resides with the student pairs.

Together, these components are intended to foster change in the classroom climate. Frequent continuing interactions between Study Buddies enable them to get to know each other and develop a working relationship over an extended time period. The fact that a Study Buddy program can be built around different content areas increases the likelihood that all children will be able to contribute to their pairs. Also, keeping pairs together for the full school year creates a group dynamic based on shared outcomes or paired contingencies. Some teachers have assigned a common grade to Study Buddy activities so that, within the program's framework, children must depend on each other to succeed. As children come to realize that they will continue to work closely with their Study Buddy, and that they must both learn material for the team to do well, they feel increasingly invested in each other's learning.

This "positive interdependence," as Slavin (1983) suggested, is the cornerstone of cooperative learning. In conventional independent learning situations, helping other children is often (a) an unnecessary hindrance, (b) a threat to one's own success (as in some zero-sum competitive goal structures), or (c) against the rules. By contrast, Study Buddy provides both an opportunity and a structure within which students are motivated and encouraged to help each other. Under such circumstances, as children come to realize that they will do well only if their Study Buddy also does well, they are more likely to interact with, teach, and explain things to each other. Finally, Study Buddy time is a time when students are responsible for their own learning. The teacher is available for support and as a resource person, but the primary responsibility for learning is with the students. This structural arrangement can enhance the child's sense of mastery and empowerment.

Because the Study Buddy program does not depend on a specific curriculum or body of content, the teacher can select program activities each week, taking into account the content, level of difficulty, amount of time, and materials needed for specific activities, and choosing those that best fit a class's cooperative work structure at a given point in time. In practice, activities reflecting many different subject areas (e.g., health, science, arithmetic, language arts, history) have all been used effectively as foci within the Study Buddy framework (Hightower et al., 1995).

Early in the program, it helps to use more structured activities with clear guidelines about how dyads can work together. Concrete activities, such as spelling and arithmetic, work well at this time. Later, as students acquire experience in working cooperatively, less structured, more creative lessons can be used, such as word problems, writing projects, science projects, or brainstorming activities. Activities for which materials are limited and sharing is necessary (e.g., science projects, computer work) are well suited to Study Buddy. The *Study Buddy Teacher's Manual* (Hightower et al., 1995) provides a rich menu of lessons that have been used for different age groups.

Choosing Study Buddy lessons well depends on an understanding of children's abilities and the relationship dynamics that develop in the class while the program is going on. Although the Study Buddy program, as noted, seeks to foster the development of cooperative work skills in all children, realistically children come to a classroom with different prior experiences and social skills. When academic subjects are taught below their ability level, they get bored; if the material is beyond their ability level, they get frustrated. The same is true for children's cooperative work skills. Thus, a core challenge in planning Study Buddy activities is to select tasks that involve a degree and type of interaction that is both optimally engaging and realistic for the children.

We have observed that many children move through a hierarchy of cooperative work styles, some quickly, others more gradually. On the basis of these observations, we have come to conceptualize children's cooperative work skills as developing through several stages. These stages serve as a rough guide to the complex network of skills needed to work cooperatively with others. Three stages that well represent this progression of cooperative work skills are *parallel work*, *structured cooperation*, and *reciprocity*.

Young children at the parallel stage tend to work side by side on a project, interacting only minimally with their Study Buddy. Because working together is unfamiliar, they may respond to requests or suggestions with indifference, puzzlement, or simply by ignoring their partner. Thus, communication between young children is often unidirectional. Although these children can, in fact, complete tasks that require some interaction, many lack the skills needed to work in truly cooperative ways.

At the more advanced, structured cooperation, or question and answer stage, children work better interactively in more structured situations in which they are capable of asking each other questions and taking turns in completing an assignment. Although their communication skills are better developed than those of children lower in the hierarchy, their interactions may still be characterized by question and answer interchanges rather than by full-fledged discussion. Thus, at this stage, children can best work together in structured activities that require relatively little decision making and in which each person's role is clear. Because these children have still had only limited cooperative work experience, they may lapse into parallel work if they are not supervised and encouraged.

Children with more advanced cooperative work skills can work together in richer, reciprocal ways. In the reciprocity stage, children have more fully developed communication skills that enable them to engage in sustained conversation and discussion and to share views more fully with each other. Moreover, because they can also better take the perspective of the other, they are more likely to be aware of their Study Buddy's strong and weak points, and to adapt their work and interaction styles to those realities. Children at this level can work together with minimal supervision, ask each other questions, and brainstorm and integrate their ideas. Importantly, they are capable of changing their modes of interaction to accommodate the requirements of specific assignments. Primary grade children do not often evidence this reciprocity. Rather, it develops gradually as students move through middle childhood.

Like other forms of child development, the cooperative work stages described are not discrete. Thus, children may occasionally regress before they move solidly into a more advanced stage, as their cooperative work skills develop further. Progression, in other words, is uneven and setbacks occur. Most classes progress with similar ups and downs during the school year. The challenge for teachers, taking children's developmental levels into account, is to select Study Buddy activities that are both interesting and challenging, as children's cooperative work skills grow.

Because Study Buddy is primarily a structural program, teachers are often challenged about how to interact with the class during program time. Whereas in normal class activities, teachers play a central instructional role either with the full class or a smaller learning group, Study Buddy requires them to step out of the traditional role and allow children to function as both teachers and students. In the beginning, this can be as difficult for teachers as it is for children. On the other hand, the structural change that Study Buddy embodies helps children to rely more on each other, develop the capacity to self-regulate, and sharpen the cooperative skills needed to complete complex tasks successfully. Ideally, the teacher as consultant should create a context to facilitate the achievement of those goals, and offer support, as needed, to help children who are having difficulty in the new role.

Consultation

Consultation, an important resource for the Study Buddy program, serves several purposes over the school year. The most basic is to maintain a sense of continuity and teamwork for the teachers and staff. Consultation also provides continuing education, as needed, in such areas as socioemotional development and peer relationships and brings classroom teachers together regularly to discuss program happenings. This is especially important for teachers just starting in Study Buddy because it provides a forum for exchanging information about what is and is not working and ways of approaching the difficult situations that come up in the course of running the program.

PROGRAM HISTORY

Study Buddy began in the Rochester City School District in 1985–1986. It started early in the year with four fourth to sixth grade classes; three other fourth to sixth grade classes were added in January. In the initial program year, teachers paired all children in same-sex dyads. The goals for the year were to pilot the new approach, develop and refine a detailed program curriculum, and establish a program evaluation framework.

In Year 2, Study Buddy expanded to nine classes; three other classes comprised a comparison group. Of the nine program teachers, six used the Year 1 curriculum and lessons; the other three developed their own lessons. Children were paired in same-sex dyads either by teacher ratings (cf. above) or by a class sociometric measure. Program evaluation showed that Study Buddy children exceeded comparison children in terms of improved class adjustment and math achievement; they also had more positive views of classmates and fewer unexcused absences. Although no outcome differences were found between the two pairing methods, teacher pairing was preferred to sociometric pairing (Hightower & Avery, 1986).

In Year 3, there were five fourth- and fifth-grade program classes and five comparison classes. Most program teachers were repeaters from Year 2. Study Buddies were paired either by teacher ratings or randomly. The latter procedure generated mixed-gender pairs for the first time. The Year 3 program ran into several major, unanticipated management problems. Teachers had a hard time fitting the program curriculum into class schedules because both the state and the local school district had introduced new sets of curricular requirements. Indeed, for that reason some teachers were not able to complete the 15-week curriculum within its 30 week allocated time span. Hence, program findings for Year 3 were largely observational and impressionistic.

Teachers who developed their own lesson plans for the program reported that (a) they had more frequent Study Buddy sessions (i.e., up to 5 times a week), and (b) children were excited about the program. They also used consultation more. Although there were several positive program outcomes (e.g., more positive sociometric ratings and teacher ratings of adjustment), those gains were less robust than they had been in the previous year. Teachers whose classes had both same- and mixed-gender pairs, preferred the former (Hightower, Avery, & Levinson, 1988).

The process of extending Study Buddy to primary graders began in 1989–1990. The program's prime setting at that time moved to a small city in a predominantly rural area. Two second grade teachers and one kindergarten teacher volunteered to participate in the program in its pilot year. Positive teacher reactions to the program led to a significant expansion between 1990 and 1994. During that period, a total of 57 teachers and more than 1,000 kindergarten to fifth-grade children participated in the program's further development.

PROGRAM EVALUATION

Study Buddy's short-term goals are to promote children's social and cooperative work skills; its long-term goals are to prevent school difficulties associated with poor peer relationships and enhance social functioning.

Program evaluations to date have focused primarily on short-term outcomes. Those evaluations, it should again be noted, have been constrained by real-world limiting factors, as for example when the program could not be completed because new curricular extensions were mandated that required time initially designated for Study Buddy. Thus, several Study Buddy program evaluations have involved "catch-as-catch-can" methods and have depended heavily on observational and impressionistic data.

Within the framework of those limits, most Study Buddy evaluations have reflected the perspectives of teachers and child participants and have assessed changes in children's school problem behaviors (acting out, anxiety) and competencies (peer social skills, frustration tolerance). Socioemotional (empathy, perceived self-worth) and academic measures have sometimes been used as secondary outcome indicators.

Study Buddy began with fourth- to sixth-grade children. In its first several years, consistent improvement was found among participants on teacher-rated dimensions of school adjustment as well as peer sociometric and achievement measures (Hightower & Avery, 1986; Hightower et al., 1988). When the program shifted focus to primary grade children and simultaneously moved to a new school setting, a second pilot period was needed. There were no formal evaluations in the first 3 years of the new program because sample sizes were too small. Although teachers reported gains in children's cooperative behaviors (i.e., the pairs were productive), sociometric data did not reflect these improvements. The 1992–1993 program was conducted in 20 classrooms. In those classes, the vast majority (over 90%) of pairs worked well together for the entire school year. Both teachers and children again reported the program to be fun, worthwhile, and productive, but these positive effects were again not confirmed by sociometric data. Although a small program evaluation study, in 1993–1994, comparing six Study Buddy and eight nonprogram classes failed to yield significant program effects on criterion outcome measures (Fagen & Hightower, 1994), teachers reported positive Study Buddy class environments and children reported that they enjoyed working in Study Buddy groups.

FUTURE DIRECTIONS

The challenging task of developing face-valid, effective interventions to foster young children's cooperative work skills is still at a relatively early stage (Battistich, Solomon, & Delucchi, 1993; Johnson & Johnson, 1989). Successful steps in that direction have important implications for school personnel and prevention researchers. Largely on the basis of clinical-impressionistic inputs, Study Buddy seems to work effectively from kindergarten to sixth grade. That impression, however, has not been supported consistently by hard empirical data involving a control group design for kindergarten- to third-grade children, and findings for fourth- to sixth-grade children have been less than robust. Carefully controlled program outcome studies are clearly needed to provide the information required to shape a more wholesome future for the Study Buddy program.

Other specific questions about the Study Buddy approach remain. Preliminary program trials with older students suggested that mixed-gender pairs had problems "settling down" initially, but that the social and academic gains they made by the end of the school year were similar to those made by like-gender dyads (Hightower et al., 1988). Conceivably, mixed-gender pairings may also work for younger children, although this possibility has not yet been explored systematically. At present, it is unclear as to when, if at all, children benefit most from cross-gender interactions or how such interactions can best be structured to facilitate short- and long-term benefits in cooperative work skills.

When recent developments in social competence training were considered in chapter 8, an evolving trend was noted for such programs to have moved away from one-shot, time-limited experiences to continuing programmatic efforts over multiple school years. That directional shift may be equally relevant for cooperative learning programs. To date, there has been little exploration of the consistent use of such an approach across grade levels, although the CDC and Seattle programs have taken starter-steps in that direction (Battistich et al., 1993; Hawkins et al., 1992). In principle, a schoolwide cooperative learning program such as Study Buddy, starting in kindergarten and continuing through the entire elementary period, should contribute appreciably to the development of more satisfying peer relationships and effective work-related skills (Gartner & Riessman, 1993). Exploring such a possibility will be labor intensive and will be accomplished only slowly over time.

Another area to explore concerns the length of time that Study Buddy pairs need to be together to optimize program gains. To date, the program has paired dyads for the full school year on the assumption that program goals are best served by close, long-term working relationships. That may be a good approach for many, but not necessarily all, children. For some youngsters, if an initial pairing is less than optimal or when contact with different partners can be helpful, there may be an advantage to having two Study Buddy pairings, each lasting half a year. Currently, however, there are no data on this issue.

Although we believe that the Study Buddy program has substantial primary preventive potential, the approach is still in an early developmental stage. Continuing program refinements come about slowly through interactions with program teachers and classroom observations. What is clearest about Study Buddy thus far is the excitement and the face-valid good sense it generates for both teachers and pupils. Study Buddy teachers have reported, quite uniformly, that because program children learn how to work better with peers, class functioning is facilitated. For that reason, some teachers who have been with Study Buddy for a while develop an evangelical fervor for the program and strive actively to get other teachers involved in it. Also, most students look forward to and enjoy Study Buddy sessions.

The program thus makes sense to its two main consumer groups: teachers and students. Moreover, qualitatively, both teachers and students have reported that most Study Buddy pairings work well. On the other hand, from a research perspective, it has not been easy to establish exactly what the phrase "works well" means or how to document such benefits empirically. For that reason, we cannot represent Study Buddy as an "open and shut" case.

Presently, we are reviewing the cooperative learning and friendship literatures, as those literatures may shed light on the social and emotional development of young children. The large majority of several hundred articles, books, and chapters in cooperative learning thus far reviewed have focused on academic outcomes among older children. Also, in the literature reviewed, short-term, micro-level interventions substantially outnumber longer term, systems-level interventions. The latter are of special interest in any attempt to assess the preventive impact of cooperative learning programs such as Study Buddy.

One hoped for outcome of this literature search is to develop a conceptual matrix within which to integrate notions about cooperative learning into the broader framework of peer relationships. Notwithstanding the substantial overlap of these two areas, there has been little exchange and cross-fertilization between them. Future cooperative learning frameworks can profit from application of literature knowledge about peer relationships. Although there is a growing literature pertaining to the development of peer relationships and friendship dyads (Newcomb & Bagwell, 1995), factors that enhance or impede such development in a classroom are not yet clear.

CONCLUDING REMARKS

The Study Buddy development has been one important element in our search for program-enhancing primary prevention options. On conceptual grounds, it well fits a primary prevention framework in that it is a class-oriented, "before the fact" (of maladjustment) program, designed to teach children a set of interactive skills with adaptive adjustment-enhancing potential, which include peer relationship and cooperative working skills.

The work thus far done in developing Study Buddy has had both exciting and vexing aspects. The positiveness and excitement come from the consistently favorable and enthusiastic reactions that the program has received from teachers and pupils. To them, Study Buddy is a "make-sense and fun" program. Moreover, teachers have consistently reported improved peer and work relationships as program outcomes. In contrast with those indicators of the program's face validity, empirical outcome findings have been at best spotty and often flat. Although it is unclear how much of this empirical shortfall reflects weaknesses and breakdowns in study designs, instrumentation, and measurements, as opposed to program insufficiencies, it is clear that Study Buddy cannot be depicted at this time as an empirically validated primary prevention approach in the same sense, for example, as CODIP. Metaphorically, it is better seen as a tender bud that has considerable growing and unfolding to do before it becomes a fully developed, fragrant flower.

11

THE ROCHESTER CHILD RESILIENCE PROJECT

The last three chapters described primary prevention interventions that have gone through extensive development and are now in active operation. This chapter describes the Rochester Child Resilience Project (RCRP), which is on a similar ultimate trajectory but not as far along as the prior ones. To date, most of the RCRP's efforts have gone into generative (fact-finding) studies designed to clarify the adaptation of inner-city children who experience major life stress, with only a few preliminary steps toward application and intervention. The proximal goal of these studies is to understand better the factors that promote and sustain healthy development in children under adverse life conditions (i.e., childhood resilience). A longer term goal is to apply such knowledge in developing preventive interventions for children at risk of maladjustment by virtue of exposure to chronic and profound life stress.

Childhood resilience is a timely concept because of the increasing numbers of children who grow up under highly adverse life conditions. More than 50% of inner-city children, for example, live in poverty; others live in the shadow of such chronic stressors as severe conflict between parents, a parent impaired by substance abuse, and neighborhood violence. Although such chronically stressful life conditions are, in general, linked to higher rates of child maladjustment, children differ markedly in their responses to stress. Whereas many children who experience adversity and disadvantage founder, others develop well, and some few even flourish. Werner and Smith (1982), pioneers in the field of childhood resilience, describe the latter as children who "worked well, played well, loved well, and expected well" in spite of major life adversity.

This chapter first considers the concept of resilience in the context of what is known about the effects of life stress on children's adjustment. Next, it summarizes current knowledge about resilience as a backdrop for considering how the RCRP got started and some of its findings to date. Finally, it describes an early exploration of a child-focused preventive intervention based on the RCRP's generative findings.

A RATIONALE FOR STUDYING CHILDHOOD RESILIENCE

Learning about the experiences, mechanisms, and processes that enable a child who grows up in a highly stressful environment to develop well emotionally, behaviorally, and cognitively has much to offer to a basic psychology of health. Because the mental health field has always been oriented predominantly to dysfunction (i.e., how problems develop and how to alleviate them), current understandings of psychological health and its components, as well as the processes that help wellness to root and develop, are limited. Focusing on resilience can help to redress this imbalance. A clear understanding of the forces that subserve resilience can also pave the way for more effective preventive interventions. PMHP's long-standing interest in prevention and wellness, plus the fact that some future programs to enhance resilience among highly stressed children are likely to be school based, are factors that first drew our attention to the study of child resilience.

Although interest in this topic is not new, concepts of resilience have evolved considerably in recent years. Early interest in resilient child outcomes grew out of research identifying factors that placed children at risk of developing serious disorders such as schizophrenia. In the course of this work, it became clear that although some children exposed to the risk of having schizophrenic parents became disordered, others did not; indeed, some of those at seemingly grave risk actually developed into very competent adults. The incongruity between high-risk life conditions and adaptive outcomes moved some observers to describe children who beat the odds as *invulnerable* or *invincible* (Anthony & Cohler, 1987; Garmezy & Nuechterlein, 1972; Werner & Smith, 1982).

Anthony (1974) sought to vivify the concept of the invulnerable child by an analogy involving three dolls—one each made of glass, plastic, and steel. To make the point, he noted that if all three dolls were exposed to the same "risk" (a blow from a hammer), consequences would vary greatly: the glass doll would be shattered and the plastic doll would have a permanent dent, whereas the hammer would bounce off the steel doll, leaving little or no mark. Although the analogy captures something real about the concept of invulnerability because that term, when used with children, conveyed an aura of infallibility, many investigators, ourselves included, gravitated to the seemingly more appropriate term "resilience." The latter offers the additional advantage of viewing adaptation to adversity along an implied continuum rather than in an either/or way (e.g., disordered vs. invulnerable).

LIFE STRESS AND CHILDREN'S ADJUSTMENT

Although the term *resilience* is sometimes used synonymously with good mental health, the concept is more useful, in our view, when used to shed light on factors that favor sound development under conditions where maladjustment is likely. Garmezy (1982) well captured this mix of competence under conditions of adversity when he described the resilient child as "the healthy child in an unhealthy setting" (p. xix).

Caplan (1981) described stress as "a marked discrepancy between the demands made . . . and the organism's capability to respond, the consequences of which will be detrimental" (p. 414). Many stressful life events and circumstances (SLE-Cs), ranging from societal conditions such as discrimination to discrete events such as sexual molestation, affect children adversely. Indeed, precisely because some traumatic stressors overwhelm children's adaptive capacities, they undermine the functioning of most children who experience them. Examples of such traumatic stressors include sustained abuse by caregivers, loss of a close family member, natural disasters, or being a child of the Holocaust (Garmezy, 1983). Many other stressors, however, including frequently occurring ones, are less predictably uniform in their effects and, hence, are best viewed as risk factors. Although children exposed to such stressors are at greater risk of impaired development, some fraction of them adjust very well. Most studies of resilience have focused on children who live under chronic high-risk conditions rather than those who have experienced acute trauma.

Many SLE-Cs that children experience, including some very important ones, occur within the family context. Examples include parent divorce, prolonged family conflict, parent unemployment and economic hardship, parent impairment from substance abuse or psychiatric disorder, and serious illness or death of a close family member. Other SLE-Cs such as neighborhood violence, exposure to drugs, and teenage gang activity are reflections of broader community contexts in which children grow up.

Some major SLE-Cs that children experience tend to co-occur either because they stem from a common source (e.g., poverty) or because one stressor triggers others. An example of the latter would be when a parent's substance abuse problem ultimately leads to job loss, serious marital conflict, or, perhaps, dissolution of a marriage. Similarly, parent divorce often sets off a chain of related stressors such as relocation, financial strain, and, importantly, loss of contact with the noncustodial parent.

Multiple stressors, including co-occurring ones, increase a child's risk of maladjustment. Indeed, the negative effects of stress were found to be more nearly multiplicative than additive in a study of children from the rural Isle of Wight and an inner-city London borough who experienced any of six major risk factors (Rutter, Cox, et al., 1975; Rutter, Yule, et al., 1975): (a) parents' marital discord, (b) low socioeconomic status, (c) large family size, (d) paternal criminality, (e) maternal psychiatric disorder, and (f) foster care. Whereas children who experienced zero or one stressor had an equally low risk of psychiatric disorder, such risk increased fourfold for children exposed to two stressors, and tenfold for children who experienced four or more stressors (Rutter, 1979). Other studies have documented similarly steep increases in risk for maladjustment among young school children, with increasing exposure to life stressors (e.g., Sterling et al., 1985). The point to highlight is that when stress exceeds a certain threshold point, many aspects of children's development and functioning may be affected adversely and the likelihood of maladjustment is much greater.

Some stressors hamper children's development through their effects on primary caregivers. For example, although poverty can, and often does, impinge directly and painfully on the child, it is even more likely to increase the child's risk for maladjustment because of its negative effects on caregivers. Other major stressors act more directly. Chronic conflict in the family, parental alcohol or drug abuse problems, and separation from primary caregivers, all have direct adverse effects on children's emotional and cognitive functioning.

CHILD COMPETENCE AND RESILIENCE

As noted earlier, one key impetus to research on child resilience came from studies of linkages between life stress and maladjustment in children. A second impetus came from studies of children's competence, which, as early as three decades ago, began to move away from mental health's classic focus on maladjustment by directing attention to antecedents and correlates of competent outcomes in children.

The Harvard Preschool Project (White, 1978; White, Kaban, & Attanuci, 1979) for example sought to identify antecedents and developmental correlates of competence in young children. Socially competent, compared with noncompetent, children had more positive self-images, were better able to express their feelings, and were more sensitive to the feelings of others. Their caretakers interacted more with them and were better able to communicate age-appropriate expectations within a context of support for the child's autonomy.

Relatedly, Murphy and Moriarty (1976) found that children who coped successfully with normative childhood challenges were characterized by a positive self-image, a clear sense of identity, effective problem-solving strategies, and the ability to engage others. Parents of these successfully adapting children provided affection, respect for their child's capabilities, age-appropriate autonomy, and clear expectations and limits.

One common feature of the studies cited is that they shifted focus from maladjustment toward components of wholesome child adaptation. As such, they set the stage for later studies of adaptive outcomes in children exposed to major life stress and identified potentially crucial factors (self-concept, ability to discern the feelings of others, nurturing involvements with a competent caregiver) that facilitate positive adaptation.

One limiting aspect of these earlier studies is that they focused on children from stable middle-class environments. That reality restricted generalization of their findings to stress-exposed children at heightened risk—exactly the group for which the concept of resilience comes most prominently into play. In parallel, a growing societal awareness of the vulnerability of highly stressed children to problems of emotional, social, and school adaptation fueled more active study of factors that relate to adaptive outcomes under such conditions. The section that follows considers four influential projects in this area: two focusing on early childhood and two on the extended childhood period.

Prior Resilience Projects

O'Grady and Metz (1987) tracked 109 children seen through the Kaiser-Permanente Infant Development Study from birth to age 7 to determine how later exposure to stress affected initially low- versus high-risk children and identify factors that facilitated positive development in the latter. At age 1 month, 51 children were classified as high risk and 58 as low risk for later adjustment problems on the basis of a multifactor screening assessment that included prenatal stress (i.e., child and maternal health factors), family psychological and life-stress problems, and maternal perceptions of the infant's temperament.

Exposure to ongoing stress in early childhood was found to magnify the negative effects of infancy risk on adjustment at ages 6 to 7 years. Conversely, social support available to the family and the child and the child's having an internal locus of control reduced the adverse effects of infancy risk and subsequent life stress on the child's later adjustment. Thus, although serious risk in infancy and ongoing exposure to stress predicted poorer adjustment in later childhood, the study identified a child characteristic (internal locus of control) and an environmental factor (availability of social support) that enhanced a child's capacity to develop successfully in spite of such adversity.

Werner and Smith's (1977, 1982, 1992) 37-year longitudinal study of 700 children born on the Island of Kauai in 1955 provides a comprehensive view of adaptation to risk factors in early childhood. Among high-risk children exposed to four or more major risk factors (e.g., prenatal stress, poverty, family instability) before age 2, roughly two thirds developed a serious behavior or learning disorder before age 18. However, 72 of these high-risk children, in the authors' words, developed into "competent, confident, and caring young adults" (Werner, 1989, p. 73). These children were resilient.

Resilient children were compared with stress-affected peers on multiple developmental and environmental variables assessed throughout childhood. The former were found to come from more stable, less crowded homes, and caregivers judged them to have had easier temperaments (i.e., more active, outgoing, and socially responsive) as infants. By middle childhood, they evidenced better problem-solving and communication skills and, in adolescence, they had a more internal locus of control, positive self-concept, and adaptive blend of masculine and feminine characteristics.

A key thread running through the lives of resilient children was the presence of responsive, nurturing care, whether from parents, extended family caregivers, or support figures outside the home (e.g., teachers, clergy). Child characteristics such as outgoingness and responsiveness, and life circumstances such as fewer prolonged separations from caregivers in infancy, enhanced the child's chances of receiving such nurturance.

As noted earlier, studies by Rutter (1985, 1987), Rutter, Cox, et al. (1975), Rutter, Yule, et al. (1975), and Rutter, Quinton, and Yule (1977) showed that a child's risk for psychiatric disorder increased geometrically with greater exposure to major risk factors. These studies also identified factors that tempered the adverse effects of stress, such as an easy temperament, and being a girl rather than a boy. Consistent with the Kauai findings, these investigators also found that the quality of the parent–child relationship was crucial to later adaptive outcomes. Thus, children who had a warm relationship with at least one parent were less adversely affected by major stressors. Extrafamilial factors, such as going to a school that promoted self-esteem and social and scholastic success, also favored resilient outcomes (e.g., lower rates of delinquency in adolescence), under stressful conditions.

Project Competence (Garmezy, Masten, & Tellegen, 1984) explored factors underlying a child's positive adjustment to stress in a mixed low- and middle-income sample. Diverse measures of children's school-related competence were found to reflect two stable factors: School Engagement and Disruptiveness. Among children who experienced stress, those with assets, such as higher IQ and SES and stable cohesive families, were more likely than their opposites to score high on Engagement and low on Disruptiveness. For this same sample, Masten et al. (1988) found that high-quality parenting functioned as a protective factor against the negative effects of high stress on Disruptiveness for girls, but not for boys. A 7-year follow-up of Project Competence children (Masten, 1989) found moderate stability in the resources (e.g., indicators of early competence, IQ, good parenting quality) that predicted good adjustment in adolescence.

In spite of differences in the populations studied, risk factors to which children were exposed and the assessment procedures used with children and families, there is substantial overlap in the findings reported across studies of childhood resilience. Together these findings converge to identify a "triad of protective factors" (Garmezy, 1983), consisting of characteristics of children and their caretaking and external environments, that enhance the likelihood of resilient outcomes under stress. Specifically, children surmount risk better if they are seen by caregivers as responsive, active, and adaptable infants (i.e., as having an easy temperament); develop such qualities as an internal locus of control, adaptive social-problem-solving skills, and positive self-image; experience continuity of competent caregiving; and have access to caring, supportive adults in their extrafamilial environment such as at school or church.

In summary, early in a child's life, continuity and high-quality caregiving function as salient protective factors in the face of major life stress. As the child develops, the acquisition of stage-salient (age-appropriate) competencies as well as the availability of support outside the family offer protective advantages that favor resilient adaptations. This developmental progression reflects how children increasingly assume such adaptive functions as maintaining emotional equilibrium and protecting against environmental dangers that originally unfold within the caregiver–child dyad (Sroufe, 1990).

The Rochester Child Resilience Project (RCRP): Generative Study

Although the studies reviewed enhanced our understanding of childhood resilience, important questions about this intriguing phenomenon remained, including the need for more detailed knowledge about attributes that help children to adapt to profound life stress. Moreover, because resilience was linked consistently to a warm, nurturant relationship with an adult caregiver, more needed to be learned about factors that enhanced the parent's capacity to nurture effectively under difficult life circumstances.

As noted earlier, few prior studies of resilience had focused on urban families that experience chronic and profound stressors such as poverty, neighborhood violence, and substance abuse. Children who grow up under such conditions are at serious risk. Because the damaging consequences of such risk were apparent in PMHP's day-to-day operation, a decision was made to focus the RCRP on highly stressed urban children, seeking first to understand the genesis of resilient outcomes and eventually to develop interventions to promote resilience in that population.

The RCRP's first effort to illuminate the concept of resilience compared two groups of highly stressed urban children with markedly disparate adjustment outcomes as fourth-to-sixth graders: stress-resilient (SR) children evidencing sound development and adjustment and stress-affected (SA) children evidencing significant early adjustment problems. Primary caregivers of these two groups of children were also compared. Later, this same approach was extended to a younger (7–8 years old) urban sample.

The high level of stress experienced by all RCRP children was a shared risk factor (Seifer & Sameroff, 1987). With regard to other socio-demographic of factors such as gender, age, and ethnicity, the two groups were comparable. The main goal of this research was to identify characteristics that differentiated these two groups of children and their environments and thus presumably contributed to the marked adjustment differences between them. Life stress was assessed using a 32-item Life Events Checklist (LEC; Work, Cowen, Parker, & Wyman, 1990) on which parents reported stressors that had occurred to their child or to the family. Although several LEC items reflected circumscribed stressors (e.g., "death of a close family member"), most assessed chronically stressful processes (e.g., "close family members have had serious arguments").

Participants for the initial RCRP came from nine urban elementary schools in 2-year waves. In each school, all families with fourth- to sixth-grade children were invited to participate at the start of each school year. Of the 2,000 families contacted, 656 agreed to participate. At the time parents gave consent, they also completed the LEC and a brief (5-item) rating of their child's adjustment. Independent global ratings of classroom adjustment were also obtained from the child's current and prior year's teachers (Work et al., 1990).

Next, the study's criterion groups were established. To be considered for inclusion in either the SR or SA group, a child had to have experienced four or more SLE-Cs—a criterion used in Werner and Smith's (1982) study of high-risk resilient children. Additionally, to classify as SR, a child had to be ranked in the top third on at least two of the three child adjustment screening measures and no lower than the middle third on the other. Conversely, to classify as SA, a child had to be ranked in the bottom third on at least two of the three screening measures and no higher than the middle third on the other.

Thus, multiple criteria were used to identify children who were seen as well or poorly adjusted in both home and school settings. These criteria identified subgroups of 75 SR and 72 SA children, comparable by grade level, gender, and ethnic composition. The combined subgroups were representative sociodemographically of the city school district from which they were drawn. Specifically, 42% were African American, 38% Caucasian, 16% Hispanic, and 4% Asian American or Native American. The median family income was $600 to $900 per month; roughly 40% of the families were on public assistance.

Our confidence that the two criterion groups had been appropriately selected was strengthened by confirming data about number of stressors experienced and the adjustment status of these children. The combined SR and SA subgroups had in fact experienced an average of nine SLE-Cs, roughly twice the number experienced by the rest of the volunteer group. Second, on the T-CRS teacher-rated measure of children's class adjustment (Hightower et al., 1986), SRs scored at least half a standard deviation above and SAs half a standard deviation below norms for their urban reference groups. These selection data confirmed that both criterion groups had experienced high levels of stress and that SRs showed consistently good and SAs consistently poor adjustment. Meeting those two preconditions set the stage for in-depth group comparisons on child assessment and parent interview measures.

Child Test and Child Interview Findings

The child test and interview measures used sought to identify factors associated with the divergent adjustment outcomes of SR and SA children and thus expand the "nomological definitional net" for childhood resilience (Cowen et al., 1992; Parker, Cowen, Work, & Wyman, 1990). This meant fleshing out the defining qualities (self-perceptions and emotional and behavioral correlates) of SR outcomes under conditions of major life stress. To this end, study children completed 11 test measures selected for their conceptual relevance to children's resilient outcomes under stress (Cowen & Work, 1988; Parker et al., 1990), and a 1-hour structured interview assessing their self-views, competencies, and perceptions of the family environment (Wyman et al., 1992).

Substantial group differences favoring SRs were found in three areas: (a) self-perception and self-regulation, (b) interpersonal competence, and (c) coping orientation. In the area of self-perception, SRs rated themselves as more competent scholastically than SAs and better able to follow rules and age-appropriate standards of behavior. They viewed their physical appearance more positively and reported higher global self-worth and self-esteem (Cowen et al., 1992). They also had more positive expectations for their future educational attainment, interpersonal relationships, employment prospects, and general happiness (Wyman et al., 1992).

In terms of relational competencies, SRs reported feeling more socially accepted by peers than SAs and more skilled in interacting with peers. They had more empathy for other children and more effective social-problem-solving skills. With regard to coping styles, SRs reported a more internal locus of control—the belief that their own actions, rather than external forces such as chance or luck, determined outcomes for them. They also had more realistic control attributions in that they were more likely to believe that they could prevent controllable problems such as getting in trouble with the law or using drugs and alcohol, and less likely to believe that they could prevent uncontrollable ones, such as an adult getting drunk or parents divorcing. SAs, by contrast, were more likely to believe that they could control either everything (i.e., both controllable and uncontrollable problems) or nothing (Cowen et al., 1992).

With regard to typical handling of problems, SRs were more likely than SAs to use effective coping strategies such as self-reliance and seeking social support and less likely to use ineffective ones such as wishful thinking, distancing, and immobilization. On the basis of child interview data, SRs evidenced a stronger sense of efficacy than SAs in terms of believing that they were competent to handle typical childhood problems such as difficult situations, new experiences, and problems with people (Wyman et al., 1992).

Although we shall not consider in depth the potential meaning of each SR versus SA difference in the three main areas of development cited, we offer several comments about these differences to highlight how SR children's resources and competencies may facilitate positive adaptation under stressful conditions. In all likelihood, these adaptive skills are relevant both to sound development in general and specifically to adaptation in the face of major life stress.

The coping competencies and styles of SR children appear to shape how they experience and respond to life stress. For example, their more realistic control attributions—specifically knowing that they cannot control uncontrollable problems—may lessen the sense of guilt and responsibility that children often have about the turmoil and stress that unfold in their environment. By contrast, their beliefs that they can prevent controllable problems from happening to them, and that their own actions importantly shape outcomes (internal locus of control), help them to deal realistically and effectively with some difficult life circumstances in the belief that what they can do makes a difference.

Relatedly, several interpersonal competencies of SR children may help both their general development and adaptation to life stress. For example, their greater empathy and knowledge of better ways to solve interpersonal problems may facilitate the formation of close relationships with relevant others—a source of support and emotional sustenance in times of stress. Moreover, SR children's positive sense of self and future expectations may shape constructively their choice of people with whom to interact, environments in which to interact, and beliefs about what they are capable of achieving. The distinctive competencies that characterize SR children can be viewed as needed foci for preventive interventions designed to enhance resilience in young children at risk.

Parent Interview Findings

A second basic RCRP goal was to identify child and family milieu antecedents of SR and SA outcomes as factors that shape and sustain these divergent developmental pathways. In-depth interviews with children's primary caregivers was the mechanism used to explore these goals (Wyman, Cowen, Work, & Parker, 1991). These interviews proceeded chronologically through the infancy, preschool, and school-age periods. For each period, the child's development, child-rearing practices, support available to parents, the parent's sense of caregiving efficacy, and family relationships were explored. Later interview segments dealt with family discipline practices and characteristics of the primary caregiver, including her own attachment history. The core objective was to identify developmental factors that differentiated SR and SA children, thereby enhancing understanding of pathways to their later divergent development.

Consistent with Werner and Smith's (1982) findings, parents of SR, compared with SA, children reported that their children had easier temperaments as infants and preschoolers (e.g., were more easily soothed, outgoing, and adaptable to change) and achieved developmental milestones (e.g., walking, talking) earlier. SR parents also reported having had more childcare support both from fathers and extended family, particularly in infancy.

Primary caregivers of SRs also reported a stronger sense of efficacy as parents by way of confidence in their ability to care for their child, and having more substantial psychosocial resources that include a composite index of self-concept, perceived support, and greater life satisfaction. They did not, however, have more favorable attachment histories as children than the parents of SAs. Indeed, many parents in both groups reported relatively poor attachment histories. Illustratively, 30% of the overall parent sample reported either having been abused themselves or having had parents who were involved in alcohol or drug abuse. Interestingly, however, parents of SRs and SAs differed in their perceptions of how their childhood affected them. Thus, SR parents, compared with SA parents with similar childhood hardship histories, were more determined to establish a good relationship with their own child.

The strongest, most consistent overall differences between SR and SA parents were in the area of parent–child relationships. Thus, SR children experienced fewer extended separations from their caregivers in infancy and their parents felt closer to them and reported being more involved with them in nurturant, age-appropriate ways. Parents of SRs used reasoning and limit setting in disciplining children; they used physical punishment less often; and they were more consistent in upholding rules. Importantly, SR parents also had more positive expectations for their children's futures; specifically, they believed that they were more likely to finish school, be gainfully employed, and be involved in close fulfilling relationships.

Data from the child interview confirmed the importance of the caregiver–child relationship in differentiating SRs and SAs. Thus, SRs reported more positive relationships with primary caregivers; more inductive, age-appropriate, and consistent family discipline practices; and perceptions of their mothers as more nurturant and interactive (Wyman et al., 1992). A related point of interest is that SR parent–child dyads had more convergent views of their relationship, personal attributes, and expressive-motor styles than did SA parent–child dyads (Cowen, Work, & Wyman, 1993).

Overall, the parent interview findings strongly supported the conclusion that a consistent, positive attachment to a primary caregiver facilitates the development of coping resources that enable a child to adapt well even in the face of exposure to major life stress. Certain child attributes, such as having an easy temperament, favor the establishment and maintenance of a positive caregiver attachment (Thomas & Chess, 1977). These early developmental characteristics of resilient children may, at least in part (i.e., transactionally), promote adaptation by enhancing a caregiver's sense of efficacy and positive regard for the child. On the other side of the coin, RCRP findings suggest that poor later adaptive outcomes for children who grow up under highly stressful life conditions stem, in good measure, from disruptions in the supports and structures that facilitate adaptive caregiver–child interactions, thus inhibiting the formation of a warm, secure parent–child relationship.

The initial RCRP study, described earlier, has been extended in several directions. One involves the application of study findings to develop a preventively oriented early child intervention designed to enhance resilience under conditions of major life stress. A second is the downward extension of the original RCRP in the form of a longitudinal study, starting with young, highly stressed second- and third-grade children. These developments are described next.

CHILD-FOCUSED PREVENTIVE INTERVENTION

An important long-term goal that fueled the start of the RCRP was to apply knowledge gained from it toward developing an effective preventive intervention for highly stressed children. With that goal in mind, a next step, however limited and tentative, was to develop and pilot an initial preventive intervention designed to enhance children's resilience. This program sought to provide highly stressed, at-risk, fourth- and fifth-grade urban children skills, competencies, and experiences that earlier RCRP findings had suggested might help them handle stress more effectively (Cowen, Wyman, Work, & Iker, 1994).

Three input strands shaped this pilot intervention: (a) a preventive orientation; (b) findings from prior (non-RCRP) school-based prevention programs; and (c) generative data from resilience research. Preventive orientation means that the program was designed to intervene with young children at risk before the need for extensive help and to provide them with resources intended to short-circuit adverse later outcomes. For reasons noted earlier, the school seemed to be a natural setting for conducting such a program.

Several existing effective school-based prevention programs, our own and others, offered (a) preliminary evidence that such programs work, and (b) useful leads about effective technology for this area. One such source was CODIP (chapter 9), notwithstanding important differences in the situations that the two programs addressed. For example, whereas all CODIP children shared the common experience of having separated or divorced parents, the new intervention was to be for children who had experienced a highly diverse range of stressors, including ongoing, chronic processes. Even so, the new program was able to draw on strategies and exercises that had worked well for CODIP, while also adding new elements designed specifically for the special needs of this new group of at-risk children.

Finally, the rationale and substance of the new program rested on prior resilience research, our own and others, identifying factors that help children adapt effectively under highly stressful conditions. Accordingly, the intervention was designed as a structured, systematic effort to provide children with experiences and skills known to be associated with resilient outcomes. These included differentiating solvable from nonsolvable problems and how to disengage from the latter, effective coping and social problem solving, learning to identify and express feelings appropriately, empathy, and self-esteem.

Although we believed that what had been learned about the attributes of resilient children would help to frame a sensible intervention, we also knew that the intervention challenge was more complex than just that. Indeed, much of what we had learned to that point suggested that there might be intrinsic limitations to a child-centered intervention for 10–12-year olds designed to enhance resilience. Illustratively, we recognized that the competencies that comprise the fiber of resilient outcomes were not likely to develop easily or permanently via an initial brief intervention conducted when children were fourth or fifth graders. This reality was underscored by research findings indicating that attributes of resilient children develop slowly over time, in the context of effective caregiving environments.

These reality constraints aside, we still considered it worthwhile to explore the effects of a limited child-centered intervention for several reasons. The first was the face-valid need to take starter steps toward preventive programming for the many children in society whose development is at grave risk because of their exposure to major life stress. The second was to determine the nature and durability of positive changes from a specific child-centered preventive intervention that might later comprise one element in a more comprehensive intervention package directed toward the child's caregiving environment.

In that spirit, an initial 20-session pilot intervention was developed and evaluated over a 1-year period, with small groups of fourth- and fifth-grade children in the schools (Iker, 1990). This pilot program, which sought basically to impart specific skills and competencies, adopted the term "tough times" as a unifying concept around which the curriculum was built. Our hope was that children would be able to find a sense of cohesion and common ground around that term. Leastwise, the concept seemed sensible to those conducting the program because of its potential, in the abstract, for reflecting the range and diversity of life stressors that program children had experienced.

The program was implemented in seven urban schools. Each group had two coleaders; most were school mental health professionals. Group leaders were given a program manual outlining a rationale, goals, and specific exercises for each session. They participated in several training sessions before the program started and biweekly 1½-hour training and supervision sessions during the intervention period.

The program consisted of three main segments: (a) identification of feelings, empathy (perspective-taking), and support; (b) coping strategies, including social problem-solving and realistic control; and (c) promoting self-esteem. Exercises designed to enhance these core competencies were presented within a structural framework which suggested that although children often experience tough times, there are ways to feel better and get help.

There were 110 eligible child volunteers for the program. All had experienced four or more SLE-Cs and were ranked in the lower or middle third in adjustment by teachers. These children were randomly assigned to intervention (*E*) or control (*C*) groups. Group size averaged 7 or 8. The program evaluation compared Es and Cs on child, teacher, and parent ratings of adjustment on the basis of pre–post intervention data for matched groups of 48 Es and 47 Cs.

In spite of the fact that group leaders and teachers reacted favorably to the intervention, the formal program evaluation failed to demonstrate positive change in participants compared to controls (Iker, 1990). These results were not entirely surprising given that group leaders had expressed concern during the intervention about a lack of cohesion (i.e., a clearly perceived common ground) in the groups. Thus, even though the need to establish a common group identity had been anticipated and steps taken to address it, the problem was not surmounted. In actual fact, the range of life stressors that program children had experienced was enormous. A specific example for one small group illustrates the point. One member, a 9-year-old girl, who had recently lost a close family member to AIDS, was visibly upset by the loss and focused uniquely on it throughout the program; another child, by contrast, had witnessed a family member being killed under violent circumstances. Because diversity of stressors experienced was the rule rather than the exception, leaders noted that the children were not optimally interconnected and, hence, could not support each other adequately, as clearly happens in groups in which children share a specific common experience such as parental divorce.

Although findings from this exploratory probe were less than scintillating, we continued to believe that a modified form of the intervention, correcting problems identified on Round 1, might have positive potential and that further exploration of the effects of a resilience-enhancing intervention was warranted. Mindful of earlier problems, the intervention was modified in several ways. Elements that had worked well (i.e., had engaged children and imparted relevant skills to them) were retained; unsuccessful ones were modified or dropped. More basically, given the lack of group cohesion that had plagued the initial trial, a key change was made in the program's guiding focus. The new focus, central both in the training of group leaders and throughout the curriculum, pivoted around an extended, concretized concept of family turmoil. In Session 1, for example, children were introduced to the notion that many families experience tough times. Concrete examples of tough times (e.g., having to move, family arguments, illness and hospitalization, problems with money) were cited, with the further structuring point that learning to deal effectively with one's role in such circumstances can help one to feel better and do better in school. By building discussions and exercises around this modified theme, it was hoped that children could identify with each other's realities better, and experience more connectedness and support than was the case on Round 1.

To sharpen the intervention's focus, the program was reduced from 20 to 12 sessions, and more early time was devoted to explaining the group's purpose and facilitating group identity. Also, to facilitate skill acquisition, exercises were adapted to be maximally relevant to the children's diverse life circumstances.

Although the program was shortened, the three main content foci of the prior intervention were preserved. Thus, Sessions 1 to 5 focused on how children can identify feelings in themselves and others, how different events and problems in families affect children's feelings, and sources of helpful support for upset feelings and troublesome experiences. Sessions 6 to 9 dealt with strategies for handling problems, including social problem solving. The last three sessions sought to consolidate program learnings, highlight children's positive qualities, and deal with their feelings about ending (Cowen et al., 1994).

This modified program was conducted over 2 years with five groups (36 children) ranging in size from six to eight. A simple pre–post evaluation design was used to assess changes in children's adjustment after the program by using both teacher and child self-ratings. At the end of the program, teachers judged participants to have fewer learning problems and a stronger task orientation. Children rated themselves as improved in perceived self-efficacy, somewhat less anxious, and less likely to be able to prevent uncontrollable problems. Leaders on this round commented that the groups were, in the main, cohesive and that children seemed to be productively engaged (Cowen et al., 1994).

Although these modestly encouraging findings should be interpreted cautiously, they at least suggest that small positive steps can be taken to enhance the capacity of young, highly stressed urban children to adapt under such conditions. We do not, in any sense, see this form of intervention as the final word on approaches to enhancing resilience among at-risk children. To the contrary, a child-focused intervention seems, at best, to be one limited aspect of a more comprehensive approach that includes facilitating and sustaining effective caregiving within a child's family system.

We again note that the work thus far done to explore resilience-enhancing options for young, highly stressed urban children is the newest and least well developed of our several primary prevention ventures to date. We present this work not at all as a *fait accompli*, but rather as a snapshot of where we are at this point in time and what we view as a promising but still very much evolving effort in an area (childhood resilience) that is high both in need of additional study and potential social significance.

RECENT RCRP FINDINGS

Although one central, long-term goal of the resilience project is to develop prevention programs that build strengths and promote resilience in at-risk children, both common sense and experience to date underscore the fact that achieving that goal will entail major challenges. To promote resilient outcomes in children effectively, we must first know about the phenomenon of resilience in its full richness and complexity. The latter awareness, in turn, can help to structure an agenda of issues that must be addressed for maximally informed, effective (proactive) resilience-enhancing interventions to evolve.

The following are issues on that agenda: How durable are early resilient outcomes in young inner-city children? What factors in both the short- and long-term act to support or undermine maintenance of such outcomes? Which child attributes operate as gateways to resilient adaptations under different risk conditions, and by what pathways do these protective qualities get shaped generally, and for different gender, age, and ethnic groups? Answers to these questions will require labor-intensive longitudinal studies.

With a keen awareness of these significant challenges, we have sought, as RCRP resources have permitted, to probe several of the above areas. The next section illustrates this work. Realistically, however, the basic agenda of unfinished business in this area (cf. above) is enormous (Gest, Neeman, Hubbard, Masten, & Tellegen, 1993); it will be addressed only slowly, over time, by many different investigators. The daunting awareness of the challenges involved in pursuing this agenda is tempered by a realization that the potential rewards of doing so can be substantial.

One recently completed longitudinal step was a 2½- to 3½-year follow-up of young adolescents for whom baseline RCRP test and interview data had been collected when they were fourth- to sixth-graders (Kerley, 1994). In this sample of highly stressed inner-city youth, now entering a period of heightened susceptibility to costly personal and social outcomes (e.g., school drop out, substance abuse), among the dimensions of social competence assessed at fourth-to-sixth grade, empathy was the strongest predictor of school adjustment in early adolescence. Specifically, children with high, compared with low, initial empathy were rated by teachers in new schools as more engaged in school and better adjusted socioemotionally. This effect was significant above and beyond the effects of life stress that children had experienced in the intervening years.

Another interesting finding was that a child's positive expectations for the future (e.g., expecting to finish school, getting a good job) as fourth-to-sixth graders predicted good socioemotional adjustment and a more internal locus of control 2½ to 3½ years later, and acted to reduce the negative effects of life stress on children's self-rated competence in early adolescence (Wyman et al., 1993). Also, having high self-esteem and achieving well in school as a fourth-to-sixth grader predicted less involvement in substance abuse risk behaviors at follow-up in early adolescence (Wyman et al., 1996).

A second recent research thrust extended the original study to second- and third-grade children in an effort to identify factors associated with resilient outcomes at that earlier age. Although the test measures used with fourth-to-sixth graders were modified to make them more appropriate developmentally for this younger sample (Hoyt-Meyers et al., 1995), the new study maintained the prime goals of identifying characteristics of children, their development, and family milieus that differentiated young SR children from their SA peers.

Two new features were built into this study. The first was a longitudinal component. An initial follow-up of child and family planned for 1½ to 2 years after the original assessment was designed to assess the stability, over time, of highly stressed children's adjustment and factors that relate to positive or negative change in adjustment. To allow room to assess such change, a second new study feature was to include a group of demographically matched highly stressed children with initially intermediate adjustment levels.

Test measures had to be modified for developmental appropriateness in this study. Within the framework of such modifications, the attributes found to differentiate second- and third-grade SR and SA children were similar to those that had earlier differentiated older SRs and SAs (Cowen et al., 1992). SR children again rated themselves as better adjusted than SAs in school and more competent along several dimensions. They had a more realistic sense of control for uncontrollable problems, had better problem-solving skills, and tended to have more empathy and a stronger sense of self-efficacy. SRs also exceeded SAs in IQ, not assessed in the earlier study.

In the parent interview, many developmental and family milieu factors associated with resilient outcomes among fourth-to-sixth graders were also found for second and third graders (Wyman et al., 1995). Thus, SR parents reported easier child temperaments in infancy, more nurturant involvements with their children, and more positive age-appropriate discipline practices. Several caregiver resources and parenting attitudes not assessed in the original RCRP also related to SR outcomes. These included better mental health, more realistic expectations, greater empathy for children, and fewer negative child-rearing beliefs, such as the belief that children should care for their parents (i.e., role-reversal).

Findings from the 1½- to 2-year follow-up (Cowen et al., 1996) were synchronous with the initial assessment data, both for child adjustment (i.e., parent, teacher, and child self-ratings) and test responses, and family milieu factors (e.g., close relationship with one's primary caregiver, more caregiver resources) that differentiated SR and SA children. This study also identified new differentiators of the two initially classified groups including a higher frequency of predelinquent behaviors (e.g., fighting and truancy) among SAs, and the use of more adaptive coping styles by SR parents (Cowen et al., 1996).

Continued tracking of these children over time will offer opportunities to learn more about factors that operate to maintain early resilient outcomes in some children, initiate a move toward resilience in others, and erode early positive adaptation in still others.

SUMMARY

RCRP findings to date suggest that knowledge about child resilience has much to offer to the fields of prevention and mental health. In relation to other PMHP developments, this thrust is still at an early unfolding stage. At the same time, its potential for moving our work another step from ontogenetically early secondary to primary prevention justifies continuing effort to understand the nature of child resilience and apply such knowledge proactively in schools.

Although much remains to be learned about childhood resilience, RCRP findings and those of other investigators highlight several important aspects of this intriguing phenomenon. One is that a warm caregiving environment plays a vital protective (resilience-favoring) role in the first years of life, indeed throughout childhood. Young children with responsive, nurturant caregivers and wholesome attachment relationships are, simply put, less vulnerable to the deleterious effects of major life stress (Werner & Smith, 1992). Continuity of caregiving also reduces risk. Quality caregiving promotes sound adaptation and lowers the risk of maladjustment by buffering the child from stressors in the immediate environment, and by promoting a sense of competence and efficacy that acts directly to enhance effective coping with stress. Otherwise put, quality caregiving enhances a child's social adaptation and perception of others as being safe and responsive. The latter world view helps the child to experience intimacy with peers and derive support from adults.

The RCRP, however, has also shown that quality caregiving under stressful life conditions depends on many factors. Caregivers with resources such as more education and sound mental health can be better parents. How parents themselves were raised as children influences their attitudes about children and childrearing practices, albeit in complex ways. Some parents clearly succeed in overcoming their own adverse experiences as neglected or abused children and are able to provide effective caregiving to their offspring.

When children enter school and increasingly as they move through middle childhood into adolescence, capacities or self-views rooted earlier and further developed over time (e.g., being able to differentiate solvable and nonsolvable problems, positive expectations for the future) serve more and more to enhance adaptation under conditions of life stress. By middle childhood, developmental trajectories for many children, though not 100% immutable, are at least well-established and difficult to change.

Some of the research findings cited have important implications for early intervention and prevention. For one thing, they suggest that interventions that seek to promote sound early attachments and quality caregiving from the start may be the most effective way to launch a child on a pathway to competence and resilience, even in the face of major life stress. Because the caregiving process goes deep and is affected by many factors (e.g., education, health, a parent's own life history), it is unlikely that brief superficial intervention programs, however well conceived and conducted, will have enduring positive effects. Otherwise put, the chances of finding quick fixes in this area are slim. Consistent with the argument being developed is the recent evidence, in the area of delinquency prevention, that early comprehensive family-oriented interventions help significantly to advance long-term, positive outcomes among children at serious early risk (Yoshikawa, 1994; Zigler, Taussig, & Black, 1992).

Further understanding of the nature, roots of, and pathways to childhood resilience, and informed application of such knowledge to family-anchored prevention programs, especially ones that start in the infancy and preschool periods, will obviously require the active involvements of key caregivers. Our future vision for this area, however, also includes an important effort by schools to apply knowledge of resilience to the articulation of programs that are continuous with and maintain and support gains from earlier family-based, preventively oriented programs.

III

CONCLUSION

12

WHERE FROM, WHERE TO?

The challenge of cumulating new knowledge never ends. Indeed, ironically, the more we learn the better we can discern things that remain to be learned. However, although learning is a necessary precondition for gainful application, such application does not follow easily or automatically. Rather, translating knowledge into practice is itself a labyrinthian process that must often overcome such formidable obstacles as budget and resource limits, organizational rigidities and inertia created by set ways, and challenges that change poses for vested interests. Indeed, the road from knowledge to application is often so strewn with obstacles that it is never negotiated.

The preceding observations are less to wax philosophical and more to establish a framework within which to offer some closing thoughts about the PMHP experience. A brief paradoxical structural summary of that experience could easily read: "We have learned so much, yet we have learned so little!" Because that statement is content free, however, we shall step down from the pedestal of abstraction to pose several more concrete questions to frame this closing chapter: What accomplishments and learnings have come out of the PMHP experience? What do these learnings mean for the here-and-now? Which significant issues need to be addressed in the future? In the light of current knowledge, what promising steps can be taken to advance adaptive outcomes for children?

WHAT HAS PMHP ACCOMPLISHED?

PMHP's roots go nearly 40 years deep. The project grew out of clinical–observational soil in which several recurrent problem themes were apparent to both school personnel and observers of the school scene. Those were not just problems of particular schools or even of particular school districts (although such problems did, of course, exist); rather, they were child-related problems evident in virtually all schools. Although there were, to be sure, variations in the exact nature, manifestation, and frequency of those problems, that should not obscure the fact that the problems had sequelae that were both detrimental to young children's development and frustrating for school personnel.

What were those endemic problems? Some children failed from the very start to profit from the school experience. Sometimes this showed up as disinterest or, more strongly, as alienation that built up like lead poisoning, eventuating in chronic school unhappiness, failure, and ultimately drop out. Short of that extreme, many children were carrying excess baggage in the form of emotional and behavioral problems that deflected energy from the mastery of stage-salient educational tasks at hand. These children were, so to speak, firing on a reduced number of cylinders.

The preceding were irrepressible problems with adverse here-and-now consequences for many children. Moreover, because a classroom is a contained ecological system, these problems spilled over onto other children and the teacher, the key elements in the system, thus adversely affecting the class as a whole. Nor were the consequences of these early problems limited to the here and now. To the contrary, many children evidencing early school adjustment problems were at risk for long-term difficulties in educational and personal development. The latter, in turn, substantially reduced the likelihood of a child's reaching his or her "farthest star."

Thus, school failure and the associated downward spiral that it generated, predisposed a tragic waste of abilities and resources for children and society, which we thought might be reduced by effective early preventive intervention. The regnant school mental health way of the time was to focus limited firepower on damage-control efforts with a few of the school's most glaring causalities (i.e., precisely those with the poorest prognosis). That approach, in our view, was sharply restricted both in sensibility and effectiveness. Our belief was that if the downward spiral of some children was not reversed by third grade, it was not likely to be reversed ever.

Because several of the system's key limiting features (e.g., professional staff shortages) were not likely to self-correct, we concluded that the systemic problems identified needed to be approached in a conceptually different way. Our goal was to engineer a realistic alternative that allocated fewer resources to trying to cure the already sick and more to cutting down the flow of problems and helping children to profit from the school experience. Two processes formed the backbone of the conceptual alternative that PMHP offered: the systematic use of early detection and screening technology to identify children at risk and, on that basis, the provision of prompt, effective, preventively oriented helping services through the use of nonprofessional child associates. Those two guiding foci, which comprised an ontogenetically early secondary prevention package, have remained central to PMHP's functioning ever since.

The preceding is not to say that the project remained static. Far from it! Many of PMHP's current practices are products of the ongoing processes of critical self-scrutiny and fine-tuning. That orientation led to the development of several program variants that extended PMHP's reach and added to its effectiveness in specific situations. At another level, the accomplishments of the basic PMHP approach paved the way for the further evolutionary steps of program dissemination and developing new primary prevention program models to expand the options available on PMHP's smorgasbord.

To describe PMHP's course as evolutionary suggests that aspects of this development can be viewed through a Darwinian lens. Thus, early program practices with limited adaptive value became extinct and more adaptive variations of core program practices emerged to extend the model's reach and effectiveness. Indeed, over time, even finer grained variations on these themes evolved in the light of needs and demand qualities of specific school environments.

PMHP's essence resides more in its structural emphases than in the literal detail of how programs operationalize those emphases. For example, systematic early detection of children's school adjustment problems is central in PMHP for two reasons: (a) unrecognized early school adjustment problems grow and fan out over time, and (b) information gleaned through systematic early detection establishes a base on which to build effective intervention. For those reasons, much time and effort have been invested, over the years, in developing useful, parsimonious, objective measures of children's school problem behaviors and competencies. These measures, designed to be responsive to school and teacher needs, have gone through many adaptive revisions. Although they are still surely less than perfect, they are at least known through the "school of hard knocks" to work well and efficiently for us and for many other school districts.

The crucial requirement for PMHP's structural model, however, is that there *be* a mechanism for systematic screening and early detection, not that that mechanism consist, for all districts, of the specific measures and processes PMHP has developed. Although we can and do offer the latter as one useful option (set of tools), districts may, for diverse reasons, prefer to use other measures better calibrated to their needs and realities.

Similar considerations pertain to other elements in PMHP's structural model. Although systematic early detection is vital in PMHP, it is an instrumental step, not an end in itself. Indeed, without constructive follow-through, it can be mischief-making; that is, galvanizing a system into readiness through an active early detection process and not following through can be an invitation to frustration, if not anger. Hence, we realized that early detection must be followed by prompt, effective preventively oriented intervention for children identified as having active or incipient school adjustment problems.

Thus, the total delivery system we envisioned was to feature prevention over amelioration and to move into action early rather than late. Professional staff shortages of the time, however, suggested that it would not be possible societally to develop such an intervention solely with professional time. For one thing, there were not enough professionals to go around and, even if there had been, few schools had the resources needed to expand professional staffs.

On the basis of a then-emerging body of literature reexamining long-held assumptions about elements needed for effective helping interactions with children, PMHP began to explore the possibility that carefully selected, trained nonprofessional child associates, working under professional supervision, could play a key role in a needed, geometrically expanded, preventively oriented helping framework. That exploration was fruitful! By now, the good sense and great potential of that way of operating has been documented many times and is central to PMHP's structural model.

PMHP's decisions about the specific format of the child associate approach were shaped by the nature of our system and our turf during that development's evolutionary period. Thus, most PMHP help-agents were women (i.e., homemakers) trained to work with children one on one. Most worked half-time and were paid at a school district's prevailing hourly rates for such employees. Their contacts with children rested on the base of a warm, caring, interactive play environment and the use of relational techniques.

For this crucial PMHP structural component too, it is important to differentiate essential from nonessential features. The critical objective of the child associate development was to provide a realistic mechanism for augmenting the reach of early effective, prevention services to children. PMHP's literal decisions about how to do this best, however, are not sacrosanct. Indeed, there is evidence from PMHP field programs that this service-expanding objective can be met in diverse ways. For example, some programs have effectively used men, college students, and retired people, not just homemakers, as help agents. Others have used associates in small-group, rather than individual, contacts with children. And, some programs have trained associates to use behavioral or short-term approaches, especially where school professionals are more at home with such approaches.

Although most PMHP associates work half time, some settings (e.g., in the inner city) have found that hiring full-time associates works better both in terms of school needs and associates' income needs. Moreover, some districts, without resources to hire child associates, have conducted PMHP programs using volunteer help agents. Although volunteer systems are susceptible to such problems as limited time commitments available, restricted program reach, scheduling problems, turnover, and scarcity of training and supervisory time, a volunteer system with all those fallibilities still has something to offer and is preferable to the alternative of no helping services.

The point to stress is that PMHP's effectiveness as an approach rests on an expanded, preventively oriented, helping pool that can swing into action promptly when intervention can help most. That objective can be met in many different ways; how that can best happen must be determined by a district's needs, resources, predilections, and realities.

The PMHP model also involves a major change in the role of school professionals, in which providing traditional one-on-one diagnostic and therapy services for the troubled few is replaced largely by a leadership role on a school team. The team's proximal goal is to provide early preventive services for many young children; its distal goal is to cut down the flow of school problems and promote optimal long-term behavioral and academic outcomes for children. These defining structural features of the PMHP model, adaptable to a wide range of school environments, comprise an intact system that offers an appealing alternative to traditional school mental health services. Its appeal resides in its potential for reaching many more children, earlier in their school careers, in ways that can cut down the flow of problems and foster adaptive competencies.

The preceding structural attributes, backed by evidence of program efficacy, paved the way for widespread dissemination of PMHP's program model. Although we view that achievement positively because it strongly suggests that PMHP has made a difference in the real world, it is not an accomplishment that is 100% free of question marks.

It is easier, for example, to report the number of program implementations than to describe what each implementation consists of or how good it is. Writing in the context of program replication, Rappaport, Seidman, and Davidson (1979) raised the question of the extent to which replications of a parent model retain the program's defining "essences." Noting that new programs range widely in this regard, these authors contrasted "manifest" adaptations (i.e., on the surface, only) with "true" adaptations (i.e., those that preserve the program's basic "spirit, ideology, values and goals"). Two contrasting sets of considerations raised earlier in this discussion relate to Rappaport et al.'s (1979) issue. On the one side, we highlighted several fundamental concepts, beliefs, and values that we see as crucial to PMHP's *raison d'être* and ways of functioning. However, we also recognized that schools vary greatly in needs, resources, beliefs, and operating styles, and that those variations necessarily affect the specific format of a program's implementation.

Thus, the tightrope that PMHP dissemination has walked reflects a standard dilemma of program dissemination. On the one hand, literal duplication of every last phenotypic element in a program model is impossible and undesirable if the practice is out of "sync" with the host system's ways of operating. On the other hand, unfettered change in program practice may ultimately transform a horse into a camel.

Sarason (1995) addressed this paradox head-on in his cogent analysis of the replication process:

> . . . when people talk of replication, they almost always mean replicating what people do (i.e., the overt, describable goings-on). In that sense, replication is impossible; it can only be approximated (i.e., things will look and happen differently). What is absolutely crucial in replication is that the assumptions, conceptions, values, and priorities undergirding what you seek to replicate are clear in your head and you take them seriously; you truly accept and believe them; *they are non-negotiable starting points.* How to do it is one thing; how to think it is another. (p. 175)

Sarason's argument converges with Rappaport et al.'s (1979) formulation. How you think it, in Sarason's words, is the key to true (as opposed to surface) program adoption. Although PMHP replications do, in fact, vary considerably in their surface manifestations, most strive to reflect the project's overarching concepts, values, and goals.

What we have said to this point falls under the umbrella of PMHP accomplishments. Perhaps the strongest *de facto* testament to PMHP is the fact that it has survived for 38 years, with ever growing numbers of implementing school districts. That could not have happened unless user districts found the model both to address important, palpable needs and to deliver significantly on its theoretical promise. Hence, we conclude that PMHP has been a good and helpful development that offers expanded early, effective, preventive services to young children—considerably more than traditional school mental health delivery systems can provide.

To the extent that the preceding overview of PMHP's accomplishments is sound, it has important, built-in implications for social planners and policy makers. If, as we have found, PMHP reaches many more children in need sooner and more effectively, thus circumventing later more serious adaptive problems, then the ideal of having such programs in all schools is a worthy policy objective for the coming decades. This is hardly a remote or far-fetched goal. Indeed, the passage, by several states, of specific PMHP-enabling legislation, with supporting budgets is a high order of social policy statement. Here, we wish only to clarify the need to build actively and systematically on several significant, social policy starter steps already effectively taken in the service of promoting widespread adoption of PMHP's model. In the long run, such policy steps have much potential for redounding positively on the wellness of many young children.

Limiting Factors

Although the preceding can all be chalked up firmly on the positive side of the ledger, it would be wrong to think of PMHP as a panacea. Far from it! Just as experience with PMHP brought us to a clearer view of its virtues, it also taught us about its limitations. Happily, we have been able to overcome some of those, such as, for example, work done to fit the approach better to the needs of acting-out children and children in crisis. Such adaptations have made PMHP a more versatile and effective approach than it was 30 years ago.

On the other hand, even though those accomplishments are real and important, there are some problems that PMHP, even with its many improvements, has not been able to address effectively. Specifying those gaps as nondefensively as possible lays the groundwork for further constructive steps in program development and reconceptualization of underlying issues and goals. The latter may lead to qualitatively different assumptions and procedures than those that have guided PMHP, as suggested in the rationale and operation of the primary prevention program extensions described in chapters 8 to 11.

Discussions of PMHP's limitations must start with the most obvious and important point: The approach simply does not work for some children and for others its benefits are limited. Although we cannot attach exact numbers to those categories (indeed such numbers surely vary across districts), data from the large-scale 5-year California program outcome studies are informative. For proximal outcomes, those data suggest that 65% of all PMHP-seen children do very well, 20% experience modest gains, and 15% profit relatively little or not at all. Those numbers, however, speak only to how children appear to their teachers when intervention ends, not to either the longer term durability or the generalizability of such proximal gains. Moreover, even if those promising early gains were all maintained, it is still the case that some children do not show significant gain in PMHP, and among those who do, gains may erode over time.

There are several reasons why PMHP may not work well for some children. Starting with an obvious one, although child-associates are effective help-agents for young children and their use in schools makes eminent good sense, that falls short of saying either that all child-associates are equally effective or that all associate–child pairings are "marriages made in heaven." Those close to the project know otherwise. In reality, associates differ in helping reflexes, some do better than others with specific types of children, and some associate–child pairings are less than idyllic. Wrong guesses made about an associate's helping skills (and such errors are sometimes slow to be acknowledged and acted on) or associate–child mismatches lower PMHP's batting average.

Although the preceding problems do, in fact, occur they do not account for most PMHP failures. Moreover, they are less shortfalls of the model per se and more failings in the mechanics of its execution that can be addressed by such concrete steps as (a) doing a better job in hiring and, when indicated, in terminating associates; (b) working toward optimal associate–child pairings; and (c) providing options for changing pairings that do not work.

More disconcerting, in our view, are several types of situations in which PMHP is relatively unsuccessful, in spite of doing the best possible job it can when the model comes into play. One such set of problems stems from misapplication of the program. PMHP was not created to be all things to all children. It is designed as a preventively oriented program, not for children with already deeply rooted problems, such as severe childhood depression or a profound conduct disorder, that impinge heavily on others. Although the latter children, in principle, were to have been referred to appropriate community settings, not all program scenarios unfold that way. One reason for that is that some people, flushed with the palpable successes they have seen, endow PMHP with more "magic" than it has and thus overtax its range of applicability. A second reason is that strong internal pressures develop in schools to do something immediate about children whose visible, profound problems are overwhelming a classroom (even if that something is only the momentary relief of getting the child out of the class for several hours each week). Team members sometimes find it hard to say "No" in such instances because doing so might alienate colleagues or tarnish the program's helpfulness image. Finally, youngsters with profound adaptive problems may be seen in some PMHP schools because there are no alternatives in that particular geographic region.

Whatever the reason, the fact remains that some fraction of youngsters for whom PMHP is not an intervention of choice, slip through the net and are seen by the project. For many of those youngsters, the program experience is, at best, a holding operation that does not change their situation materially. Although such instances are also likely to show as project failures, they too are more a failure of the model's application and monitoring, than an intrinsic failure of the model per se.

A final important concern about PMHP's limits reflects changing social conditions, the effects of which are increasingly apparent in schools. The problem is this: Many children in today's society grow up in the shadow of exposure to such chronic stressors as poverty, neighborhood and family violence, substance abuse, squalid living conditions, and child neglect or abuse. These stressors exact heavy tolls. Moreover, they often co-occur with a climate of disinterest in or devaluation of education. Thus, many profoundly stressed children start school with 2½ strikes against them. Furthermore, it is not hard for them to pick up the last half strike quickly. These children, now seen in increasing numbers, are the ones whom educators view as highly susceptible to school failure and its associated life fallout if their course is not reversed by third grade.

The children we are describing start life with omnipresent problems— not necessarily psychological problems, but surely ponderous ones that are experienced daily in many forms. Although PMHP may have palliative value for them, its long-term helping potential is seriously limited. Indeed, given the magnitude and chronicity of the problems these children experience, a skeptic has every reason to ask why 20 meetings with an adult, no matter how caring, should be expected to turn the child's life situation around. Shooting elephants with a pea-gun is the metaphor that comes to mind in this situation, or, in Winston Churchill's immortal words: "Too little and too late."

For the children described, PMHP is a limited approach and outcomes with them are likely to reflect that reality. This problem is more serious than prior ones because it does, in fact, reflect an intrinsic limitation of the program model rather than a flaw in the mechanics of its application. Whereas the latter can be patched up by better quality control or other types of "Elmer's glue," limitations in the model's applicability push one to reexamine its assumptions and, on that basis, to develop new and better ways to address problems that the existing system cannot resolve. Major realignment processes of this type are sometimes called *paradigm shifts* (Kuhn 1971).

Emerging Directions

The preceding comments have two purposes. First, they describe what we see as limitations of the PMHP model. Highlighting these limitations is not to "bad mouth" an innovative approach that has done a first-rate job in many respects. Rather, it is to say that the model has some limits and a first step in addressing such limits is to delineate what they are. Having summed up PMHP's strengths and limitations as realistically as we can, the rest of this chapter focuses on steps that flow naturally from that summary.

That analysis can profitably start by differentiating among the levels at which school mental health issues can, theoretically, be addressed. School mental health's earliest and still dominant way was to use its finite resources reactively with the school's most serious, visible problems. Both because resources for dealing with such problems were insufficient, and pay-offs from focusing scarce resources on children with the poorest prognoses were low, it became appealing, if not obligatory, to consider prevention as an alternative. PMHP, targeted systematically to young children in schools, was our embodiment of that alternative.

Although PMHP is an important and very useful, reach-expanding alternative to traditional school mental health services, we realized that it also had several limitations: (a) it remained, in good measure, a reactive program (albeit one that reacted earlier and hence more effectively); (b) it reached only one segment of the school population; and (c) it was a circumscribed, time-limited approach that worked better for some children than others. Those realities had already raised important questions in our minds when the first PMHP volume was written—questions such as

- How could the fulcrum of our effort be moved toward more proactive programming?
- How might beneficial effects of school mental health programming accrue to all children, not just those with evident or incipient problems?
- How might the durability and robustness of a program's positive effects be enhanced? (Cowen, Trost, et al., 1975).

Our objective in posing those questions was not to replace PMHP, but rather to modify and extend the range of school-based programming to reach more children in before-the-fact, health-building ways.

The preceding questions gently nudged our purview from its original exclusive focus on ontogenetically early secondary prevention toward primary prevention. There, it joined programmatic efforts by others, many centered in schools, linked by the shared goal of enhancing the wellness of young children (Lorion, 1990; Price et al., 1988). Although a full review of those developments is beyond the scope of this volume, it may be helpful in developing thoughts about the future to cite several projects exemplifying current trends in school-based preventive programming that may stand as harbingers for the future.

As noted in chapter 8, the early social problem-solving approach went through important progressions and metamorphoses. These changes, leading to second generation programs (Elias & Clabby, 1992), are substantive not cosmetic and extensive rather than limited. For example, the early, specific focus on enhancing social or interpersonal problem-solving skills has broadened to include an extended family of competencies that come together under the label of social competencies. The latter term embraces such diverse skills as empathy and social awareness, stress management, impulse control, information processing, communication, and conflict resolution.

There were several reasons for widening the initial SPS viewing lens. One was the recurrent early finding that encapsulated SPS programs had limited initial value, some of which did not endure over time (Durlak,

1983). A second reason was an expanding generative knowledge base show-ing relationships between other (i.e., non-SPS) social competence indi-cators and positive adjustment outcomes. These variables differed in terms of when, developmentally, it was best to introduce them. Such considera-tions helped to forge the new training principles and formats that char-acterize second-generation, school-based social competence programs. For one thing, these programs train diverse skills and competencies, not just one, including skills designed to promote physical as well as psychological wellness and, as such, do not well fit the Procrustean bed that finite, one-shot programs impose. Rather, they become elements in a more compre-hensive curricular plan that (a) extends over multiple school years, (b) introduces new skills at developmentally appropriate times, (c) includes refreshers for skills previously taught at simpler levels, and (d) creates sup-portive school and class climates to build on program learnings after the formal program ends.

The preceding are constructive, reality-grounded steps in the evolu-tion of more effective competence-building programs. The following ex-amples can be cited: A multi-year program to teach self-control, social awareness, and group participation skills as well as problem-solving and decision-making skills (Elias et al., 1991) was found, 6 years later, to have increased self-efficacy and prosocial behavior and reduced pathology, ag-gression, and vandalism in participants. A similar program for sixth- and seventh-grade urban children, featuring training in stress management, problem solving, appropriate assertiveness, friendship formation, substance use, and health (Caplan et al., 1992), was found to strengthen children's abilities to solve problems, deal with anxiety, resolve conflict, and exercise impulse control. The program also enhanced children's popularity with peers and reduced their proneness to substance or alcohol abuse.

These examples illustrate the important and still unfolding develop-ment of comprehensive, multiyear, school-based programs to promote chil-dren's social competence. Cowen (1994) cites other examples of successful programs of this type. Encouraging findings from this work prompted Weiss-berg and Elias (1993) to sketch the contours of what can be thought of as third-generation, social competence training programs. As envisioned, such programs would be comprehensive and continuous from kindergarten to twelfth grade, introducing new components in parallel with the maturation of children's interests and cognitive skills. Their core goal is to provide children with cognitive, affective, and behavioral skills that centrally undergird physical and psychological well-being.

The social competence thrust is one of several new families of proac-tive school programs that go well beyond PMHP. Another that bears men-tion is the comprehensive Child Development Project (CDP), which seeks to modify the entire school environment rather than just enhance chil-dren's social competence (Battistich, Solomon, Watson, Solomon, &

Schaps, 1989; Developmental Studies Center, 1994; Solomon, Watson, Delucchi, Schaps, & Battistich, 1988). One distinguishing feature of this project is that it reflects the synchronized effort of an entire school, across all grade levels. Initially developed in the San Ramon, California School District, the CDP is now being conducted in a number of districts around the country.

The CDP's overarching, instrumental goal is to create a caring school community on the basis of significant involvements of parents, teachers, and children. Following Deci and Ryan's (1985) motivation theory, school and class environments were designed to enhance children's feelings of autonomy, belongingness, and competence. To enhance autonomy, a schoolwide developmental discipline approach was used with responsibility for setting and upholding class rules vested in the children. This step presumably helps students to feel valued (empowered) and creates a base on which to build solutions reflecting a commitment to democratic values.

Several schoolwide (kindergarten to sixth grade) steps were taken to promote belongingness. One was to use cooperative learning formats; another was to establish a schoolwide Buddies program pairing older and younger children. Also, the school's reading and instructional programs were geared throughout to the objective of helping children to understand themselves, others, and positive prosocial values better. The CDP's most pivotal assumption is that children will engage better and profit more from the school experience if they have a genuine stake in what they are doing and find their educational experiences interesting and rewarding. Project outcome findings support the feasibility of that assumption.

Systematic monitoring, including both reports by outside observers and student feedback, showed that the program had been implemented as intended. Specifically, program classes exceeded control classes in terms of warmth and supportiveness, number of mutual help activities, use of cooperative learning formats, extent to which prosocial values and interpersonal understanding were highlighted, opportunities provided for student autonomy and inputs, and use of discipline that promoted responsible behavior rather than external rewards and punishments (Developmental Studies Center, 1994). These differentiating program elements were found to extend across grade levels.

Among the project's important substantive findings, program children were judged to be more cooperative and considerate than control children, better able to defend their views and handle conflicts, and more willing for peers to be involved in group decision making. They also had more friends, felt less anxious socially and better accepted by peers, were more socially competent, and evidenced a deeper understanding of others. They were higher in self-esteem and empathy and, importantly, evidenced a stronger sense of community than comparison children. They did every bit as well as the latter academically, in fact better in some areas (e.g., reading comprehension).

Children from 12 CDP and 12 comparison schools were tracked in a 3-year follow-up study, as seventh and eighth graders in new schools (Battistich, Schaps, Watson, & Solomon, 1995). There were significantly lower rates of alcohol and marijuana use among children from program schools, with similar strong trends for tobacco use and delinquency or violence-related behaviors, such as carrying a weapon. In addition, continuing program benefits were found on prior sensitive variables such as conflict-resolution skills and self-esteem. Positive outcome findings were strongest in schools with high fidelity of program implementation. A related study (Battistich, Solomon, Kim, Watson, & Schaps, 1995) documented positive program effects on student motivation and attitude indicators in schools at different poverty levels, including those with high proportions of disadvantaged students. In this study, student perceptions of their schools as caring communities centrally predicted positive program outcomes and operated to mitigate some typical negative effects of poverty.

CDP's demonstrated early success paved the way for its extension, in a large-scale replication study, to three more California districts and districts in New York, Florida, and Kentucky. Although these new implementations are still unfolding, early evidence suggests that they are succeeding in enhancing children's sense of autonomy, sense of school as a community, liking of school, achievement motivation, concern for others, and conflict-resolution skills (Developmental Studies Center, 1994).

The groundbreaking CDP, based on major modifications of school and class environments, is not the only example of a comprehensive, proactively oriented, school-based program. Others include both all-purpose programs and ones targeted specifically to preventing specific adverse outcomes such as substance abuse or delinquency (e.g., Gottfredson, 1986; Hawkins et al., 1992). These school-based, primary prevention program developments, although still in an early stage, go well beyond PMHP's primary prevention programming efforts to date. The strengths of this development reside in its proactivity, targeting to all children, continuity of focus, and persistence over time.

Several other school-based, primary prevention programs that involve reactive, as well as proactive features, and specific targeting are cited to illustrate the range of program options being explored. The Home Improvement Program for Preschool Youngsters (HIPPY) is an academically targeted skill-building approach, designed to prepare children better for school entry (Lombard, 1981). Indigenous neighborhood parents do home visits over a 2-year period to teach mothers with limited educational backgrounds how to use structured curricular materials to train school readiness skills in their children. This role is empowering for mothers; it models steps that parents can take to help their children get a good start in school and, ultimately, further their education. The program, developed in Israel, was evaluated in a longitudinal study that followed children from ages 4 to 16. HIPPY children were found to exceed control children in academic achievement and school adjustment and had fewer grade retentions and dropouts. In parallel, mothers of HIPPY, compared with control, children had more positive self-concepts, pursued their education further, and were more involved in community activities (Lombard, 1981).

Olweus (1993) developed a school-based, primary prevention program in Norway, based on generative studies of bullying in the schools (Olweus, 1978, 1979). The demonstration that bullying was widespread, with significant negative consequences both for perpetrators and victims, gave rise to a large-scale prevention (system-change) program conducted in 42 Norwegian elementary and junior high schools. The program included school-, class-, and individual-level interventions built around four program objectives: (a) increasing awareness of bully–victim problems and their effects, (b) gaining the help of parents and teachers in addressing those problems, (c) developing clear anti-bullying rules and enforcing them, and (d) providing victims support and protection (Olweus, 1993).

Program outcomes 2 years later included an average 50% reduction in direct and indirect bullying incidents, both in and out of school, comparable reductions in other antisocial behaviors (e.g., vandalism, theft, drunkenness), and improvements in classroom social climates, interpersonal relationships, schoolwork, and satisfaction. These are important findings in their own right and in relation to the growing problems of school violence in modern society.

CHALLENGES FOR THE FUTURE

The programs considered above illustrate important forward strides in school-based prevention programming that differ from PMHP in goals, targeting, timing, and substantive activities. They do not, however, compete with PMHP. Rather, by going beyond PMHP, they enrich the available smorgasbord of school-based prevention options.

One common feature that most of these programs, including PMHP, share, for better and worse, is that they are school based or oriented. That fact reraises a serious question touched on only lightly earlier: Are there circumstances in which even the most carefully thought out, well-conducted school program will have, at best, limited potential value for some children? One such instance involves children in modern society who come to school from contexts of profound everyday stress, unprepared, tuned out, and at grave risk of failure. Many of these are children for whom PMHP and other school-based prevention programs have restricted potential.

From the start, three defining elements have dominated PMHP's coat of arms: *prevention, young children,* and *schools.* Those elements have been helpful directional beacons in our continuing search for more effective school mental health ways. However effective that search, we have learned that PMHP cannot solve all problems that school mental health services are called on to engage. One message inherent in that reality is that school mental health cannot be seen as an island unto itself; rather, it is more realistic and fruitful to see it as one potentially useful element in a broader social matrix that, for many children, significantly shapes the problems and perceptions they bring to school and sharply restricts what schools can do once those problems have locked in. PMHP learnings and bruises, over many years, push that second awareness into figure.

Prevention and wellness issues, even for those who are fully cathected to the concepts, can thus be framed at different levels. How they are framed will importantly shape both the issues to be addressed and the methods used to address them. The concrete choice in this case is the extent to which preventive efforts should be built around promoting wellness and adaptation in school contexts or around promoting wellness and adaptation, *period!*

Those two alternatives provide different viewing lenses and structure different goals and activities. Our belief, and the PMHP experience is a crucial factor in bringing us to it, is that a comprehensive wellness approach, within which school wellness is one significant component, is a strategy of choice for individuals and for society. That view is predicated on the awareness that wellness in school is not independent of the wellness or lack thereof that a child brings to school. Hence, even though schools have much to offer in a comprehensive quest for wellness enhancement, and that potential should be developed to the hilt, they are best seen as one important instrumentality in a much broader process, rather than as a "be-all and end-all" for all children.

Although we applaud PMHP's accomplishments and believe them to justify social policy changes that can better equip schools for the twenty-first century, we realize that PMHP is not a comprehensive solution for all the vexing problems of school maladaptation and failure. Wellness in the infancy and preschool years powerfully shape wellness in school and what children can derive from the school experience. Those earlier experiences are significant aspects of a continuous developmental process. For that reason, it is likely that many things that show up as failings of wellness in school can better be addressed in children's lives and experiences before they enter school (Schweinhart et al., 1993) than after the fact when the most a school can do is to redress false starts.

Although our faith remains both in a preventive focus with young children and in schools as settings in which prevention goals can be advanced significantly, the recognition of many instances in which schools alone are not enough has led to several small, but significant, refocusings of our long-standing directional beacons. In that refocusing, wellness enhancement, not just prevention, still targeted primarily to young children, is the overarching goal. Achieving that goal, however, will need to involve settings other than just schools (wherever it takes to get the job done). The rest of this chapter clarifies and expands this modest reformulation and highlights the considerations that bring us to it.

Promoting Wellness

The bedrock question we pose is, What can be done from the start and throughout to maximize the likelihood that children will develop in wholesome ways? Promoting wellness is a more basic objective than the one that launched PMHP (i.e., promoting school adaptation). A multipronged search for pathways to wellness is an objective that must increasingly capture our imagination, challenge our ingenuity, and guide our effort in the decades to come. The constructive model that PMHP has carved out can play a useful, though less than comprehensive, role in such an overall quest.

At several points in this discussion, the terms wellness and wellness enhancement have been used rather than primary prevention. This drift in terminology has been intentional. Early usage of the term primary prevention featured two related goals: cutting down the flow of dysfunction in situations of known risk and building health and wellness from the start (Cowen, 1973, 1985, 1986). Although both these goals continue to be acknowledged intellectually, most of the field's energies and resources in recent years have gone to the efforts to prevent specific *DSM-IV* (American Psychiatric Association, 1994) type disorders in people at risk for such disorders (Coie et al., 1993; Mrazek & Haggerty, 1994). Although that is a laudable objective, it is one with restrictions of timing, targeting, and mode of implementation. A wellness enhancement approach (Cowen, 1994) is not limited by those restrictions; it is population oriented and necessarily entails multifaceted strands that come into play in different formats and at different times, for different groups.

Tactics and strategies to improve the human condition can be conceptualized along several dimensions: reactive–proactive, individual versus population centered, uni- versus multidimensional, and temporally restricted versus ongoing. Psychotherapy, one well-known strategy within a broadly construed wellness-enhancement framework, is basically reactive, targeted to individuals, unidimensional, and temporally restricted. It is a relatively narrow approach that reaches a limited number of people, selectively so with regard to age, extent of problem evolution, and having the means to afford it. Indeed, the acronym YAVIS (young, attractive, verbal, intelligent, and successful) was once coined spoofingly to describe those for whom psychotherapy worked best.

Although PMHP is also designed primarily for individuals, it operates comfortably in a preventive mode because it is targeted to young children before problems root and fan out, and is equipotentially available to all children in implementing schools. For these reasons, PMHP's early effective intervention harbors considerable potential long-term benefit.

Several of the school-based primary prevention programs we have developed differ from PMHP in that they are more proactive than reactive and are targeted to entire classes or groups with common risk factors. Wellness-enhancement programs, anchoring the identified continuum, are proactive, directed to all people, not just individuals; are health building in intent; and have no temporal restrictions; on the contrary, the approach pulls for temporal continuity. Such programs include diverse contents and formats designed to fit the realities of different age and sociodemographic groups and different circumstances across the life span.

Elsewhere (Cowen, 1994), the broad contours and substantive directions of a wellness-enhancement framework were outlined. A comprehensive approach of this type requires inputs at many different levels and coordination across levels. At the broadest level, wellness outcomes are strongly molded by the social context in which children grow and develop. The social context formed by chronic poverty, lack of opportunity, and the absence of hope or a "fair shake in life" does not favor wellness outcomes such as satisfaction with life or happiness. Indeed, such contexts are more likely to predispose desperate measures, including a search for escape that can take the form of antisocial behaviors and actions. Wellness outcomes are also shaped by the ways in which major social settings, such as schools, are structured and how they actually operate. Additionally, at a more micro-level, such outcomes are powerfully shaped by the family milieu in which a child's earliest and most formative experiences first unfold and continue to unfold throughout childhood and youth.

In planning a wellness enhancement approach, Cowen (1994) identified five pathways that differ in their defining operations, targeting, and points of primary temporal relevance. The two key pathways to wellness in the early years involve establishing wholesome attachments and acquiring age-appropriate competencies. These two steps, vital in their own right, also lay down a solid base on which later wellness enhancing steps can rest. However helpful PMHP is for many children, it cannot by itself form those two key wellness pillars.

A comprehensive wellness enhancement strategy must begin with early efforts to strengthen children's attachments and competence development in ways that help centrally to form a child's senses of competence, belongingness, being loved, and being able to handle age-relevant problems. The child who has such feelings and self-views has a major adaptive advantage that is per se empowering. Major shortfalls in a child's early wellness development in these two crucial areas seriously limit what PMHP or, for that matter, any other helping intervention can provide. This reality, more than any other, moves us to replace school with "wherever it takes," as the locus in our long-standing imprimatur. One such place, for sure, is the home. Others are the key settings in a child's world before the formal school experience begins (e.g., day care, preschool).

In the past few years, this awareness has moved us in the direction of a leadership role in a large-scale, United Way–sponsored community consortium project called the Rochester Early Enrichment Program (REEP). In this project, 14 community agencies, operating in domains that significantly affect children's early development (e.g., pregnancy counseling, well-baby clinics, preschool health and education settings), have been working together to promote a coordinated set of early wellness-directed steps to better prepare children for school entry and increase the likelihood that they will benefit educationally and personally from the school experience.

In later childhood, as children mature, they interact increasingly with systems, settings, and people beyond the family. Those later experiences are also relevant to furthering wellness objectives, even though limits in the child's initially laid-down wellness base may restrict their potential helpfulness. In a wellness context, pertinent questions about extrafamilial settings to which children are exposed (schools are a good case in point) include the extent to which they can be structured to favor wellness outcomes in the many, and provide mechanisms for redressing limitations in wellness development to date and pointing children in adaptive, competence-enhancing directions. The latter is PMHP's focal objective.

Another important pathway to wellness involves the development of a sense of empowerment, feeling in control, and being able to make decisions that shape one's life. Although this ideal can be approached early on by promoting age-appropriate autonomy in children, pervasive and sometimes uncontrollable issues of disempowerment become salient later when diverse groups (e.g., minorities, children, the elderly, disabled people) have sharply limited access to essential commodities such as hope, justice, and opportunity. Given known associations between disempowerment and adaptive problems, policies and practices are needed to augment empowerment among the disempowered and, thereby, enhance the likelihood of wellness outcomes.

A final important wellness strand, being able to cope with major life stress, differs from those already described in that it can be pertinent to any person, in any walk of life, at any point in time. People vary enormously in their ability to deal with major life stress. Successful mastery of such stress, either because early experiences prepare a child to cope effectively or because relevant adaptive skills are acquired through training, increases the likelihood of later wellness outcomes. This is one reason why the study of pathways to resilient outcomes among profoundly stressed children has attracted much recent interest (Cicchetti & Garmezy, 1993). The intriguing phenomenon of resilient outcomes under highly stressful conditions is important in its own right and for its potential contributions to a richer psychology of wellness.

The wellness strands described should be seen as mutually supporting elements in an elaborate network rather than as competing approaches. Each piece is needed to complete a complex jigsaw puzzle. Moreover, there are interdependencies among those pieces such that failure in early wellness development may sharply restrict later wellness and, conversely, early wellness acquisition paves the way for continuing, later wellness. The latter, thought-provoking point is confirmed by the conclusions of two recent reviews (Yoshikawa, 1994; Zigler et al., 1992). Both these reviews reported stronger delinquency-prevention effects from several early, comprehensive wellness-oriented programs for families, such as the Perry Preschool Project (Schweinhart et al., 1993), targeted only to early school adaptation when they were conducted, than from later (i.e., preadolescent and adolescent) programs targeted specifically to delinquency prevention among youth at risk.

Pursuing the full richness of a wellness-enhancement orientation thus requires going well beyond schools, including PMHP. Doing so will entail active, systematic, wellness-enhancing steps much earlier than is now the case, indeed probably starting before the child is born (Olds, 1988), to involve primary caregivers in the instrumental actions and processes that subserve children's healthy attachment formation and competence acquisition.

Although negotiating those steps successfully is fundamental to sound wellness starts in children, when that does not happen, schools can still play important supporting roles within the large wellness framework being proposed. Those steps include the development of class and school environments, as well as educational programs (e.g., social competence training) designed to promote wellness outcomes in all children. There is growing reason to believe that such programs should begin early, be comprehensive, introduce new wellness-related skills and competencies as children's developmental readiness permits, and offer continuing booster shots to build on and solidify prior learnings.

Within such a comprehensive framework, the PMHP model offers a very useful resource in ontogenetically early secondary prevention for children in whom an early preventive experience can reroute trajectories onto a pathway toward wellness. That such an early course correction can be a significant turning point for many youngsters is the basis for suggesting that planners and policy makers consider seriously, as several states have already done, widespread incorporation of PMHP's program model in the schools.

Looking Backward and Looking Forward: Final Remarks

The long PMHP trip did not take place in a vacuum. Rather, project experiences served well to frame new questions and launch new initiatives in what can be seen as a dynamic, ever-evolving scenario. Those new steps helped to make PMHP a better, more effective venture of the type it was intended to be. In parallel, however, program experience also clarified what PMHP could not be. Importantly, however paradoxical or counterintuitive the next statement may seem, we came more to see PMHP as the right answer to the wrong or, at least, an artificially narrow and restrictive question: What can be done to build a "better mousetrap" in *school* mental health? Here, the word school is italicized because it harbors a hidden assumption, which constrains PMHP, that the school period is meaningful in and of itself, without reference to the shaping inputs that precede it. For children whose prior shaping inputs have been reasonably solid, PMHP can indeed be an effective source of help at an important time. For those who lack that base of preparedness, PMHP may be insufficient. We thus end up depicting PMHP as a good answer to an insufficient question and, in so doing, hopefully put a more heuristic question into focus: What can be done to maximize children's wellness and fulfillment from the start?

Authors have had the experience of giving a manuscript (book, chapter, article) their finest shot and feeling reasonably satisfied with the finished product, only to look later at that work and perceive, sometimes in shock, what they had failed to say, or worse yet, that what once looked so right and now looked so wrong. We now have a rare opportunity to revisit the concluding wisdoms and seeming certainties of the PMHP volume written 20 years ago, which seem in hindsight to have or have not withstood the test of time. Such a sobering exercise can readily force one to "eat crow" or to give up on the temptation to crystal-ball gaze ever again. In this case, the potential embarrassment of such a review is outweighed (if only slightly) by a need to put the sum of the PMHP experience into perspective and, on that base, to generate several concluding thoughts that point toward a hopefully better tomorrow.

One key conclusion of the prior volume (Cowen, Trost, et al., 1975) was that PMHP offered options that traditional school mental health services did not, including particularly systematic early detection of school adjustment problems and sharply expanded, early, effective preventively oriented helping services to the many children identified by that process as being at risk. That conclusion is even more valid today than it was in 1975, for several reasons. For one, today's PMHP is a stronger, more diversified program than it was 20 years ago. It offers more solid options for working with a broader range of children and situations than could previously be reached. Moreover, it has been shown to work effectively in very diverse circumstances; it can flexibly fit many situations still respecting a school's resources, ecology, and operating realities and maintain its usefulness for children and school personnel. Notwithstanding such diversity, program outcome studies done by many people in many settings have provided a continuing stream of evidence of PMHP's efficacy.

All the preceding, we believe, adds up to high marks for PMHP and argues strongly for its place in tomorrow's school mental health world, without suggesting that today's PMHP should be its forever version. Rather, we see the process of strengthening PMHP as open and ongoing, fueled by day-to-day experience with the project, and developing a sense of what does and does not work. An example is our current belief that the PMHP process can be enhanced by more extensive, meaningful parent involvements.

A second question posed in the prior volume was whether PMHP should be seen as an ideal school mental health model. We answered that question with a firm no, arguing for the need to shift future efforts increasingly from repairing to building (health), and to do so by "articulating school environments that permit children to grow and develop optimally from the start" (Cowen, Trost, et al., 1975). Both these points, insofar as they go, still make sense today (e.g., MacIver, Reuman, & Main, 1995). Indeed, a good deal of our current effort involves primary prevention steps that flow logically from that view.

The hedge in the above paragraph pivots around the key words "insofar as they go." Time and experience suggest that such efforts may fall short in two key regards. First, even though steps taken to modify school environments constructively (i.e., changes that favor positive educational and wellness outcomes) remain central in an overall school-anchored primary prevention plan, other approaches (e.g., skill-building programs and programs to defuse the negative effects of stress and strengthen children's coping capacities) with similar objectives need also to be developed vigorously.

Indeed, our own efforts to develop primary prevention program options for schools over the past 20 years have reflected several theoretically appealing approaches, including exploration of class environment changes. Such developments can both enrich health building options available to PMHP schools and extend them to all children, not just those who evidence early warning signs. That accomplishment too is a source of pride. Even so, PMHP's evident limitations suggest that the total symphony is still unfinished, and that the conceptual matrix in which PMHP unfolded is too narrow.

This leads to a second level of modification of conclusions reached in the 1975 volume. For those who work in schools, the ideal of promoting children's mental health makes eminently good sense in its own right and for the academic benefits it may facilitate; indeed, it defines a mandate. However, helping actions that school mental health professionals can offer are limited by starting points and givens and, by the time a child reaches the age of 5, some crucial givens are firmly established. The point to highlight here is that there is some artificiality and arbitrariness to the very concept of school mental health. Although such a thing, to be sure, exists, it is not a thing unto itself. Otherwise put, many issues that school mental health is called on to engage reactively reflect the realities of a child's life to that point and the things that define the child's current life.

By extension, we can say that questions about how to strengthen school mental health approaches—focal questions that PMHP and its derivatives have sought to address over the years—although legitimate in their own right, are limited. A better, richer, more heuristic question, albeit a more complex and challenging one, is what can be done to enhance the development of wellness from the start. This question is different from and more basic than school mental health. Schools can play a useful and important role in articulating and implementing steps that support and are consistent with the objectives of a comprehensive life-span, wellness-enhancement thrust. This is the level at which the PMHP model with its extensions and elaborations can make its greatest contribution.

Hence, we envision a contributory future place for PMHP programs as one important, but not dominant or exclusive, element in a comprehensive social effort to enhance children's wellness in the twenty-first century. Society's real challenge is to promote wellness in the many. To realize that goal will require articulation of effective wellness enhancement strategies that (a) begin at birth (or before) and continue through childhood, (b) recognize continuities between early wellness and school adaptation, and (c) better prepare children to profit from the school experience. Given such a starter base, schools can gainfully pursue many options for building on and solidifying good early starts and providing constructive course modifiers, such as PMHP, for children with gaps in their early experience. Thus, schools harbor some, but not all, important potential roles in the pursuit of wellness. In like manner, PMHP and the later primary prevention models it has spawned offer one set, but not all, of the options that can augment a school's potential contributions to the development of wellness in children.

REFERENCES

Achenbach, T. M., & Edelbrock, C. S. (1983). *Manual for the Child Behavior Checklist and Revised Child Behavior Profile*. Burlington: University of Vermont, Department of Psychiatry.

Achenbach, T. M., McConaughy, S. H., Howell, C. T. (1987). Child/adolescent behavioral and emotional problems: Implications of cross-informant correlations for situational specificity. *Psychological Bulletin, 101*, 213–232.

Albee, G. W. (1959). *Mental health manpower trends*. New York: Basic Books.

Albee, G. W. (1982). Preventing psychopathology and promoting human potential. *American Psychologist, 37*, 1043–1050.

Allen, G. J., Chinsky, J. M., Larcen, S. W., Lochman, J. E., & Selinger, H. V. (1976). *Community psychology and the schools: A behaviorally oriented multilevel preventive approach*. Hillsdale, NJ: Erlbaum.

Allen, V. L. (Ed.). (1976). *Children as teachers: Theory and research on tutoring*. New York: Academic Press.

Alpert-Gillis, L. J., Pedro-Carroll, J. L., & Cowen, E. L. (1989). Children of Divorce Intervention Program: Development, implementation, and evaluation of a program for young urban children. *Journal of Consulting and Clinical Psychology, 57*, 583–587.

Amato, P. R., & Keith, B. (1991a). Parental divorce and adult well-being: A meta-analysis. *Journal of Marriage and the Family, 53*, 43–58.

Amato, P. R., & Keith, B. (1991b). Parental divorce and the well-being of children: A meta-analysis. *Psychological Bulletin, 110*, 26–46.

American Psychiatric Association. (1994). *Diagnostic and Statistical Manual of Mental Disorders* (4th ed.). Washington, DC: Author.

Anthony, E. J. (1974). A risk-vulnerability intervention model. In E. J. Anthony & C. Koupernik (Eds.), *The child in his family: Children at psychiatric risk* (pp. 99–122). New York: Wiley.

Anthony, E. J., & Cohler, B. J. (Eds.). (1987). *The invulnerable child*. New York: Guilford Press.

Armistead, L., McCombs, A., Forehand, R., Wierson, M., Long, N., & Fauber, R. (1990). Coping with divorce: A study of young adolescents. *Journal of Clinical Child Psychology, 19*, 79–84.

Arnhoff, F. N., Rubenstein, E. A., & Speisman, J. C. (1969). *Manpower for mental health*. Chicago: Aldine.

Aronson, E., Blaney, M., Stefan, C., Sykes, J., & Snapp, N. (1978). *The jigsaw classroom*. Beverly Hills, CA: Sage.

Barker, R. G., & Gump, P. V. (1964). *Big school, small school*. Stanford, CA: Stanford University Press.

299

Battistich, V., Schaps, E., Watson, M., & Solomon, D. (1996). Prevention effects of the Child Development Project: Early findings from an ongoing multisite demonstration trial. *Journal of Adolescent Research, 11*, 12–35.

Battistich, V., Solomon, D., & Delucchi, K. (1993). Interaction processes and student outcomes in cooperative learning groups. *The Elementary School Journal, 94*, 19–32.

Battistich, V., Solomon, D., Kim, D., Watson, M., & Schaps, E. (1995). Schools as communities, poverty levels of student populations, and students' attitudes, motives and performance: A multilevel analysis. *American Educational Research Journal, 32*, 627–658.

Battistich, V., Solomon, D.S., Watson, M., Solomon, J., & Schaps, E. (1989). Effects of an elementary school program to enhance prosocial behavior and children's cognitive social problem solving skills and strategies. *Journal of Applied Developmental Psychology, 10*, 147–169.

Baumeister, R. F., & Leary, M. R. (1995). The need to belong: Desire for interpersonal attachments as a fundamental human motivation. *Psychological Bulletin, 117*, 497–529.

Berrueta-Clement, J. R., Schweinhart, L. J., Barnett, M. W., Epstein, A. S., & Weikart, D. P. (1984). *Changed lives: The effects of the Perry Preschool Program on youths through age 19.* Ypsilanti, MI: High/Scope Educational Research Foundation.

Black, A. E., & Pedro-Carroll, J. L. (1993). The role of parent–child relationships in mediating the effects of marital disruption. *Journal of the American Academy of Child and Adolescent Psychiatry, 32*, 1019–1027.

Bloom, B. L. (1980). Social and community interventions. *Annual Review of Psychology, 31*, 111–142.

Bloom, B. L., Hodges, W. F., & Caldwell, R. A. (1982). A preventive program for the newly separated. *American Journal of Community Psychology, 10*, 251–264.

Bower, E. M. (1960). *Early identification of emotionally handicapped children.* Springfield, IL: Charles C Thomas.

Bowlby, J. (1982). *Attachment and loss: Vol. 1. Attachment* (2nd ed.). New York: Basic Books.

Bronfenbrenner, U. (1979). *The ecology of human development: Experiments by nature and design.* Cambridge, MA: Harvard University Press.

Brown, L. P., & Cowen, E. L. (1988). Children's judgments of event upsettingness and personal experiencing of stressful events. *American Journal of Community Psychology, 16*, 123–135.

Brown, L. P., & Cowen, E. L. (1989). Stressful life events, support and children's school adjustment. *Journal of Clinical Child Psychology, 18*, 214–220.

Caplan, G. (1964). *Principles of preventive psychiatry.* New York: Basic Books.

Caplan, G. (1981). Mastery of stress: Psychosocial aspects. *American Journal of Psychiatry, 138*, 413–420.

Caplan, M. Z., Weissberg, R. P., Grober, J. S., Sivo, P. J., Grady, K., & Jacoby, C. (1992). Social competence promotion with inner-city and suburban young adolescents: Effects on social adjustment and alcohol use. *Journal of Consulting and Clinical Psychology, 60,* 56–63.

Carden-Smith, L. K., & Fowler, S. A. (1984). Positive peer pressure: The effects of peer monitoring on children's disruptive behavior. *Journal of Applied Behavior Analysis, 17,* 213–227.

Casey, R. J., & Berman, J. S. (1985). The outcome of psychotherapy with children. *Psychological Bulletin, 98,* 388–400.

Chandler, C., Weissberg, R. P., Cowen, E. L., & Guare, J. (1984). The long-term effects of a school-based secondary prevention program for young maladapting children. *Journal of Consulting and Clinical Psychology, 52,* 165–170.

Cicchetti, D., & Garmezy, N. (Eds.). (1993). Milestones in the development of resilience [Special issue]. *Development and Psychopathology, 5.*

Clarfield, S. P. (1974). The development of a teacher referral form for identifying early school maladaptation. *American Journal of Community Psychology, 2,* 199–210.

Cohen, S. (1988). *Statistical power analysis for behavioral sciences* (2nd ed.). Hillsdale, NJ: Erlbaum.

Coie, J. D., & Dodge, K. A. (1988). Multiple sources of data on social behavior and social status in the school: A cross-age comparison. *Child Development, 59,* 815–829.

Coie, J. D., Watt, N. F., West, S. G., Hawkins, J. D., Asarnow, J. R., Markman, H. J., Ramey, S. L., Shure, M. B., & Long, B. (1993). The science of prevention: A conceptual framework and some directions for a national research program. *American Psychologist, 48,* 1013–1022.

Coronet Video. (1980a). *After the divorce* [Video]. Deerfield, IL: Author.

Coronet Video. (1980b). *When parents separate* [Video]. Deerfield, IL: Author.

Cotton, J. L., & Cook, M. S. (1982). Meta-analyses and the effects of various reward systems: Some different conclusions from Johnson et al. *Psychological Bulletin, 92,* 176–183.

Cowen, E. L. (1968). The effectiveness of secondary prevention programs using nonprofessionals in the school setting. *Proceedings of the 76th Annual Convention of the American Psychological Association, 2,* 705–706.

Cowen, E. L. (1971). Emergent directions in school mental health: The development and evaluation of a program for early detection and prevention of ineffective school behavior. *American Scientist, 59,* 723–733.

Cowen, E. L. (1973). Social and community interventions. In P. Mussen & M. Rosenzweig (Eds.), *Annual Review of Psychology, 24,* 423–472.

Cowen, E. L. (1978). Some problems in community program evaluation research. *Journal of Consulting and Clinical Psychology, 46,* 792–805.

Cowen, E. L. (1980). The wooing of primary prevention. *American Journal of Community Psychology, 8,* 258–284.

Cowen, E. L. (1985). Person-centered approaches to primary prevention in mental health: Situation-focused and competence-enhancement. *American Journal of Community Psychology, 13,* 31–48.

Cowen, E. L. (1986). Primary prevention in mental health: Ten years of retrospect and ten years of prospect. In M. Kessler & S. E. Goldston (Eds.), *A decade of progress in primary prevention* (pp. 3–45). Hanover, NH: University Press of New England.

Cowen, E. L. (1991). In pursuit of wellness. *American Psychologist, 46,* 404–408.

Cowen, E. L. (1994). The enhancement of psychological wellness: Challenges and opportunities. *American Journal of Community Psychology, 22,* 149–179.

Cowen, E. L., Davidson, E. R., & Gesten, E. L. (1980). Program dissemination and the modification of delivery practices in school mental health. *Professional Psychology, 11,* 36–47.

Cowen, E. L., Dorr, D., Clarfield, S. P., Kreling, B., McWilliams, S. A., Pokracki, F., Pratt, D. M., Terrell, D., & Wilson, A. (1973). The AML: A quick screening device for early detection of school maladaptation. *American Journal of Community Psychology, 1,* 12–35.

Cowen, E. L., Dorr, D. A., & Pokracki, F. (1972). Selection of nonprofessional child aides for a school mental health project. *Community Mental Health Journal, 8,* 220–226.

Cowen, E. L., Dorr, D., Sandler, I. N., & McWilliams, S. (1971). Utilization of a nonprofessional child-aide school mental health program. *Journal of School Psychology, 9,* 131–136.

Cowen, E. L., Dorr, D. A., Trost, M. A., & Izzo, L. D. (1972). A follow-up study of maladapting school children seen by nonprofessionals. *Journal of Consulting and Clinical Psychology, 39,* 235–238.

Cowen, E. L., Gardner, E. A., & Zax, M. (Eds.). (1967). *Emergent approaches to mental health problems.* New York: Appleton-Century-Crofts.

Cowen, E. L., & Gesten, E. L. (1980). Evaluating community programs: Tough and tender perspectives. In M. Gibbs, J. R. Lachemeyer, & J. Sigal (Eds.), *Community psychology: Theoretical and empirical approaches* (pp. 363–393). New York: Gardner Press.

Cowen, E. L., Gesten, E. L., & DeStefano, M. A. (1977). Nonprofessional and professional help agents' views of interventions with young maladapting school children. *American Journal of Community Psychology, 5,* 469–479.

Cowen, E. L., & Hightower, A. D. (1986). Stressful life events and young children's school adjustment. In S. M. Auerbach & A. L. Stolberg (Eds.), *Crisis intervention with children and families* (pp. 85–101). New York: Hemisphere.

Cowen, E. L., Hightower, A. D., Johnson, D. B., Sarno, M., & Weissberg, R. P. (1989). State level dissemination of a program for early detection and prevention of school maladjustment. *Professional Psychology, 20,* 513–519.

Cowen, E. L., Huser, J., Beach, D. R., & Rappaport, J. (1970). Parental perceptions of young children and their relation to indices of adjustment. *Journal of Consulting and Clinical Psychology, 34*, 97–103.

Cowen, E. L., Izzo, L. D., Miles, H., Telschow, E. F., Trost, M. A., & Zax, M. (1963). A preventive mental health program in the school setting: Description and evaluation. *Journal of Psychology, 56*, 307–356.

Cowen, E. L., & Lorion, R. P. (1974). Which kids are helped? *Journal of Special Education, 8*, 187–192.

Cowen, E. L., Lorion, R. P., & Dorr, D. (1974). Research in the community cauldron: A case history. *Canadian Psychologist, 15*, 313–325.

Cowen, E. L., Lorion, R. P., Dorr, D., Clarfield, S. P., & Wilson, A. B. (1975). Evaluation of a preventively oriented, school based mental health program. *Psychology in the Schools, 12*, 161–166.

Cowen, E. L., Lotyczewski, B. S., & Weissberg, R. P. (1984). Risk and resource indicators and their relationship to young children's school adjustment. *American Journal of Community Psychology, 12*, 353–367.

Cowen, E. L., Orgel, A. R., Gesten, E. L., & Wilson, A. B. (1979). The evaluation of an intervention program for young schoolchildren with acting-out problems. *Journal of Abnormal Child Psychology, 7*, 381–396.

Cowen, E. L., Pedersen, A., Babigian, H., Izzo, L. D., & Trost, M. A. (1973). Long-term follow-up of early detected vulnerable children. *Journal of Consulting and Clinical Psychology, 41*, 438–446.

Cowen, E. L., Pedro-Carroll, J. L., & Alpert-Gillis, L. J. (1990). Relationships between support and adjustment among children of divorce. *Journal of Child Psychology and Psychiatry, 31*, 727–735.

Cowen, E. L., & Schochet, B. V. (1973). Referral and outcome differences between terminating and nonterminating children seen by nonprofessionals in a school mental health project. *American Journal of Community Psychology, 1*, 103–112.

Cowen, E. L., Spinell, A., Wright, S., & Weissberg, R. P. (1983). Continuing dissemination of a school-based early detection and prevention model. *Professional Psychology, 14*, 118–127.

Cowen, E. L., Trost, M. A., & Izzo, L. D. (1973). Nonprofessional human-service personnel in consulting roles. *Community Mental Health Journal, 9*, 335–341.

Cowen, E. L., Trost, M. A., Lorion, R. P., Dorr, D., Izzo, L. D., & Isaacson, R. V. (1975). *New ways in school mental health: Early detection and prevention of school maladaptation.* New York: Human Sciences Press.

Cowen, E. L., Weissberg, R. P., & Guare, J. (1984). Differentiating attributes of children referred to a school mental health program. *Journal of Abnormal Child Psychology, 12*, 397–409.

Cowen, E. L., Weissberg, R. P., Lotyczewski, B. S., Bromley, M. L., Gilliland-Mallo, G., DeMeis, J. L., Farago, J. P., Grassi, R. J., Haffey, W. G., Weiner, M. J., & Woods, A. (1983). Validity generalization of a school-based preventive mental health program. *Professional Psychology, 14*, 613–623.

Cowen, E. L., & Work, W. C. (1988). Resilient children, psychological wellness and primary prevention. *American Journal of Community Psychology, 16*, 591–607.

Cowen, E. L., Work, W. C., Hightower, A. D., Wyman, P. A., Parker, G. R., & Lotyczewski, B. S. (1991). Toward the development of a measure of perceived self-efficacy in children. *Journal of Clinical Child Psychology, 20*, 169–178.

Cowen, E. L., Work, W. C., & Wyman, P. A. (1993). Similarity of parent and child self-views in stress affected and stress resilient urban families. *Acta Paedopsychiatrica, 55*, 193–197.

Cowen, E. L., Work, W. C., Wyman, P. A., Parker, G. R., Wannon, M., & Gribble, P. A. (1992). Test comparisons among stress-affected, stress-resilient and non-classified 4th–6th grade urban children. *Journal of Community Psychology, 20*, 200–214.

Cowen, E. L., Wyman, P. A., Work, W. C., & Iker, M.R. (1994). A preventive intervention for enhancing resilience among young highly stressed urban children. *Journal of Primary Prevention, 15*, 247–260.

Cowen, E. L., Wyman, P. A., Work, W. C., Kim, J., Fagen, D. B., & Magnus, K. (1996). *Follow-up study of young stress-affected and stress resilient children.* Manuscript submitted for publication.

Cowen, E. L., Zax, M., Izzo, L. D., & Trost, M. A. (1966). Prevention of emotional disorders in the school setting: A further investigation. *Journal of Consulting Psychology, 30*, 381–387.

Damon, W. (1977). *The social world of the child.* San Francisco: Jossey-Bass.

Deci, E. L., & Ryan, R. (1985). *Intrinsic motivation and self-determination in human behavior.* New York: Plenum Press.

DeStefano, M. A., Gesten, E. L., & Cowen, E. L. (1977). Teachers' views of the treatability of children's school adjustment problems. *Journal of Special Education, 11*, 275–280.

Developmental Studies Center. (1994). *The Child Development Project: Summary of findings in two initial districts and the first phase of an expansion to six additional districts nationally.* Oakland, CA: Developmental Studies Center.

Donahue, G. T. (1967). A school district program for schizophrenic, organic and seriously disturbed children. In E. L. Cowen, E. A. Gardner, & M. Zax (Eds.), *Emergent approaches to mental health problems* (pp. 352–368). New York: Appleton-Century-Crofts.

Donahue, G. T., & Nichtern, S. (1965). *Teaching the troubled child.* New York: Free Press.

Dorr, D. A. (1972). An ounce of prevention. *Mental Hygiene, 56*, 25–27.

Dorr, D., & Cowen, E. L. (1972). Teachers' perception of a school mental health project. *Journal of School Psychology, 10*, 76–78.

Dorr, D., & Cowen, E. L. (1973). Nonprofessional mental health workers' judgments of change in children. *Journal of Community Psychology, 1*, 23–26.

Dorr, D., Cowen, E. L., & Sandler, I. N. (1973). Changes in nonprofessional mental health workers' response preference and attitudes as a function of training and supervised field experience. *Journal of School Psychology, 11,* 118–122.

Dorr, D., Cowen, E. L., Sandler, I. N., & Pratt, D. M. (1973). Dimensionality of a test battery for nonprofessional mental health workers. *Journal of Consulting and Clinical Psychology, 41,* 181–185.

Duerr, M. (1993). *Early mental health initiative: Year-end evaluation report.* Chico, CA: Duerr Evaluation Resources, California Department of Mental Health.

Durlak, J. A. (1983). Social problem-solving as a primary prevention strategy. In R. D. Felner, L. A. Jason, J. N. Moritsugu, & S. S. Farber (Eds.), *Preventive psychology: Theory, research and practice* (pp. 31–48). Elmsford, NY: Pergamon Press.

Elias, M. J., & Clabby, J. F. (1992). *Building social problem-solving skills: Guidelines from a school-based program.* San Francisco: Jossey-Bass.

Elias, M. J., Gara, M. A., Schuyler, T. F., Branden-Muller, L. R., & Sayette, M. A. (1991). The promotion of social competence: Longitudinal study of a school-based program. *American Journal of Orthopsychiatry, 61,* 409–417.

Emery, R. E. (1982). Interparental conflict and the children of discord and divorce. *Psychological Bulletin, 92,* 310–330.

Emery, R. E., & Forehand, R. (1994). Parental divorce and children's well being: A focus on resilience. In R. J. Haggerty, L. R. Sherrod, N. Garmezy, & M. Rutter (Eds.), *Stress, risk, and resilience in children and adolescents* (pp. 64–99). Cambridge, UK: Cambridge University Press.

Ensminger, M. E., Kellam, S. G., & Rubin, R. B. (1983). School and family origins of delinquency: Comparisons by sex. In K. T. VanDusen & S. A. Mednick (Eds.), *Prospective studies of crime and delinquency* (pp. 17–41). Boston: Kluwer-Nijhoff.

Epstein, L. (1978). The effects of intraclass peer tutoring on the vocabulary development of learning disabled children. *Journal of Learning Disabilities, 11,* 518–521.

Eron, L. D., & Huesmann, L. R. (1990). The stability of aggressive behavior: Even unto the third generation. In M. Lewis & S. M. Miller (Eds.), *Handbook of developmental psychopathology* (pp. 147–156). New York: Plenum.

Fagen, D. B., & Hightower, A. D. (1994, August). *Cooperative learning and the importance of peer relationships.* Paper presented at the meeting of the American Psychological Association, Los Angeles, CA.

Fairweather, G. W. (1972). *Social change: The challenge to survival.* Morristown, NJ: General Learning Press.

Fairweather, G. W., Sanders, D. H., & Tornatzky, L. G. (1974). *Creating change in mental health organizations.* New York: Pergamon Press.

Farie, A. M., Cowen, E. L., & Smith, M. (1986). The development and implementation of a rural consortium program to provide early, preventive school mental health services. *Community Mental Health Journal, 22,* 94–103.

Felner, R. D., Ginter, M. A., Boike, M. F., & Cowen, E. L. (1981). Parental death or divorce and the school adjustment of young children. *American Journal of Community Psychology, 9,* 181–191.

Felner, R. D., Norton, P. L., Cowen, E. L., & Farber, S. S. (1981). A prevention program for children experiencing life crisis. *Professional Psychology, 12,* 446–452.

Felner, R. D., Stolberg, A. L., & Cowen, E. L. (1975). Crisis events and school mental health referral patterns of young children. *Journal of Consulting and Clinical Psychology, 43,* 305–310.

Flores de Apodaca, R. (1979). *Interpersonal cognitive problem solving training for school maladjusted primary graders.* Unpublished doctoral dissertation, University of Rochester.

Franklin, K. M., Janoff-Bulman, R., & Roberts, J. E. (1990). Long-term impact of parental divorce on optimism and trust: Changes in general assumptions or narrow beliefs? *Journal of Personality and Social Psychology, 59,* 743–755.

Fromm-Reichmann, F. (1959). Loneliness. *Psychiatry, 22,* 1–15.

Furstenberg, F. F. (1990). Divorce and the American family. *Annual Review of Sociology, 16,* 379–403.

Garmezy, N. (1982). Foreword. In E. E. Werner & R. S. Smith, *Vulnerable but invincible: A study of resilient children* (pp. xiii–xix). New York: McGraw-Hill.

Garmezy, N. (1983). Stressors of childhood. In N. Garmezy & M. Rutter (Eds.), *Stress, coping and development in children* (pp. 43–84). New York: McGraw-Hill.

Garmezy, N., Masten, A. S., & Tellegen, A. (1984). Studies of stress-resistant children: A building block for developmental psychopathology. *Child Development, 55,* 97–111.

Garmezy, N., & Nuechterlein, K. (1972). Invulnerable children: The facts and fiction of competence and disadvantage. *American Journal of Orthopsychiatry, 42,* 328–329.

Gartner, A., & Riessman, F. (1993). Peer tutoring: Toward a new model. Washington, DC: ERIC Clearinghouse on Teaching and Teacher Education.

Gest, S. D., Neeman, J., Hubbard, J., Masten, A. S., & Tellegen, A. (1993). Parenting quality, adversity and conduct problems in adolescence: Testing process oriented models of resilience. *Development and Psychopathology, 5,* 663–682.

Gesten, E. L. (1976). A Health Resources Inventory: The development of a measure of the personal and social competence of primary grade children. *Journal of Consulting and Clinical Psychology, 44,* 775–786.

Gesten, E. L., Cowen, E. L., Orgel, A. R., & Schwartz, E. (1979). Help-agents' views about clinical interactions with acting-out children. *Journal of Abnormal Child Psychology, 7,* 397–404.

Gesten, E. L., Flores de Apodaca, R., Rains, M. H., Weissberg, R. P., & Cowen, E. L. (1979). Promoting peer related social competence in schools. In M. W. Kent & J. E. Rolf (Eds.), *The primary prevention of psychopathology: Vol. 3.*

Social competence in children (pp. 220–247). Hanover, NH: University Press of New England.

Gesten, E. L., Rains, M. H., Rapkin, B. D., Weissberg, R. P., Flores de Apodaca, R., Cowen, E. L., & Bowen, R. (1982). Training children in social problem-solving competencies: A first and second look. *American Journal of Community Psychology, 10*, 95–115.

Ginott, H. G. (1959). The theory and practice of "therapeutic intervention" in child treatment. *Journal of Consulting and Clinical Psychology, 23*, 160–166.

Glick, P. C., & Lin, S. (1986). Recent changes in divorce and remarriage. *Journal of Marriage and the Family, 48*, 737–747.

Glidewell, J. C., & Swallow, C. S. (1969). *The prevalence of maladjustment in elementary schools: A report prepared for the Joint Commission on the Mental Health of Children.* Chicago: University of Chicago Press.

Goldstein, M. J. (1982). *Preventive intervention in schizophrenia: Are we ready?* (NIMH Primary Prevention Series). Washington, DC: U.S. Government Printing Office.

Goodenough, F. L. (1926). *Measurement of intelligence by drawings.* Yonkers-on-Hudson, NY: World Book Co.

Gottfredson, D. C. (1986). An empirical test of school-based environmental and individual interventions to reduce the risk of delinquent behavior. *Criminology, 25*, 705–731.

Greenberg, J. R., & Mitchell, S. A. (1983). *Object relations and psychoanalytic theory.* Cambridge, MA: Harvard University Press.

Grych, S., & Fincham, S. (1992). Interventions for children of divorce: Towards greater integration of research and action. *Psychological Bulletin, 111*, 434–454.

Hamblin, R. L., Hathaway, C., & Wodarski, J. (1971). Group contingencies, peer tutoring, and accelerating academic achievement. In E. Ramp & B. L. Hopkins (Eds.), *A new direction for education: Behavior analysis* (pp. 41–53). Lawrence: The University of Kansas Press.

Hansell, S. (1984). Cooperative groups, weak ties, and the integration of peer friendships. *Social Psychology Quarterly, 47*, 316–328.

Hartup, W. W. (1983). Peer relations. In P. H. Mussen (Series Ed.) & E. M. Hetherington (Vol. Ed.), *Handbook of child psychology: Vol. 4. Socialization, personality, and social development* (pp. 103–196). New York: Wiley.

Hartup, W. W., & Moore, S. G. (1990). Early peer relations: Developmental significance and prognostic implications. *Early Childhood Research Quarterly, 5*, 1–17.

Hawkins, J. D., Catalano, R. F., Morrison, D. M., O'Donnell, J., Abbott, R. D., & Day, L. E. (1992). The Seattle Social Development Project: Effects of the first four years on protective factors and problem behaviors. In J. McCord & R. E. Tremblay (Eds.), *The prevention of anti-social behavior in children* (pp. 139–161). New York: Guilford Press.

Hetherington, E. M. (1972). Effects of parental absence on personality development in adolescent daughters. *Developmental Psychology, 7*, 313–326.

Hetherington, E. M., (1989). Marital transitions: A child's perspective. *American Psychologist, 44*, 303–312.

Hetherington, E. M., & Clingempeel, W. G. (1992). Coping with marital transitions. *Monographs of the Society for Research in Child Development, 57*, 1–299.

Hetherington, E. M., Cox, M., & Cox, R. (1979). Family interaction and the social, emotional, and cognitive development of children following divorce. In V. Vaughn & T. Brazelton (Eds.), *The family: Setting priorities* (pp. 89–128). New York: Science and Medicine.

Hetherington, E. M., Cox, M., & Cox, R. (1982). Effects of divorce on parents and children. In M. Lamb (Ed.), *Nontraditional families* (pp. 233–288). Hillsdale, NJ: Erlbaum.

Hightower, A. D. (1994). [Scales characteristics of the Parent–Child Rating Scale (P-CRS): Factor structure and validity estimates.] Unpublished raw data.

Hightower, A. D., & Avery, R. R. (1986, August). The Study Buddy Program. In W. C. Work (Chair), *Prevention programs in elementary schools: From conceptualization to implementation.* Symposium conducted at the annual meeting of the American Psychological Association, Washington, DC.

Hightower, A. D., Avery, R. R., & Levinson, H. R. (1988, April). *An evaluation of the Study Buddy Program: A preventive intervention for 4th and 5th grades.* Paper presented at the meeting of the National Association of School Psychologists, Chicago, IL.

Hightower, A. D., Cowen, E. L., Spinell, A. P., Lotyczewski, B. S., Guare, J. C., Rohrbeck, C. A., & Brown, L. P. (1987). The Child Rating Scale: The development and psychometric refinement of a socioemotional self-rating scale for young school children. *School Psychology Review, 16*, 239–255.

Hightower, A. D., Fagen, D. B., Lee, Ja., Lee, Ju., Gervase, A. M., & Slocum, B. (1995). *Study Buddy Manual.* Unpublished manuscript.

Hightower, A. D., Work, W. C., Cowen, E. L., Lotyczewski, B. S., Spinell, A. P., Guare, J. C., & Rohrbeck, C. A. (1986). The Teacher–Child Rating Scale: A brief objective measure of elementary children's school problem behaviors and competencies. *School Psychology Review, 15*, 393–409.

Hobbs, N. (1966). Helping disturbed children: Psychological and ecological strategies. *American Psychologist, 21*, 1105–1115.

Hobbs, N. (1967). The reeducation of emotionally disturbed children. In E. M. Bower & W. G. Hollister (Eds.), *Behavior science frontiers in education* (pp. 335–356). New York: Wiley.

Holmes, T. H., & Rahe, R. H. (1967). The Social Readjustment Rating Scale. *Journal of Psychosomatic Research, 11*, 213–218.

Holzberg, J. D., Knapp, R. H., & Turner, J. L. (1967). College students as companions to the mentally ill. In E. L. Cowen, E. A. Gardner, & M. Zax (Eds.), *Emergent approaches to mental health problems* (pp. 91–109). New York: Appleton-Century-Crofts.

Hoyt, L. A., Cowen, E. L., Pedro-Carroll, J. L., & Alpert-Gillis, L. J. (1990). Anxiety and depression in young children of divorce. *Journal of Clinical Child Psychology, 19,* 26–32.

Hoyt-Meyers, L. A., Cowen, E. L., Work, W. C., Wyman, P. A., Magnus, K., Fagen, D. B., & Lotyczewski, B. S. (1995). *Test correlates of resilient outcomes among highly stressed 2nd–3rd grade urban children.* Manuscript submitted for publication.

Iker, M. (1990). *A preventive intervention for young profoundly stressed urban children.* Unpublished doctoral dissertation, University of Connecticut, Storrs.

Isaacs, S. (1939). *Social development in young children.* New York: Harcourt, Brace.

Jenkins, J. R., Mayhall, W. F., Peschyn, C. M., & Jenkins, L. M. (1974). Comparing small group and tutorial instruction in resource rooms. *Exceptional Children, 40,* 245–250.

Johnson, D. B., Carlson, S. R., & Couick, J. (1992). *Program Development Manual for the Primary Intervention Program.* Sacramento: California Department of Mental Health.

Johnson, D. W., & Johnson, R. T. (1974). Instructional goal structure: Cooperative, competitive, or individualistic. *Review of Educational Research, 44,* 213–240.

Johnson, D. W., & Johnson, R. T. (1989). *Cooperation and competition: Theory and research.* Edina, MN: Interaction Book Company.

Johnson, D. W., Maruyama, G., Johnson, R. T., Nelson, D., & Skon, S. (1981). Effects of cooperative, competitive, and individualistic goal structures on achievement: A meta-analysis. *Psychological Bulletin, 89,* 47–62.

Johnson, R. T., Johnson, D. W., Scott, L. E., & Ramolae, B. A. (1985). Effects of single-sex and mixed-sex cooperative interaction on science achievement and attitudes and cross-handicap and cross-sex relationships. *Journal of Research in Science Teaching, 22,* 207–220.

Joint Commission on Mental Illness and Health. (1961). *Action for mental health.* New York: Basic Books.

Kellam, S. G., Branch, J. D., Agrawal, K. C., & Ensminger, M. E. (1975). *Mental health and going to school: The Woodlawn program of assessment, early intervention, and evaluation.* Chicago: University of Chicago Press.

Kellam, S. G., Branch, J. D., Agrawal, K. C., & Grabill, M. E. (1972). Woodlawn Mental Health Center: An evolving strategy for planning community mental health. In S. E. Golann & C. Eisdorfer (Eds.), *Handbook of community mental health* (pp. 711–727). New York: Appleton-Century-Crofts.

Kellam, S. G., Simon, M. B., & Ensminger, M. E. (1983). Antecedents in first grade of teenage substance use and psychological well being: A ten-year community-wide prospective study. In D. F. Ricks & B. S. Dohrenwend (Eds.), *Origins of psychopathology: Research and public policy* (pp. 73–97). New York: Cambridge University Press.

Kerley, J. (1994). *Social competencies and life stress as predictors of school adjustment in urban early adolescents: A prospective-longitudinal study.* Unpublished doctoral dissertation, The Fielding Institute, Santa Barbara, CA.

Kiesler, C. A. (1992). Some observations about the concept of the chronically mental ill. In M. Kessler, S. E. Goldston, & J. M. Joffe (Eds.), *The present and future of prevention: In honor of George W. Albee* (pp. 55–68). Newbury Park, CA: Sage.

Kiesler, C. A., Simpkins, C., & Morton, T. (1989). The psychiatric in-patient treatment of children and youth in general hospitals. *American Journal of Community Psychology, 17,* 821–830.

Kohut, H. (1984). *How does analysis cure?* Chicago: University of Chicago Press.

Krauss, D. M., & Weissberg, R. P. (1988). *A replication of a school-based preventive mental health program for primary-grade children.* Hartford, CT: State Department of Education.

Kuhn, T. S. (1971). *The structure of scientific revolutions* (2nd. ed.). Chicago: University of Chicago Press.

Kurdek, L. A., & Berg, B. (1983). Correlates of children's adjustment to their parents' divorces. In L. A. Kurdek (Ed.), *New directions in child development: Vol. 19. Children and divorce* (pp. 47–60). San Francisco: Jossey-Bass.

Kurdek, L. A., & Berg, B. (1987). Children's beliefs about parental divorce scale: Psychometric characteristics and concurrent validity. *Journal of Consulting and Clinical Psychology, 55,* 712–718.

Levine, M., & Perkins, D. V. (1987). *Principles of community psychology: Perspectives and applications.* New York: Oxford University Press.

Levitt, E. E. (1971). Research on psychotherapy with children. In A. E. Bergin & S. L. Garfield (Eds.), *Handbook of psychotherapy and behavior change: An empirical analysis* (pp. 474–494). New York: Wiley.

Lewis, W. W. (1967). Project Re-Ed: Educational intervention in discordant child rearing systems. In E. L. Cowen, E. A. Gardner, & M. Zax (Eds.), *Emergent approaches to mental health problems* (pp. 352–368). New York: Appleton-Century-Crofts.

Liem, G. R., Yellott, A. W., Cowen, E. L., Trost, M. A., & Izzo, L. D. (1969). Some correlates of early detected emotional dysfunction in the schools. *American Journal of Orthopsychiatry, 39,* 619–626.

Lockheed, M. E., & Harris, A. M. (1984). Cross-sex collaborative learning in elementary classrooms. *American Educational Research Journal, 21,* 275–294.

Lombard, A. D. (1981). *Success begins at home.* Lexington, MA: Lexington Books.

Lorion, R. P. (1973). Socioeconomic status and traditional treatment approaches reconsidered. *Psychological Bulletin, 79,* 263–270.

Lorion, R. P. (1974). Patient and therapist variables in the treatment of low-income patients. *Psychological Bulletin, 81,* 344–354.

Lorion, R. P. (Ed.). (1990). *Protecting the children: Strategies for optimizing emotional and behavioral development.* New York: Haworth.

Lorion, R. P., Caldwell, R. A., & Cowen, E. L. (1976). Effects of a school mental health project: A one-year follow-up. *Journal of School Psychology, 14,* 56–63.

Lorion, R. P., & Cowen, E. L. (1976). Comparison of two outcome groups in a school-based mental health project. *American Journal of Community Psychology, 4,* 65–73.

Lorion, R. P., Cowen, E. L., & Caldwell, R. A. (1974). Problem types of children referred to a school based mental health program: Identification and outcome. *Journal of Consulting and Clinical Psychology, 42,* 491–496.

Lorion, R. P., Cowen, E. L., & Caldwell, R. A. (1975). Normative and parametric analyses of school maladjustment. *American Journal of Community Psychology, 3,* 291–301.

Lorion, R. P., Cowen, E. L., & Kraus, R. M. (1974). Some hidden "regularities" in a school mental health program and their relation to intended outcomes. *Journal of Consulting and Clinical Psychology, 42,* 346–352.

Lotyczewski, B. S., Cowen, E. L., & Weissberg, R. P. (1986). Adjustment correlates of physical and health problems in young children. *Journal of Special Education, 20,* 241–250.

MacIver, D. J., Reuman, D. A., & Main, S. R. (1995). Social structuring of the school: Studying what is, illuminating what could be. In J. T. Spence, J. M. Darley, & D. F. Foss (Eds.), *Annual Review of Psychology, 46,* 375–400.

Magoon, T. M., Golann, S. E., & Freeman, R. W. (1969). *Mental health counselors at work.* Elmsford, NY: Pergamon Press.

Manson, S. M. (Ed.). (1982). *New directions in prevention among Native American and Alaska native communities.* Portland: University of Oregon, Oregon Health Sciences.

Masten, A. S. (1989). Resilience in development: Implications of the study of successful adaptation for developmental psychopathology. In D. Cicchetti (Ed.), *Rochester Symposium on Developmental Psychopathology* (Vol. 1, pp. 261–294). Hillsdale, NJ: Erlbaum.

Masten, A. S., Garmezy, N., Tellegen, A., Pelligrini, D. S., Larkin, K., Larsen, A. (1988). Competence and stress in school children: The moderating effects of individual and family qualities. *Journal of Child Psychology and Psychiatry, 29,* 745–764.

McKim, B. J., & Cowen, E. L. (1988). A brief parent rating scale for assessing young children's adjustment. *Special Services in the Schools, 4,* 55–70.

McLanahan, S. S., & Bumpass, L. (1988). Intergenerational consequences of family disruption. *American Journal of Sociology, 94,* 130–152.

McLaughlin, T. F. (1981). The effects of individual and group contingencies on reading performance of special education students. *Contemporary Educational Psychology, 6,* 76–79.

McLaughlin, T. F., Herb, C., & Davis, C. (1980). The effects of individual and group contingencies on spelling performance for a special education class. *B. C. Journal of Special Education, 4,* 263–270.

McWilliams, S. A. (1972). A process analysis of nonprofessional intervention with children. *Journal of School Psychology, 10,* 367–377.

Meller, P. J., Laboy, W., Rothwax, Y., Fritton, J., & Mangual, J. (1994). *Community School District Four: Primary Mental Health Project, 1990–1994.* New York: Community School District #4.

Mijangos, L. B., & Farie, A. (1992). *Supervision.* Rochester, NY: Primary Mental Health Project.

Moos, R. H. (1979). *Evaluating educational environments.* San Francisco: Jossey-Bass.

Moos, R. H., & Trickett, E. S. (1974). *Classroom Environment Scale.* Palo Alto, CA: Consulting Psychologists Press.

Mrazek, P. J., & Haggerty, R. J. (Eds.). (1994). *Reducing risks for mental disorders: Frontiers for preventive intervention research.* Washington, DC: National Academy Press.

Murphy, L. B., & Moriarty, A. E. (1976). *Vulnerability, coping, and growth: From infancy to adolescence.* New Haven, CT: Yale University Press.

National Mental Health Association. (1995). *Getting started: The NMHA directory of model programs to prevent mental disorders and promote mental health.* Alexandria, VA: National Mental Health Association.

Newcomb, A. F., & Bagwell, C. L. (1995). Children's friendship relations: A meta-analytic review. *Psychological Bulletin, 117,* 306–347.

Newcomb, A. F., Bukowski, W. M., & Pattee, L. (1993). Children's peer relations: A meta-analytic review of popular, rejected, neglected, controversial, and average sociometric status. *Psychological Bulletin, 113,* 99–128.

O'Grady, D., Metz, J. R. (1987). Resilience in children at high risk for psychiatric disorder. *Journal of Pediatric Psychology, 12,* 3–23.

Ojeman, R. H. (1967). Incorporating psychological concepts in the school curriculum. *Journal of School Psychology, 5,* 195–204.

Olds, D. L. (1988). The prenatal/early infancy project. In R. H. Price, E. L. Cowen, R. P. Lorion, & J. Ramos-McKay (Eds.), *Fourteen ounces of prevention: A casebook for practitioners* (pp. 9–23). Washington, DC: American Psychological Association.

Olweus, D. (1978). *Aggression in the schools: Bullies and whipping boys.* Washington, DC: Hemisphere.

Olweus, D. (1979). Stability of aggressive reaction patterns in males: A review. *Psychological Bulletin, 86,* 852–875.

Olweus, D. (1993). *Bullying at school: What we know and what we can do.* Cambridge, MA: Blackwell.

Orgel, A. R. (1980). Haim Ginott's approach to discipline. In D. Dorr & M. Zax (Eds.), *Comparative approaches to discipline for children and youth* (pp. 75–100). New York: Springer.

Pardes, H., & Pincus, H. A. (1981). Brief therapy in the context of national mental health issues. In S. H. Budman (Ed.), *Forms of brief psychotherapy* (pp. 7–22). New York: Guilford Press.

Parker, G. R., Cowen, E. L., Work, W. C., & Wyman, P. A. (1990). Test correlates of stress affected and stress resilient outcomes among urban children. *Journal of Primary Prevention, 11,* 19–35.

Parker, J., & Asher, S. R. (1987). Peer acceptance and later personal adjustment: Are low accepted children at risk? *Psychological Bulletin, 102,* 357–389.

Pedro-Carroll, J. L., & Alpert-Gillis, L. J. (in press). Preventive interventions for children of divorce: A developmental model for 5 and 6 year old children. *Journal of Primary Prevention.*

Pedro-Carroll, J. L., Alpert-Gillis, L. J., & Cowen, E. L. (1992). An evaluation of the efficacy of a preventive intervention for 4th–6th grade urban children of divorce. *Journal of Primary Prevention, 13,* 115–130.

Pedro-Carroll, J. L., & Cowen, E. L. (1985). The children of divorce intervention program: An investigation of the efficacy of a school-based prevention program. *Journal of Consulting and Clinical Psychology, 53,* 603–611.

Pedro-Carroll, J. L., Cowen, E. L., Hightower, A. D., & Guare, J. C. (1986). Preventive intervention with latency-aged children of divorce: A replication study. *American Journal of Community Psychology, 14,* 277–290.

Pedro-Carroll, J. L., Sutton, S. E., & Black, A. E. (1993). *The Children of Divorce Intervention Program: Preventive outreach to early adolescents—Final report.* Rochester, NY: Rochester Mental Health Association.

Pedro-Carroll, J. L., Sutton, S. E., & Wyman, P. A. (1996). *A two year follow-up investigation of a preventive intervention for children of divorce.* Manuscript submitted for publication.

Peterson, J. L., & Zill, N. (1986). Marital disruption, parent–child relationships, and behavior problems in children. *Journal of Marriage and the Family, 48,* 295–307.

Pigott, H. E., Fantuzzo, J. W., & Clement, P. W. (1986). The effects of reciprocal peer tutoring and group contingencies on the academic performance of elementary school children. *Journal of Applied Behavioral Analysis, 19,* 93–98.

Poser, E. G. (1966). The effect of therapist training on group therapeutic outcome. *Journal of Consulting Psychology, 30,* 283–289.

President's Commission on Mental Health. (1978). *Report to the President* (Vol. 1, Stock No. 040-000-00390-8). Washington, DC: U.S. Government Printing Office.

Price, R. H., Cowen, E. L., Lorion, R. P., & Ramos-McKay, J. (Eds.). (1988). *Fourteen ounces of prevention: A casebook for practitioners.* Washington, DC: American Psychological Association.

Price, R. H., & Smith, S. A. (1985). *A guide to evaluating prevention programs in mental health.* Rockville, MD: National Institute of Mental Health.

Primary Mental Health Project. (1995). *Screening and evaluation measures and forms.* Rochester, NY: Author.

Rappaport, J. (1977). *Community psychology: Values, research, and action.* New York: Holt, Rinehart & Winston.

Rappaport, J. (1981). In praise of paradox: A social policy of empowerment over prevention. *American Journal of Community Psychology, 9*, 1–25.

Rappaport, J. (1987). Terms of empowerment/exemplars of prevention: Toward a theory of community psychology. *American Journal of Community Psychology, 15*, 121–148.

Rappaport, J., Chinksy, J. M., & Cowen, E. L. (1971). *Innovations in helping chronic patients: College students in a mental hospital.* New York: Academic Press.

Rappaport, J., Seidman, E., & Davidson, W. S. (1979). Demonstration research and manifest vs. true adoption: The natural history of a research project designed to divert adolescents from the legal system. In R. F. Muñoz, L. R. Snowden, & J. G. Kelly (Eds.), *Social and psychological research in community settings: Designing and conducting programs for social and personal well-being* (pp. 101–144). San Francisco, CA: Jossey-Bass.

Rieff, P. (1959). *Freud: The mind of the moralist.* New York: Viking Press.

Reiff, R. (1967). Mental health manpower and institutional change. In E. L. Cowen, E. A. Gardner, & M. Zax (Eds.), *Emergent approaches to mental health problems* (pp. 74–88). New York: Appleton-Century-Crofts.

Reiff, R., & Riessman, F. (1965). The indigenous nonprofessional: A strategy of change in community action and community mental health programs. *Community Mental Health Journal* (Monograph No. 1).

Riessman, F. (1965). The "helper therapy" principle. *Social Work, 10*, 27–32.

Riessman, F. (1967). A neighborhood-based mental health approach. In E. L. Cowen, E. A. Gardner, & M. Zax (Eds.), *Emergent approaches to mental health problems* (pp. 162–184). New York: Appleton-Century-Crofts.

Rioch, J., Elkes, C., & Flint, A. A. (1965). *National Institute of Mental Health pilot project in training mental health counselors.* (U.S. Department of Health, Education & Welfare, Public Health Service Publication No. 1254). Washington, DC: U.S. Government Printing Office.

Rioch, M. J. (1967). Pilot projects in training mental health counselors. In E. L. Cowen, E. A. Gardner, & M. Zax (Eds.), *Emergent approaches to mental health problems* (pp. 110–127). New York: Appleton-Century-Crofts.

Robins, L. N. (1966). *Deviant children grown up.* Baltimore, MD: Williams & Wilkins.

Rolf, J. E. (1972). The social and academic competence of children vulnerable to schizophrenia and other behavior pathologies. *Journal of Abnormal Psychology, 80*, 225–243.

Rolf, J. E. (1976). Peer status and the directionality of symptomatic behavior: Prime social competence predictors of outcome for vulnerable children. *American Journal of Orthopsychiatry, 46*, 74–88.

Rosnow, R. L., & Rosenthal, R. (1993). *Beginning behavioral research: A conceptual primer.* New York: Macmillan.

Rubin, Z. (Ed.). (1974). *Doing unto others: Joining, molding, conforming, helping, loving.* Englewood Cliffs, NJ: Prentice-Hall.

Rubin, Z. (1980). *Children's friendships*. Cambridge, MA: Harvard University Press.

Rutter, M. (1979). Protective factors in children's responses to stress and disadvantage. In M. W. Kent & J. E. Rolf (Eds.), *Primary prevention of psychopathology: Vol. 3. Social competence in children* (pp. 49–74). Hanover, NH: University of New England.

Rutter, M. (1985). Resilience in the face of adversity: Protective factors and resistance to psychiatric disorder. *British Journal of Psychiatry, 147*, 598–611.

Rutter, M. (1987). Psychosocial resilience and protective mechanisms. *American Journal of Orthopsychiatry, 57*, 316–331.

Rutter, M., Cox, A., Tupling, C., Berger, M., & Yule, W. (1975). Attainment and adjustment in two geographical areas: I. The prevalence of psychiatric disorder. *British Journal of Psychiatry, 126*, 493–509.

Rutter, M., Quinton, D., & Yule, B. (1977). *Family pathology and disorder in children*. New York: Wiley.

Rutter, M., Yule, B., Quinton, D., Rowlands, O., Yule, W., & Berger, M. (1975). Attainment and adjustment in two geographical areas: III. Some factors accounting for area differences. *British Journal of Psychiatry, 126*, 520–533.

Ryan, W. (1971). *Blaming the victim*. New York: Random House.

Sanders, R. (1967). New manpower for mental health service. In E. L. Cowen, E. A. Gardner, & M. Zax (Eds.), *Emergent approaches to mental health problems* (pp. 128–143). New York: Appleton-Century-Crofts.

Sandler, I. N. (1972). Characteristics of women working as child-aides in a school based preventive mental health program. *Journal of Consulting and Clinical Psychology, 39*, 56–61.

Santrock, J. W., & Warshak, R. A. (1979). Father custody and social development in boys and girls. *Journal of Social Issues, 35*, 112–125.

Sanua, V. D. (1966). Sociocultural aspects of psychotherapy and treatment: A review of the literature. In L. E. Abt & L. Bellak (Eds.), *Progress in clinical psychology* (Vol. 8, pp. 151–190). New York: Grune & Stratton.

Sarason, S. B. (1971). *The culture of the school and the problem of change*. Boston: Allyn-Bacon.

Sarason, S. B. (1982). *The culture of the school and the problem of change* (2nd ed.). Boston: Allyn-Bacon.

Sarason, S. B. (1983). *Schooling in America: Scapegoat and salvation*. New York: Free Press.

Sarason, S. B. (1986, August). *And what is in the public interest?*. Paper presented at the meeting of the American Psychological Association, Washington, DC.

Sarason, S. B. (1990). *The predictable failure of educational reform*. San Francisco: Jossey-Bass.

Sarason, S. B. (1995). *Parental involvement and the political principle*. San Francisco: Jossey-Bass.

Schofield, W. (1964). *Psychotherapy: The purchase of friendship*. Englewood-Cliffs, NJ: Prentice-Hall.

Schunk, D. H., & Hanson, A. R. (1985). Peer models: Influence on children's self-efficacy and achievement. *Journal of Educational Psychology, 77,* 313–322.

Schweinhart, L. J., Barnes, H. V., & Weikart, D. P. (with Barnett, W. S., & Epstein, A. S.). (1993). *Significant benefits: The High/Scope Perry Preschool study through age 27.* Ypsilanti, MI: High/Scope Press.

Seifer, R., & Sameroff, A. J. (1987). Multiple determinants of risk and invulnerability. In E. J. Anthony & B. J. Cohler (Eds.), *The invulnerable child* (pp. 51–69). New York: Guilford Press.

Seitz, V., & Apfel, N. H. (1994). Parent focused intervention: Diffusion effects on siblings. *Child Development, 65,* 677–683.

Sharan, S. (1980). Cooperative learning in small groups: Recent methods and effects on achievement, attitudes and ethnic relations. *Review of Educational Research, 50,* 241–271.

Sharan, S. (Ed.). (1990). *Cooperative learning: Theory and research.* New York: Praeger.

Shore, M. F. (1972). The federal scene. *Professional Psychology, 4,* 383–384.

Shure, M. B., & Spivack G. (1978). *Problem-solving techniques in childrearing.* San Francisco: Jossey-Bass.

Silverman, P. R. (1988). Widow-to-Widow: A mutual help program for the widowed. In R. H. Price, E. L. Cowen, R. P. Lorion, & J. Ramos-McKay (Eds.), *Fourteen ounces of prevention: A casebook for practitioners* (pp. 175–186). Washington DC: American Psychological Association.

Simon, N. (1976). *All kinds of families.* Niles, IL: Whitman.

Slater, E. J., & Calhoun, K. S. (1988). Familial conflict and marital dissolution: Effect on the social functioning of college students. *Journal of Social and Clinical Psychology, 6,* 118–126.

Slavin, R. E. (1983). When does cooperative learning increase student achievement? *Psychological Bulletin, 94,* 429–445.

Solomon, D., Watson, M. S. Delucchi, K. L., Schaps, E., & Battistich, V. (1988). Enhancing children's prosocial behavior in the classroom. *American Educational Research Journal, 25,* 527–554.

Spielberger, C. D. (1973). *State–Trait Anxiety Scale for Children: Preliminary Manual.* Palo Alto, CA: Consulting Psychologists Press.

Spivack, G., Platt, J. J., & Shure, M. B. (1976). *The problem-solving approach to adjustment.* San Francisco: Jossey-Bass.

Spivack, G., & Shure, M. B. (1974). *Social adjustment of young children: A cognitive approach to solving real life problems.* San Francisco: Jossey-Bass.

Sroufe, L. A. (1990). An organizational perspective on the self. In D. Cicchetti & M. Beeghly (Eds.), *The self in transition: Infancy to childhood* (pp. 281–307). Chicago: University of Chicago Press.

Sterling, S. E. (1986). *School-based intervention program for early latency-aged children of divorce.* Unpublished doctoral dissertation, University of Rochester.

Sterling, S. E., Cowen, E. L., Weissberg, R. P., Lotyczewski, B. S., & Boike, M. (1985). Recent stressful life events and young children's school adjustment. *American Journal of Community Psychology, 13*, 87–98.

Stolberg, A. L., & Mahler, J. (1994). Enhancing treatment gains in school-based intervention for children of divorce through skill training, parental involvement and transfer procedures. *Journal of Consulting and Clinical Psychology, 62*, 147–156.

Strain, P. S. (Ed.). (1981). *The utilization of classroom peers as behavior change agents.* New York: Plenum.

Strayhorn, J. M. (1988). *The competent child: An approach to psychotherapy and preventive mental health.* New York: Guilford Press.

Sullivan, E. T., Clark, W. W., & Tiegs, E. W. (1957). *California Short-Form Test of Mental Maturity.* Monterey, CA: California Test Bureau.

Sullivan, H. S. (1953). *The interpersonal theory of psychiatry.* New York: Norton.

Swift, C. F. (1980). Primary prevention: Policy and practice. In R. H. Price, R. F. Ketterer, B. C. Bader, & J. Monahan (Eds.), *Prevention in mental health: Research, policy and practice* (pp. 207–236). Beverly Hills, CA: Sage.

Tableman, B. (1980). Prevention activities at the state level. In R. H. Price, R. F. Ketterer, B. C. Bader, & J. Monahan (Eds.), *Prevention in mental health: Research, policy and practice* (pp. 237–252). Beverly Hills, CA: Sage.

Talmage, H., Pascarella, E. T., & Ford S. (1984). The influence of cooperative learning strategies on teacher practices, student perceptions of the learning environment and academic achievement. *American Educational Research Journal, 21*, 163–179.

Task Panel Report: Learning Failure and Unused Learning Potential (1978). *Task Panel Reports submitted to the President's Commission on Mental Health* (Vol. 3, pp. 661–704, Stock No. 040-000-00392-4). Washington, DC: U.S. Government Printing Office.

Terrell, D. L. (1973). *A comparison of individual, group and individual plus group interventions by nonprofessional child-aides.* Unpublished doctoral dissertation, University of Rochester.

Terrell, D. L., McWilliams, S. A., & Cowen, E. L. (1972). Description and evaluation of group-work training for nonprofessional aides in a school mental health program. *Psychology in the Schools, 9*, 70–75.

Thomas, A., & Chess, S. (1977). *Temperament and development.* New York: Brunner/Mazel.

Thomas, C. F. (1989). *An evaluation of the effectiveness of the Primary Intervention Program in improving the school and social adjustment of primary grade children: Final report.* Los Alamitos, CA: Southwest Regional Education Laboratory.

Thomas C. F., & Brock, W. M. (1987). *Primary Intervention Program: Program development manual.* Los Alamitos, CA: Southwest Regional Education Laboratory.

Tremblay, R. E., Pihl, R. O., Vitaro, F., Dobkin, P. L. (1994). Predicting early onset of male antisocial behavior from preschool behaviors. *Archives of General Psychiatry, 51*, 732–739.

Trickett, E. S., & Moos, R. H. (1974). Personal correlates of contrasting environments: Student satisfaction in high school classrooms. *American Journal of Community Psychology, 2*, 1–12.

Umbarger, C. C., Dalsimer, J. S., Morrison, A. P., & Breggin, P. R. (1962). *College students in mental hospitals.* New York: Grune & Stratton.

Van Vleet, P., & Kannegieter, R. (1969). *Investments in prevention: The prevention of learning and behavior problems in young children.* San Francisco: PACE ID Center.

Wallerstein, J. S. (1983). Children of divorce: The psychological tasks of the child. *American Journal of Orthopsychiatry, 53*, 230–243.

Wallerstein, J. S., & Blakeslee, S. (1989). *Second chances: Men, women, and children a decade after divorce—Who wins, who loses, and why?* New York: Ticknor & Fields.

Wallerstein, J. S., & Kelly, J. B. (1980). *Surviving the breakup: How children actually cope with divorce.* New York: Basic Books.

Wannon, M. (1990). *Children's control beliefs about controllable and uncontrollable events: Their relationship to stress resilience and psychosocial adjustment.* Unpublished doctoral dissertation, University of Rochester.

Weissberg, R. P., Caplan, M. Z., & Harwood, R. L. (1991). Promoting competence enhancing environments: A systems-based perspective on primary prevention. *Journal of Consulting and Clinical Psychology, 59*, 830–841.

Weissberg, R. P., Cowen, E. L., Lotyczewski, B. S., & Gesten, E. L. (1983). Primary Mental Health Project: Seven consecutive years of program outcome research. *Journal of Consulting and Clinical Psychology, 51*, 100–107.

Weissberg, R. P., & Elias, M. J. (1993). Enhancing young children's social competence and health behavior: An important challenge for educators, scientists, policy makers and funders. *Applied and Preventive Psychology, 2*, 179–190.

Weissberg, R. P., Gesten, E. L., Carnrike, C. L., Toro, P. A., Rapkin, B. D., Davidson, E., & Cowen, E. L. (1981). Social problem-solving skills training: A competence building intervention with 2nd–4th grade children. *American Journal of Community Psychology, 9*, 411–424.

Weissberg, R. P., Gesten, E. L., Liebenstein, N. L., Schmid, K. D., & Hutton, H. (1980). *The Rochester Social Problem-Solving (SPS) Program: A training manual for teachers of 2nd–4th grade children.* Rochester, NY: Primary Mental Health Project.

Weissberg, R. P., Gesten, E. L., Rapkin, B. D., Cowen, E. L., Davidson, E., Flores de Apodaca, R., & McKim, B. J. (1981). Evaluation of a social problem-solving training program for suburban and inner-city third-grade children. *Journal of Consulting and Clinical Psychology, 49*, 251–261.

Weissberg, R. P., Pike, K. M., & Bersoff, D. M. (1986). *The evaluation of the Primary Mental Health Project during 1984–85 in Connecticut.* Hartford, CT: State Department of Education.

Werner, E. E. (1989). High-risk children in young adulthood: A longitudinal study from birth to 32 years. *American Journal of Orthopsychiatry, 59,* 72–81.

Werner, E. E., & Smith, R. S. (1977). *Kauai's children come of age.* Honolulu: University Press.

Werner, E. E., & Smith, R. S. (1982). *Vulnerable but invincible: A study of resilient children.* New York: McGraw-Hill.

Werner, E. E., & Smith, R. S. (1992). *Overcoming the odds: High risk children from birth to adulthood.* Ithaca, NY: Cornell University Press.

White, B. L. (1978). *Experience and environment: Major influences on the development of the young child* (Vol. 2). Englewood Cliffs, NJ: Prentice Hall.

White, B. L., Kaban, B. T., & Attanuci, J. S. (1979). *The origins of human competence: Final report of the Harvard Preschool Project.* Lexington, MA: Heath.

Willems, E. P. (1967). Sense of obligation to high school activities as related to school size and marginality of student. *Child Development, 38,* 1247–1260.

Winer, J. I., Hilpert, P. L., Gesten, E. L., Cowen, E. L., & Schubin, W. E. (1982). The evaluation of a kindergarten social problem-solving program. *Journal of Primary Prevention, 2,* 205–216.

Winer-Elkin, J. I., Weissberg, R. P., & Cowen, E. L. (1988). Evaluation of a planned short-term intervention for school children with focal adjustment problems. *Journal of Clinical Child Psychology, 17,* 106–115.

Winnicott, D. W. (1965). *The maturational processes and the facilitating environment.* New York: International Universities Press.

Work, W. C. (1986). *The social problem solving cognitive measure.* Unpublished manuscript, University of Rochester.

Work, W. C., Cowen, E. L., Parker, G. W., & Wyman, P. A. (1990). Stress resilient children in an urban setting. *Journal of Primary Prevention, 11,* 3–17.

Work, W. C., Levinson, H. R., & Hightower, A. D. (1995). *What I Usually Do: A measure of elementary children's coping strategies.* Manuscript submitted for publication.

Work, W. C., Lotyczewski, B. S., & Raymond, C. (1995). *Long term effectiveness of an early preventive intervention for rural school children.* Manuscript submitted for publication.

Work, W. C., & Olsen, K. H. (1990). Development and evaluation of a revised social problem solving curriculum for fourth graders. *Journal of Primary Prevention, 11,* 143–157.

Wright, S., & Cowen, E. L. (1982). Student perception of school environment and its relationship to mood, achievement, popularity and adjustment. *American Journal of Community Psychology, 10,* 687–703.

Wright, S., & Cowen, E. L. (1985). The effects of peer teaching on student perceptions of class environment, adjustment and academic performance. *American Journal of Community Psychology, 13,* 413–427.

Wright, S., Cowen, E. L., & Kaplan, E. M. (1982). Perceptions of classroom environments and their relationship to children's mood, achievement, popularity and adjustment. *Journal of Primary Prevention, 3,* 18–34.

Wyman, P. A., Cowen, E. L., Work, W. C., Hoyt-Meyers, L., Magnus, K., & Fagen, D. (1995). *Developmental and caregiving factors differentiating parents of young stress affected and stress resilient urban children: A replication and extension.* Manuscript submitted for publication.

Wyman, P. A., Cowen, E. L., Work, W. C., & Kerley, J. H. (1993). The role of children's future expectations in self-system functioning and adjustment to life-stress. A prospective study of urban at risk children. *Development and Psychopathology, 5,* 649–661.

Wyman, P. A., Cowen, E. L., Work, W. C., & Parker, G. R. (1991). Developmental and family milieu interview correlates of resilience in urban children who have experienced major life-stress. *American Journal of Community Psychology, 19,* 405–426.

Wyman, P. A., Cowen, E. L., Work, W. C., Raoof, A., Gribble, P. A., Parker, G. R., & Wannon, M. (1992). Interviews with children who experienced major life stress: Family and child attributes that predict resilient outcomes. *Journal of the American Academy of Child and Adolescent Psychiatry, 31,* 904–910.

Wyman, P. A., Work, W. C., Kerley, J., Hightower, A. D., Cowen, E. L., & Lotyczewski, B. S. (1996). *Predicting substance abuse risk behaviors among inner-city adolescents from childhood competencies and family life-stress: A longitudinal study.* Manuscript submitted for publication.

Yamamoto, K. (1979). Children's ratings of the stressfulness of experiences. *Developmental Psychology, 15,* 581–582.

Yellott, A. W., Liem, G. R., & Cowen, E. L. (1969). Relationships among measures of adjustment, sociometric status and achievement in third graders. *Psychology in the Schools, 6,* 315–321.

Yoshikawa, H. (1994). Prevention as cumulative protection: Effects of early family support and education on chronic delinquency and its risks. *Psychological Bulletin, 115,* 28–54.

Zax, M., & Cowen, E. L. (1976). *Abnormal psychology: Changing conceptions* (2nd ed.). New York: Holt, Rinehart & Winston.

Zax, M., Cowen, E. L., Beach, D. R., & Rappaport, J. (1972). Longitudinal relationships among aptitude, achievement and adjustment measures of school children. *Journal of Genetic Psychology, 121,* 145–154.

Zax, M., Cowen, E. L., Izzo, L. D., & Trost, M. A. (1964). Identifying emotional disturbance in the school setting. *American Journal of Orthopsychiatry, 34,* 447–454.

Zax, M., Cowen, E. L., Rappaport, J., Beach, D. R., & Laird, J. D. (1968). Follow-up study of children identified early as emotionally disturbed. *Journal of Consulting and Clinical Psychology, 32*, 369–374.

Zigler, E., Taussig, C., & Black, K. (1992). A promising preventative for juvenile delinquency. *American Psychologist, 47*, 997–1006.

Zill, N., Morrison, D. R., Coiro, M. J. (1993). Long-term effects of parental divorce on parent-child relationships, adjustment, and achievement in young adulthood. *Journal of Family Psychology, 7*, 91–103.

Zill, N., & Schoenborn, C. A. (1990). Health of our nation's children: Developmental, learning and emotional problems, United States, 1988. *Advance Data From Vital and Health Statistics, 190*, 1–18.

APPENDIXES

APPENDIX A
Playroom Equipment, Materials, and Supplies

Play areas in PMHP schools are equipped differently. These variations, among other things, reflect cross-setting differences in the amount of space and storage room available to the program, space layouts, and the personal preferences and styles of child associates. Table A1 is a composite list of equipment, materials, and supplies used in diverse PMHP settings. Although more items are listed than most play areas can hold, the list includes many items of potential interest to users.

Several caveats accompany the lists. It is very important to have play materials that encourage children's self-expression. Playroom materials should also reflect diverse modalities, including materials and toys that enable children to express aggression. Finally, toys, games, puppets, and books should reflect the ethnic make-up of the community being served.

325

TABLE A1
Suggested Playroom Equipment, Materials, and Supplies

Facility Items

Table and chairs
Chalkboard
Tape recorder and blank tapes
Rocking chair
Sink area
Supply of paper cups, paper towels, and tissue

Plants
Record player
Bean bag chair
Playhouse
Shelving or furniture to use as props for pretend

Materials

Pictures (to explore different feelings)
Sand tray (12″ × 18″ × 3″)
Assorted small plastic animals
Puppets
Playhouse, doll house with furniture and human figures (ethnically appropriate)
Craft sticks (like popsicle sticks)

Nerf bats, swords
Baby doll (boy or girl) and doll bed
Hand mirror or wall mirror
Dress-up clothes and assorted scarves
Doctor's kit
Wiffle balls, rubber balls, plastic bat and ball
Balloons

Jump rope
Punch bags
Toy soldiers
Relaxation records
Bottles of soap bubbles
Assorted stickers
Empty food containers (for use in playhouse)
Assorted small wooden shapes or plastic shape sets
Small square blocks
Constructing sets
Cardboard boxes
Play telephones
Cars and trucks

Art Materials

Finger paints
Tempera paint in primary colors
Colored pencils
Modeling clay
Chalk
Playdough

Paint brushes
Construction paper
Scissors
Paste
Crayons (large size)
Water colors

Games

Dice
Sets of jacks and balls
Pick-up sticks

Checkers
Object matching card game
Playing cards

Books

APPENDIX B
Child-Associate Information

APPENDIX B1
PMHP Child-Associate Job Description

General Supervisory Control

The child associate works under the supervision of the mental health team (the school psychologist, social worker, and elementary counselor).

Specific Supervision

Specific supervision of child associates is provided by the school-based mental health team, sometimes supported by a senior associate. PMHP consultants may also provide additional *ad hoc* supervision.

General Duties

Child associates, working under professional supervision, meet regularly with referred children to pursue goals established jointly by the team and the referring teacher. These goals involve maximizing children's educational and personal development. Child associates also participate in training exercises and project conferences designed to strengthen their child-serving skills.

Specific Duties of Child Associates

- Establish rapport and a warm, meaningful relationship with referred children to reduce problem behaviors in class and elsewhere and to strengthen their behavioral adaptation, educational performance, and social relationships.
- Use play, conversation, games, tutoring, and other approaches to further goals established with individual children experiencing school adjustment problems.

- Converse with children and establish an atmosphere that encourages expression of feelings and ideas.
- Build confidence and self-esteem in children in one-to-one and group interactions.
- Provide feedback to mental health team, principal, teachers, and other school personnel and, at the discretion of the team, to parents about children's progress in the program.
- Participate with other PMHP team members and consultants in assignment, progress, and termination conferences for referred children.
- When indicated by supervisors, meet with other school personnel and with parents to gain additional information about referred children to understand their behavior.
- Participate in training activities and periodic in-service, instructional workshops provided by PMHP staff and school districts.
- Write progress notes and reports for children being seen and provide pertinent information in program evaluation studies.
- Have regularly scheduled supervision with a school-based mental health professional, with supervisory modes (i.e., formats, frequency, etc.) determined by the team.

Entry Requirements

- Child associates are selected on the basis of interpersonal and experiential, rather than educational, qualities. Associates need not be high school or college graduates. Training is provided to prepare the associates for work in a school.
- Applicants for child-associate positions should have personal warmth, enjoy working with children, be reliable and adaptable, and be able to empathize with children. If they are parents, they should give evidence of having been successful in that role. They should also be in good health and relatively free of personal problems.
- All prospective applicants are screened initially through one or more in-depth interviews.

APPENDIX B2
Child-Associate Interviewer Rating Form

Applicant:_____   Date:_____

Interviewer:_____

	Unfavorable				Favorable		
1. Personal warmth	1	2	3	4	5	6	7
2. Enjoys working with children	1	2	3	4	5	6	7
3. Concern about others	1	2	3	4	5	6	7
4. Understands and accepts individual differences	1	2	3	4	5	6	7
5. Empathy for children	1	2	3	4	5	6	7
6. Works well with others	1	2	3	4	5	6	7
7. Independence	1	2	3	4	5	6	7
8. Reliability	1	2	3	4	5	6	7
9. Adaptability	1	2	3	4	5	6	7
10. Openness to new knowledge	1	2	3	4	5	6	7
11. Interview openness	1	2	3	4	5	6	7
12. Estimate of potential effectiveness as a child associate	1	2	3	4	5	6	7

COMMENTS:_____

_____

_____

_____

_____

_____

APPENDIX C1
AML Behavior Rating Scale—Revised (AML-R)

CHILD'S NAME _____ TODAY'S DATE ___/___/___
(MM) (DD) (YY)

SCHOOL _____ TEACHER _____

| SEX | DATE OF BIRTH | GRADE | STUDENT ID NUMBER |

SEX: (M) (F)

RACE
- WHITE
- AFRICAN AM.
- NATIVE AM.
- ASIAN
- HISPANIC
- OTHER

GRADE:
Pre-K, K, 1, 2, 3, 4, 5, 6-8, 9-12, Other

Please rate the child's behavior, as you have observed and experienced it <u>since the beginning of school</u> according to the following scale, by filling in the appropriate number:

(1) **Never** - You have literally never observed this behavior in this child.

(2) **Seldom** - You have observed this behavior once or twice.

(3) **Moderately often** - You have seen this behavior more often than once a month, but less often than once a week.

(4) **Often** - You have seen this behavior more often than once a week, but less often than daily.

(5) **Most or all of the time** - You have seen this behavior with great frequency, averaging once a day or more often.

This child:	Never	Seldom	Moderately often	Often	Most or all of the time
1. gets into fights or quarrels with classmates	1	2	3	4	5
2. has to be coaxed to play or work with peers	1	2	3	4	5
3. is confused with school work	1	2	3	4	5
4. is restless	1	2	3	4	5
5. is unhappy	1	2	3	4	5
6. gets off-task	1	2	3	4	5
7. disrupts class discipline	1	2	3	4	5
8. feels hurt when criticized	1	2	3	4	5
9. needs help with school work	1	2	3	4	5
10. is impulsive	1	2	3	4	5
11. is moody	1	2	3	4	5
12. has difficulty learning	1	2	3	4	5

- USE NO. 2 PENCIL ONLY
- ERASE CHANGES COMPLETELY

COPYRIGHT © 1993 BY PRIMARY MENTAL HEALTH PROJECT, INC. ALL RIGHTS RESERVED.

	A	M	L	TOTAL
RAW SCORE				
PERCENTILE				

APPENDIX C2
Child Rating Scale (CRS)

First Name _____ **Last Name** _____

School _____ **Teacher** _____

Today's Date _____ / _____ / _____
MONTH   DAY   YEAR

	SCREENING	INITIAL	MIDDLE	FINAL
	Ⓢ	Ⓘ	Ⓜ3 Ⓜ2	Ⓕ

SEX	AGE	GRADE
Ⓑ Ⓖ	⑤	K ☐
	⑥	1 ☐
RACE	⑦	2 ☐
White ①	⑧	3 ☐
African Am. ②	⑨	4 ☐
Native Am. ③	⑩	5 ☐
Asian ④	⑪	6-8 ☐
Hispanic ⑤	⑫	Sp. Ed. ☐
Other ⓞ	⑬	Other ☐

STUDENT ID NUMBER

(columns of bubbles numbered 0–9)

IMPORTANT — PLEASE READ

- ◀ USE NO. 2 PENCIL ONLY ▬
- Erase any changes completely.

EXAMPLE

WRONG		RIGHT
◑ ☑ ⊠		●

PLEASE DECIDE HOW MUCH EACH SENTENCE BELOW DESCRIBES YOU.

	USUALLY NO	SOMETIMES	USUALLY YES
If it is <u>USUALLY NOT</u> like you, fill in the N.	●	Ⓢ	Ⓨ
If it is <u>SOMETIMES</u> like you, fill in the S.	Ⓝ	●	Ⓨ
If it is <u>USUALLY</u> like you, fill in the Y.	Ⓝ	Ⓢ	●

	USUALLY NO	SOMETIMES	USUALLY YES
A. I like to swim	Ⓝ	Ⓢ	Ⓨ
B. I'm good at drawing pictures	Ⓝ	Ⓢ	Ⓨ

COPYRIGHT © 1993 BY A. DIRK HIGHTOWER. ALL RIGHTS RESERVED.

	USUALLY NO	SOMETIMES	USUALLY YES
1. I behave in school	Ⓝ	Ⓢ	Ⓨ	▬
2. I get scared in school	Ⓝ	Ⓢ	Ⓨ	▬
3. I have many friends	Ⓝ	Ⓢ	Ⓨ	▬
4. I like to do school work	Ⓝ	Ⓢ	Ⓨ	▬
5. I bother classmates who are working	Ⓝ	Ⓢ	Ⓨ	▬
6. I'm afraid of making mistakes	Ⓝ	Ⓢ	Ⓨ	▬
7. My classmates tease me.....................................	Ⓝ	Ⓢ	Ⓨ	▬
8. I get bored in class	Ⓝ	Ⓢ	Ⓨ	▬
9. I do what I'm supposed to in school.......................	Ⓝ	Ⓢ	Ⓨ	▬
10. I worry about things at school	Ⓝ	Ⓢ	Ⓨ	▬
11. Other kids are mean to me..................................	Ⓝ	Ⓢ	Ⓨ	▬
12. School is fun	Ⓝ	Ⓢ	Ⓨ	▬
13. I get in trouble in class......................................	Ⓝ	Ⓢ	Ⓨ	▬
14. My feelings get hurt easily.................................	Ⓝ	Ⓢ	Ⓨ	▬
15. My classmates like me	Ⓝ	Ⓢ	Ⓨ	▬
16. I like to answer questions in class	Ⓝ	Ⓢ	Ⓨ	▬
17. I follow the class rules	Ⓝ	Ⓢ	Ⓨ	▬
18. I'm nervous at school..	Ⓝ	Ⓢ	Ⓨ	▬
19. Other kids choose me last for games.....................	Ⓝ	Ⓢ	Ⓨ	▬
20. I hate school...	Ⓝ	Ⓢ	Ⓨ	▬
21. I call other students names	Ⓝ	Ⓢ	Ⓨ	▬
22. I feel like crying at school..................................	Ⓝ	Ⓢ	Ⓨ	▬
23. I make friends easily	Ⓝ	Ⓢ	Ⓨ	▬
24. I get tired of going to school	Ⓝ	Ⓢ	Ⓨ	▬

APPENDIX C3
Teacher–Child Rating Scale (T-CRS)

STUDENT ID NUMBER

[Bubble grid for student ID number, digits 0–9]

GRADE
- PRE-K ☐
- K ☐
- 1 ☐
- 2 ☐
- 3 ☐
- 4 ☐
- 5 ☐
- 6-8 ☐
- 9-12 ☐

● ◄ USE NO. 2 PENCIL ONLY ► ● Erase changes completely

CHILD'S NAME _____
(LAST)   (FIRST)

TEACHER _____

SCHOOL _____ DATE __/__/__
MONTH DAY YEAR

| Screening | Initial | Middle | Final |
| | | (M3) (M2) | |

SEX ☐ M ☐ F

I. Please rate this child on the following:

	Not a Problem	Mild	Moderate	Serious	Very Serious Problem
1. Disruptive in class	1	2	3	4	5
2. Withdrawn	1	2	3	4	5
3. Underachieving (not working to ability)	1	2	3	4	5
4. Fidgety, difficulty sitting still	1	2	3	4	5
5. Shy, timid	1	2	3	4	5
6. Poor work habits	1	2	3	4	5
7. Disturbs others while they are working	1	2	3	4	5
8. Anxious, worried	1	2	3	4	5
9. Poor concentration, limited attention span	1	2	3	4	5
10. Constantly seeks attention	1	2	3	4	5
11. Nervous, frightened, tense	1	2	3	4	5
12. Difficulty following directions	1	2	3	4	5
13. Overly aggressive to peers (fights)	1	2	3	4	5
14. Does not express feelings	1	2	3	4	5
15. Poorly motivated to achieve	1	2	3	4	5
16. Defiant, obstinate, stubborn	1	2	3	4	5
17. Unhappy, sad	1	2	3	4	5
18. Learning academic subjects	1	2	3	4	5

II. Please rate the following items according to how well they describe the child:

	Not at All	A Little	Moderately Well	Well	Very Well
1. Accepts things not going his/her way	1	2	3	4	5
2. Defends own views under group pressure	1	2	3	4	5
3. Completes work	1	2	3	4	5
4. Has many friends	1	2	3	4	5
5. Ignores teasing	1	2	3	4	5
6. Comfortable as a leader	1	2	3	4	5
7. Well organized	1	2	3	4	5
8. Is friendly toward peers	1	2	3	4	5
9. Accepts imposed limits	1	2	3	4	5
10. Participates in class discussions	1	2	3	4	5
11. Functions well even with distractions	1	2	3	4	5
12. Makes friends easily	1	2	3	4	5
13. Copes well with failure	1	2	3	4	5
14. Expresses ideas willingly	1	2	3	4	5
15. Works well without adult support	1	2	3	4	5
16. Classmates wish to sit near this child	1	2	3	4	5
17. Tolerates frustration	1	2	3	4	5
18. Questions rules that seem unfair/unclear	1	2	3	4	5
19. A self-starter	1	2	3	4	5
20. Well liked by classmates	1	2	3	4	5

APPENDIX C4
Background Information Form (BIF)

Part 1:

CHILD'S NAME _____
(Last)   (First)

TODAY'S DATE ___ / ___ / ___

TEACHER _____ SCHOOL _____

PARENT/GUARDIAN _____ PHONE _____

ADDRESS _____

⓪	⓪	⓪	⓪	⓪
①	①	①	①	①
②	②	②	②	②
③	③	③	③	③
④	④	④	④	④
⑤	⑤	⑤	⑤	⑤
⑥	⑥	⑥	⑥	⑥
⑦	⑦	⑦	⑦	⑦
⑧	⑧	⑧	⑧	⑧
⑨	⑨	⑨	⑨	⑨

Part 2: ◀ USE NO. 2 PENCIL ONLY ▮▮▮ Erase any changes completely.

SEX Ⓜ Ⓕ

RACE
White ①
African Am. ②
Native Am. ③
Asian ④
Hispanic ⑤
Other ⓪

GRADE
Pre-K Ⓟ
K Ⓚ
1 ①
2 ②
3 ③
4 ④
5 ⑤
6-8 ⑧
9-12 ⑫
Other ⓪

DATE OF BIRTH

⓪	⓪	⓪	⓪	⓪	⓪
①	①	①	①	①	①
	②	②	②	②	②
	③	③	③	③	③
	④	④	④	④	④
	⑤	⑤	⑤	⑤	⑤
	⑥	⑥	⑥	⑥	⑥
	⑦	⑦	⑦	⑦	⑦
	⑧	⑧	⑧	⑧	⑧
	⑨	⑨	⑨	⑨	⑨

STUDENT ID NUMBER

⓪	⓪	⓪	⓪	⓪	⓪	⓪	⓪	⓪
①	①	①	①	①	①	①	①	①
②	②	②	②	②	②	②	②	②
③	③	③	③	③	③	③	③	③
④	④	④	④	④	④	④	④	④
⑤	⑤	⑤	⑤	⑤	⑤	⑤	⑤	⑤
⑥	⑥	⑥	⑥	⑥	⑥	⑥	⑥	⑥
⑦	⑦	⑦	⑦	⑦	⑦	⑦	⑦	⑦
⑧	⑧	⑧	⑧	⑧	⑧	⑧	⑧	⑧
⑨	⑨	⑨	⑨	⑨	⑨	⑨	⑨	⑨

Part 3: Parent information:

☐ Both natural or adoptive parents in home
☐ Single parent family – divorce or separation
☐ Single parent family – other (e.g., death, never married)
☐ Natural/Adoptive parent with stepparent
☐ Foster placement
☐ Other _____

Part 4: Educational characteristics:

	No	Yes	If "Yes" — then answer below:
1. Has repeated a grade	Ⓝ	Ⓨ	Grade Repeated Ⓚ ① ② ③ ④ ⑤
2. Has transferred schools	Ⓝ	Ⓨ	Number of Transfers ① ② ③ ④
3. Has been in Project before	Ⓝ	Ⓨ	
4. Speech/Language	Ⓝ	Ⓨ	
5. Special day class	Ⓝ	Ⓨ	
6. Resource Specialist Program	Ⓝ	Ⓨ	
7. Remedial Education	Ⓝ	Ⓨ	
8. Learning Disabled or Perceptually Handicapped	Ⓝ	Ⓨ	
9. Emotionally or Behaviorally Handicapped	Ⓝ	Ⓨ	
10. Other Counseling	Ⓝ	Ⓨ	
11. Reduced or free lunch	Ⓝ	Ⓨ	
12. English as a Second Language	Ⓝ	Ⓨ	
13. Other	Ⓝ	Ⓨ	

Part 5: Child characteristics:

	No	Yes	
1. Frequent legal absences	Ⓝ	Ⓨ	
2. Frequent illegal absences	Ⓝ	Ⓨ	
3. Visits school nurse often	Ⓝ	Ⓨ	
4. On-going medical problems	Ⓝ	Ⓨ	. . . If "Yes" — specify _____
5. Child is easy to like	Ⓝ	Ⓨ	
6. Number of siblings	⓪ ① ② ③ ④ ⑤		

COPYRIGHT © 1993 BY PRIMARY MENTAL HEALTH PROJECT, INC. ALL RIGHTS RESERVED.

SCANTRON® FORM NO. F-5299-CCS   [Scantron asks that you please RECYCLE this product.]   3193·C E4501·12 11 10 9 8 7 6 5 4 3 2

APPENDIX C5
Parent–Child Rating Scale (P-CRS)

DO NOT WRITE IN THESE SPACES

USE NO. 2 PENCIL ONLY

Child's name _____

School _____ Teacher _____

Relationship to child: ☐ Mother ☐ Father ☐ Other _____

Child's sex: ☐ Boy ☐ Girl   Date __/__/__

Each of the following statements describes ways in which children behave. For each description, fill in the response which best describes your child.

	Not at all true of my child	A little true of my child	Somewhat true of my child	Quite true of my child	Very true of my child
1. Disruptive at home	1	2	3	4	5
2. Withdrawn	1	2	3	4	5
3. Fails to work to ability	1	2	3	4	5
4. Has difficulty sitting still	1	2	3	4	5
5. Shy	1	2	3	4	5
6. Poor work habits	1	2	3	4	5
7. Disturbs others	1	2	3	4	5
8. Worries	1	2	3	4	5
9. Limited attention span	1	2	3	4	5
10. Seeks attention	1	2	3	4	5
11. Nervous, becomes tense	1	2	3	4	5
12. Difficulty following directions	1	2	3	4	5
13. Aggressive with peers	1	2	3	4	5
14. Does not express feelings	1	2	3	4	5
15. Poorly motivated	1	2	3	4	5
16. Stubborn	1	2	3	4	5
17. Unhappy, sad	1	2	3	4	5
18. Has difficulty learning	1	2	3	4	5
19. Mood is balanced and stable	1	2	3	4	5
20. Defends own views	1	2	3	4	5
21. Completes assigned work	1	2	3	4	5
22. Has many friends	1	2	3	4	5
23. Ignores teasing	1	2	3	4	5
24. A leader among peers	1	2	3	4	5
25. Well organized	1	2	3	4	5
26. Is friendly toward peers	1	2	3	4	5
27. Accepts imposed limits	1	2	3	4	5
28. Participates in discussions	1	2	3	4	5
29. Functions well with distractions	1	2	3	4	5
30. Makes friends easily	1	2	3	4	5
31. Copes well with failure	1	2	3	4	5
32. Expresses ideas willingly	1	2	3	4	5
33. Works well without adult support	1	2	3	4	5
34. Tries to help other kids	1	2	3	4	5
35. Tolerates frustration	1	2	3	4	5
36. Questions rules that seem unfair	1	2	3	4	5
37. A self-starter	1	2	3	4	5
38. Well liked by peers	1	2	3	4	5

© Copyright 1993 by Primary Mental Health Project, Inc. All rights reserved

HAGA EL FAVOR DE DEJAR LOS ESPACIOS EN BLANCO.

Use Lápiz No. 2

Nombre del niño(a) _____

La escuela _____ El profesor(a) _____

Su relación con el niño(a): ☐ Madre
☐ Padre
☐ Otra _____

El sexo del niño(a): ☐ Varón ☐ Hembra Fecha del dia ___/___/___

Cada una de las frases siguientes describe maneras en que los niños se comportan. Para cada descripción haga un circulo en el número de la respuesta que mejor describe a su hijo(a).

	No describe a mi hijo/a	Describe un poco a mi hijo/a	Describe bien a mi hijo/a	Describe bastante bien a mi hijo/a	Describe muy bien a mi hijo/a
1. Causa trastornos en casa	1	2	3	4	5
2. Reservado (introvertido)(a)	1	2	3	4	5
3. Trabaja debajo de su capácidad	1	2	3	4	5
4. Tiene dificultad para sentarse quieto	1	2	3	4	5
5. Es tímido(a)	1	2	3	4	5
6. Tiene malos habitos de trabajo	1	2	3	4	5
7. Molesta a los otros	1	2	3	4	5
8. Se preocupa	1	2	3	4	5
9. Su atención es limitada	1	2	3	4	
10. Busca atención	1	2	3	4	5
11. Es nervioso(a), está tenso(a)	1	2	3	4	5
12. Tiene dificultad siguiendo direcciones	1	2	3	4	
13. Es agresivo(a) con sus compañeros	1	2	3	4	5
14. No expresa emociones	1	2	3	4	5
15. No se motiva facilmente	1	2	3	4	5
16. Terco(a)	1	2	3	4	5
17. Triste	1	2	3	4	5
18. Tiene dificultad para aprender	1	2	3	4	
19. Sus emociones son balanceadas y estables	1	2	3	4	5
20. Defiende su opinión	1	2	3	4	5
21. Termina tareas asignadas	1	2	3	4	5
22. Tiene muchos amigos	1	2	3	4	5
23. No hace caso a las burlas	1	2	3	4	5
24. Es lider entre sus compañeros	1	2	3	4	5
25. Es bien organizado(a)	1	2	3	4	5
26. Es amable con sus compañeros	1	2	3	4	5
27. Acepta las limitaciones impuestas	1	2	3	4	5
28. Participa en discusiones	1	2	3	4	5
29. Funciona bien con distracciones	1	2	3	4	5
30. Hace amigos facilmente	1	2	3	4	5
31. Tolera bien los fracasos	1	2	3	4	5
32. Expresa sus ideas con mucho gusto	1	2	3	4	5
33. Trabaja bien sin el apoyo de los adultos	1	2	3	4	5
34. Trata de ayudar a otros niños	1	2	3	4	5
35. Tolera las frustraciones	1	2	3	4	5
36. Hace preguntas a cerca de las reglas injustas	1	2	3	4	5
37. Tiene iniciativa	1	2	3	4	5
38. Es apreciado por sus compañeros	1	2	3	4	5

© Derechos de Primary Mental Health Project 1993. Todos los derechos reservados.

APPENDIX C6
Associate–Child Rating Scale (A-CRS)

CHILD'S
NAME _____ TEACHER _____
    (LAST)   (FIRST)

TODAY'S
DATE ___/___/___
  (MM) (DD) (YY)

CHILD ASSOCIATE _____ NUMBER OF SESSIONS TO DATE _____

SCHOOL _____ **Sex** Ⓜ Ⓕ

STUDENT ID NUMBER

Time of Form Completion: Initial   Final
(fill in one)   Ⓘ   Ⓕ

Life Events:

	No	Yes	Don't Know
1. Death of a family member	Ⓝ	Ⓨ	Ⓞⓚ
If yes, specify _____			
2. Serious illness in the family	Ⓝ	Ⓨ	Ⓞⓚ
If yes, specify _____			
3. Lacks after school supervision	Ⓝ	Ⓨ	Ⓞⓚ
4. Child is easy to like	Ⓝ	Ⓨ	Ⓞⓚ

Based on your <u>direct contacts</u> with this child to date, please rate each of the behaviors according to <u>how well</u> it describes the child <u>now</u> by filling in the corresponding number:

Describes child:	Not at All	A Little	Moderately Well	Well	Very Well
1. Looks forward to coming	①	②	③	④	⑤
2. Aggressive................................	①	②	③	④	⑤
3. Is fearful................................	①	②	③	④	⑤
4. Completes task	①	②	③	④	⑤
5. Expresses feelings openly.................	①	②	③	④	⑤
6. Tests limits	①	②	③	④	⑤
7. Anxious, worries about things	①	②	③	④	⑤
8. Copes well with failure..................	①	②	③	④	⑤
9. Participates enthusiastically.............	①	②	③	④	⑤
10. Fidgety, difficulty sitting still	①	②	③	④	⑤
11. Nervous, tense	①	②	③	④	⑤
12. Competes fairly.........................	①	②	③	④	⑤
13. Good rapport with me (child worker).....	①	②	③	④	⑤
14. Disruptive during sessions	①	②	③	④	⑤
15. Sad, unhappy	①	②	③	④	⑤
16. Tolerates frustration	①	②	③	④	⑤
17. Maintains eye contact when speaking	①	②	③	④	⑤
18. Stubborn, obstinate	①	②	③	④	⑤
19. Feelings are hurt easily.................	①	②	③	④	⑤
20. Mood is balanced and stable...........	①	②	③	④	⑤

- Erase changes completely
- USE NO. 2 PENCIL ONLY

	PART.	LIMITS	ANXIETY	SELF-
RAW SCORES				

COPYRIGHT © 1994 BY PRIMARY MENTAL HEALTH PROJECT, INC. ALL RIGHTS RESERVED.

APPENDIX C7
Professional Summary Report (PSR)

Student _____ School _____

Child Associate _____ Supervising Professional _____ Today's Date _____

Instructions:

This report should be completed by the **supervising professional.** It should summarize how this student is perceived by the supervising professional, child associate, and teacher(s).

● USE NO. 2 PENCIL ONLY
● ERASE CHANGES COMPLETELY

STUDENT ID NUMBER								

TITLE OF PERSON COMPLETING FORM

- Psychologist
- Social Worker
- Counselor
- Other

_____
(please specify)

Section I: Indicate changes in the student's behavior since the time of referral by filling in the appropriate space for each item. If a behavior never applied to this student, fill in "NA," not applicable.

	MUCH WORSE	WORSE	SAME	IMPROVED	GREATLY IMPROVED	NA
1. Acting-out/aggressive behaviors	1	2	3	4	5	NA
2. Shy, withdrawn, or anxious behaviors	1	2	3	4	5	NA
3. Task orientation	1	2	3	4	5	NA
4. Frustration tolerance	1	2	3	4	5	NA
5. Assertive social skills	1	2	3	4	5	NA
6. Peer social skills	1	2	3	4	5	NA
7. Initiative and participation	1	2	3	4	5	NA
8. Self-confidence	1	2	3	4	5	NA
9. Interest in school	1	2	3	4	5	NA
10. Academic performance	1	2	3	4	5	NA
11. Overall school behavior	1	2	3	4	5	NA
12. Attendance	1	2	3	4	5	NA
13. Other _____	1	2	3	4	5	NA

Section II: Fill in the most appropriate choice for each item below:

1. Child is leaving Project at this time because
   - child has met his/her goals.
   - school year is ending.
   - child is moving or has moved.
   - child has transferred to another helping service (e.g., special education, another school program, outside Mental Health agency).
   - other (please specify) _____

2. Recommendation for this child is to
   - terminate from Project.
   - continue in Project next fall.
   - evaluate child's progress in the fall as a basis for decision about Project continuation.
   - continue in Project in next school, if available.
   - other (please specify) _____

Comments: _____

_____

_____

Copyright © 1993 by Primary Mental Health Project, Inc. All rights reserved.

AUTHOR INDEX

Numbers in italics refer to listings in reference sections.

343

Huser, J., 134, *303*
Hutton, H., *318*

Iker, M. R., 267, 269, *304, 309*
Isaacs, S., 239, *309*
Issacson, R. V., *303*
Izzo, L. D., 11, 45, 58, 94, 133–134, *303, 310, 320*

Jacoby, C., *301*
Janoff-Bulman, R., 229, *306*
Jenkins, J. R., 239, *309*
Jenkins, L. M., *309*
Johnson, D. B., 70, 77, 81, 169, 183, 239–240, *309*
Johnson, D. W., *309*
Johnson, R. T., *309*
Joint Commission on Mental Illness and Health, 47, *309*

Kaban, B. T., 259, *319*
Kannegieter, R., 131, *318*
Kaplan, E. M., 150, *320*
Keith, B., 213, *299*
Kellam, S. G., 11, *305,309*
Kelly, J. B., 213, 217, 227, *318*
Kerley, J. H., 234, *310, 320*
Kiesler, C. A., 13, *310*
Kim, D., 289, *304*
Knapp, R. H., 48, *308*
Kohut, H., *310*
Kraus, D. M., 120, 134, 145, *310–311*
Kuhn, T. S., 285, *310*
Kurdek, L. A., 216, *310*

Laboy, W., *312*
Laird, J. D., 132, *321*
Larcen, S. W., *311*
Larkin, K., *311*
Larsen, A., *311*
Leary, M. R., 239, *300*
Levine, M., 9, *310*
Levinson, H. R., 139, 250, *308, 319*
Levitt, E. E., 117, *310*
Lewis, W. W., 48, *310*
Liebenstein, N. L., *318*
Liem, G. R., 134, *310, 320*
Lin, S., 212, *307*

Lockhead, M. E., 240, *310*
Lombard, A. D., 2, 89–290, *310*
Lorion, R. P., 9, 117, 120, 129, 131, 134, 145, 286, *303, 310–311, 313*
Lotyczewski, B. S., 141, 147, 151, 152–153, *303–304, 308–309, 311, 317–320*

Magnus, K., *309*
Magoon, T. M., 49, *311*
Mahler, J., 233, *317*
Main, S. R., *311*
Mangual, J., *312*
Manson, S. M., 9, *311*
Marauyama, G., *309*
Markman, H. J., *301*
Masten, A. S., 261, 271, *306, 311*
Mayhall, W. F., 239, *309*
McConaughy, S. H., 138, *299*
McKim, B. J., 137, *311, 318*
McLanahan, S. S., 214, *311*
McLaughlin, T. F., 240, *311*
McWilliams, S. A., 66, 112, 135, *302, 312, 317*
Meller, P. J., 142, *312*
Metz, J. R., 259, *312*
Mijangos, L. B., 97, *312*
Mitchell, S. A., 239, *307*
Moore, S. G., 238, 241, *307*
Moos, R. H., 149–150, *312, 318*
Moriarty, A. E., 215, 259, *312*
Morrison, A. P., *318*
Morrison, D., 48, 215, *307, 321*
Morton, T., 13, *310*
Mrazek, P. J., 129, 292, *312*
Murphy, L. B., 259, *312*

National Mental Health Association, 7, *312*
Neeman, J., 271, *306*
Nelson, D., 239, *309*
Newcomb, A. F., 241, 253, *312*
Norton, P. L., 116, *306*

O'Donnell, J., *307*
O'Grady, D., 259, *312*
Ojemann, R. H., 194, *312*
Olds, D. L., 295, *312*
Olsen, K. H., 203–204, *319*

SUBJECT INDEX

ABOUT THE AUTHORS

Emory L. Cowen, PhD, is professor of psychology and director of the University of Rochester Center for Community Study. He was a founder of the Primary Mental Health Project (PMHP) and directed the project for its first 34 years. Dr. Cowen is past president of Division 27 of the American Psychological Association (APA) and the recipient of its Distinguished Contributions and Seymour B. Sarason awards. He also received the APA Award for Distinguished Contributions in Psychology in Public Interest.

A. Dirk Hightower, PhD, is the current director of PMHP and a senior research associate and associate professor of psychology at the University of Rochester. Previously, he was research director at PMHP for 9 years. Dr. Hightower is on the editorial board of several school and community psychology journals. He has been active with various National Association of School Psychology and APA Division 16 committees and is past president of the New York Association of School Psychologists. He is a consultant in program evaluation and research for local and state agencies and currently is serving a second term on the Rush-Henrietta New York City School Board.

JoAnne L. Pedro-Carroll, PhD, is a senior research associate and associate professor of psychology and psychiatry at the University of Rochester. She is the founder and director of the Children of Divorce Intervention Program, an award-winning prevention program for children in kindergarten through eighth grade. Dr. Pedro-Carroll provides consultation and training locally and nationally on prevention and family issues and has written extensively about children of divorce. She is a fellow of the American Psychological Association.

William C. Work, PhD, is adjunct professor at the State University of New York at Brockport. From 1989 to 1995, he was the research director for PMHP at the University of Rochester Center for Community Study. Dr. Work was coprincipal investigator on two 3-year grants examining the correlates and determinants of stress resilience in urban children. He has authored or coauthored a number of articles on social problem solving and stress and coping in children. He currently serves as associate editor of the *Journal of Community Psychology*. His major research foci are in the areas of social competence development, stress and coping in young children and their families, and preventive intervention research.

Peter A. Wyman, PhD, is senior research associate and associate professor of psychology and clinical assistant professor of psychiatry at the University of Rochester. Since 1988, he has been codirector of the Rochester Child Resilience Project, a series of studies investigating the phenomenon of resilient adaptations among inner-city, at-risk children. Dr. Wyman is the author and coauthor of a number of articles on the topic of child resilience. Since 1995, he has also been director of research at PMHP.

William G. Haffey, MS, is director of PMHP for the Monroe County Board of Cooperative Services No. 1, the lead agency for PMHP in the state of New York. Mr. Haffey started as a school psychologist with PMHP in 1971. He has primary current involvements in PMHP program development, maintenance, quality control, and dissemination activities both in Monroe County and in the entire state of New York.